Amazon Sumerian by Tutorials

By Brian Moakley & Gur Raunaq Singh

Amazon Sumerian by Tutorials

By Brian Moakley & Gur Raunaq Singh

Notice of Rights

Notice of Liability

Trademarks

ISBN: 978-1-942878-87-2

Table of Contents

Section III: Creating an Augmented Reality Experience 363

About the Cover

For some time, there was a viral video circulating on the internet of a woman hatching a chameleon in the palm of her hand. In the video, the egg is impossibly small and smooth, slowly splitting as the hatchling does its best to push out his head. It takes longer than you might think; the hatchling takes breaks and rests in between working to be born. At one point, the woman helps the hatchling by gently peeling the shell and cooing words of encouragement. And after some time, there he is: a chameleon. He is the color of the shallow part of the sea, his eyes working separately to see the world, and his body already swaying in the chameleon's side-to-side rhythm. But if you watch closely, you can see the most amazing part: His blue-green skin begins to speckle, lighten and become peach and fleshy. The hatchling is barely two minutes old and his body already knows to try to blend in with the hand that holds him.

Like this chameleon, Amazon's Sumerian is new, vibrant, smart, beautiful and ready to take on the world.

Though they are nearly silent, relatively small — ranging from just 15 mm to 21 inches — and try their best to blend in, no other creature shows us more blatantly how creative the act of adaption can be. And nature has given them an impressive set of tools: zygodactylous feet, rapidly extrudable tongues, prehensile tails, independently mobile eyes and stereoscopic vision. They are fast, focused, nimble, fierce, deliberate and wild.

Their changing skin is, of course, their most notable feature, making and unmaking combinations with a diverse palette of pink, blue, red, orange, green, black, brown, light blue, yellow, turquoise and purple. They adapt for protection, in response to temperature, and to show their mood and intention. Their exterior is multi-dimensional, with two layers within their skin. Of most importance is the top layer, which contains a lattice that expands and contracts, with growing and shrinking spaces changing how wavelengths of light are reflected and absorbed. The chameleon himself is always the same; the chameleon we see seems endlessly new.

Amazon Sumerian seeks to equip you with the same intuitive and immersive tools that will help you, too, create realistic, multi-dimensional and visually stimulating experiences. But there is one point in which Amazon Sumerian and chameleons differ greatly: with Amazon Sumerian, you will not blend in. The multitude of experiences to be made with these tools is endless — and waiting in your hands to be born.

Dedication

"To my mom and dad, for giving me the tools, patience and love to make my way through this uncertain world."

— Brian Moakley

"For my Mom, thanks for all the french fries. For my Dad, thanks for all the scooter rides. And for my friends, thanks for all the good times."

— Gur Raunaq Singh

About the Authors

Brian Moakley is an author of this book. He is a writer and video instructor at Razeware. Brian was also an author and final pass editor of Unity Games by Tutorials and he has produced many videos and articles on wide variety of subjects at raywenderlich.com. Off work, Brian enjoys spending time with his wife and two kids.

Gur Raunaq Singh is an author of this book. Raunaq is a Software Engineer from New Delhi, India. Having worked as a Unity developer in the past, he has worked on a number of award winning Augmented Reality applications. He is currently exploring the world of Computer Vision and Machine Learning. You can find him on Twitter: @raunaqness

About the Editor

Tammy Coron is the technical editor of this book. She is an independent creative professional and the host of Roundabout: Creative Chaos. She's also a Development Editor at The Pragmatic Bookshelf, a Sr. Editor at Razeware, and a content contributor at Creative Bloq, Lynda.com, iMore, and raywenderlich.com.

About the Artists

Jake Nolt is the internal designer of this book. He is a 3D designer working for a decade in video game and application development. He is also an assistant professor of animation and the proprietor of a small indie game studio. When not developing or teaching, Jake enjoys spending time with family, gaming, and being outdoors.

Vicki Wenderlich is the designer and artist of the cover of this book. She is Ray's wife and business partner. She is a digital artist who creates illustrations, game art and a lot of other art or design work for the tutorials and books on raywenderlich.com.

Early Access Edition

You're reading an early access edition of *Amazon Sumerian by Tutorials*. As we continue to add chapters to the early access edition of this book, we'll notify you and let you know how to access the updated versions.

We hope you enjoy the preview of this book, and that you'll come back to help us celebrate more releases of *Amazon Sumerian by Tutorials* as we work on the book!

What You Need

To follow along with this book, you'll need:

- Firefox 61 or newer
- Chrome 69 or newer

You will need the following hardware requirements for either of those browsers:

- A PC running Windows 7 or higher. A Pentium 4 processor that SSE2 capable. 512 MB of RAM (2 GB for 64-bit).
- A Mac running macOS 10.10 or higher. An Intel x86 processor. 512 MB of RAM.

If you plan on doing virtual reality work, your system requirements may increase. See your VR headset's requirements for more information.

Sumerian supports the following VR headsets:

- HTC Vive
- Vive Pro
- Oculus Rift
- Oculus Rift S
- Oculus Go
- Oculus Quest
- Samsung Gear VR

- Lenovo Mirage Solo
- Google Daydream

If you plan to follow along with the augmented reality projects, you will need either an Android or iOS device.

- If using an iOS device, make sure to use a device that supports ARKit.
- If using an Android device, make sure to use a device that supports ARCore.

Android augmented reality apps require Android Studio 3.5. This application has the following requirements:

- 8 GB of RAM
- 4 GB of available disk space **minimum**
- 1280 x 800 **minimum** screen resolution
- Intel i5 or higher (U series or higher) recommended

iOS augmented reality requires that you have a Mac and Xcode 11. Xcode 11 has the following requirements:

- macOS running 10.14.4 or higher

> **Note**: Being browser-based, Sumerian may work on other platforms not listed here. These are unsupported platforms that may or may not have issues.

Book License

By purchasing *Amazon Sumerian by Tutorials*, you have the following license:

- You are allowed to use and/or modify the source code in *Amazon Sumerian by Tutorials* in as many apps as you want, with no attribution required.
- You are allowed to use and/or modify all art, images and designs that are included in *Amazon Sumerian by Tutorials* in as many apps as you want, but must include this attribution line somewhere inside your app: "Artwork/images/designs: from *Amazon Sumerian by Tutorials*, available at www.raywenderlich.com".
- The source code included in *Amazon Sumerian by Tutorials* is for your personal use only. You are NOT allowed to distribute or sell the source code in *Amazon Sumerian by Tutorials* without prior authorization.
- This book is for your personal use only. You are NOT allowed to sell this book without prior authorization, or distribute it to friends, coworkers or students; they would need to purchase their own copies.

All materials provided with this book are provided on an “as is” basis, without warranty of any kind, express or implied, including but not limited to the warranties of merchantability, fitness for a particular purpose and noninfringement. In no event shall the authors or copyright holders be liable for any claim, damages or other liability, whether in an action of contract, tort or otherwise, arising from, out of or in connection with the software or the use or other dealings in the software.

All trademarks and registered trademarks appearing in this guide are the properties of their respective owners.

Book Source Code & Forums

The resource files for each chapter can be found here:

- https://store.raywenderlich.com/products/amazon-sumerian-by-tutorials-source-code

Forums

We've also set up an official forum for the book at https://forums.raywenderlich.com. This is a great place to ask questions about the book or to submit any errors you may find.

Foreword

AWS has millions of active customers every month. Our customers are being pulled into immersive mediums for just about everything – training, simulations, IoT digital twins, and product configurations – you name it. Yet, many of our developers don't have a gaming or 3D background, nor have the time to deal with app stores or the time-intensive processes blocking their content from reaching end users. Quick! Secure! That's what they want, that's what they need – to deliver the best experiences to their end-users across the globe.

We placed a bet. Gambling? No. Transformation of the web? Yes. When we heard about WebXR, we got excited about a future where AR/VR would transform the way our customers engage with their customers, and how developers would make that a reality. We live in a 3D world, why weren't we developing a 3D world?

We built Amazon Sumerian with this in mind — it's essentially a full-on game engine in a browser, accessible, adaptable, and achievable by the masses. Everyone gets to come to the party, and that's how we like it. We get a lot of credit for Sumerian being a nod to earlier civilizations, known for their innovations in language, governance, architecture... the 360-degree circle! It sounds chest-pounding — Sumerians were the creators of civilization as modern humans understand it. That's giving us too much credit. In all honesty, I'm a huge fan of Snow Crash, this hyper currency dystopian novel by Neal Stephenson depicting a future where pizza delivery is the only viable business left, also run by the mafia. It's where the world's fastest pizza delivery driver is also the self-proclaimed world's greatest sword fighter, and society escapes into this virtual world called the metaverse. At some point in the novel, a virus that affects both your physical and virtual person is introduced to the metaverse using the ancient Sumerian language. Anyway, we didn't want a name using acronyms like AR, VR or XR because they've almost already become passé.

Next, it will be ZX, but don't ask me what that means, it just sounds futuristic.

Sumerian is a bit early, some say nascent. WebXR is just coming out. Oculus Quest and VIVE Focus are finally giving customers untethered access to high-quality content. Firefox Reality is making it possible for customers to ship content using nothing more than a URL. It's happening quickly and the passion, the energy, the determination, is hard to contain. We publish dozens of tutorials and do weekly Twitch streams. It's not enough, we're all thirsting for more. Ray Wenderlich's team is helping us get more end to end examples to customers looking to build immersive experiences in the browser. I'm super excited about this book and looking forward to feedback. Join the few thousand Sumerian developers on our Slack channel (slack.sumerian.aws) or hit me up directly on Twitter @kylemroche.

- Kyle and the Sumerian Team

Introduction

In 2017, Amazon introduced Sumerian to the world. It was positioned as a new graphics engine that allowed users to create unique 3D experiences in a modern web browser. The news was somewhat surprising because not only a year earlier, Amazon released a different 3D engine called Lumberyard aimed to make cutting edge 3D games.

So why use Sumerian when Lumberyard is available? Both are free and only cost money based on the Amazon Web Service usage rates.

Yet, 3D engines like Lumberyard, Unity and Unreal are designed for professional game developers. These engines have steep learning curves and require developers to know a modern programming language like C# or C++. Becoming proficient in a programming language, the editor and all the game development frameworks takes years of focused study.

Unlike these other engines, Sumerian provides a gentle on-ramp to 3D development. Sumerian provides a visual scripting language and then allows users to use web technologies such as HTML, CSS, and JavaScript to bring their experiences to the next level.

Creating graphical experiences

In the past twenty years, 3D technology is being used everywhere. People are getting used to interacting with 3D worlds. As computers have grown in power, the hardware and tooling have dropped in price, allowing anyone to construct virtual worlds. People have come to expect 3D interactions.

Imagine the following scenario. You are looking to buy a house and find a house for sale that on the outside, matches what you are looking for. In the listing, you see a link for a virtual tour. When you click on it, you are brought to a 3D reproduction of the house. In it, a virtual real estate agent walks you through each room, giving you information about it. When the tour concludes, the virtual agent asks you if you are interested in a real-life tour and then takes down your name and phone number. A day later, you get a call.

Or imagine you need to replace a part in your lawnmower. Inside the part instructions, you find a link to a 3D instructional video. Navigating to it, you are presented with a 3D reproduction of the lawnmower with step by step instructions on how to replace the part.

Sumerian is designed to create these types of experiences and it allows you to even create them in virtual and augmented reality. Better still, Sumerian is designed in a way that allows anyone to make these experiences.

Book structure

This book is split into four main sections:

Section 1: Creating an Escape Room

Sumerian comes with lots of different systems. A good way to learn them is to create an escape room. This provides an easy way to cover a range of diverse components. This section will not only how to create experiences in Sumerian, but it will also how to **think** in Sumerian.

This section also provides extensive coverage of Sumerian's visual scripting language. At first glance, the visual scripting language may seem overwhelming, but once you understand the structure and organization behind it, you'll be creating dynamic scenes with ease. You'll even convert your scenes to virtual reality.

Section 2: Building an Education Experience

This section covers the nuts and bolts of building an educational experience. This section explores how to use lighting, cameras, and sound to direct the user's attention. It also incorporates custom models, animation and shows how to use the Sumerian particle system to great effect.

This section also introduces the Sumerian API. It shows how you can leverage the API to add new features not included with the engine. The section also provides a JavaScript primer that will help you get started writing code in Sumerian.

Section 3: Creating an Augmented Reality Experience

One of the coolest things Sumerian offers is the ability to create augmented reality apps for mobile devices. This section will put you to the task of creating a virtual shoe store. Users will be able to try on new shoes with their phone. You'll learn the basics of augmented reality and also how to store data for a Sumerian scene outside of Sumerian using AWS.

Section 4: Creating a Virtual Travel Agent

This final section walks you through the process of creating an interactive travel agent. This is a fully interactive agent that asks questions and responds to answers. In this experience, you'll leverage AWS to create the speech, respond to the user and return a list of recommended destinations.

How to read this book

It's best to start with the first chapter and make your way through the book in order. The book assumes no 3D experience or programming knowledge. This book intends to give you everything you need to know to create interesting dynamic scenes. Hopefully, you'll have as much fun reading it as we did writing it. Enjoy!

Section I: Creating an Escape Room

Sumerian provides many tools to create rich 3D experiences. From an easy-to use-3D editor to an easy-to-understand visual scripting engine, Sumerian has everything you need to build unique scenes.

In this section, you'll cut your teeth on Sumerian by building an escape room. An escape room is a room filled with puzzles that you must solve to escape. Over the next eight chapters, these puzzles will each highlight a different aspect of the engine to give you an overview of what's possible with Sumerian. These chapters assume that you have no programming or 3D development experience. They'll walk you through the whole process, from creating a new Amazon account to enjoying your published your scene.

Here's what the following chapters will cover:

Chapter 1: Getting Started with Amazon Sumerian: Every journey starts with a first step. In this case, that means creating an AWS account and setting up a IAM user account.

Chapter 2: Building an Escape Room: This chapter introduces you to the 3D objects that you'll use to construct your escape room.

Chapter 3: Entities & Materials: This chapter introduces you to entities and how to use materials to give them some color.

Chapter 4: Adding Interactivity With Behaviors: Scenes are best when they are interactive. The chapter shows you how to use behaviors to make your scene dynamic.

Chapter 5: Creating Branching Logic with Attributes: This chapter shows you how to create logical behaviors that change based on user input.

Chapter 6: Physics: Here, you'll get an overview of the Sumerian physics engine, from adding gravity to a scene to throwing objects on command.

Chapter 7: Virtual Reality: Sumerian comes with built-in virtual reality tools. This chapter walks you through the process of turning your escape room into a virtual reality experience.

Chapter 8: Post Effects & Publishing a Scene: Once you've completed your scene, you'll add effects to make it pop. You'll also learn how to optimize your scene and publish it.

Chapter 1: Getting Started with Amazon Sumerian

By Brian Moakley

Amazon Sumerian is an excellent tool that you can use to create unique user experiences. With Sumerian, you can create a virtual shop where users can interact and buy products as if they were in a real store. You can use it to augment the real world so that when a user points their phone at a movie poster and they'll see movie times, short trailers or animated models. You can even create a three-dimensional world and embed it in a web page, allowing users to navigate a virtual floor plan without having to install custom software.

Ten years ago, you would have needed a team of programmers to do even a fraction of what's offered by Amazon Sumerian. You would have needed custom software built for a specific platform, requiring users to download a large amount of software. Now, you can do it all in your browser; but better still, you don't need a team of developers. You only need this book and a little quiet time to read through all of the examples.

This book intends to teach the Sumerian platform from the ground up. It will enable you to create unique experiences. By doing so, you'll become proficient with Sumerian.

Some of you may be breaking out into a cold sweat, thinking, “But I’m not a programmer.” That’s OK – Amazon designed Sumerian for beginners. It provides a way for you to visually code your experiences as if you were writing traditional code. This book will walk you through the basics, and by the end, you’ll be writing your own code.

Others may be thinking, “I am a programmer and I want to dive deep.” Sumerian has you covered. It provides an extensive API where you can leverage Amazon Web Services (AWS) you may be already using. You can record items to DynamoDB. You can run Amazon Polly to provide text-to-speech capabilities. You can even leverage the powers of Amazon Lex to provide an Alexa-like interface into your 3D world. This is all done using JavaScript and leveraging Sumerian’s API. You’ll learn how to do all of these things in this book.

Throughout this book, you'll learn Sumerian by building four different experiences. In the first experience, you’ll create an escape room.

What’s an escape room, you ask? It’s not a cheesy movie from 2019. Rather, it’s a physical room where you and some friends must solve clues to escape. The clues, often cryptic, may lead to keys or combinations that open boxes filled with other clues that lead to your eventual escape.

Every escape room needs to have a theme, and yours is no different. The escape room you’ll build takes place in a well-known Swedish furniture store. These stores are known to be quite large, and it’s easy to get lost in them.

In this scenario, you decided to take a break and sit down on a sofa. There, you fell asleep. When you wake, the store is closed and locked up and the alarms are active as well. Stepping on the floor will alert the nearby police force.

You read somewhere that the showrooms are locked down, but can be unlocked by solving some cryptic clues. Your mission is to solve these clues and, hopefully, escape.

Creating an AWS Account

Before you can build custom experiences, you need to create an AWS account. If you already have an AWS account, feel free to skip to the "Creating an IAM account" section in this chapter to learn about the required Sumerian permissions.

To create your AWS account, you'll need to provide not only a valid email address but a phone number as well. This provides an additional layer of verification.

To get started, visit the following URL: https://aws.amazon.com. While the design of the page may have changed since the writing of this book, there's likely still a button on the page inviting you to create a free AWS account. Click that button.

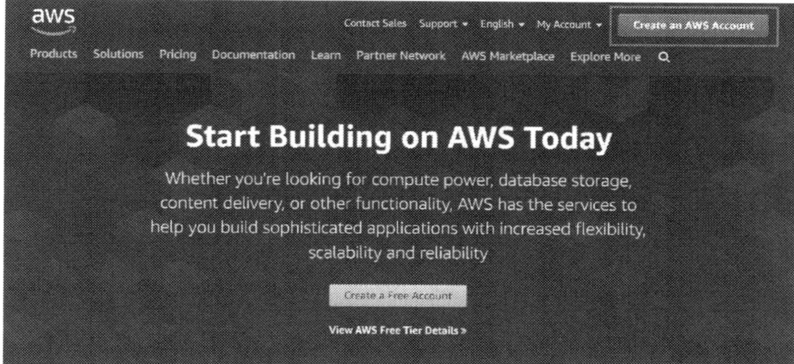

Now, fill out all the details to create your AWS account.

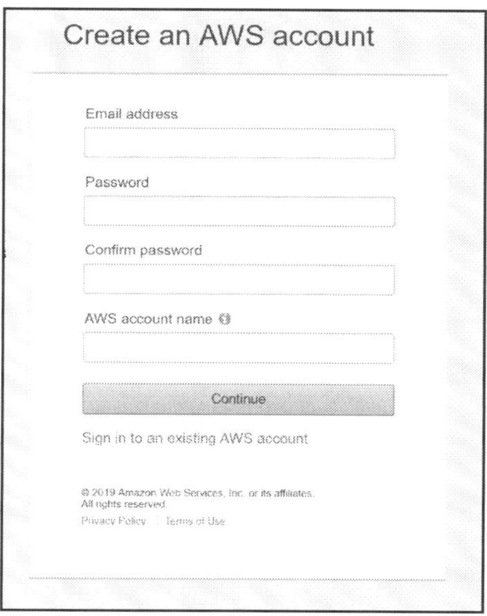

Once you've added the initial details, AWS will ask you to enter more registration information. The first prompt asks you to create either a business account or a personal account.

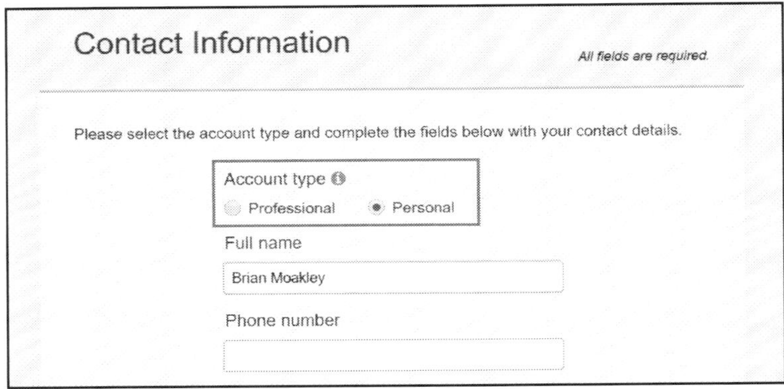

Both accounts have the same features and functions. If you select a business account, AWS will prompt you to provide additional information about your company. For this book, select the **personal account** option.

Fill out the rest of the form, being sure to provide a valid phone number. Once you submit the form, AWS will ask you for your payment information.

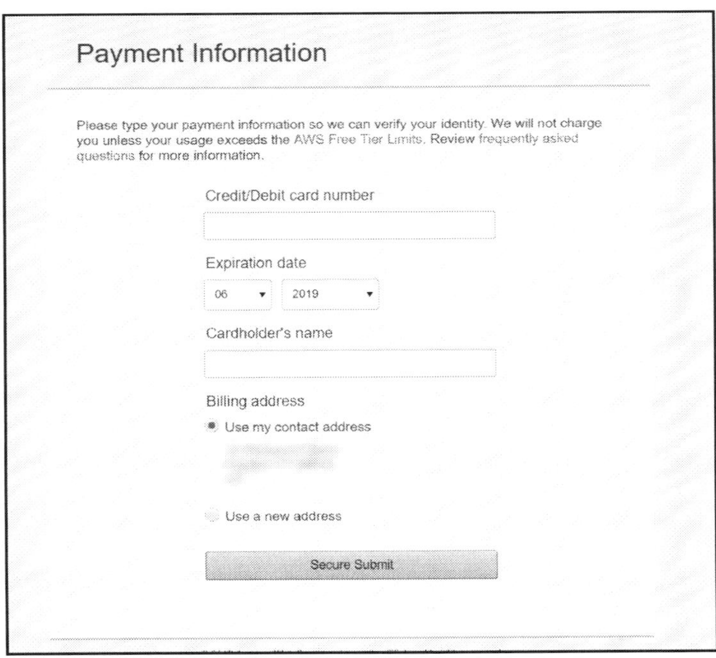

The account is free — registering won't cost you anything. Amazon only charges your credit card after you exceed the free usage tier.

Once you've filled out the payment information, click **Secure Submit** to continue.

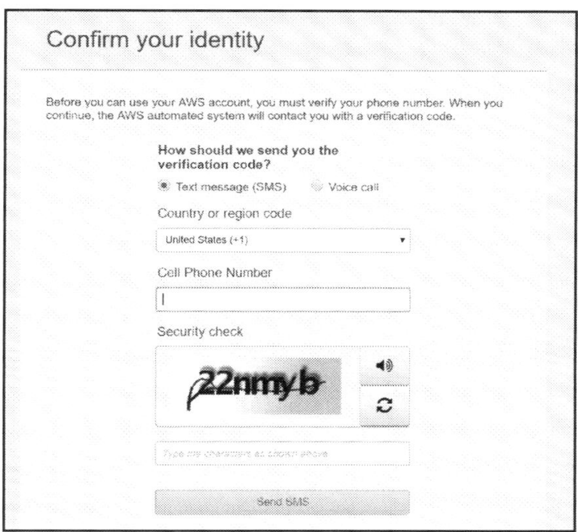

After you submit your payment information, you'll need to verify your identity. You can do this via a text message or a voice call. Select the **Text message (SMS)** option. Fill out the form and click **Send SMS**.

As soon as you click the button, you'll see a form where you enter the verification code.

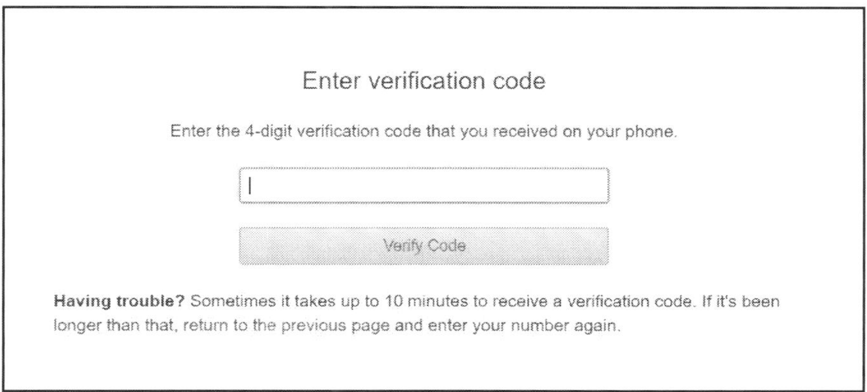

You should receive a text message once you submit the form. If you don't immediately receive a text, give it a few minutes. If you still don't receive the code, click the link sending you back to the previous page, and re-enter your phone number.

If all goes well, you'll see a green checkmark, letting you know that Amazon has verified your account.

Click **Continue** to move on to the next step.

With your account verified, your next task is to select a support plan.

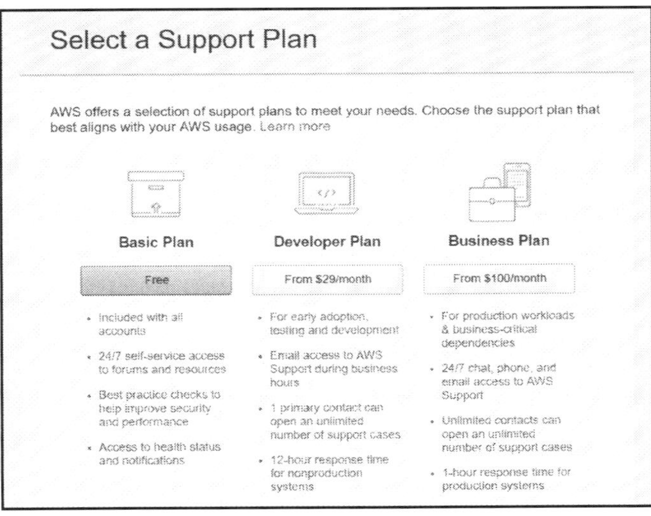

You can use the support plan for technical guidance or troubleshoot issues with a service. Since you're just learning the platform, there's no need for a paid account. Select the **Basic Plan** and click **Free**.

Congratulations! You've created a new account. You should see something like the following:

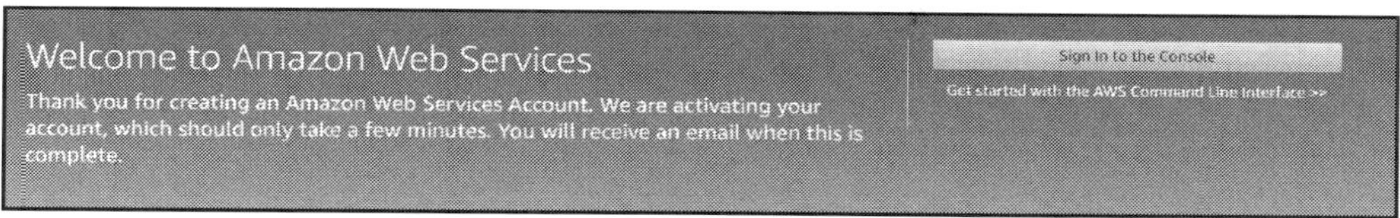

Although you've created your account, you haven't logged into it. Click **Sign In to the Console** and provide your login credentials.

Once you log into the system, you'll see the AWS Console. From here, you can launch Sumerian and get started, but before you do that, you need to create an additional user account.

Creating an IAM account

When you created your AWS account, you created what's known as a *root account*. The root account has access to all of the various services. The account also has access to your payment information, your personal information, and even your password. This is a very sensitive account.

The problem compounds when you're working with a team. By sharing your username and password, you're unnecessarily exposing this confidential information.

To avoid this, AWS requests that you create additional accounts that are known as Identity and Access Management (IAM) accounts. This lets you limit each account to only the services it needs. Each account has its own password, which doesn't affect the root account in any way, and the IAM accounts don't have access to any billing or personal information like the root account does.

Even if you're working by yourself, it's a good idea to use IAM accounts and only switch to the root account when you need to manage account access or billing information.

Note: IAM accounts provide many features that go well beyond the scope of this book. You can create groups, delegate access and responsibilities and manage security levels. Read the official IAM documentation to learn about the features and best practices. You can access the user guide here: https://docs.aws.amazon.com/IAM/latest/UserGuide/introduction.html

To start creating your first IAM account, head to the IAM console by following the URL: https://console.aws.amazon.com/iam/home#/home. Click the **Users link** in the left column.

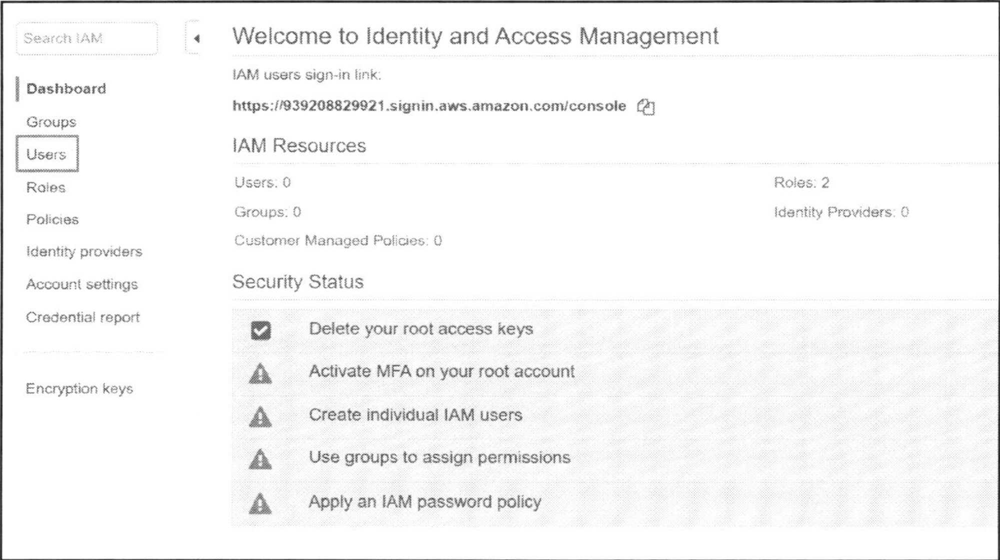

You'll see a page that allows you to create IAM users. Click **Add user** to create a new IAM user.

First, you'll need to give the user a name. You can enter your first name or any other username that makes sense to you.

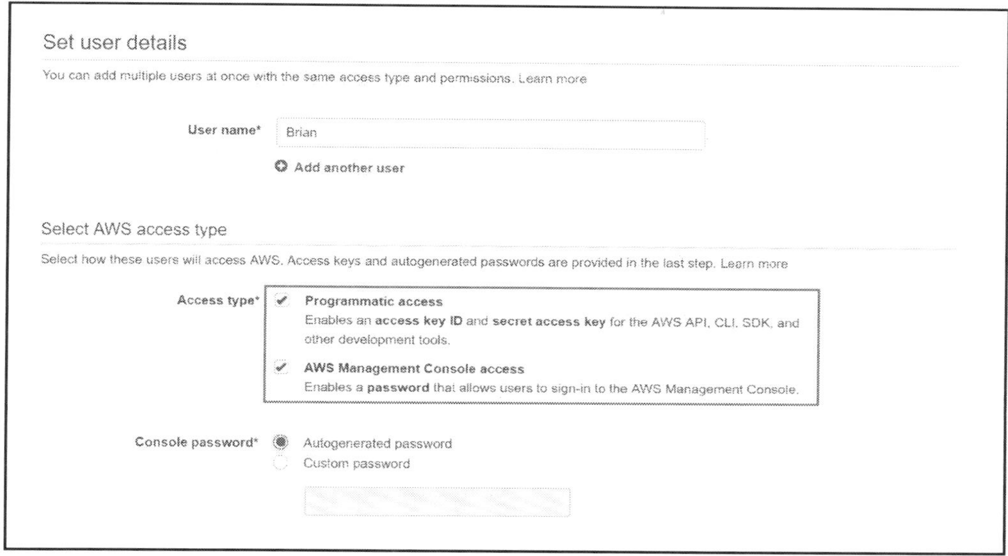

Once you've entered the username, you must set the access type for the user. Add **Programmatic access** and **AWS Management Console** to the account.

Programmatic access is useful if you need to access AWS features in your apps. For instance, you may be writing an iPhone app, but you still need to upload data to AWS. In that case, you'd need programmatic access.

The AWS management console allows the user to access the AWS site to make changes such as configuring AWS services. Since you'll be playing around with lots of different AWS services, you'll need access to the AWS management console.

Finally, you need to create a new password for the IAM account. You can provide your own or have a password auto-generated for you.

Once you have everything set, click **Next: Permissions**. By default, IAM users can't do anything with AWS. You must provide permission to the user.

AWS gives users only the permissions they need to accomplish their tasks. That way, if an IAM account is compromised due to a stolen password, it will have a minimal impact. It's like setting a credit card to buy only groceries.

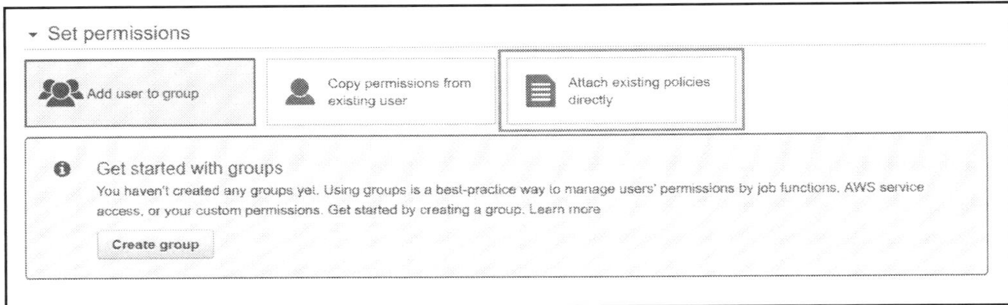

Now, select **Attach existing policies directly**.

You'll see a list of policies that you can assign to the account. In the Filter policies box, type **Sumerian**, which will filter out all of the unnecessary policies. Check the box for the **AmazonSumerianFullAccess** policy.

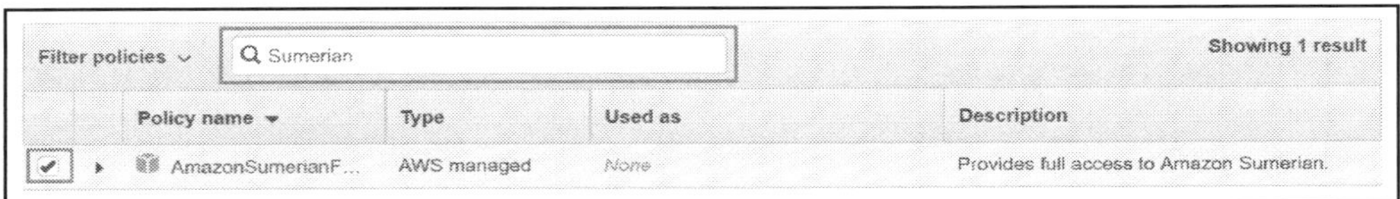

Once you're done, click **Next: Tags**. This form allows you to add metadata tags such as a physical mailing address. For now, click **Next: Review**. The review page summarizes everything you've set up. If you need to make any adjustments, click *Previous* to return to the previous screen.

With everything all set up, click **Create user** to create your new IAM user account. It may take a few moments for AWS to create the user, but once it has been set up, you'll get a confirmation page. You'll also receive a link for the IAM account to sign in as well as a CSV file with all of the credentials.

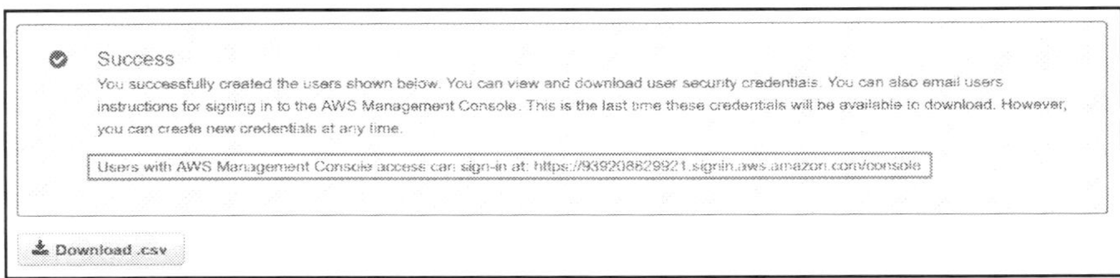

> **Important Note**: This is the last time you'll have an opportunity to download the CSV file that contains the login credentials, so it's essential to download this file now. If you lose the credentials, you can reset the IAM account password using your root account.

Click the **sign-in at** link to sign in with your new IAM account. AWS will prompt you to change your password. After you sign in, you'll see the AWS console, except this time, you're using the IAM account.

Well done! You're ready to get started using Amazon Sumerian.

Key points

- The first account that you will create is your **root account**. Only use this account to change billing or account information.
- Use an **IAM account** to do all your development
- Permissions are assigned to IAM accounts to access the various web services.
- To use Sumerian, your IAM account must have **AmazonSumerianFullAccess** permissions.
- Make sure to **download your user credentials** when you create an IAM account.

Where to go from here?

Working with Sumerian all starts with creating an AWS account. While you may not initially use AWS services in your scenes, down the road you may want to utilize these services to record data and capture user audio recordings.

If you want to learn more about IAM accounts and all the various features, Amazon provides a nice tutorial over here: https://docs.aws.amazon.com/IAM/latest/UserGuide/tutorials.html

That said, creating an AWS account is the first step. The second step is learning Sumerian, which you'll do in the next chapter.

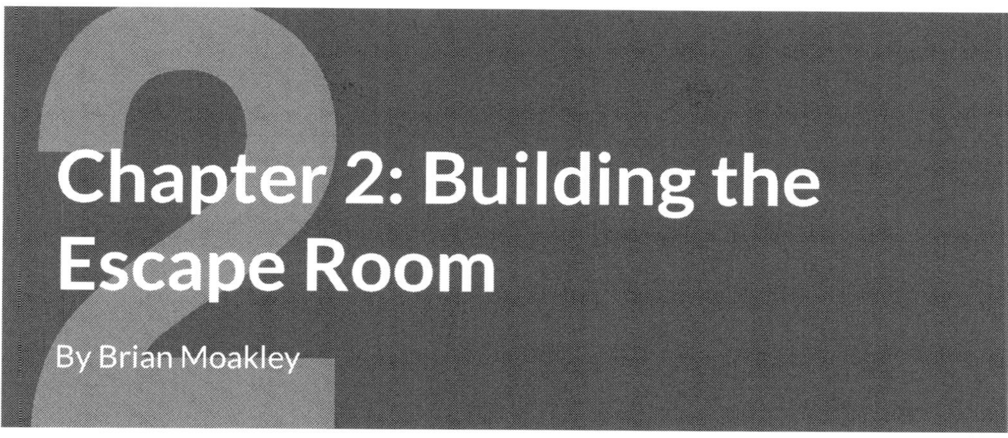

Chapter 2: Building the Escape Room

By Brian Moakley

In the previous chapter, you went through the process of creating an AWS account. If you skipped the chapter because you already had an AWS account, you'll need to add Sumerian permissions to your IAM account; otherwise, you won't be able to access the engine. If you do run into permission errors, please refer to the "Creating an IAM Account" section of the previous chapter.

Launching Sumerian

To start working with Sumerian, log into your IAM account, where the AWS Console will greet you. In the **Find Services** filter box, type **Sumerian** to bring up the Sumerian service.

Click on **Amazon Sumerian** and the Sumerian dashboard greets you. The dashboard is the central hub for your Sumerian projects. A collection of scenes defines each project; a scene is a 3D experience that you design.

To get started creating your escape room, click **Projects**.

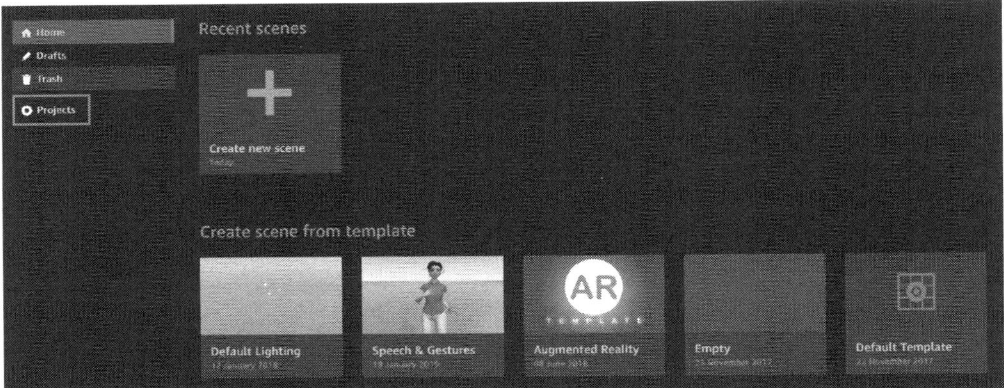

Since Sumerian creates a project for you by default, you'll see a project list already. Click **New Project** to create a project for your escape room.

When you click the link, you'll see a prompt asking for the project name. Name your project **Showroom Skedaddle** and click **Create**.

Click Create; it may take a few moments to complete. After the project is ready, you'll see a scene list. Click **Create new scene**.

As with the project creation, you'll need to create a name. Give the scene the same name as the project: **Showroom Skedaddle**. Click **Create**, and you'll come to the Sumerian editor.

Using the Sumerian editor

When you first arrive at the editor, it may feel a little overwhelming. There's a lot of information here, so it's best to get a high-level overview of the various functions. As you progress, you'll dive deeper into each one.

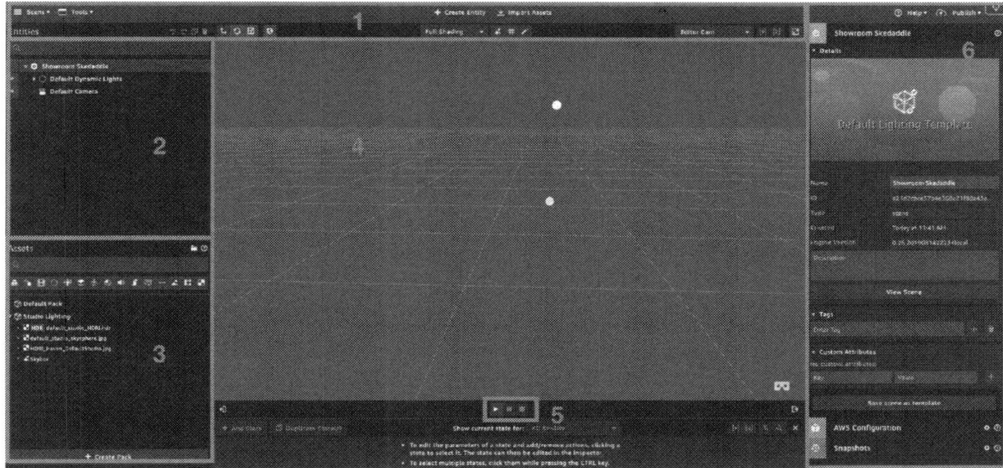

Here's a complete breakdown of what you can find in the Sumerian editor:

1. This is where your menu items and toolbars live. This is where you can save your current scene, jump to another scene, create various pre-customized entities, or manipulate those entities. What's an entity? I'm glad you asked (that was you, wasn't it?). An entity is an object that's part of your scene, such as a camera, light or cube. If you're coming from Unity, you can think of these entities as GameObjects.

2. This is the Entities panel. This a list of the current entities in the scene. Entities act very much like folders in so much as an entity can exist inside of another entity. This provides an excellent mechanism for organizing your scene. If you're coming from Unity, you can think of this as the hierarchy window. The eyeball to the left of each entity controls its visibility. If you need to make an entity invisible, click the eyeball. You click it again to make it reappear. Keep in mind, this doesn't work in real life!

3. Beneath the Entities panel is your Assets panel. The Assets panel contains all of the raw assets that make up your scene. You can think of the Assets panel like a bookcase with books you might need and the Entities panel like a desk with the books you're actively reading. If you're coming from Unity, you can think of this as your Project Browser window.

4. This is the 3D space where you'll create your experience. The white dots indicate the default lights in the scene.

5. When you're working with the editor, it's either in edit mode or play mode. In edit mode, you can add your entities, position them and configure all of your scripts. In Play mode, the scene will play and you will be able to interact with it. The editor controls play, stop or pause your scene.

6. This is the Inspector panel, which allows you to configure your entities. For instance, you may want to change the color of a mug or set the sounds that you want to play.

First, you need to create your room. The floor is an excellent place to start. At the top of the editor, click **Create Entity**.

Clicking the button gives you a list of predefined entities that you can create. Click the icon that looks like a **cube**. This is the box entity.

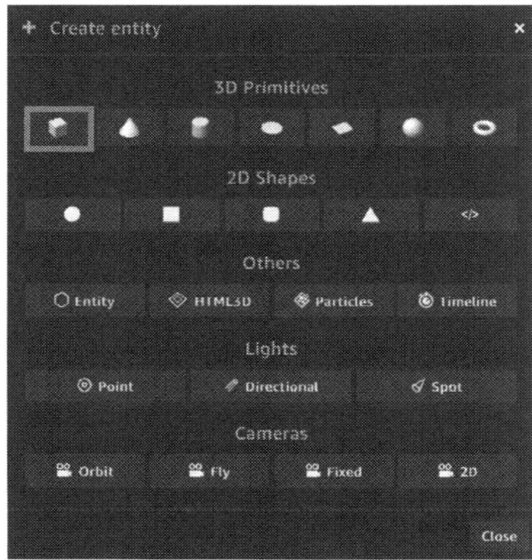

This places a box entity in the center of the world. The box is very far away from your vantage point. **Scroll up** on your mouse wheel. You'll zoom toward the box. Now, **scroll down**. This zooms you out.

> **Note**: If you're working on macOS, you may find your scroll directions to be exactly the opposite. The key point is that the scroll wheel lets you zoom.

Now, press the **F** key. You'll zoom right to the object. Using the F shortcut is a great time saver when you have lots of entities on the canvas.

This book will introduce you to a variety of shortcuts. Do your best to memorize them, as they'll dramatically increase the speed and efficiency of your workflow. I call the F key my "focus key", as it focuses on the object. That's an easy way to remember it.

You can orbit around the box to see the surrounding geometry or view the model from different vantage points. **Right-click** your mouse and **drag your mouse** in a circle. Conversely, you can **alt-left click** to orbit the camera as well.

You can also pan around the canvas. Press your **middle mouse button**, and **drag your mouse** left then right. You can get the same effect by **shift-left clicking** and then moving your mouse. This moves your view on a horizontal axis. By holding the middle mouse button and dragging up and down, you can move your view on the vertical axis.

By using those keyboard and mouse commands, you'll be able to navigate throughout your scene. For now, return to the box. Press the **F** key. If nothing happens, make sure that the **box is selected** in the Entities panel, and then press the F key again.

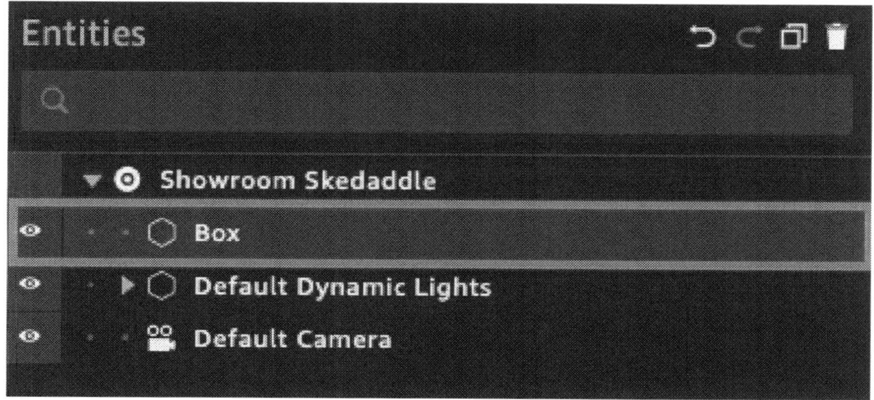

You'll also notice three colored arrows pointing from the box. This is the transform of the entity.

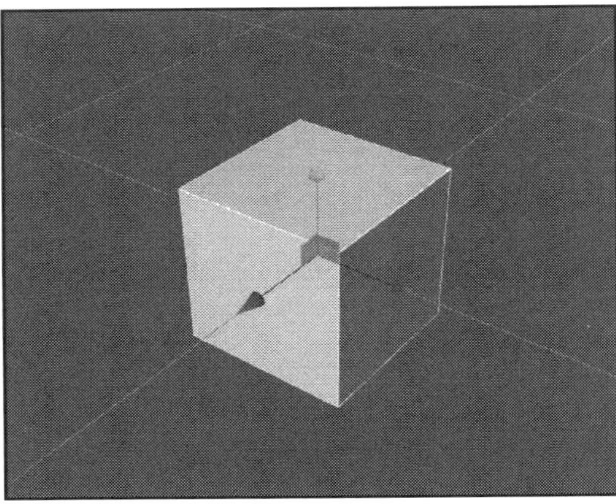

The arrows allow you to move the box on the canvas. Place your cursor over the blue arrow and **hold the left mouse button.** You'll notice the arrow turns yellow, which means it's actively selected.

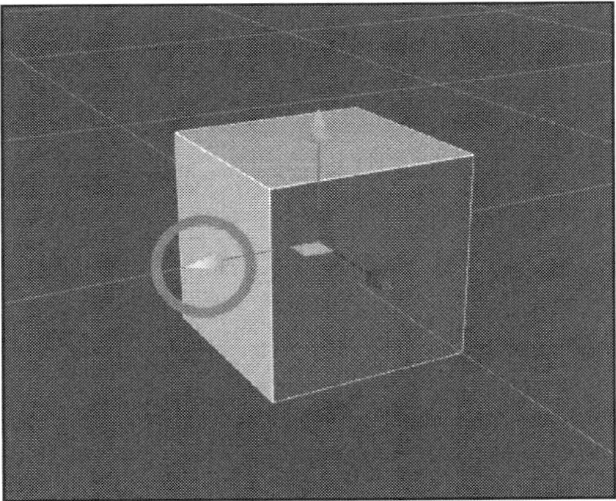

Drag the mouse up or down and you'll move the box only on that z-axis – you won't be able to move the box in any other direction. The green arrow restricts movement to the y-axis, and the red is the x-axis. You'll quickly find that manipulating objects in a 3D space is challenging, so using these arrows will save you time.

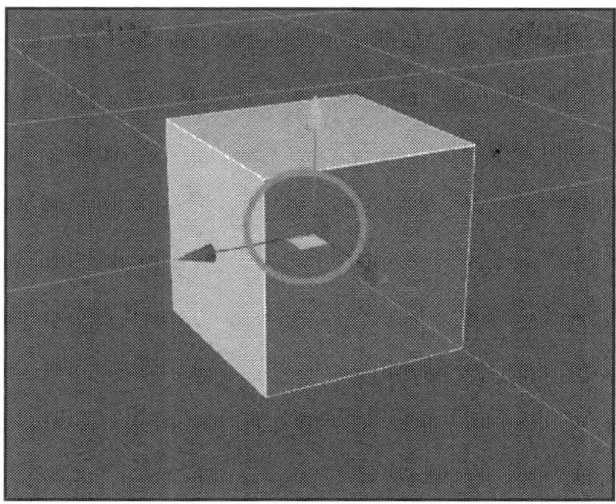

In the center of the transform, you'll notice colored three colored squares. The squares allow you to move the box on two axes at once.

The color of the square indicates the axis that won't move. By selecting the red square, which is the x-axis, you can move the box only on the y- and z-axes. Experiment by clicking each of the color squares and then moving your mouse.

OK, back to the business of creating your escape room floor. The box needs to shrink in height and expand in width. Thankfully, you have tools to do this.

With the box selected, click **Scale (R)** from the toolbar.

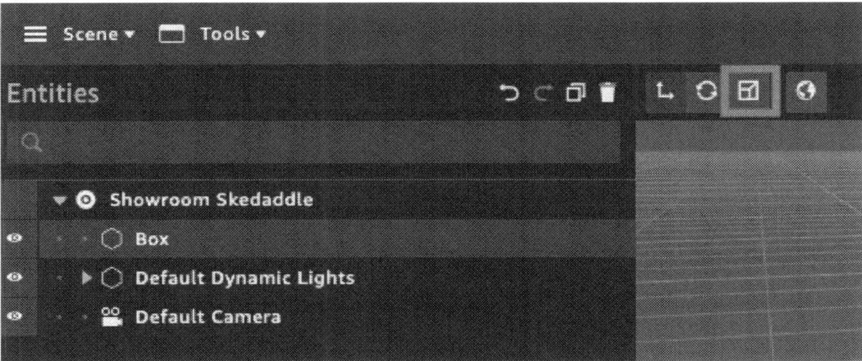

You'll notice the transform arrows have now changed to boxes. This lets you know that you're using the scale tool. Other tools change the transform in different ways.

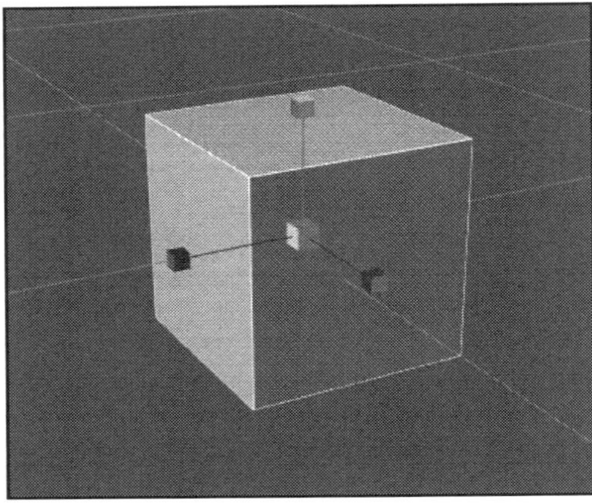

As with the transform arrows, each colored box indicates the axis to scale the box. The center gray box allows you to scale the entire cube.

Decrease the height of the cube and **expand the size** of it until it covers four squares in the grid. Don't worry about exact sizes. Just eyeball it for now.

You'll notice in the Entities panel that your floor is still named Box. **Double-click** it and rename it to **Floor**. It's a good habit to name your entities, especially when you have a lot of them in a scene.

Now, you need to create some walls. Click **Create Entity** and select **Add box** from the options. You'll need to scale and translate (move) it to form a wall. When you need to translate it, press **Translate (W)** in the toolbar.

When complete, your room will look like this:

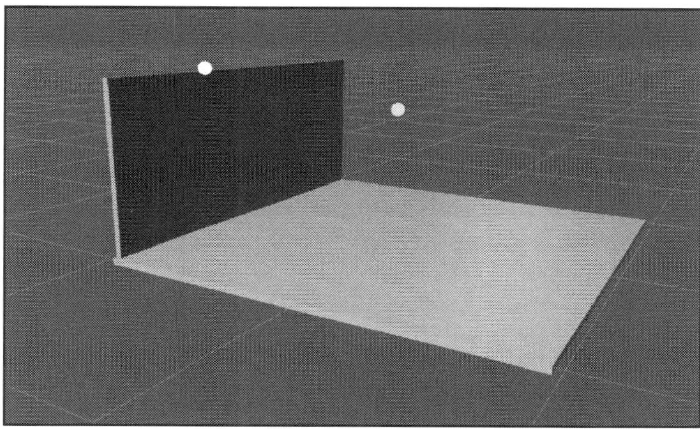

In the Entities panel, double-click the newly added **box** entity and name it **Wall 1**.

One side of the wall is black because it is blocking the light

To make an adjacent wall, you need to duplicate the existing wall. Duplicating the wall raises some issues, which you'll learn about in later chapters.

For now, select your wall and press **Duplicate all selections** in the toolbar.

The Entities panel gains a new entity, smartly named Wall 2. You'll notice that the canvas shows only one entity, the wall you already created. There's a new entity except it's in the exact position of the current wall. **Move** the new wall to the center of the floor.

Next, you need to rotate it to form a side wall. You could click **Rotate (E)** in the toolbar:

Or you could use the keyboard shortcuts:

- **W**: Translate.
- **E**: Rotate.
- **R**: Scale.
- **Q**: Cycle between them.

These shortcuts may seem strange, but they all correspond to keys above your left hand on the keyboard. This makes the keys easy to access.

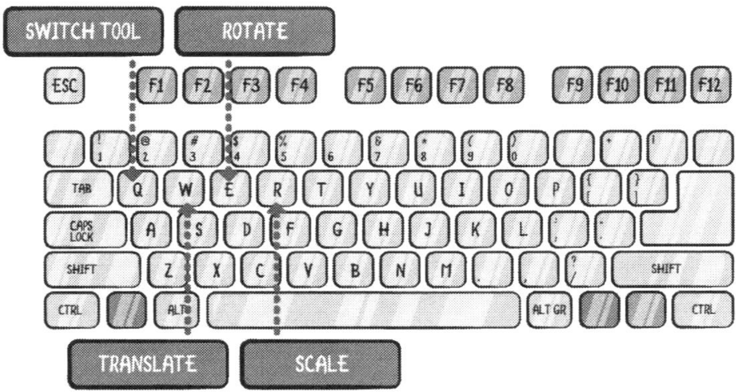

Sumerian also provides an extensive undo/redo system. You can access the undo and redo icons near the top of the editor.

With Wall 2 selected, press the **E** key. You'll see that the transform component has transformed into a rotation component.

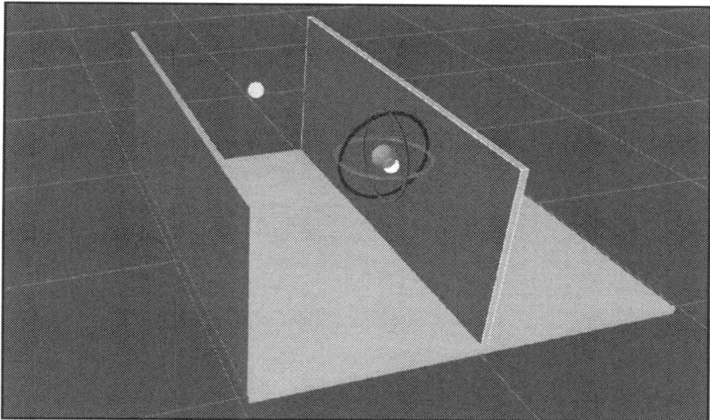

As you can probably deduce by now, each color corresponds to an axis. Click on the green ring (y-axis) and rotate the wall until it's perpendicular to the other wall. Then align it against the floor edge — and look at that, you have half of a room.

Your mission now is to add the two other walls. You can either duplicate the existing walls or create new walls from box entities. When you're done, your room will look like this:

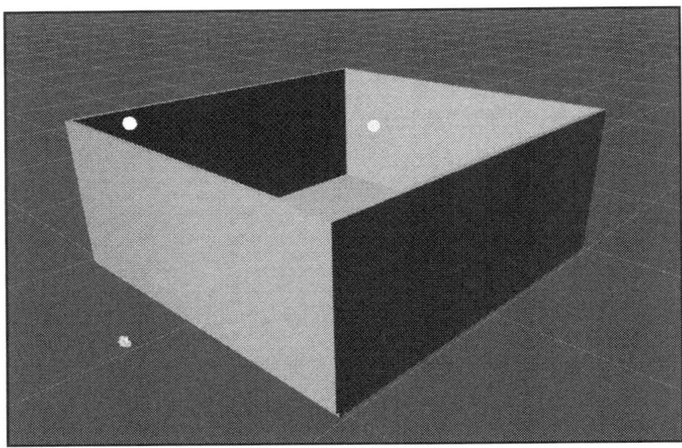

Congratulations! You've built your first room. Zoom the camera into the center of the room and click **Play** in the bottom toolbar.

Now, move the mouse to look around the room. You can continue to orbit, pan and zoom, but the movements are much smoother. This is what a user will experience. When you're done, click **Stop**, also located in the bottom toolbar, to return to the editor.

Creating a secret door

At this point, you have the basic room created, but there's no way to escape it. It's just an empty room hanging out in space. You need to create a way for the user to escape.

Select one of the walls and press the **R** key. **Scale** the width of the wall until it's about half of its previous width.

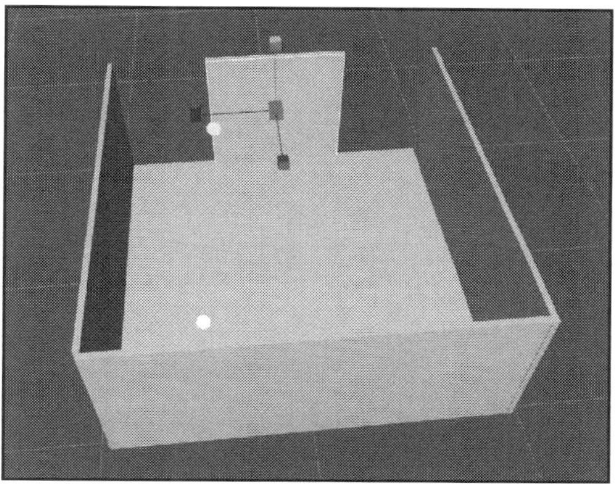

Translate the wall (**W**) and move it to the corner of the room. Now you have one half of the wall. Don't worry about it being precisely half.

With the wall still selected, click **Duplicate all selections** (from here on out, I'll refer to it simply as Duplicate). **Translate** the duplicated wall until it fills the missing gap. You may need to scale the walls until they exactly fill the gap.

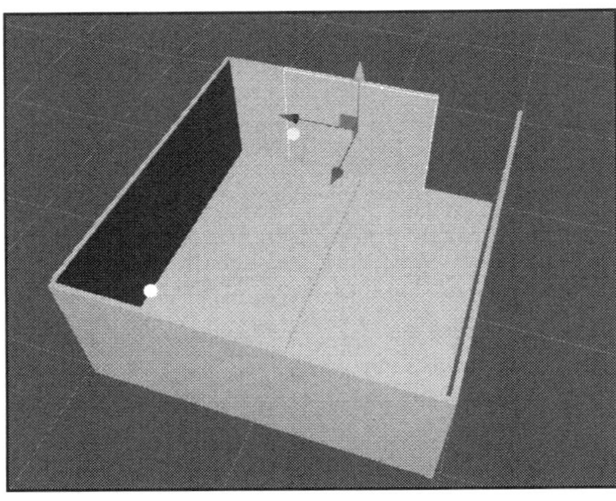

You now have a newly-completed wall made up of two individual walls. When the user solves the puzzle, the walls will slide open. Your completed room will look like this:

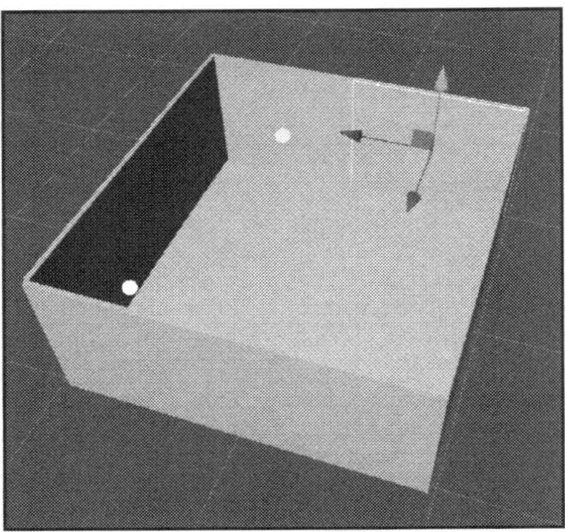

Don't worry if it looks a little different right now. In the next chapter, you'll build your room with exact specifications.

Challenges

It's important to practice what you've learned, so some chapters in this book may have challenges associated with them.

I recommend trying all of the challenges. While following a step-by-step tutorial is educational, you'll learn a lot more by solving a problem on your own. Also, each chapter will continue where the previous chapter's challenges left off, so you'll want to stay in the loop!

If you get stuck, you can find solutions in the resources for this chapter – but to get the most from this book, give it your best shot before you look.

Challenge 1: Adding the ceiling

Your escape room looks great, but it lacks one thing: A ceiling. Your task is to create that ceiling using the skills you've learned. Start by creating a box entity and moving on from there.

Solution

Start by creating a 3D box. Click **Create Entity** and select the box model. You may not see the box right away because it may be under the floor.

With the box selected, **translate** it to where the ceiling should be.

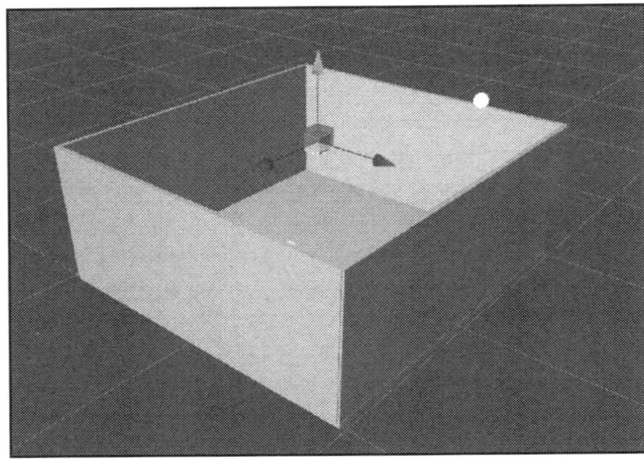

Next, press **R** to size the box so that it fits the size of the room.

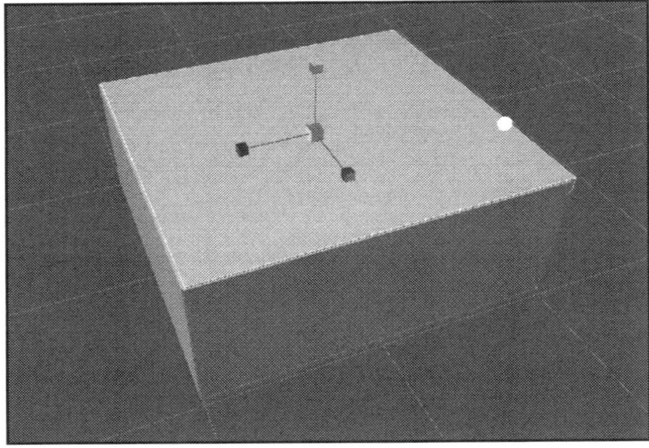

In the Entities panel, double-click the new **box** and rename it to **Ceiling**.

Finally, that ceiling is blocking your view. Click the eyeball to the left of it to make it disappear.

You're ready for the next challenge!

Challenge 2: Creating a secret hallway

When your secret door opens, the user will see an empty space, as if the room is hanging over a massive abyss. It's better to display a hallway so that the showroom looks like it's connected to a larger space.

Your challenge is to create this new hallway. When you're done, your escape room will look like this:

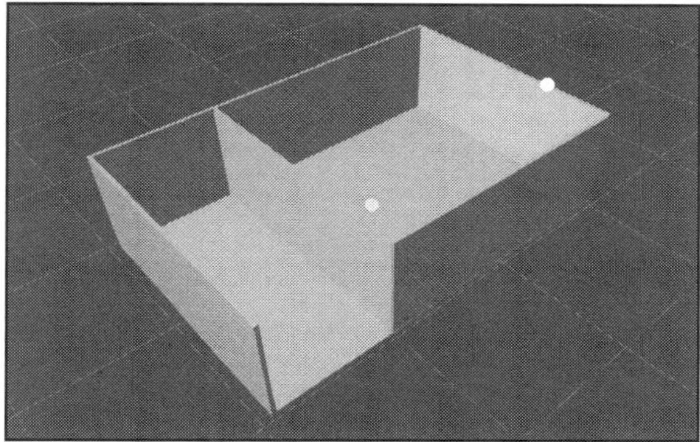

In the previous challenge, you manipulated a box. Try completing this challenge by duplicating existing entities.

Solution

To build your secret hallway, you could create new entities, but it's much easier to duplicate existing ones. Duplication saves time so you're not repeating existing work.

Select the floor and **duplicate** it. **Translate the floor** so that it's flush against the secret wall. In the Entities panel, rename it to **Secret Hall Floor**.

With the secret floor still selected, **scale** the floor until it's as narrow as the hall and **translate** it against the wall.

Now, to deal with the wall. Select **Wall 1** and **duplicate** it. **Translate** it to the other side of the secret hall floor.

Finally, select **Wall 2** and **duplicate** it. **Translate** and **scale** it to fill the empty space at the end of the hall.

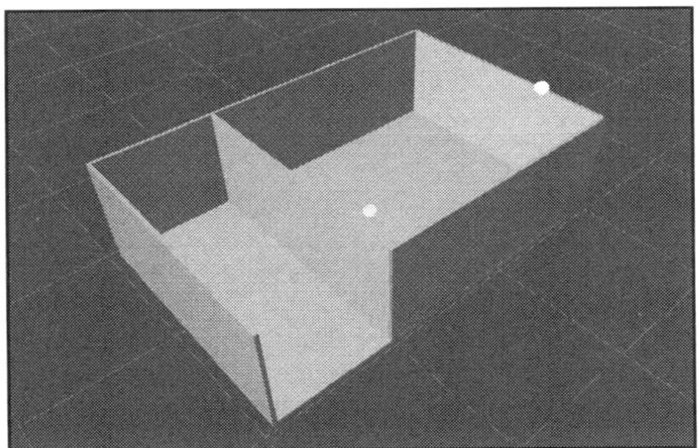

Key points

- An entity is an object that exists in your scene.
- The **Entities panel** contains all the various entities being **actively used** in your scene.
- The **Assets panel** contains all the various objects (entities, sounds, scripts, etc) that **you can add to your scene**.
- The Inspector panel allows you to **change various properties** on your entities.
- Click the **Create Entity** button to create new entities.
- Use the **arrow and transform tools** to move, scale and rotate your entities.

Where to go from here?

It's hard to believe that in just one chapter, you've learned how to create entities, you've learned how to position and manipulate those entities and find your way around the interface.

If you are interested in learning more about the Sumerian interface, the Amazon Sumerian team has created an informative tutorial that you can find here: https://docs.sumerian.amazonaws.com/tutorials/create/getting-started/sumerian-interface/

The fun is only starting. In the next chapter, you'll add some color to your escape room and even do some interior decorating with the built-in assets.

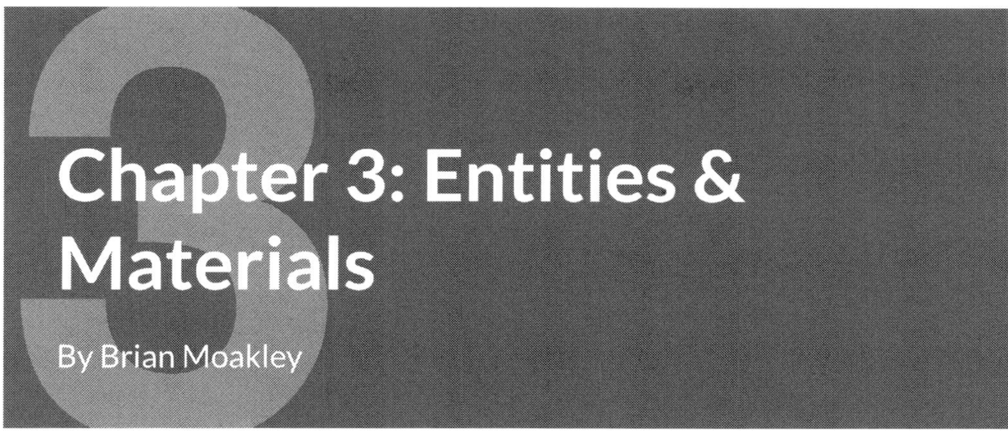

Chapter 3: Entities & Materials

By Brian Moakley

At this point in the book, you have a constructed room that isn't very interesting. It's just a collection of white walls that contain a secret hallway. Your goal is to make the escape room give off a more Swedish-furniture-store vibe.

To do this, you'll need to learn more about entities, materials and even how to import models provided by the Amazon Sumerian team.

Diving deeper into entities

Entities. What are they good for? As it turns out, they are good for absolutely everything. Everything you've done so far has used entities.

You constructed your simple escape room with boxes, but those boxes are entities. The default lights that allow you to see are also entities. The camera which captures your scene is an entity. Even the folders in your Entities panel are entities. Entities are everywhere; but what does it *mean* to be an entity?

The answer is simple: An entity, in its barest form, represents a point in space in your scene.

Every entity contains a transform that provides its x, y, and z location. This is the physical address where the entity lives in your scene. You'll learn about this a moment.

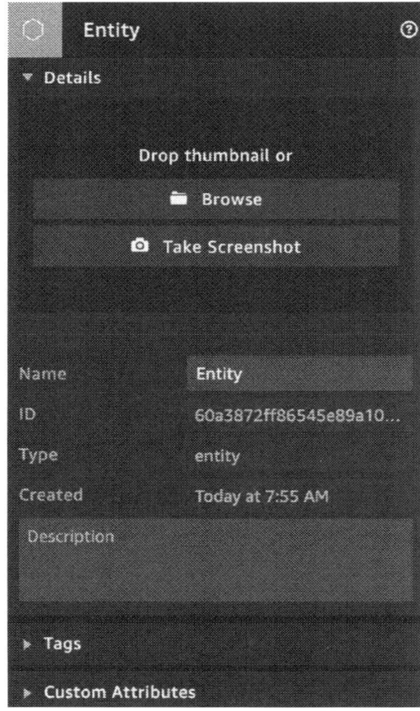

Entities also contain metadata. You can give an entity a name and a description, and provide custom tags as well. Every entity is unique. When you create an entity, Sumerian creates a unique identifier for it as well as recording when the entity was created.

As you can imagine, your scenes will use a lot of entities. Sumerian provides up to 1,000 of them. If you find yourself reaching the limit, you may want to either downsize your scene or break your scene into smaller scenes.

Note: You can import entities as assets, but not all assets are entities. When you import items, such as 3D models or images, into your scene, they'll appear in the Assets panel. You can think of this as a warehouse for your scene. You can only drag entities and skyboxes onto the canvas.

Components

Being that everything in your scene is an entity, you might wonder how Sumerian treats a camera differently from a box.

Entities are modified by components. These components can make the entity display a 3D model, play a sound, move through space and do a whole lot of other things. In essence, an entity is a single point in space whose behavior you provide by way of components.

If your scene isn't open, start your scene from the Sumerian dashboard In the Entities panel, select the **Wall 1** entity. You'll notice that the right-hand side of your screen provides all this new information.

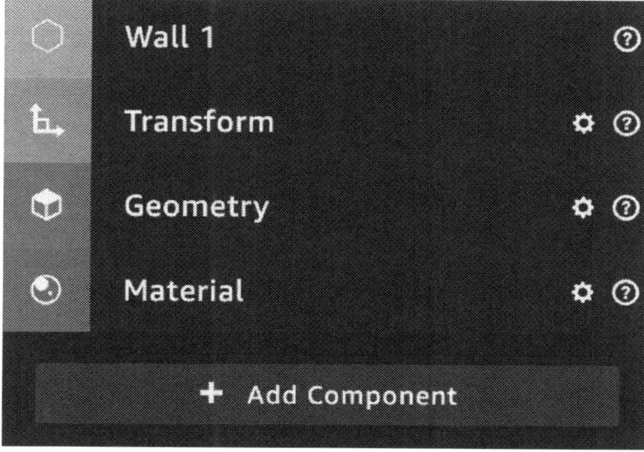

This panel is called the Inspector panel. The Inspector lists all the various components attached to Wall 1. You'll notice the following components: Transform, Geometry, and Material.

The Inspector panel allows you to customize the values of all these components. In short, you convert your wall into a camera by simply adding, changing and removing existing components.

Click the **Geometry** component and from the drop-down, select **Remove**.

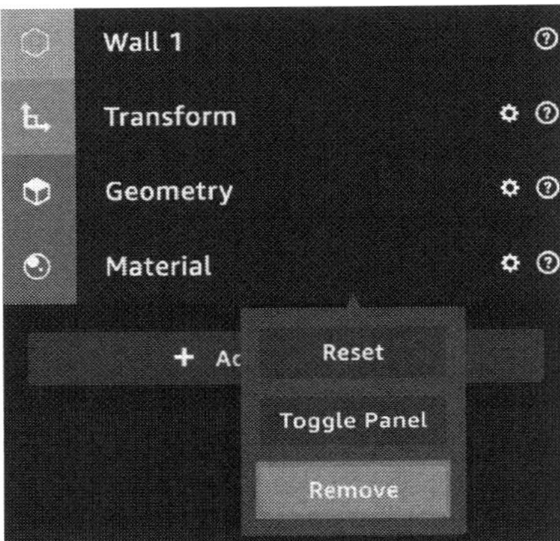

It looks like your wall has disappeared, but what happened is that you deleted the 3D model of the wall. Don't worry, you can get it back. Just press **Control-Z** to undo.

> **Note**: Sumerian will run on any modern browser such as Google Chrome or Firefox. This means that you can run Sumerian on a wide range of platforms. For the sake of simplicity, I'll refer to Windows-based shortcuts. Please refer to the shortcuts of your platform.

The question mark icon in the component heading represents the documentation. Click this icon when you need to look up any details about the component.

Getting in sync

In the last chapter, you shaped boxes to match the shape of the escape room. While you may have matched the shape of the escape room, your escape room has a different size and position from the one featured in this book. It's best to be on the same page.

To get in sync, you'll use the Transform component, which every entity contains. As mentioned, every entity is a point in space and the transform allows you to modify that location.

Since Sumerian is a 3D engine, you'll be working in 3D space. You can visualize a 2D system by looking at a simple graph over your monitor.

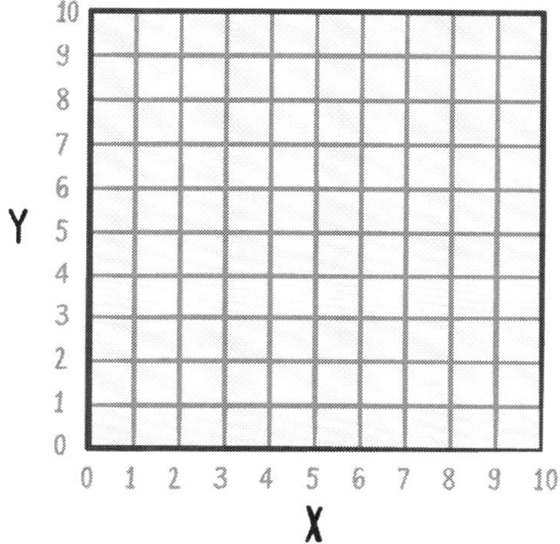

The x-axis represents the horizontal coordinates and the y-axis represents the vertical coordinates.

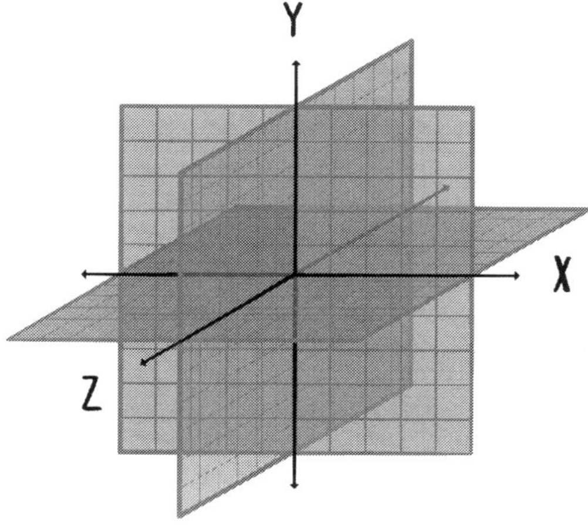

For a 3D system, you now need an additional coordinate system, where the z-axis goes into the monitor or out towards you.

Select the **Floor** and in the transform component, set the position to (**-0.367**, **-0.03**, **-0.027**). These numbers are arbitrary. The floor ended up in this position as I was building the project.

> **Note**: The transform component also contains one cool feature: You can scrub the values. Select the value inside of a field, then hold down the left mouse button and try moving your mouse either up or down. This allows you to rapidly change a value. This is great to do when you make broad changes. Remember, if you change a value too much, Control-Z is your friend.

Next, set the scale (the third row) to the following values: (**8.888**, **0.045**, **7.084**)

Your transform should look as follows:

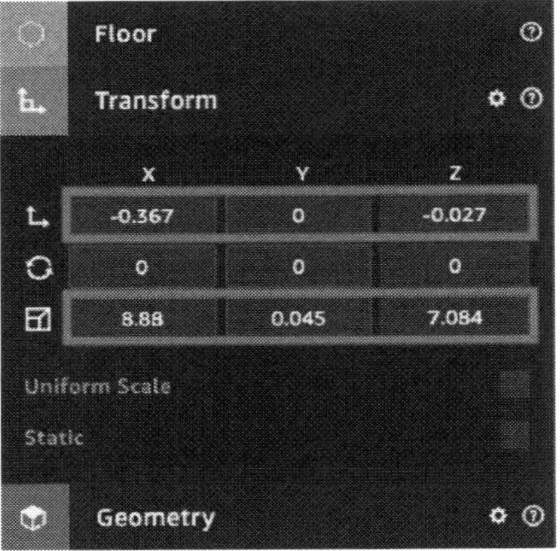

Now, in the Entities panel, **delete** all the entities *except* the following: **Default Dynamic Lights, Floor and Camera**. To delete an entity, **select** an entity in the Entities panel and press your **delete** key. Each time you delete an entity, you'll be prompted with a confirmation dialog.

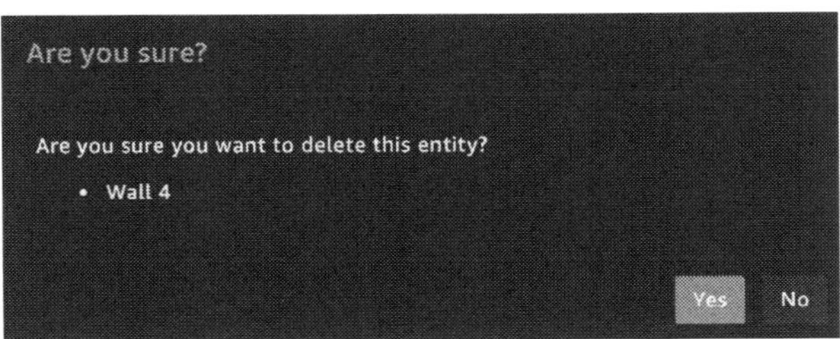

Make sure to click the **Yes** button for each delete.

Next, create the following entities using the box as your template.

> **Note**: Forgot how to create a box? Click the **Create Entity** button on the top of the editor and in the dialog, select the **cube** icon in the **3D Primitives** section.

Entity Name	Position X	Position Y	Position Z	Rotation X	Rotation Y	Rotation Z	Scale X	Scale Y	Scale Z
Wall 1	-4.752	1.379	0.015	0	90	0	7.093	2.83	0.124
Wall 2	-1.734	1.377	-3.608	0	0	0	6.143	2.827	0.124
Wall 3	1.393	1.377	-2	0	90	0	3.345	2.827	0.124
Wall 4	1.393	1.377	1.61	0	90	0	3.88	2.827	0.124
Wall 5	-0.367	1.377	3.493	0	0	0	8.887	2.827	0.124
Wall 6	4.131	1.377	0.007	0	90	0	7.093	2.827	0.124
Ceiling	-0.3	2.77	-0.06	0	0	0	9.007	0.045	7.112

Your escape room should look like the following:

Hide the ceiling so you can get a better glimpse of the room. To hide the ceiling, click the **eyeball** next to the **Ceiling** entity. Your escape room now looks like the following:

Your escape room could use some nice columns. Add the following using the box entity:

Entity Name	Position X	Position Y	Position Z	Rotation X	Rotation Y	Rotation Z	Scale X	Scale Y	Scale Z
Column 1	-3.372	1.362	-1.249	0	0	0	0.204	2.79	0.212
Column 2	-3.372	1.362	2.332	0	0	0	0.204	2.79	0.212
Column 3	0.302	1.362	2.332	0	0	0	0.204	2.79	0.212
Column 4	0.302	1.362	-1.267	0	0	0	0.204	2.79	0.212

Congrats! You now have a completed escape room with columns.

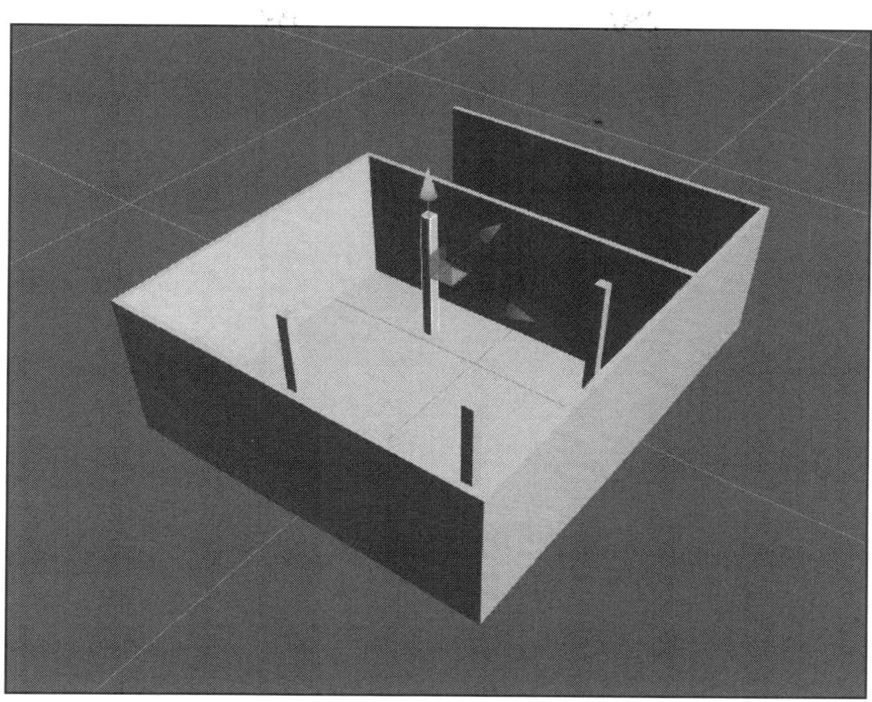

Parenting entities

While your escape room is looking good, your Entities panel looks like a mess.

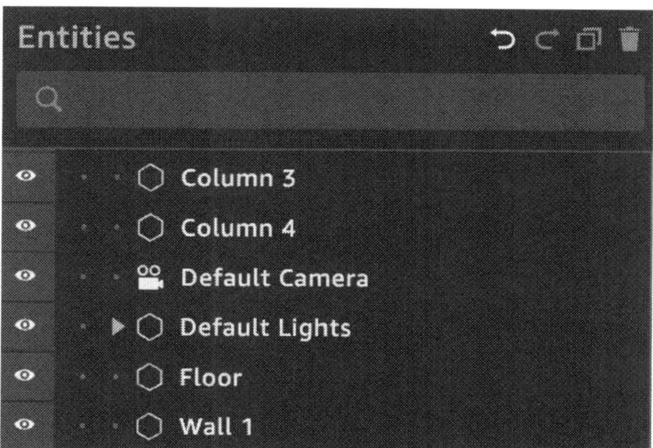

Mind you, this is with a dozen or so entities. Imagine working with hundreds of them. Thankfully, you can organize an entity by using entities.

Every time that you create an entity, it's all by itself. Don't worry, the entity is quite happy. Nevertheless, you can provide a parent to the entity. From this perspective, entities work very much like folders in that you can create a tree structure.

Click **Create Entity** and this time click the **Entity** button. This creates an empty entity.

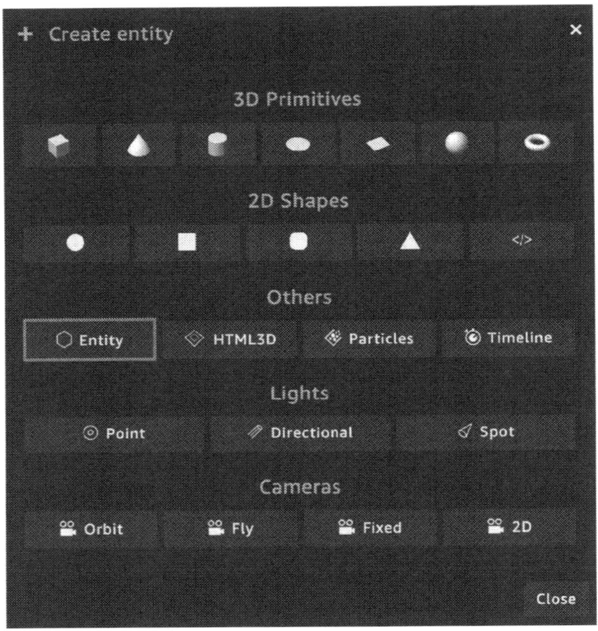

You'll now have a new entity in the Entities panel named — wait for it — Entity. **Rename** it to **Columns**.

Now, drag each column into your new Columns entity.

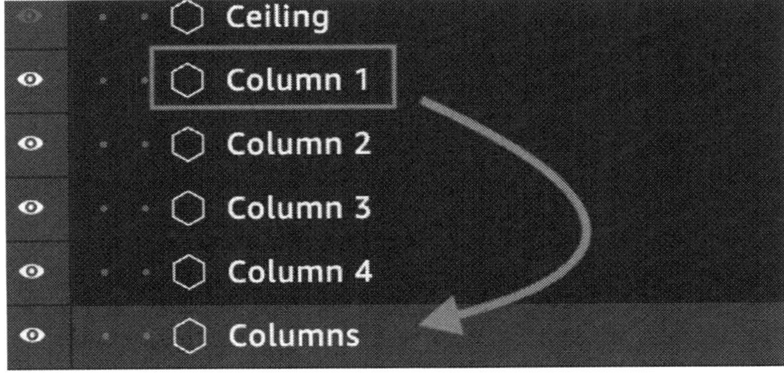

Once you have all your columns organized, you'll find that you can expand and collapse the Columns entity by clicking on the disclosure triangle next to the name.

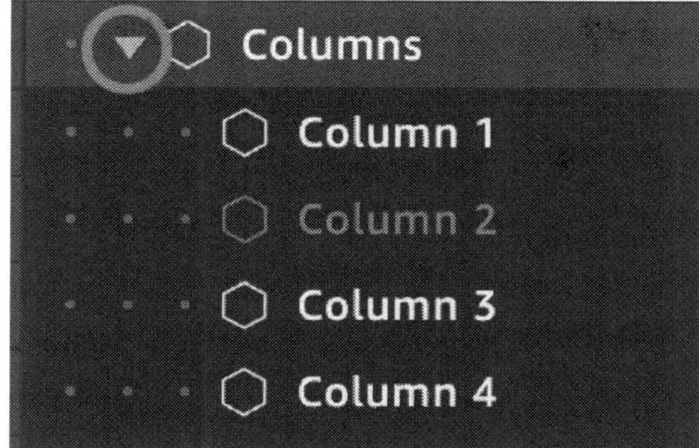

Parent entities can also influence their children. Click the **Columns** entity, and you'll notice that a transform appears on the canvas. Remember, an entity occupies a point in space — even empty entities.

Now, **move** the **Columns** entity in any direction. You'll notice that all of the columns move with it. When you've finished moving, just press **Control-Z** to return to the previous state.

Next, create a new empty entity and give it the name: **Walls**. Drag the following entities into it: **Wall 1, Wall 2, Wall 3, Wall 4, Wall 5 and Wall 6**.

Create another empty entity and call it **Room Geometry**. Drag the following entities into it: **Walls, Columns, Floor and Ceiling**.

Your Entities panel should look like the following:

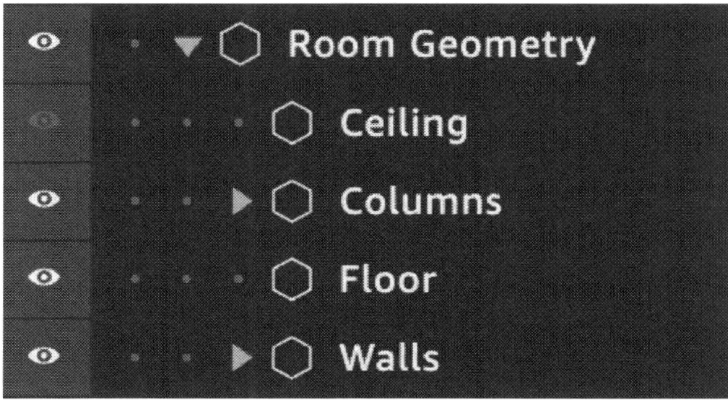

Adjusting the Lights

Lighting is incredibly important when developing your scenes. This book has an entire chapter just on lights. For now, you'll make some small adjustments to get rid of those sharp shadows.

First, you'll rename the Default Dynamic Lights entity. There are two ways to do this. First, you can double-click the entity name in the Entities panel. The second way is to select the entity and rename it in the Inspector Panel.

Select the **Default Dynamic Lights** entity and in the Inspector panel, rename it to **Default Lights**.

Select the **Key - Directional** entity and set the rotation to (**-38**, **16.958**, **-18**). In the Light component, set the Intensity to **1.15**. This sets the light's overall brightness.

Next, select the **Rim - Directional**. Set the rotation to (**-35.112**, **154.697**, **9.967**). Set the Intensity to **.5**.

Finally, click the **Create Entity** button and select the **Directional Light**. A directional light is like the sun.

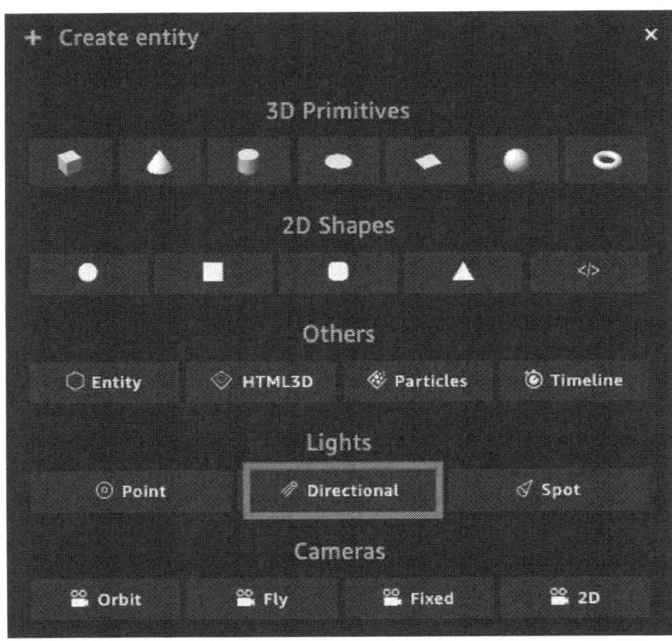

Rename the light to **Fill - Directional**. Set the rotation to (**-21.913**, **-70.363**, **5.503**). Set the Intensity to **.35**.

This produces even lighting throughout your escape room.

Selecting nested entities

Having your entities organized into other entities makes it easier to understand in the Entities panel, but it does cause some problems when you try to select an entity.

For instance, in your canvas, **click on a column** to select it. Make sure you do this with nothing else selected.

You'll notice in the entities panel that the column isn't selected at all. The Room Geometry entity is selected instead.

Double-click on the column again, and now the Columns entity is selected. **Double-click** one last time and your column will be selected. As you can see, double-clicking an entity brings you one level deeper in the Entities panel.

Now, it's time to bring some color and texture to your escape room. You'll do this by using materials.

Using materials

When working with a 3D environment, you provide models that are composed of geometry and materials. The geometry tells the engine how to draw the object. The materials determine how the model looks. These materials paint the model as well as determine how the textures appear under various light conditions.

It's easy to confuse materials with textures. A texture is an image such as a JPG or PNG that you import into a scene. A material uses textures to provide detail to a model.

When you create a box entity, Sumerian creates a 3D model of a box then applies a white material to it.

In the Entities panel, select the **Floor** entity and in the inspector, expand the **Material** component. You'll see that you have lots of options.

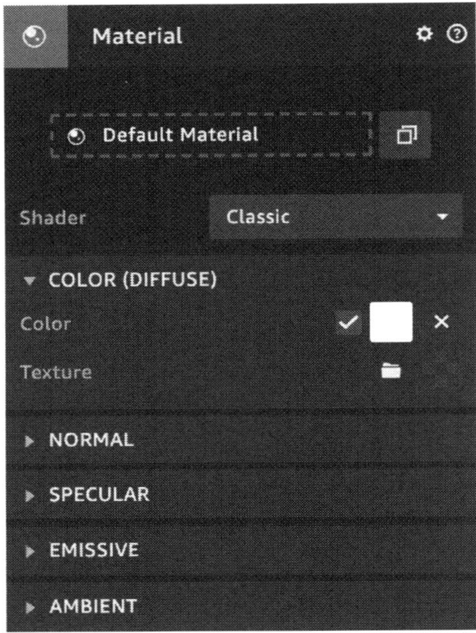

You'll learn more about some of these options later, but for now, give the floor a different color. Expand **Color**, and set the color by clicking the **white color box**. From the color picker, select a **red color**.

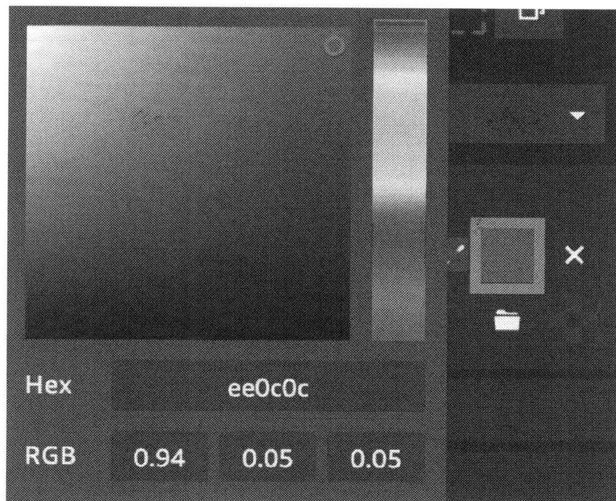

Now you have a red floor and when you orbit the camera around the room, you'll notice that the light sheen off the floor. This is due to the material.

With one click of the mouse, you've brought some color into your world.

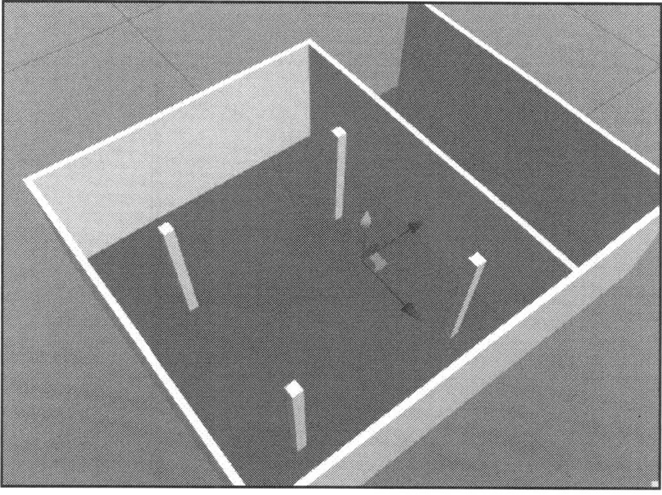

While the red floor might make for a good Edgar Allen Poe story, for this tutorial, you'll use a texture instead. Don't worry! You don't have to supply your own texture; Sumerian provides a bunch for you to use.

At the top of the editor, click **Import Assets**.

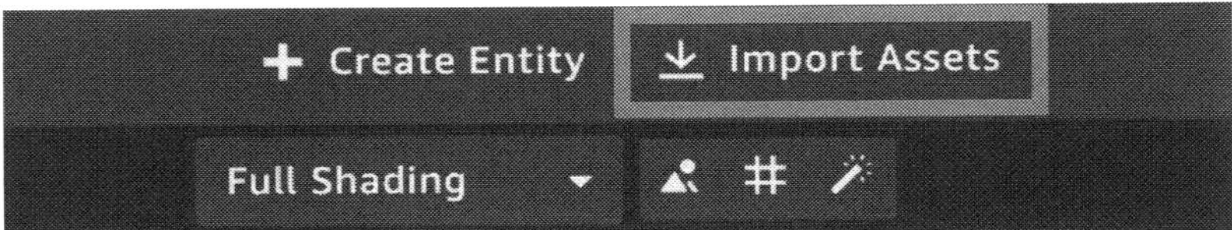

A dialog will appear with all the various assets that you can include with your project. In the search field, type: **material**.

You've now filtered the assets to show a bunch of material packs. Some are labeled PBR.

When working with materials, Sumerian provides two options: Classic and PBR. A material encapsulates a program called a shader that runs on your graphics card. This program determines how your textures will appear on the model. Classic is the rendering option that originally shipped with the engine. PBR stands for Physical Based Rendering. This is a relatively recent method of rendering graphics that tries to accurately depict how surfaces are affected by light.

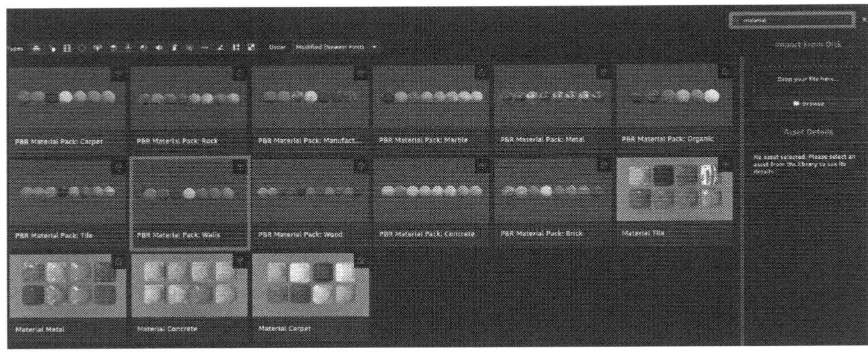

Double-click on the **PBR Material Pack: Walls**. When you import the package, the editor will inform you that the new materials have been imported into your assets panel. Click **OK** to continue.

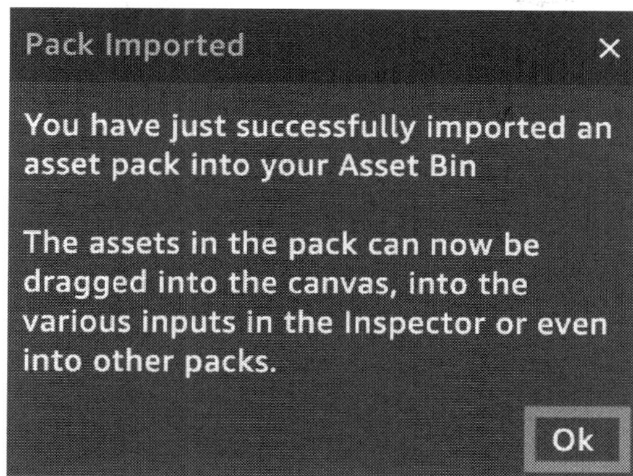

Click the **Import Assets** button again and this time, import the **PBR Material: Concrete** and **PBR Material: Wood** packages as well.

When you import an asset, you import a pack into your project. When you add assets to your own project, you put them in the default pack. As you import assets, you'll import packs related to those assets.

If you look in the Assets panel, you'll see that you now have additional packs: **Default Pack, PBR Material Pack: Walls, PBR Material Pack: Wood and PBR Material Pack: Concrete.**

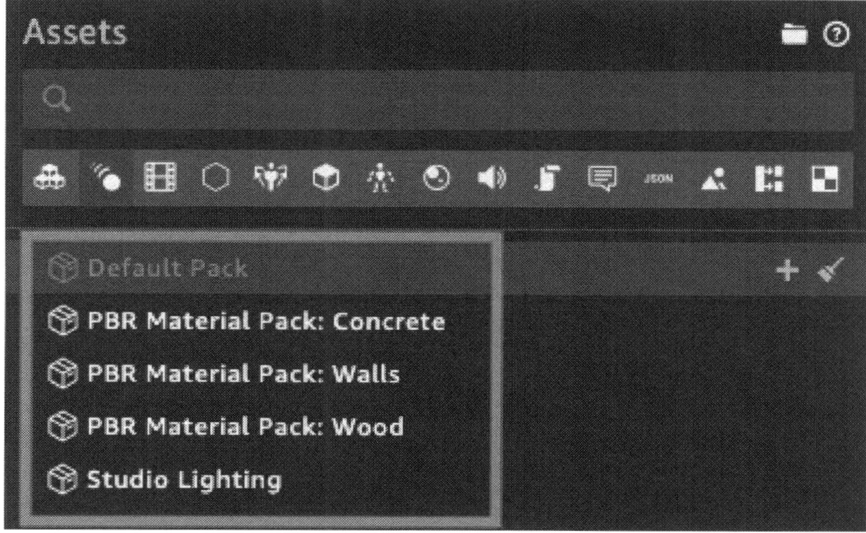

You can also create your own asset packs and export them to other projects as well. For instance, you can create an animated login form that you can use in other projects. Instead of recreating the form, you could simply create a custom pack, add the entities and assets to it and then export the pack. Once exported, all your other projects can import it from the import assets menu.

> **Note**: By default, when you add entities to your canvas, they will not be added to your assets pack. To add them to your custom pack you must drag the entity to the pack.

Now that you have materials imported, your next task is to put them to use. The first entity is the floor. Select the **Floor** entity and expand the **Material** component.

Next, in the Assets panel, you want to assign one of your imported materials. To do this, click the **Materials** tab.

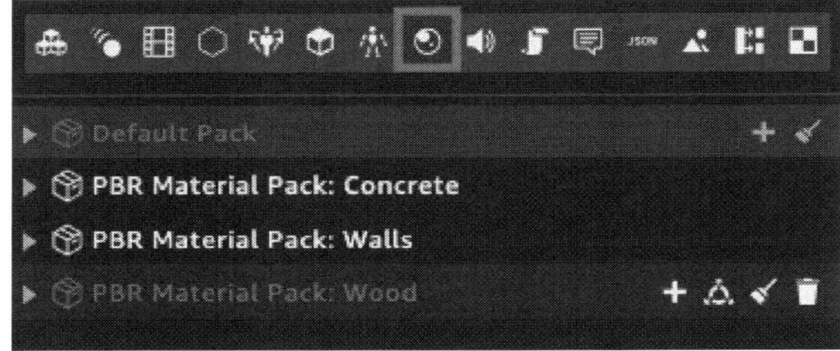

The Assets panel will now display only materials. In the **PBR Material Pack: Concrete Pack**, find the **Concrete_Polished_MAT** material and drag it to the **Default Material** field.

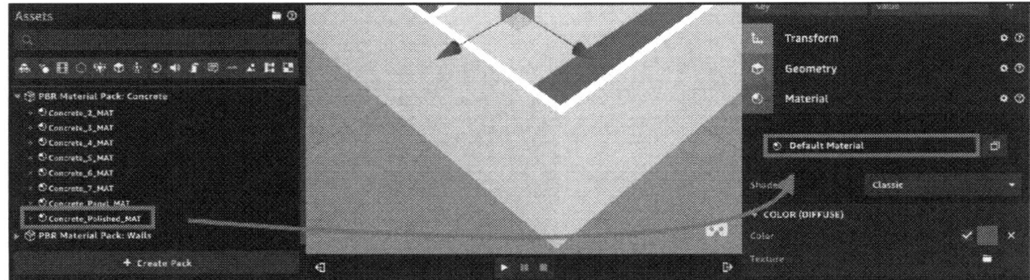

Now do the same for the ceiling. Once you assign the texture, you'll notice that the ceiling is darker than the floor.

Now for the walls. Select **Wall 1** and in the **PBR Material Pack: Walls Pack**, assign the **Walls_Stucco_Cream_MAT** material component. Do this for the rest of the walls. Your room should look like the following:

For the columns, assign the **Wood_Pine_MAT** material to all of the columns. Your escape room should now look like this:

Congrats! Your escape room has texture. You'll notice that there are a lot of materials in the asset panel. Remember, when you created the box entities, new materials were created for you.

You could go on and delete them, but you should make sure they nothing is using them. Select the **Walls_Stucco_Cream_MAT** material and then click the **chain-link** icon. You'll see all the entities that are currently using the material.

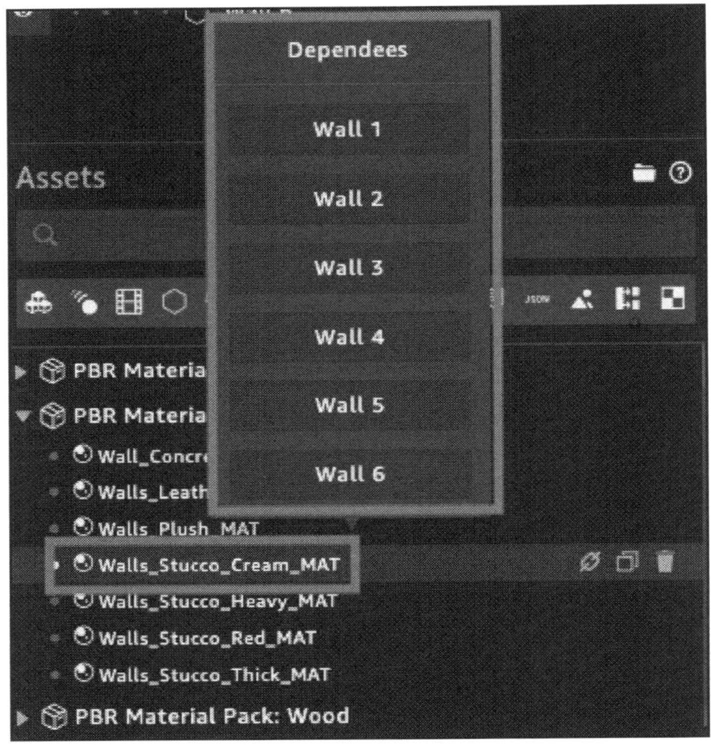

This works for all assets in the asset pane, not just materials.

Now in the **Default Pack**, select the **Default Material** and click the chain link icon. This time, there are no dependencies found.

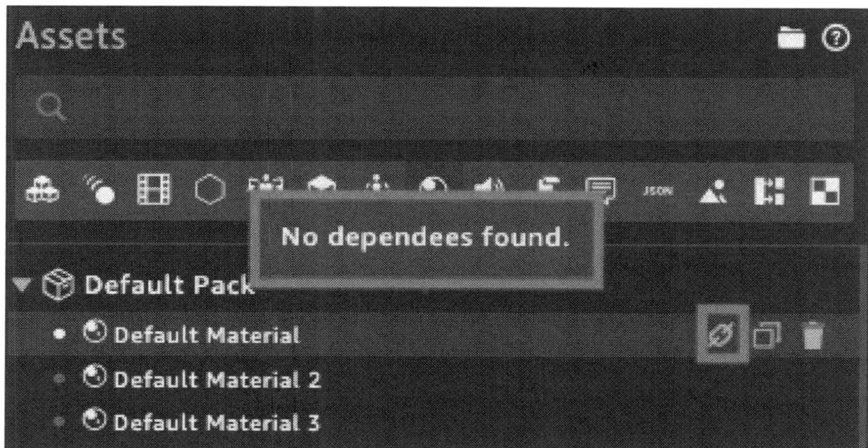

Select the **Default Material** and click the **trash can** icon to delete it.

You still have a lot of unused materials left. Instead of checking if anything is using each asset, you can simply delete all unused assets from the Default package. In the Default Package header, click the **broom icon**.

The following dialog will give you a list of all the assets you're about to delete. Press **Yes** to delete the unused assets.

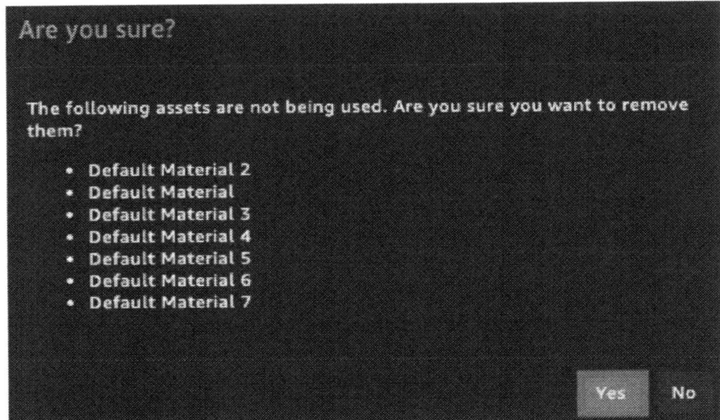

Now you have a much cleaner Assets panel, just in time to import models.

Adding models

Now comes the fun part — decorating your escape room. You have two options when it comes to models: You can import your own models or you can use models included with the engine.

If you choose to use your own models, you need to provide them in either OBJ or FBX format. When you import your model, Sumerian will convert it into an asset pack that contains all the various assets that form it. Keep in mind, you can't import a super high-res model of the Death Star. Your models should be low poly (not a lot of geometry) and the file size cannot exceed 50 MB.

> **Note**: Sumerian does charge money for hosting your models and using related AWS services. There's a lot you can do with the free tier. After that, the prices are quite reasonable. That said, it never hurts to check the pricing page to get an idea of how much a scene may cost.

If you don't want to use your own models, you can use the models provide by Sumerian.

Click the **Import Assets** button and search for **Rug**. Click **Add** to import it into your project. Once you add it, you'll gain a new asset pack. This one is aptly called Rug.

The big question of the hour — how do you add it to the scene? You need to provide an entity. Thankfully, the asset package provides an entity for you. In the Asset panel, click the **entity** tab and drag the **rug_ViewRoom.fbx** onto the canvas.

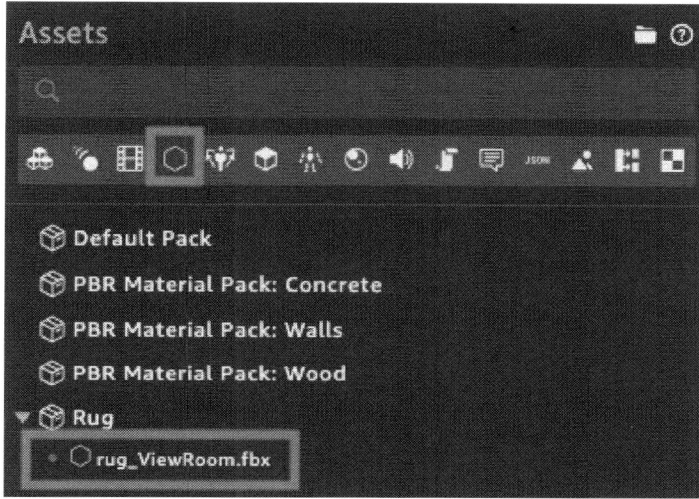

Once you drag your entity on the canvas, you'll notice that the rug has an interesting name. In the inspector, change the name back to **Rug**.

At this point, you will assign a position to the rug. It's **essential** that the entity is parentless. You'll learn why in the next chapter. For now, add each model to the top-level (parentless), assign a position to it and then place it in an entity.

With the rug selected, set the position to: (**-4.421**, **0**, **3.104**). Next, set the scale to: (**1.796**, **1**, **1.378**). Your room should now have a nice rug on the floor.

With the position set, in the Entities panel, put your new **Rug** entity into the **Room Geometry** entity. You set the position first because the parent coordinate system is different from a child's coordinate system. You'll learn about this in detail in the next chapter.

At this point, you'll import a few more models to decorate your room. First, import the following assets and drag an instance to your scene. Don't worry about the position. You'll handle that in a moment. Rename them according to the following:

Asset Name	Entity Name
ASIN: B072ZRPFJL	Bookcase
Table Cafe	Statue Table
ASIN: B071W5VD5C	Left Comfy Chair
ASIN: B071W5VD5C	Right Comfy Chair
ASIN: B0728NWFCG	Couch
Cabinet	Cabinet 1
Cabinet	Cabinet 2
Door Desk Medium	TV Table

Now set the following positions:

Entity Name	Position X	Position Y	Position Z	Rotation X	Rotation Y	Rotation Z	Scale X	Scale Y	Scale Z
Bookcase	-1.498	0	3.11	0	180	0	0.015	0.011	0.011
Statue Table	-1.554	0.023	1.496	0	0	0	0.47	0.47	0.47
L. Comfy Chair	-0.599	0	1.141	0	-120	0	0.008	0.008	0.008
R. Comfy Chair	-2.523	0	1.141	0	120	0	0.008	0.008	0.008
Couch	-1.544	-0.001	-0.517	0.540	90	0.055	0.01	0.01	0.01
Cabinet 1	0.044	0	-3.282	0	90	0	0.738	0.738	0.738
Cabinet 2	-3.298	0	-3.282	0	90	0	0.738	0.738	0.738
TV Table	-1.487	0.777	-1.695	0	0	0	1	1	0.452

Now create a new empty entity and call it: **Furniture**. Inside the Furniture entity, create another entity and call it: **Cabinets**. Parent your entities according to the following table:

Parent Entity	Child Entities
Furniture	Bookcase
	Statue Table
	Left Comfy Chair
	Right Comfy Chair
	Couch
	TV Table
Cabinets	Cabinet 1
	Cabinet 2

You've now decorated your room. Granted, you'll add more elements to it eventually, but this gives you a good start.

The cool thing about those models prefixed with "ASIN" is that you can buy them on Amazon. Search for "ASIN: B071W5VD5C" on Amazon and you'll see your comfy chair in its native habitat.

Challenge

Challenge: Swedish artwork

If you've ever been to a Swedish furniture store, you'll notice that there are lots of abstract paintings hanging on the walls. Your challenge is to recreate the following abstract painting that uses the various shapes provided by Sumerian. Make sure to place it on **Wall 1**. Use only the 3D primitives. Place the painting in an entity named **Painting** inside of the Furniture entity.

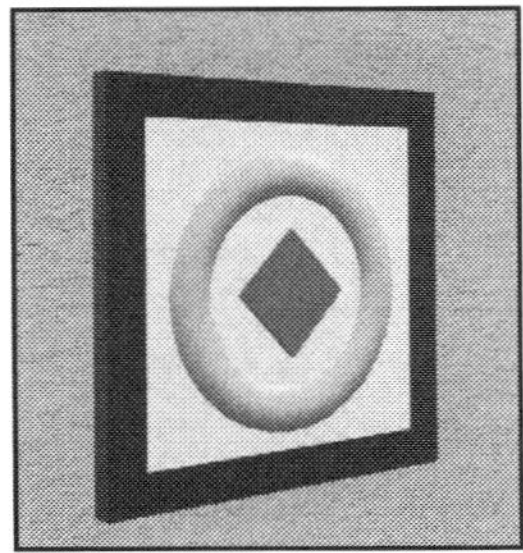

Once you've created your painting, go through the challenge completion so you can get the exact coordinates. You'll use this painting later in the book.

Solution

If you haven't done it yet, create an empty entity and call it **Painting**. You'll add items to it in a moment. For now, create the painting.

Start by creating a **new box entity**. Name it **Left Frame Edge**. Set the position to: (**-4.669**, **1.466**, **0.954**). Set the scale to: (**0.112**, **1.400**, **0.141**). Set the color to **#000000**.

In the Assets panel, select the **Materials** tab and change the name of the Default Material to **Black Frame**. **Duplicate the Frame Edge** and give it the name: **Right Frame Edge**. Set its position to: (**-4.669**, **1.466**, **-0.334**).

With the Right Frame Edge still selected, **duplicate it**. Rename it to: **Top Frame Edge**. Set the position to: (**-4.669**, **2.108**, **0.300**). Set the rotation to: (**90**, **0**, **00**).

Duplicate the Top Frame Edge, and rename the duplicate to **Bottom Frame Edge**. Move it to the following position: (**-4.669**, **0.832**, **0.307**).

You should now have an empty picture frame.

Next, create a **next box entity** and rename it to **Painting Background**. Set the position to: (-**4.670**, **1.461**, **0.305**). Set the scale to: (**0.112**, **1.176**, **1.175**). In the Assets panel, select the Materials tab and rename the material to **Painting Background**.

Now create a **torus** (that's the donut-looking entity). Set the position to: (-**4.757**, **1.451**, **0.306**). Set the rotation to: (**0**, **90**, **0**). Set the scale to: (**0.820**, **0.820**, **0.820**). In **Material**, set the color to **#4fb47b**. In the Assets panel, rename the material to **Painting Donut**.

Finally, create a **new box entity**. Name it **Red Diamond**. Set the position to: (**-4.630**, **1.444**, **0.304**). Set the rotation to: (**45**, **0**, **0**). Set the scale to: (**0.313**, **0.313**, **0.313**). Set the color to **#ff0000**. At long last, rename the new material to **Red Diamond**.

You're almost done! Drag your **Painting** entity into the **Furniture** entity. Next, drag all of the parts of your painting into the Painting entity. And that's it! You have a new painting.

When you're finished, make sure to **save** your scene.

Key points

- Every entity represents a **single point in space**.
- An entity's behavior is created by **adding, removing and altering components**.
- An **entity can have child entities** which provides a great way to organize related entities.
- A material is a special object that **affects how an entity looks** in the scene.
- Sumerian supports **OBJ** and **FBX** model formats.

Where to go from here?

You now have an escape room with some furniture. One of the more fun aspects of working with Sumerian is incorporating models and building your scene. If you would like to practice setting up a scene, the Sumerian team put together a piece on creating a TV-viewing room. You can read it here: https://docs.sumerian.amazonaws.com/tutorials/create/getting-started/sumerian-basics-tv-room/

Unfortunately, your room is static. In the next chapter, you'll add some interaction by way of State Machines and behaviors.

Chapter 4: Adding Interactivity with Behaviors

By Brian Moakley

Your furniture showroom is looking good. The floors and walls are nicely textured. It features a nice, colorful rug. There's plenty of furniture and even a nice abstract painting on the wall. There's only one thing that it is lacking: A means to escape!

Part of the fun of working with Sumerian is adding interactive elements. Sumerian allows you to do this in two ways: You can create state machines to visually organize your logic, or you could write individual scripts.

A **state machine** is a way to code your interactivity without writing a single line of code. With Sumerian's state machine, you define individual states and trigger transitions to switch between them:

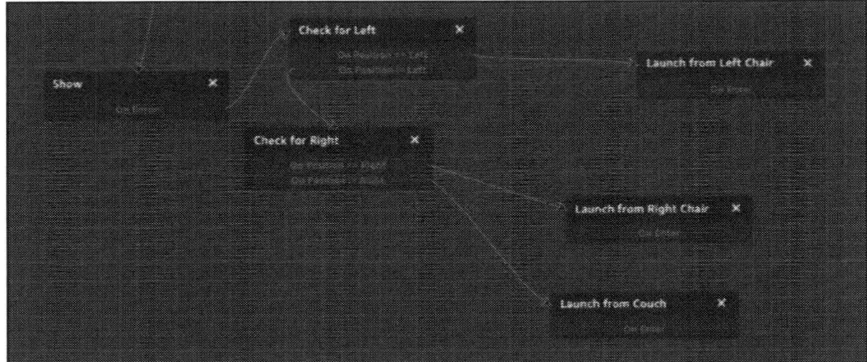

While the state machine allows for visual logic, scripting allows you to define your own behavior as well as incorporate other AWS services. The big question of the hour is which approach should you use? The answer is simple enough: Both!

The state machine provides an easy way to construct your logic, while scripting allows you to build additional behavior that isn't provided by Sumerian. You can even incorporate your scripts into the state machine giving you the best of both worlds.

Setting up the Player Camera

At this point, you have a complete room. You now need to set a starting point for the player. Remember, the idea of the escape room is that you're locked overnight in a Swedish furniture store. Stepping on the rug might set off the alarms, so you will jump from furniture to furniture to try to escape.

> **Note**: This is a somewhat contrived situation. You can create a player controller that works using a traditional mouse and keyboard. This results in a very complex state machine. By using teleportation, you'll get a good idea of how to create state machines. It also provides a great segue into virtual reality since teleportation is often preferred to avoid motion sickness.

To get started, navigate to the Sumerian dashboard, and click on your current scene to open the editor.

The first thing you need to do is set up the camera. You'll notice that you already have a camera in the scene. This is the **Editor Camera**. If you click the play button, the scene will start where you had last moved the camera. This means you will have to position the camera in the start location each time that you start the scene.

A better approach is to add a new camera. In the **Entities panel**, select the **Default Camera** and click the **duplicate button**.

Name the new camera: **Player Camera**.

This new camera will follow the Editor Camera. You want the camera to be in a fixed location. With your new camera selected, uncheck the **Follow Editor Camera** property.

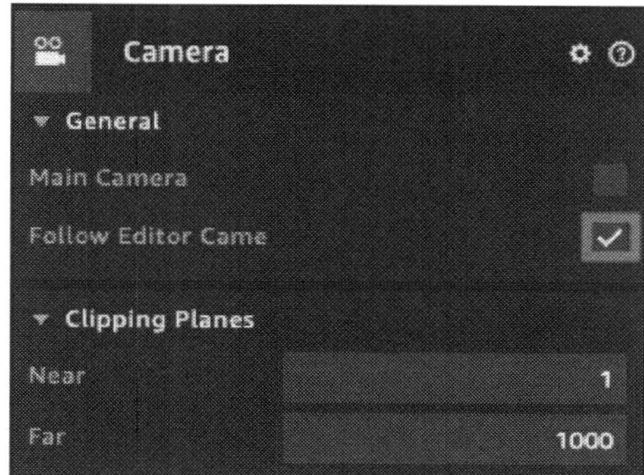

> **Note**: Cameras are a fundamental aspect of working with Sumerian. Cameras (as well as lights) are covered in depth in Chapter 10, "Lights, Camera, Action!"

You can only have one main camera in a scene. The main camera is what users of your scene will see. Right now, the Default Camera is the main camera. You want the Player Camera to be the default camera. Every camera contains a camera component and only one camera can be the main camera.

So, in the Camera component, check the **Main Camera** checkbox. By ticking this checkbox, any other camera designated as the main camera will become unchecked.

By default, this kind of camera orbits around a point. This is provided by a script attached to the camera. It's better to use a mouse look script.

In the **Script** component, remove the **OrbitNPanControlScript** by clicking the **X** in its right-hand corner.

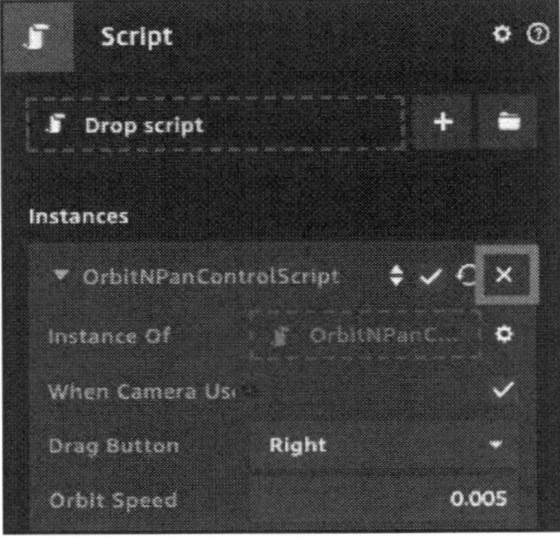

Still within the Script component, click + to add a new script. From the list of options, choose **Mouse Look Control**.

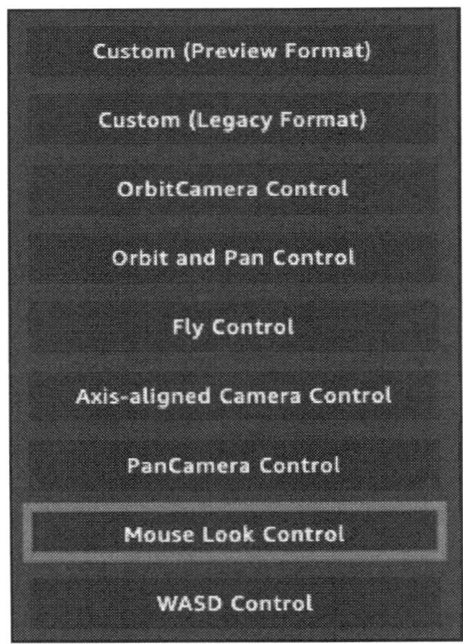

The **MouseLookScript** is configured to activate when the user presses the left mouse button. You'll need that button so that users can click on elements.

In the MouseLookScript, set the **Mouse Button** to **Right**.

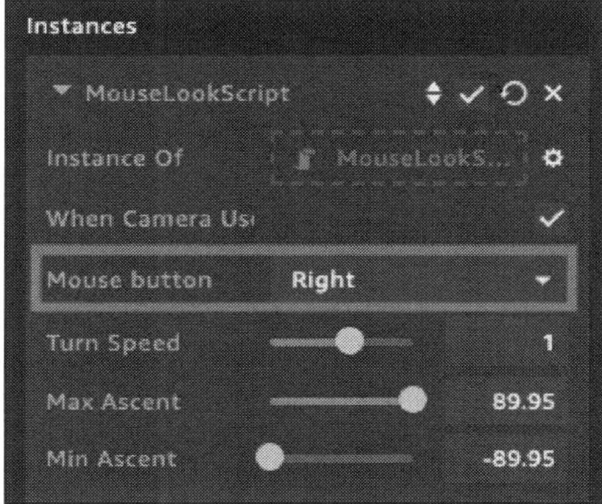

Finally, set the position to (**-2.626**, **1.606**, **1.043**) and the rotation to (**-15.720**, **0**, **0**).

Now, play the scene. You'll find yourself hovering over a comfy chair. To make sure everything works, try looking around by pressing the right mouse button.

Adding interactivity

Adding interactivity is quite simple with Sumerian. You create a behavior and assign it to an entity. A behavior is composed of individual states — each containing actions such as animating an entity, playing some music or even speaking dialogue. Sumerian comes with a lot of pre-built actions and, with the power of scripting, you can even add your own actions.

To get started with creating your own behavior, select the **Couch** entity and, in the inspector panel, click **Add Component**. You'll see that you have a lot of options. In this case, choose **State Machine**

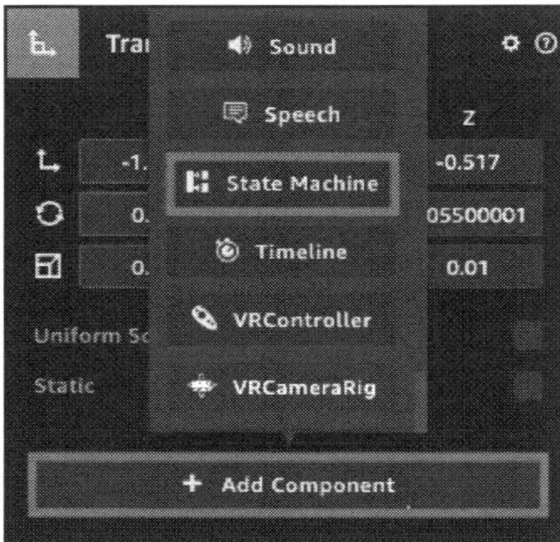

Your couch will now get a state machine component added to it. You can either add existing behaviors or create your own. Click the + button next to the Drop Behavior field. This creates your first behavior.

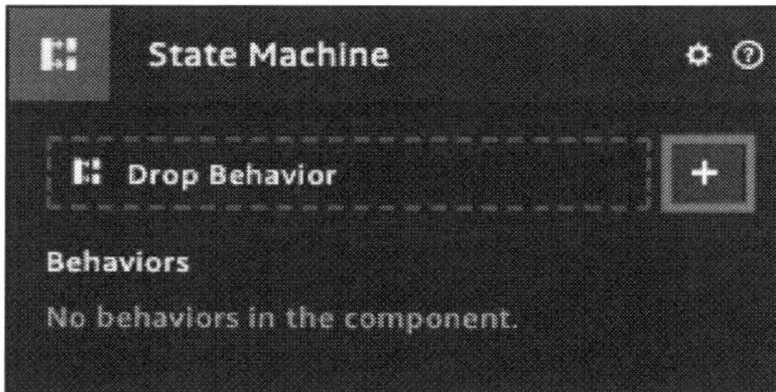

Once you create a new behavior, the State Machine Editor will open at the bottom of the editor. It even comes with a state aptly named State 1.

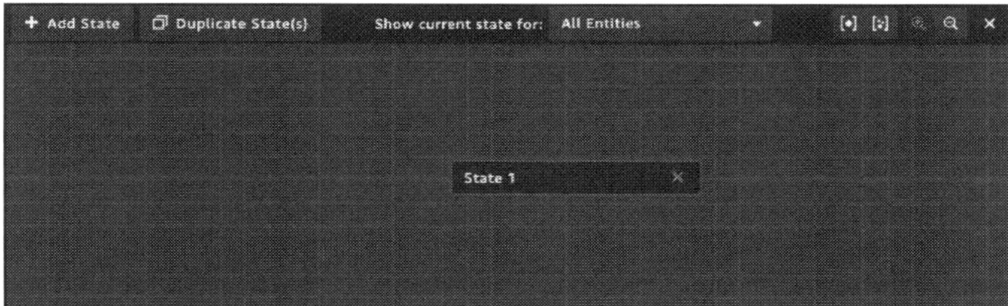

Before you start playing around with states, it's a good idea to name the state. Often with Sumerian projects, you'll acquire lots of behaviors and states. When something goes wrong — say, for instance, your teleportation isn't working — you'll know that the logic is found the Teleport behavior, versus searching in Behavior 1, Behavior 2, etc.

In the inspector, change the name of the behavior to **Couch**.

In the State Machine Editor, make sure to select **State 1** by clicking on it. You'll see that you get information about the state in the inspector. Change the name of the state to **Click on Couch**. Now click the **Add Action** button.

The following dialog provides a whole bunch of actions that you can use with your behaviors. Take a moment to click through all the various categories and check out all of the various actions you can use. Once you know these, you'll use the search field to speed things up.

For now, click on the **Controls** category, and then click on the **Click/Tap on entity**. Finally, click the **Add** button at the bottom of the dialog.

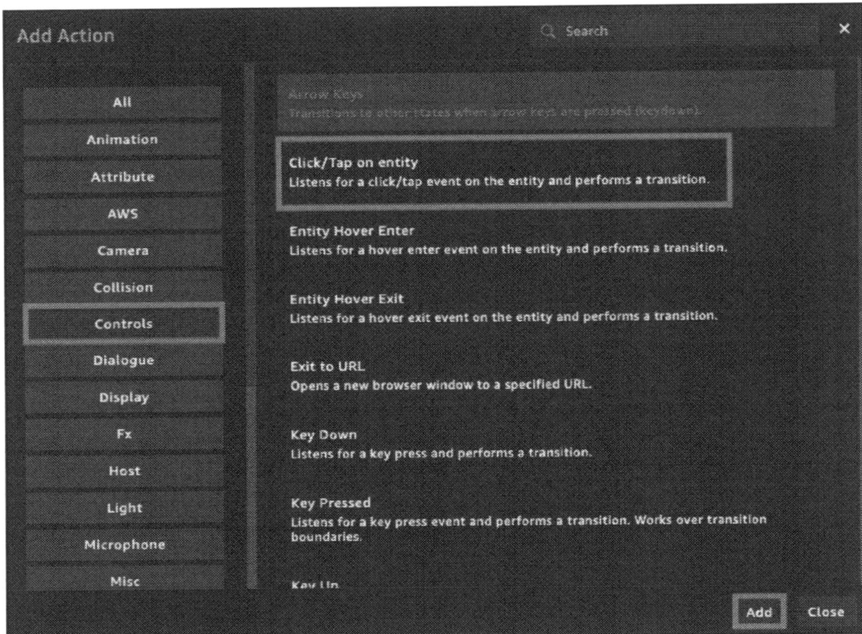

You'll notice that your state now has a statement that reads: "On Click / Tap Entity." This is your action. This means the couch will respond to all clicks. Yet, nothing will happen when the user clicks.

Click the **Add State** button to add another state.

Change the name to **Hide Couch** and click the **Add Action** button. In the **Display** category, select **Hide**.

Now, you have two states with actions but the states aren't connected. In the **Click on Couch** state, click and drag the text that reads **"On Click / Tap Entity"** to the **Hide Couch** state.

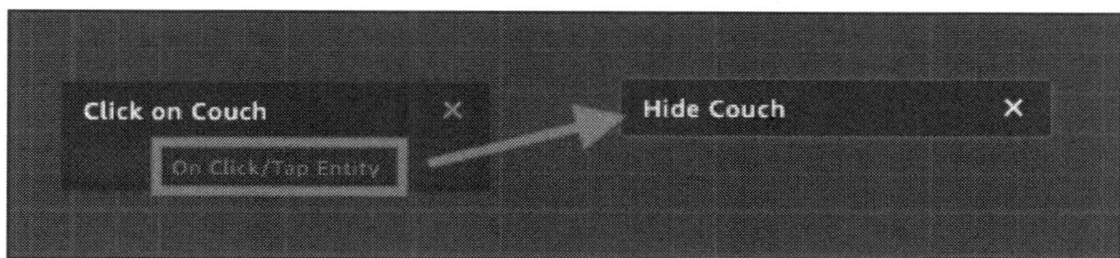

This will draw an arrow between the two states. When the user clicks on the couch, the state will transition to the Hide Couch and the couch will disappear.

Play the scene. Notice that there is a difference in the behavior. When the scene is playing, you'll notice that the Click on Couch state has a green outline around it.

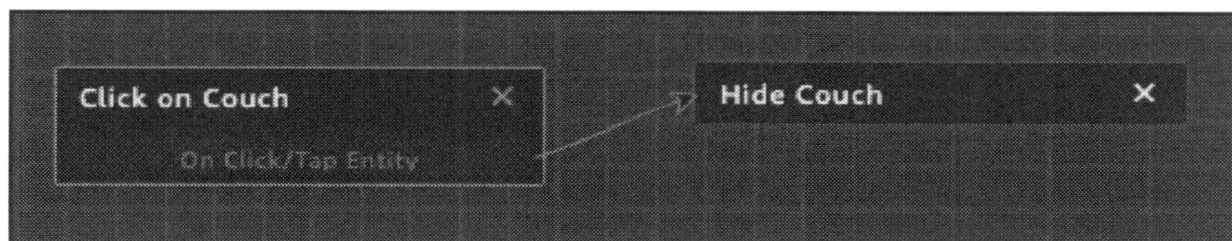

This lets you know the active state of the behavior. Right now, the behavior is waiting for the click event. **Click** on the couch and you will see it disappear. Also, notice that the Hide Couch state is the active state.

When a state transition occurs, all the actions will run in the order listed in the state.

Of course, the objective isn't to make the couch disappear (although that'd be a good magic trick). Your goal is to teleport the player. This raises an interesting conundrum.

Behaviors are designed to just work on the current entity. Later you'll see how some actions and custom scripts can affect other entities, but these are exceptions. In this current situation, when a user clicks on the couch, you'll want to move the camera to it. Thankfully, there is a way to communicate between entities and that's accomplished by sending messages.

Sending messages

Messages are the primary means in which entities communicate with other entities. Messages are interesting in that a receiving entity can't reply to the message and the sender has no idea who is receiving the message. This may seem a little bit strange. But this keeps the entities separate from each other. This means that changes to one entity won't affect another.

You can think of a message like an announcement. When an event occurs, an entity broadcasts a message. Any number of entities can listen for the message and react when they receive the message.

For example, in the case of the couch, when the user clicks on the couch, the couch will broadcast a `CouchClicked` message. Every entity in the scene can respond to it. Since the camera is interested in the event, it will listen to the CouchClicked event. When the message is broadcast, the camera will receive the message and then change its position.

To get started withs messages, you'll need to edit your couch behavior. You can select the couch and then click the pencil icon next to the behavior name. There is another way to access your behavior. In the Assets Panel, click the Behavior tab and then in the Default Pack, click the pencil icon next to the couch behavior:

This opens the State Machine Editor. Select the **Hide the Couch** state and rename it to **Send Couch Click Message**. Click the **Add Action** button and, in the **Transitions** category, select the **Emit Message** action.

You'll see that there is a new action underneath the **Hide** action. It contains only one field named **Channel**. This is the name of the message.

Note: You can only broadcast the message name when using a behavior. When working with scripts, you can send data with the message. You'll do this in Chapter 12, "The Sumerian API."

Set the Channel to **MoveToCouch**. You may be wondering why all the letters are squeezed together. Typically, spaces can cause problems in computer languages and so when broadcasting messages it's just a good practice to remove spaces to avoid any potential issues.

Right now, there are two actions in the selected state. The first action hides the entity while the second action sends out a message. These actions will start with the first message and run every subsequent action in order.

Note:: As you'll soon see, Listen actions will run concurrently.

You can reorder the actions by clicking on the two arrows and dragging the action.

For now, you don't need the hide action, so delete it by clicking the **x** icon next to the reorder icon. Doing so will leave you with just one action. There is only one problem with the current behavior, when the user clicks on the couch the behavior will emit a message but nothing else will occur.

You want the emit action transition back to the click action. That way, the couch will be able to be clicked multiple times. When you added a click action, the action provided its own transition. The **Emit Message** action doesn't have such a transition. You'll need to add your own transition.

Click the **Add Action** button and, in the Transitions category, select the transition **Transition** action. Now your state will have an **On Enter** transition. Click on the **On Enter** transition and drag to the **Click on Couch** state.

You now have two states referring to each other.

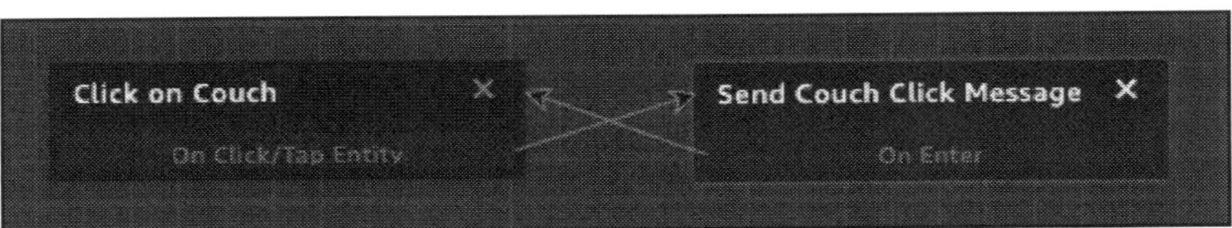

Now that you are sending messages, you'll need the camera to respond to the message. In the Assets Panel, click the **Behaviors** tab and then click the + button in the **Default Pack** header.

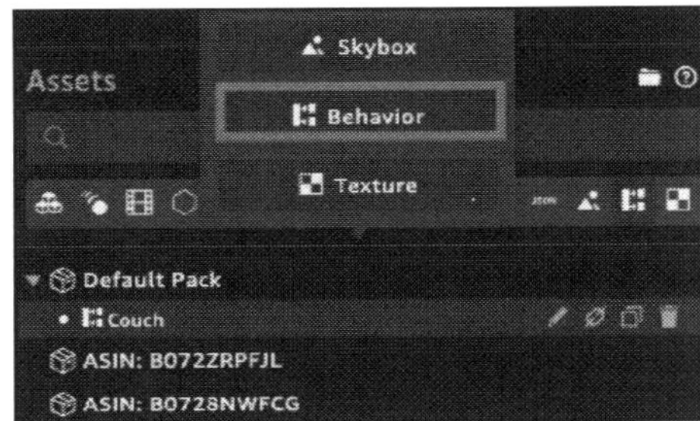

As you can see, there is more than one way to create a behavior or assets in general.

Rename your new behavior to **Player Camera**. Make sure to edit the behavior to access the **State Machine Editor**.

Like the Couch behavior, you have a state already provided for you. Rename it to **Listen for Clicks**.

> **Note**: When naming your state, it helps to be clear with the intention of the state. That way, you'll understand the state's intention at a glance

Click **Add Action** and in the **Transitions** category, select the transition **Listen** action. In the **Message channel** field, give it the name **MoveToCouch**.

Now, click the **Add State** button to create a new state. Give it the name **Move to Couch**. This is the part when you move the camera. Thankfully, there's a move action!

With **Move to Couch** selected, click the **Add Action** button. In the **Animation** category, add the **Move** action. Set the position to (**1.380**, **1.606**, **-0.116**). Make sure to **uncheck** all the other values. This will make it so that the camera will jump to the nearby chair.

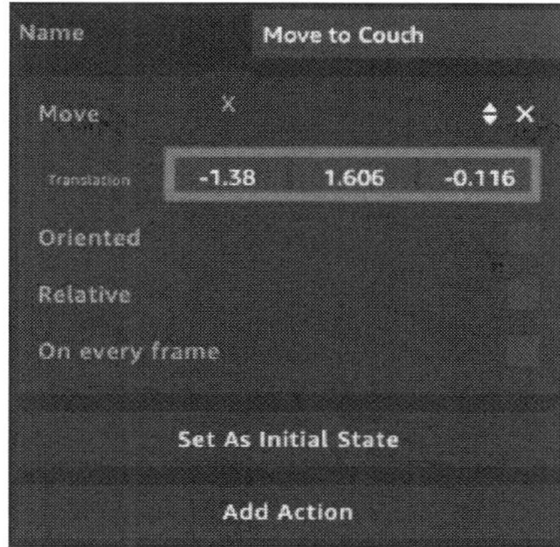

Since you need to transition back to the **Listen for Clicks** state, click the **Add Action** button. In the **Transitions** category, add the **Transition** action. Drag a connection between the **Move to Couch** state and **Listen for Clicks** state.

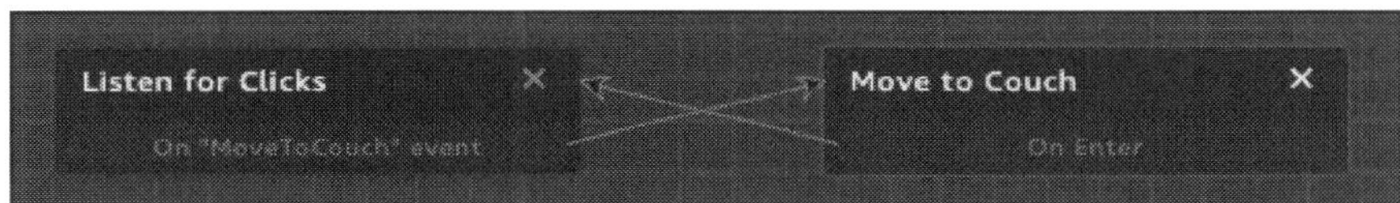

Now, to add the behavior to the Place Camera. First, select the **Player Camera** in the Entities Panel. Its information should appear in the inspector. In the Assets Panel, select the **Player Camera** behavior and drag it to the bottom of the inspector. You will see an **Add component** message appear in the inspector panel.

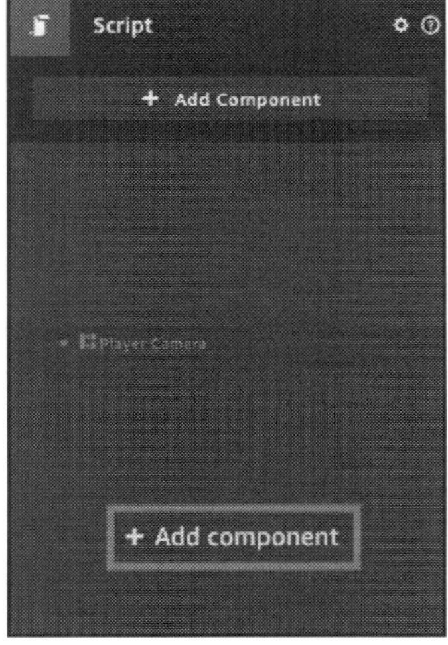

When you release the mouse button, a State Machine component will be added to the entity with your behavior assigned to it.

Now, run the scene and click on the couch. The camera will teleport.

Completing the teleportation

At this point, the couch is the only item that you can click. You need to send out messages for the left comfy chair and the right comfy chair.

In the Assets Panel, select the **Couch** behavior and click the **duplicate button**. Rename this new behavior to **Left Comfy Chair**. **Duplicate** the **Couch behavior** again and rename it **Right Comfy Chair**.

Select the **Left Comfy Chair** behavior and in the State Machine Editor, rename the **Click on Couch** state to **Click on Left Comfy Chair**. Make sure to also rename **Send Couch Click Message** to **Send Left Comfy Chair Message**. Finally, in the **Send Couch Click Message** state, change the message channel to **MoveToLeftComfyChair**.

Next, do the same for the **Right Comfy Chair**. Rename all of the states to reference the **Right Comfy Chair** and change the message channel to **MoveToRightComfyChair**.

> **Note**: You'll notice that the behaviors are almost the same except for a few small details. This is a problem. Later, you need to change the logic of the behavior. Instead of changing it in one place, you will now have to change it in multiple places. This is a sign that the behavior is better expressed as a script. You'll learn how to do this in Chapter 12, "The Sumerian API." For the time being, you'll use duplicated behaviors.

Once you have both the Left Comfy Chair and Right Comfy Chair behaviors configured, select the **Player Camera** behavior in the Assets Panel.

In the **State Machine Editor**, select the **Move to Couch** state and press the **Duplicate State(s)** button:

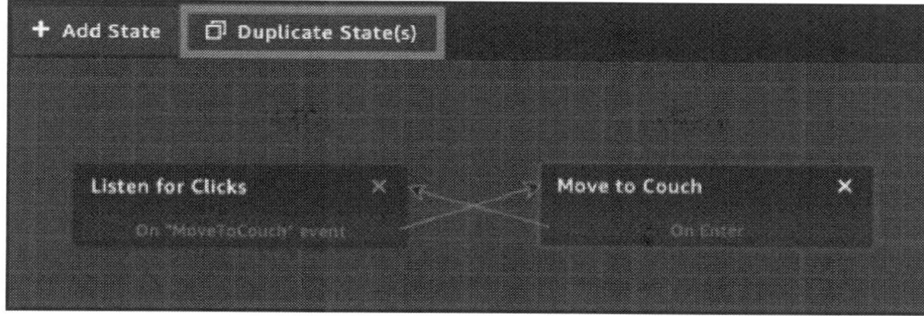

Doing so will create a new state, all transitioning to Listen for Clicks. Select the state, and for the **Move** action, set the **Translation** to (**-2.626**, **1.606**, **1.043**). Rename the state to **Move to Left Comfy Chair**.

Duplicate the state and rename it to **Move to Right Comfy Chair**. Set the **Translation** to (**-0.638**, **1.606**, **1.043**).

Your behavior should look like the following:

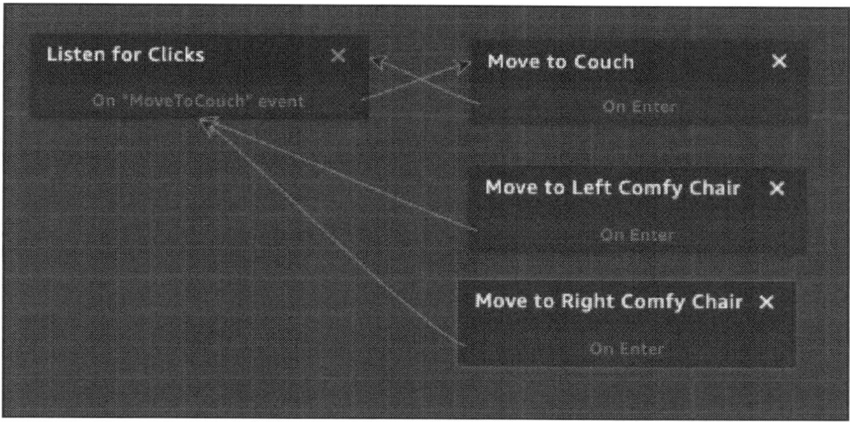

At this point, you have transitioned from your new move states, but there are no transitions to the move states.

Select the **Listen for Clicks** state. **Add** two **Listen** actions. Set one channel to be **MoveToLeftComfyChair** and the other to be **MoveToRightComfyChair**.

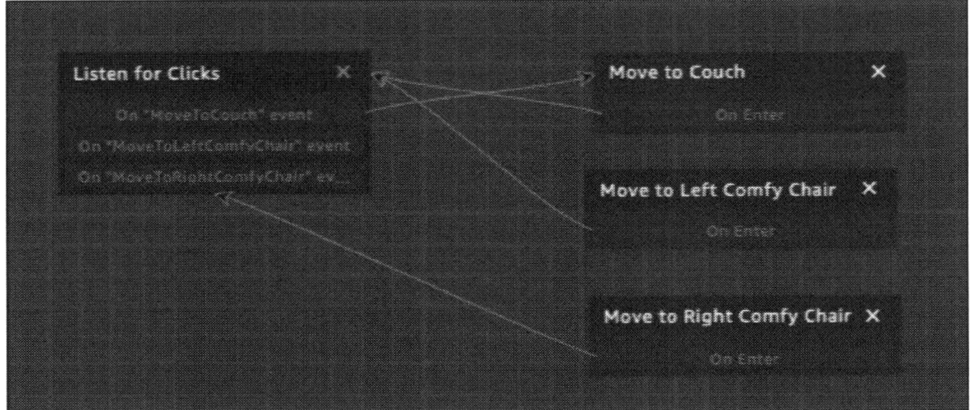

Next, create a transition from **On "MoveToLeftComfyChair" event** to **Move to Left Comfy Chair**. Do the same from **On "MoveToRightComfyChar" event** to **Move to Right Comfy Chair**.

Your behavior should now look like the following:

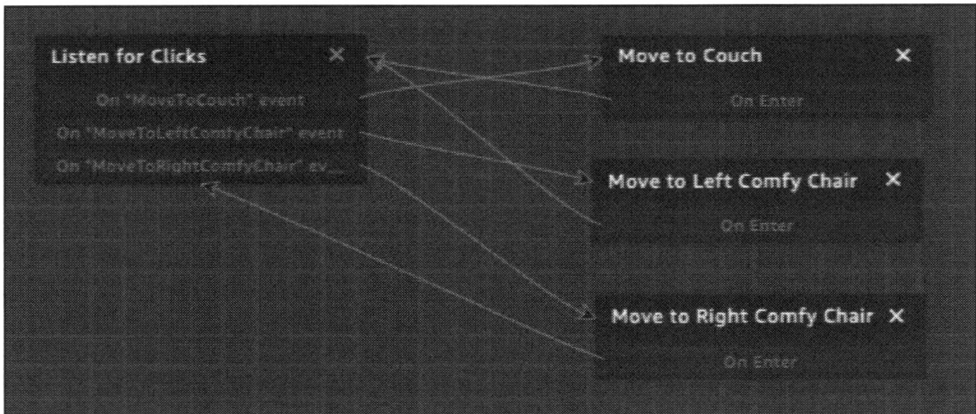

Now you have a completed behavior!

> **Note**: If you found that you made a mistake and dragged a transition to the incorrect state, simply click on the arrowhead of the transition. This will delete the transition.

Finally, select the **Behaviors** tab in the **Asset Panel**. Select the **Left Comfy Chair** in the **Entities panel**. Drag the **Left Comfy Chair behavior** to the **Inspector Panel**. Do the same for the **Right Comfy Chair**, using the **Comfy Chair behavior**.

Now, run your scene. You will be able to hop between all the furniture.

Light switch puzzle

Now that the user can effectively move, it's time to put the first puzzle into the game. The escape room features three puzzles and the first is easiest. It's just a switch that needs to be pressed.

With your scene open, click **Import Assets**. Search for the **Light Switch** asset and add it to your project.

In the assets inspector, switch to the **Entity** tag and drag a **light switch** entity to the canvas. Set the position to (**0.301**, **1.392**, **-1.156**).

Now to provide the behaviors. When the user clicks on the light switch, the switch should rise. The actual switch is in the midpoint, so select the **light_switch** child entity. Set the rotation to (**32**, **0**, **0**).

When the user clicks the switch, the switch should animate upwards. The light switch itself is too small for a user to click so it's better to add it to the entire switch panel.

Select the **light switch** parent entity in the Entities Panel. In the inspector, click **Add Component** and select **State Machine**. In the State Machine component, click the **+** button to create a new behavior.

The State Machine editor will open. In the inspector, rename the behavior to **Light Switch Panel**.

Select **State 1** and rename it to **Click on Light**. Press the **Add Action** button and in the **Controls** category, add a **Click** action.

Click the **Add State** button. Select the new state and rename it to **Emit Activate Message**. Click the **Add Action** button and, in the **Transitions** category, add a **Emit Message** action. In the Emit Message action, set the **Channel** to **ActivateSwitch**.

Drag a transition from the **Click on Light** to the other. Your behavior should look like the following:

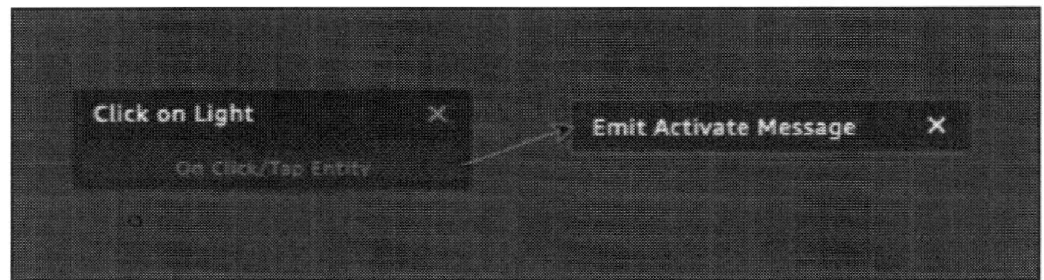

Clicking the overall switch will fire a message. Now, you need to create a behavior in the child switch to listen to the message. As you can see, a project can acquire quite a few behaviors.

Click the child **light_switch** and click the **Add Component** button. Add a **State Machine** and then click the **+** button to create a new behavior. Name the behavior **Light Switch**.

In the State Machine editor, select **State 1**. Rename it to **Listen for Light Switch Click**. Click the **Add Action** button and, in the **Transitions** category, add a **Listen** action. In the channel, add **ActivateSwitch**.

Now, click the **Add State** button and rename your new state to **Rotate Light Switch**.

So far, you've moved an entity but that was an instant movement. In this case, you want the switch to animate over time. There is an action for this.

Click the **Add Action** button and select the **Animations** category. You'll notice that there are two **Rotate** actions. One is called **Rotate** and the other is called **Tween Rotate**.

The Rotate action will instantly rotate the switch much like the Move action moved the entity. To animate movement, you must select a tween variant of the action. **Tween** is an animation term. It's a shortening of the word between. It's the process of generating the intermediate frames between two images.

That is, you provide a start point and then an endpoint, and the engine will generate the animation for you.

Select **Tween Rotate**. You'll get a lot of options with this action. For now, set the **Rotation** to (-32, 0, 0), **uncheck** the **Relative** option and set the **Time (Seconds)** to **0.3**.

> **Note:** You'll learn all about the various animation options in Chapter 13, "Animation & Particle Systems."

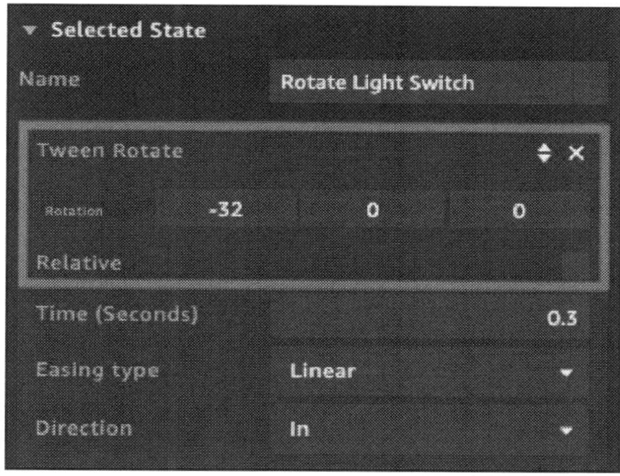

Drag a **transition** from the first state to the current one. It should look like the following:

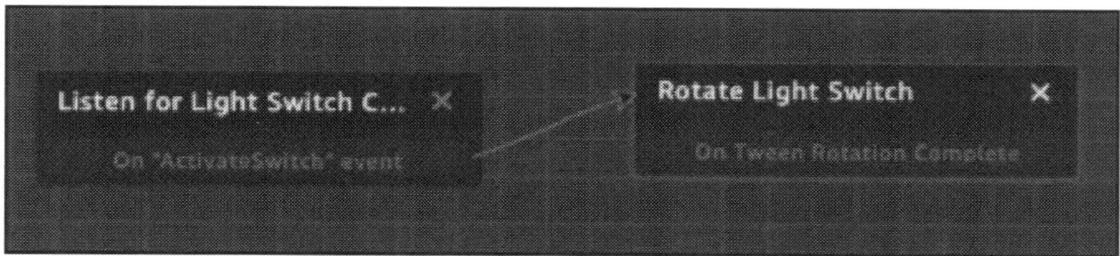

Now, play your scene and click on the light switch. You'll see that you have a working light switch that required not a single line code.

Revealing the next clue

When the players click on the light switch, they will expect something to happen. In this escape room, it will reveal the clue for the second puzzle.

For this to happen, you'll need to add a few more assets to the scene. Click the **Import Assets** button and search for the asset: **Television Hanging**. Select the television and click the **Add** button.

In the Assets Panel, drag the **television_wall_ViewRoom.fbx** entity onto the canvas. Rename the entity to **Television**. Finally, set the position to (**-2.646**, **1.076**, **-3.425**). Set the scale to (**0.691**, **0.691**, **0.691**)

Now, with your television in place, you want to rotate it on the left once the user activates the light switch. All you need to do is have the television listen to the **ActivateSwitch** event.

With the television still selected, click the **Add Component** button and select the **State Machine**. Click the **+** button to add a new behavior and name it **Television**.

Open the Television behavior in the State Machine Editor. Rename the default state to **Listen for Light Switch**. With the state selected, click the **Add Action** button and in the **Transitions** category, add the **Listen** event. Set the **Message Channel** to **Activate State**.

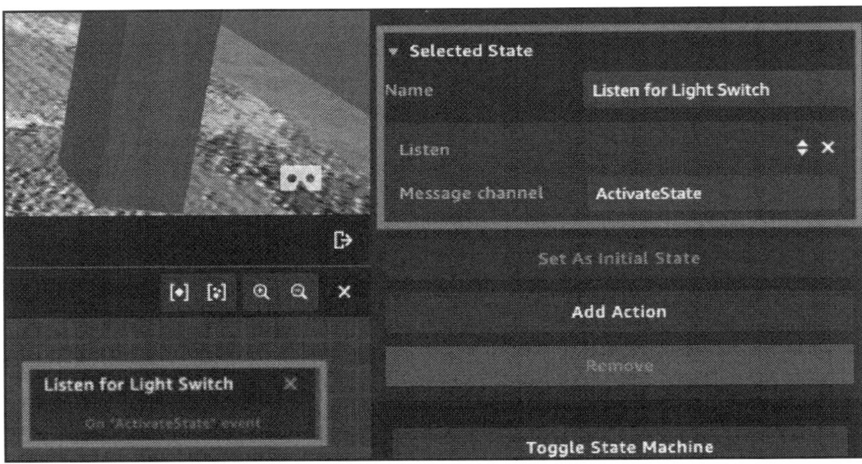

Click the **Add State** button and name it **Rotate Television**. Click the **Add Action** button and, in the **Animation** category, add a **Tween Rotate** action. In the Tween Rotate action, set the **Rotation** to (**0**, **-90**, **0**).

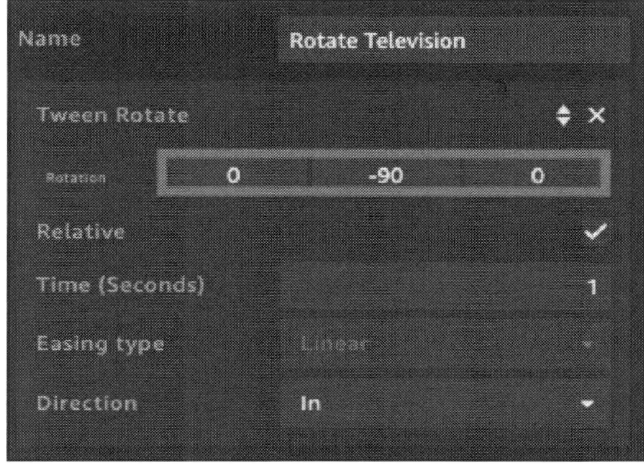

Finally, drag a transition for the **Listen for Light Switch** state to the **Rotate Television** state.

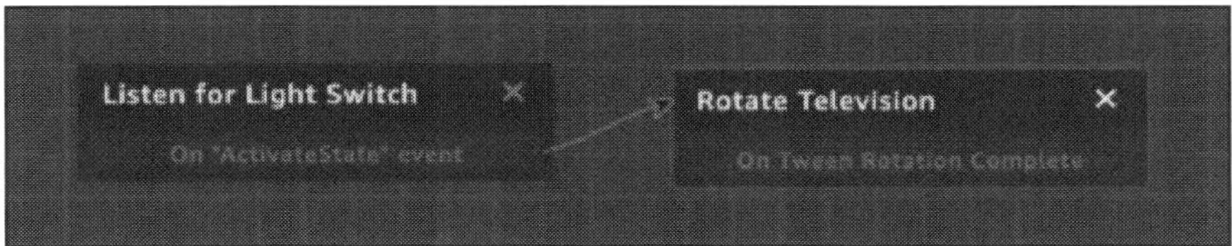

Now, run your game and flick the switch. The television rotates to reveal ... nothing! It's time for you to add a clue.

Nested coordinate systems

In escape rooms, clues are meant to be both obvious but also obtuse. That way, the escapees can all share an a-ha moment when they figure it out.

This clue is a simple image with three colored shapes. The shapes don't matter. It's the color that's important. The clue is just an image. You have to import it into the engine.

In the Assets Panel, click the **folder icon**. This opens the file browser. Navigate to the Resources folder and select **clue.png**. Now, if you click the **Texture** tab in the Assets Panel, you'll see your imported image.

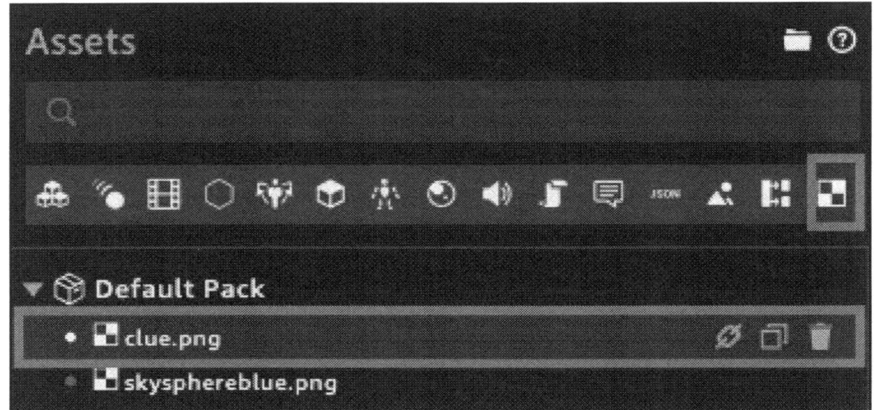

At this point, you have a 2D image. If you drag it onto your canvas, you'll get an error. Remember, only entities can be added to your scene. You'll need to create one. What you need are some geometry and material. You could use a box entity, but a quad is a better fit.

A quad entity is a rectangle. It has no depth and is perfect for signs and images.

Click **Create Entity** and, in the 3D Primitives category, select the **quad**

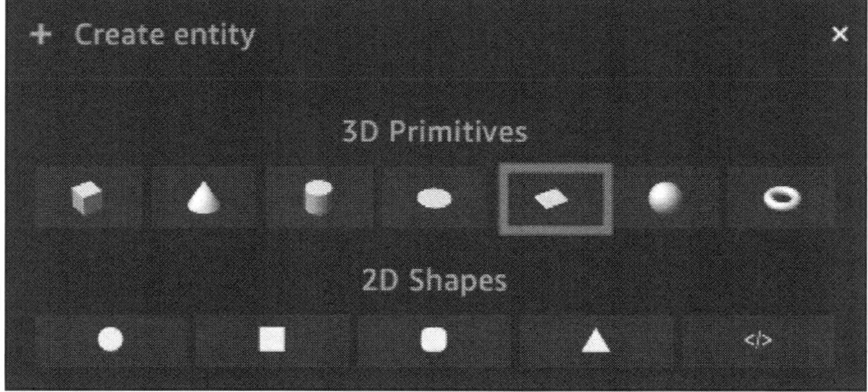

This will add a quad to your scene. If you look at the scene from behind, you may just see the outline of a white rectangle.

Quads are only meant to viewed from the front. The quad won't be rendered from behind which is why you can see through it. This is an optimization. There's no point in rendering a surface if it isn't meant to be seen.

You'll often see this in a game when you glitch through the world. You'll see through all the walls of a level because you are seeing the back-faces of all of them.

If you can't see the quad, simply rotate around it until you can see the plain white face. Now to add the clue.

First, rename the Quad to **Clue**. Next, in the quads material, drag the **clue.png** texture to the material **Texture** property. Set the scale to: (**1.378**, **0.730**, **1**). Finally, rename Default Material 2 to **Clue**.

At this point, your quad should look like the following:

Now, you need to position the clue. The clue should go directly behind the television. So far you've been just entering the position via coordinates provided by this book. This time, you'll use another entity's coordinate system.

When you assign an entity to be a child of another entity, the child's coordinate system becomes expressed in terms of the parent's coordinate system.

It's easier to think about this in 2D coordinates. Entity A is located at a position of (1, 1). Entity B is located at a position of (-1, -1).

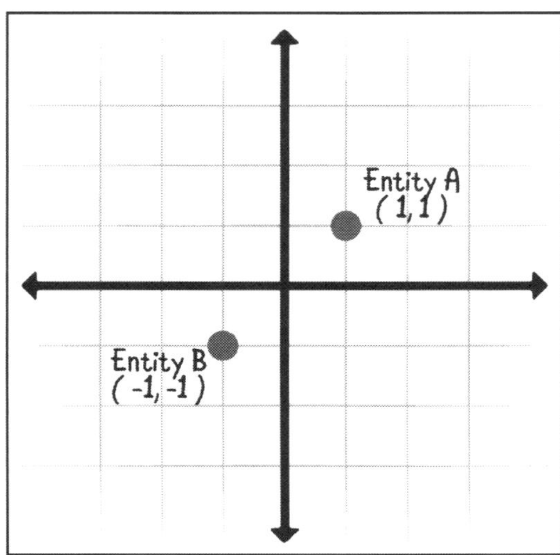

When you make Entity B a child of Entity A, Entity B's position doesn't change, but the center of the coordinate system does.

To Entity B, the origin point of the world (0, 0) is the location of the parent entity. This means its coordinates are expressed in terms of the parent. Entity A's coordinates are (0,0). Entity B's new coordinates are (-2, -2).

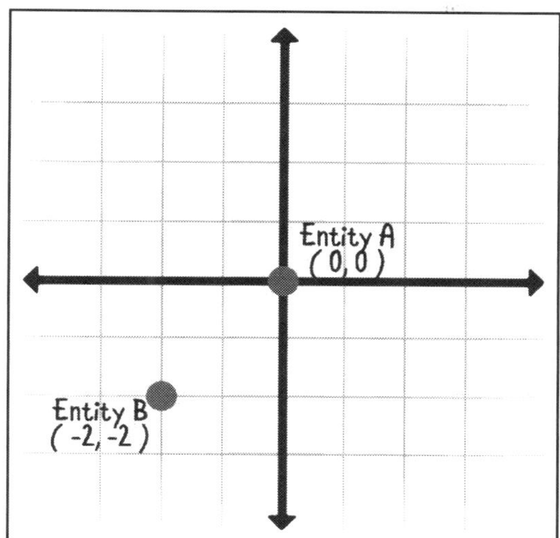

This is why you set the position of the entity *before* you made it a child of another entity. Had you made the entity a child first and *then* set the coordinates, the entity would have been misplaced since all the coordinates in this book are provided in the world space.

You can use this to your advantage when you need entities to be positioned at the same place as other entities. In the Entities Panel, drag the clue entity to be a child of the television.

Right away, the clue's coordinates will update since the television is the parent.

Transform

	X	Y	Z
Position	-2.646736	1.076	-3.425
Rotation	0	-9	0
Scale	0.691	0.691	0.691

Now set the position of the Clue to be (**0, 0, 0**). This moves the entity to the place of the television.

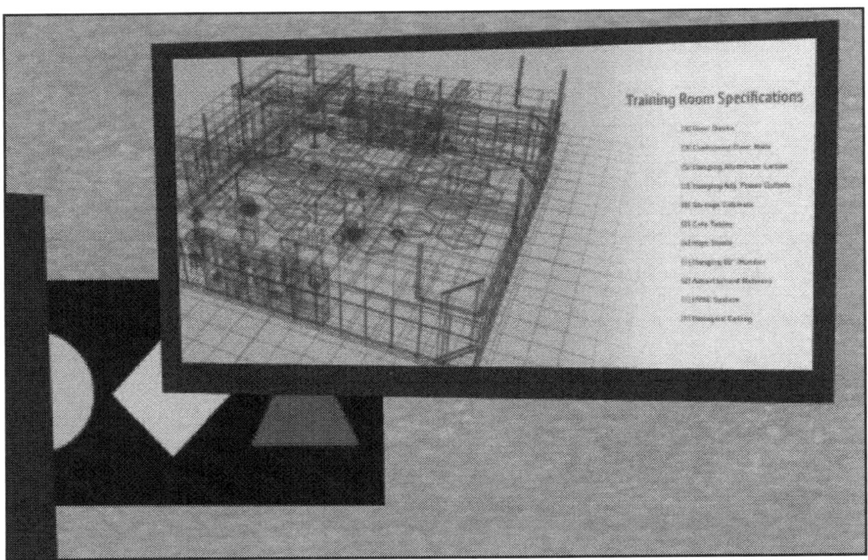

Using the position controls, move the clue to the center of the television. Once in position, **un-parent the Clue**. You can do this by dragging the Clue entity to the scene name.

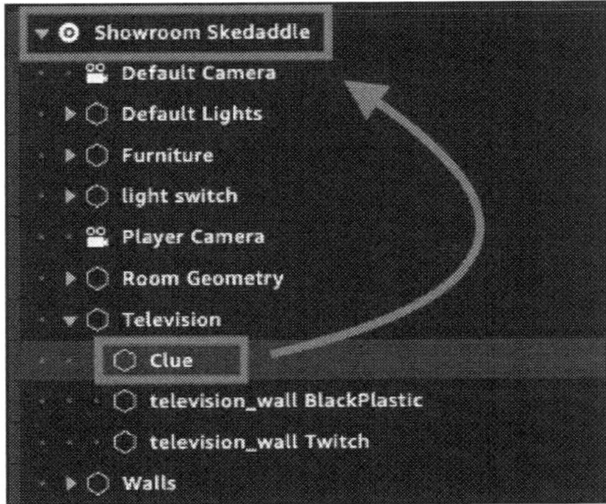

Now, play your scene and flick the switch. This time, you'll see a clue.

Congrats on making it this far! In the next chapter, you'll add additional complexity by the way of attributes and branching logic.

Key points

- A state machine is a component that **provides interactivity** to any entity.
- The interactivity is saved into a file known as a **behavior**.
- An entity can have multiple behaviors added to it.
- A behavior is composed of individual **states** that have **actions** added to them.
- A **message** is an action sent between behaviors.
- Child entities adopt the coordinate system of their parent entity.

Where to go from here?

Behaviors allow for dynamic interactions with your 3D scene. You'll be writing lots of behaviors with Sumerian. The Sumerian team has provided two additional tutorials. One tutorial covers the interface that can be found here: https://docs.sumerian.amazonaws.com/tutorials/create/beginner/state-graph-editor-interface/

The other tutorial provides details on state machines that can be found here: https://docs.sumerian.amazonaws.com/tutorials/create/beginner/state-machine-basics/

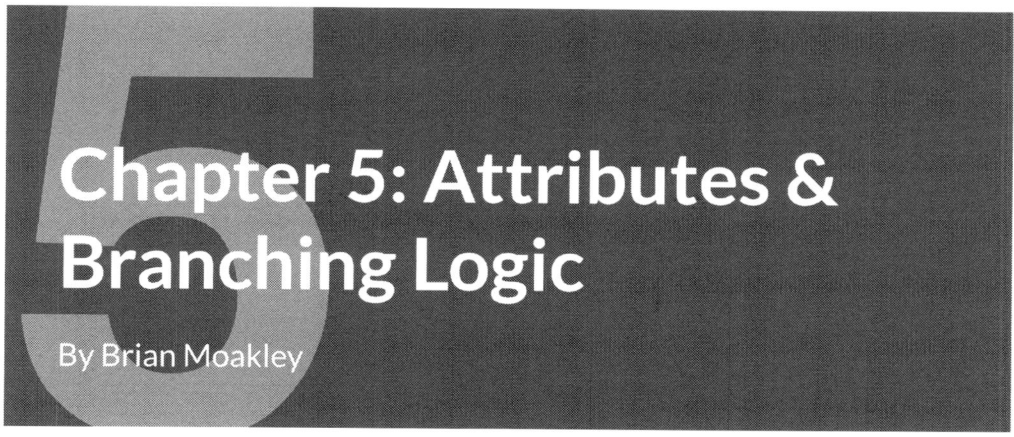

Chapter 5: Attributes & Branching Logic

By Brian Moakley

Creating behaviors to provide interactivity is one of the cooler things you can do with Sumerian. The visual State Machine editor makes it easy to track how states transition into other states. Adding additional states is just a matter of creating new states and integrating them with the rest via transitions.

Unfortunately, the current behaviors in your escape room are somewhat simple. While they do provide interactivity, their linearity limits them. Thankfully, Sumerian provides a tool to add complexity to your behaviors with attributes; by using these attributes, you'll learn how to make branching choices in your behaviors.

In this chapter, you'll use attributes to construct your second puzzle. When you last left off, the light switch caused the television to move, revealing a cryptic clue.

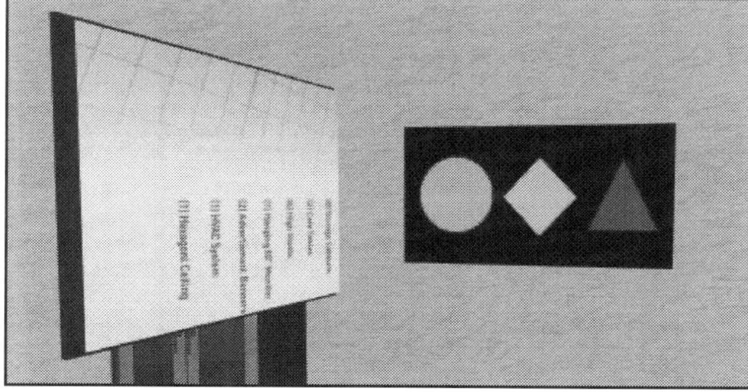

The shapes on the clue don't mean anything – it's the colors that are important. The user will need to click three objects in the room, each of which matches a color. The user will need to click the colors in order. If they click the wrong color, the puzzle will reset. As you can imagine, this behavior is going to be a bit complicated.

Setting up the puzzle pieces

To get started with the puzzle, you need to provide three different objects for the user to click.

From the Sumerian Dashboard, open the **Showroom Skedaddle** scene.

Click **Import Assets** and search for **statue**. Once you find it, select it, and click **Add** to add it to your available assets.

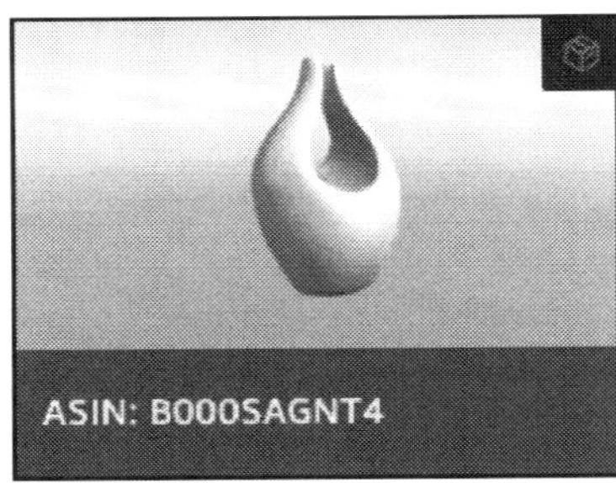

Click **Import Assets** again and, this time, search for **ASIN: B073P2DNTD**. This search returns a lamp. Select it, and click **Add**.

You'll need an end table to hold the lamp. Click **Import Assets**, search for **Table Curved**, select the asset, then click **Add**.

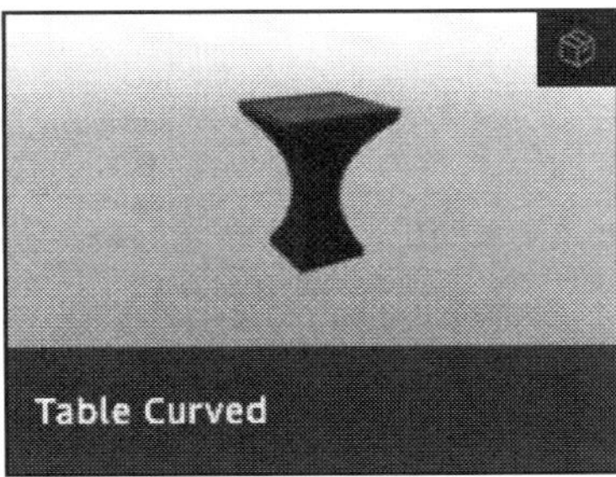

Click **Import Assets** one final time and search for **ASIN: B00PCS8PDY**. This search returns a vase. Click **Add**.

Arranging the room

You now have four objects you can use in your puzzle, so your next task is to arrange the room. In the Assets panel, select the **Entities** tab.

Drag a **Table Curved** entity onto the canvas and set its position to (**-0.321**, **0**, **-0.625**). Rename the entity to **Side Table** and drag it into the **Furniture** entity. This will hold the lamp.

Next, drag a **B073P2DNTD.obj** entity from the Assets panel onto the canvas. Rename the entity to **Desk Lamp**. Set its position to (**-0.316**, **0.532**, **-0.624**) and drag it into the **Furniture** entity.

Finally, drag a **vase_ViewRoom.fbx** entity onto the canvas. Rename this entity to **Vase**. Set its position to (**-1.557**, **0.199**, **-1.592**) and set the scale to (**0.594**, **0.594**, **0.594**).

Expand the Vase entity in the Entities panel and select **B00PCS8PDY:Bottle B00PCS8PDY:Stone1**.

In the Inspector, expand the Material component. In the COLOR (DIFFUSE) section, click on the **white color box** and set the color to **#0046dd**.

You now have a blue vase. Drag it into the **Furniture** entity.

Now, drag a **smooth_statue_ViewRoom.fbx** entity onto the canvas. Set its position to (**-1.563**, **0.517**, **1.466**) and set the scale to (**0.675**, **0.675**, **0.675**). Rename it to **Statue**.

In the Entities panel, **expand the Statue entity**. Select the **B000SAGNT4:Artwork** entity child.

In the Inspector, expand the Material component. In the COLOR (DIFFUSE) section, set the Color to **#79fd4d**. Now, drag the **Statue** entity into the **Furniture** entity.

When you're all done, your escape room will look like this:

Now comes the fun part: Creating the behaviors!

Setting up the emitters

Now that you have all the elements in place, you need to start building the puzzle. Each element in the puzzle will emit a message when the user clicks it. A central entity will listen for the messages and determine when the user has solved the puzzle. When this occurs, the puzzle manager will emit a puzzle complete message, triggering the third and final puzzle.

Start by clicking **Create Entity** then, in the Others category, select **Entity**. Give it the name **Color Puzzle Manager** and select it. In the Inspector, click **Add Component** and select **State Machine**.

In the State Machine component, click the + button to add a new behavior. Rename this new behavior to **Color Puzzle Manager**.

When you're done, the entity will look like this:

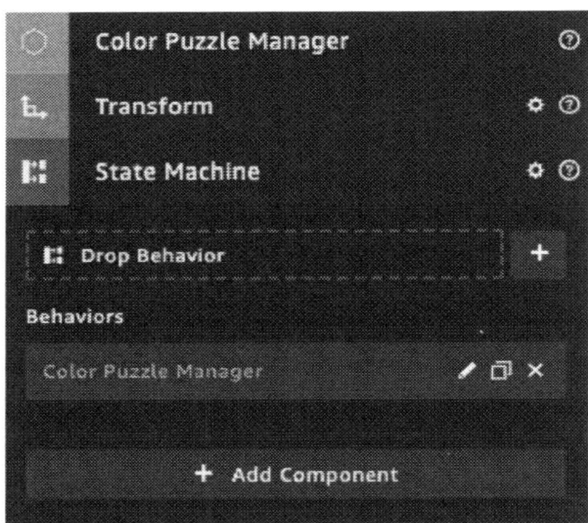

Now, to create the emitting behaviors!

In the Assets panel, select the **Behaviors** tab. In the Default Pack, click the + button and select **Behavior** from the list. Rename your new behavior to **Blue Trigger**.

In the State Machine editor, select **State 1** and rename it to **Listen for Click**. Click **Add Action** and, in the **Controls** category, select the **Click/Tap on Entity** action. Once selected, click **Add**.

You need to add another state to this behavior, so click **Add State**. Rename this state to **Emit Click Message**. Click **Add Action** and, in the Transition category, select the **Emit Message** action and click **Add**. Set Channel to **ClickedBlue**.

Click **Add Action** again and, in the Transitions category, select the **Transition** action and click **Add**.

Drag transitions between both states. Your behavior should look like this:

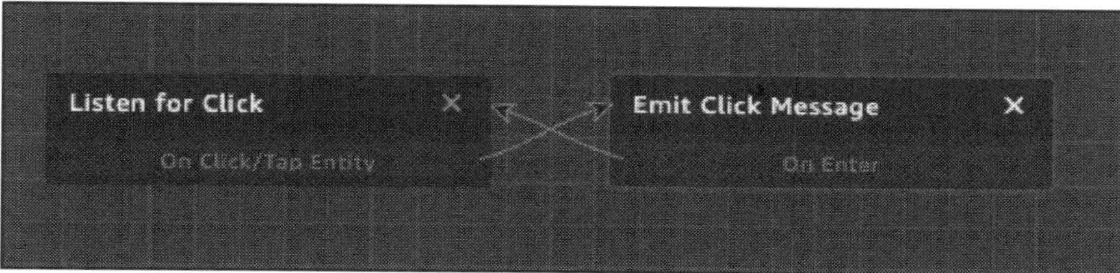

In the Asset panel, select the **Blue Trigger** behavior and press the **duplicate** button.

Rename the duplicate behavior to **Green Trigger**. Edit the behavior and change Channel in the Emit Click Message action to **ClickedGreen**.

In the Asset panel, duplicate the **Green Trigger** behavior and rename it to **Yellow Trigger**. Edit the behavior and change Channel in the Emit Click Message action to **ClickedYellow**.

Now, assign the **Yellow Trigger** behavior to the **Desk Lamp**. Assign the **Green Trigger** behavior to the **Statue**. Finally, assign the **Blue Trigger** behavior to the **Vase**.

Building logic with attributes

When you first read about entities, you learned that they represent a single point in space. Later, you saw how you could customize your entities by using components. You also learned that entities can contain metadata such as a description of the entity and when it was created.

In short, entities have many useful features, but here's one additional feature that will take your scenes to the next level: With entities, you can store data by way of attributes.

When you create an attribute on an entity, you can use that attribute to store whatever data is relevant to your scene. For instance, you can store whether the user has clicked on a certain entity. You can use them to save user preferences, such as music or sound volume. You can also use them to keep track of any interaction in your scene and make choices based on them.

You have three different types of attributes at your disposal: You can use them to store numbers, true or false values, and text. Using these values, you can create rich interactive scenes.

Unfortunately, attributes do not persist between sessions. Every time a user restarts your scene, the attributes will be reset. If you want data to persist between sessions, you'll need to save outside of Sumerian by using one of the many services provided by AWS. You'll learn how to leverage AWS later in this book.

In this puzzle, you'll be using attributes to store two different values. The first attribute will store the color that the user just clicked. You'll use another attribute to store the previous color that the user clicked.

The puzzle reaches a winning condition when the current clicked color is blue and the previous clicked color is yellow.

Defining attributes

Before you can use an attribute, you must define that attribute. There are two ways to define attributes. You can either use a **Set x Attribute** action in a behavior or you can manually set an attribute on an entity.

When manually setting an attribute, you can only use string (text) attributes. When using an action, you can set text (string attribute), a number (numeric attribute) or a true or false value attribute (boolean attribute).

In the Entities panel, select the **Color Puzzle Manager**. In the Inspector, expand the **Custom Attributes** section.

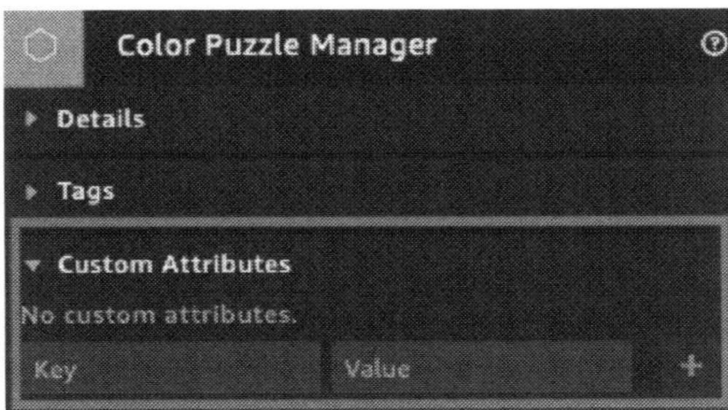

Defining an attribute means giving it a name and providing a value.

For Key, use **CurrentClicked**. For Value, use **None**. Click the + button. For the next attribute, set Key to **PreviousClicked**, and set Value to **None**. Click the + button to add it.

Your entity now has two different attributes assigned to it.

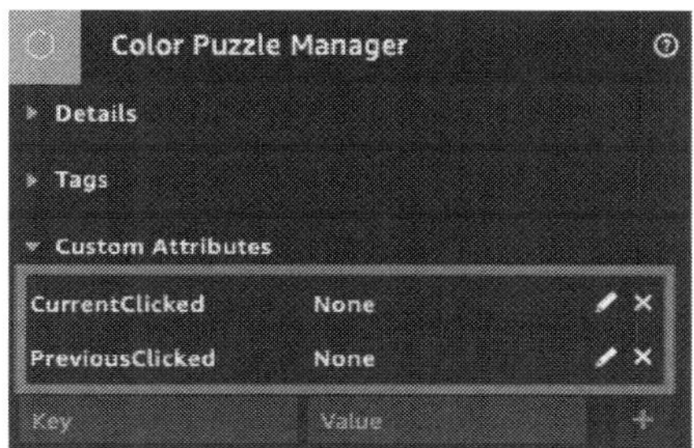

Building a branching behavior

Attributes work well with behaviors; you can create behaviors that run actions based on the value of certain attributes.

When evaluating attributes, there are four types of results. You don't need to respond to all of them; you may be interested in only one result.

The first result is an **equal** result, which you express using **==**. This is a sign that's used in many programming languages to test for equality. The definition of equality is pretty strict – the value "Green" is different from the value "green", for example, since one is uppercase and the other is lowercase.

The second result is a **not equal** result. You express this using **!=**.

The third result is a **greater than** result expressed using **>**.

The final result is the **less than** result expressed using **<**.

You express the branching logic in transitions. You simply drag one of these results to another state.

Clicking puzzle pieces

For your escape room, you're going to use branching behaviors to determine what happens when a user clicks on one of the puzzle pieces.

To get started, switch to the **Behaviors** tab in the Asset panel, then click on **Color Puzzle Manager** to start editing it.

Rename State 1 to **Listen for Clicks** then click **Add Action**. In the Transitions category, select the **Listen** action and click **Add**. Set the action's Message channel to **ClickedGreen**.

Create two more listen actions. For blue, set the Message channel to **ClickedBlue**. For yellow, set it to **ClickedYellow**.

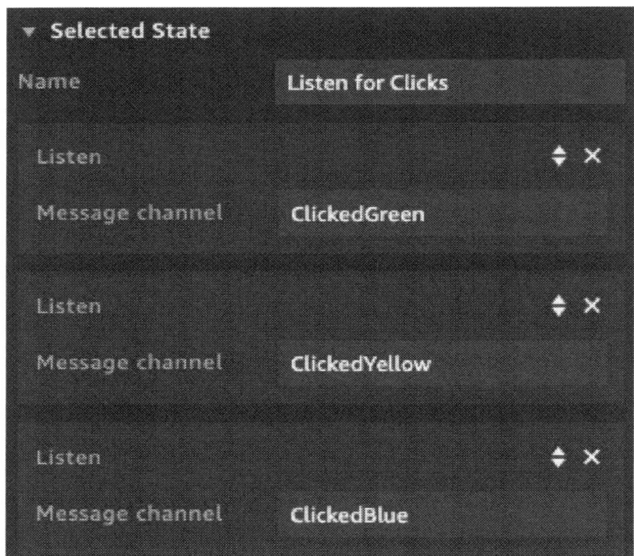

Once a click is registered, you need to save the currently-clicked color (say that ten times fast). To do this, **add three new states** and name them: **Set to Green**, **Set to Yellow** and **Set to Blue**.

Create transitions from the **ClickedGreen** to the **Set to Green** state. Do the same for the yellow and blue states.

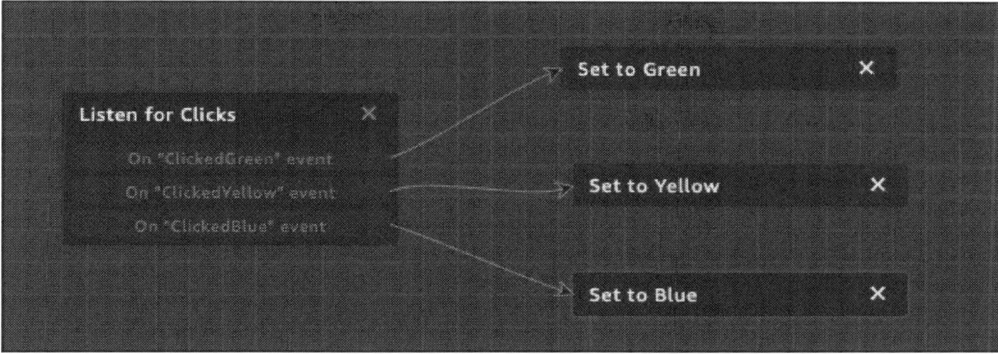

You now want to set the `CurrentClicked` attribute to the color that the user clicked. You'll do this by using an action. Select the **Set to Green** state and click **Add Action**. In the Add Action dialog, select the **Attribute** category.

You'll notice that you have lots of related actions that you can run on attributes.

Scroll down then select and add the **Set String Attribute** action. This is another way to define attributes. If the attribute isn't defined, this action will create one.

In the action, set Name to **CurrentClicked** and set Value to **Green**.

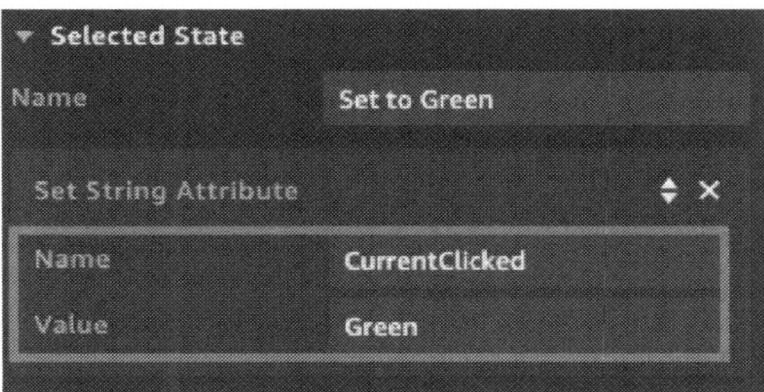

Do the same for both the **Set to Yellow** and **Set to Blue** states.

Setting up the order of the puzzle pieces

At this point, when the user clicks a color, it will set the current color. Remember, you need to keep track of the previous color, too. Currently, when the user clicks the green statue, it will set the current color. When they click the yellow lamp, the `CurrentClick` attribute is still set to the statue until it's updated.

What you need to do is copy the `CurrentClicked` attribute to the `PreviousClicked` attribute. Thankfully, there's an attribute action for that.

Select the **Set to Green** action and click **Add Action**. Select the **Duplicate Attribute** action and click **Add**.

In the Duplicate Attribute action, set the Source Attribute to **CurrentClicked** and set the Destination Attribute to be **PreviousClicked**.

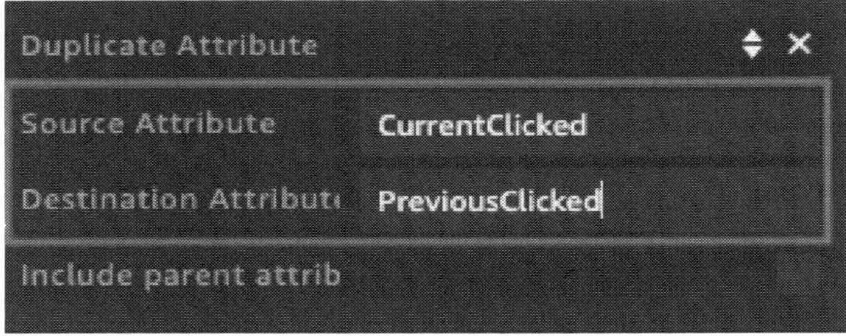

> **Note**: If the attribute doesn't exist, then the attribute won't be copied. You need to create the attribute first.

There is a small bug (mistake) with your implementation. The `CurrentClicked` attribute is being set before you copy the value to the `PreviousClicked` attribute. You need to change the order of the actions.

Using the double arrows on the Duplicate Attribute action, **drag it above the Set String Attribute**.

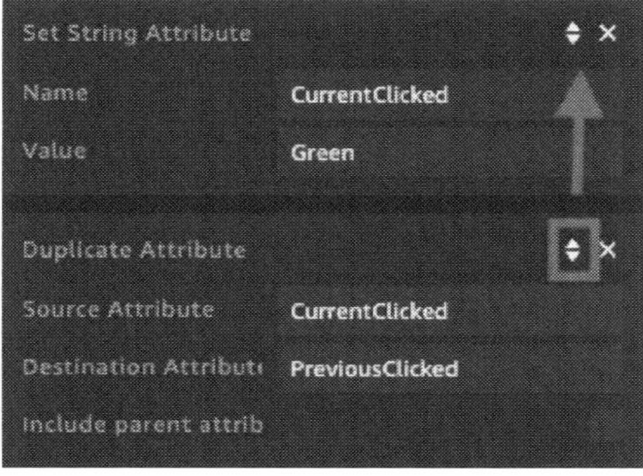

Do this for the **Set to Yellow** and **Set to Blue** states.

Adding transitions for each state

Finally, these three states need transitions. For each state, click **Add Action**, and in the Transitions category, select the **Transition** action, and then click **Add**.

Now it's time to construct the overall puzzle logic. First, you need to check the Green click. When the user clicks the green statue, you have to check if they clicked a previous color. If so, the puzzle resets. Otherwise, they can proceed to the next step.

Click **Add State** and name your state **Check for Previous Click**. Now you need to test the `PreviousClick` attribute. Click **Add Action**, then in the Attribute category, select the **Compare String Attribute to a Constant** and click **Add**.

If the `PreviousClicked` is `None`, that means the puzzle has just started. Otherwise, the user's puzzle progress is reset.

In your new action, enter **PreviousClicked** in the Attribute field.

The constant is the value you're testing against. In this case, you're testing for "None", so enter **None** in the Constant field.

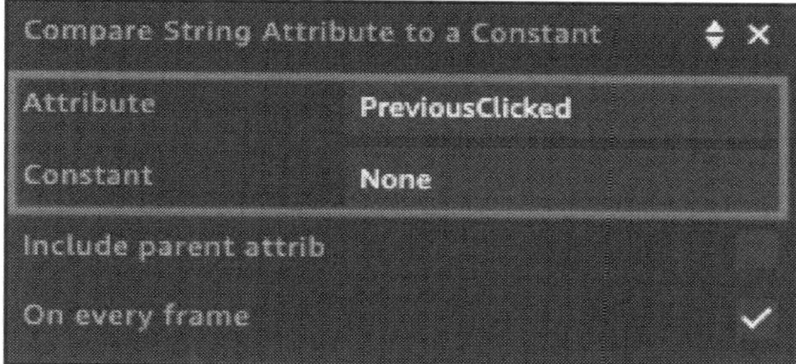

Now, your state has two different transition options. Remember, == indicates that the values are equal, whereas `!=` indicates that the values are not equal.

Drag a transition from **On PreviousClicked == None** to the **Listen for Clicks** state. This is the correct path.

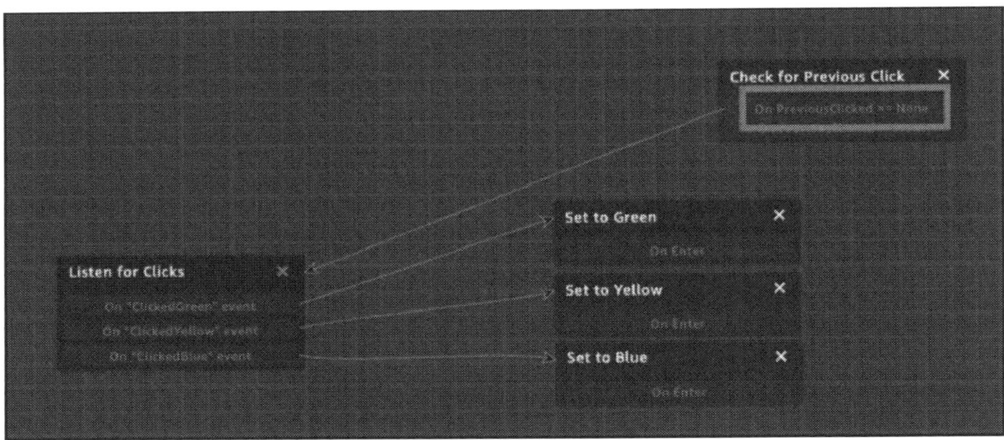

If the user clicks the wrong color, you'll need to reset the puzzle. Click **Add State** and name your state to **Reset Attributes**.

Click **Add Action** and, from the Attribute category, select and add a **Set String Attribute**. Set Name to **CurrentClicked** and Value to **None**.

Add another **Set String Attribute** action. This time, set Name to **PreviousClicked** and Value to **None**.

Finally, add a **Transition** action to the state. When you're done, your state will look like this:

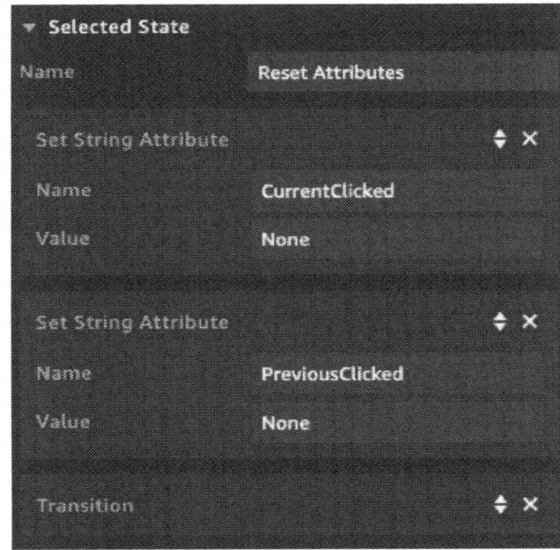

Pulling everything together

Now, it's time to link everything up. Drag a transition from **Set to Green** to **Check for Previous Click**. In Check for Previous Click, drag a transition from **On PreviousClicked != None** to **Reset Attributes**. Finally, drag a transition from **Reset Attributes** to **Listen for Clicks**. When you're done, your behavior will look like this:

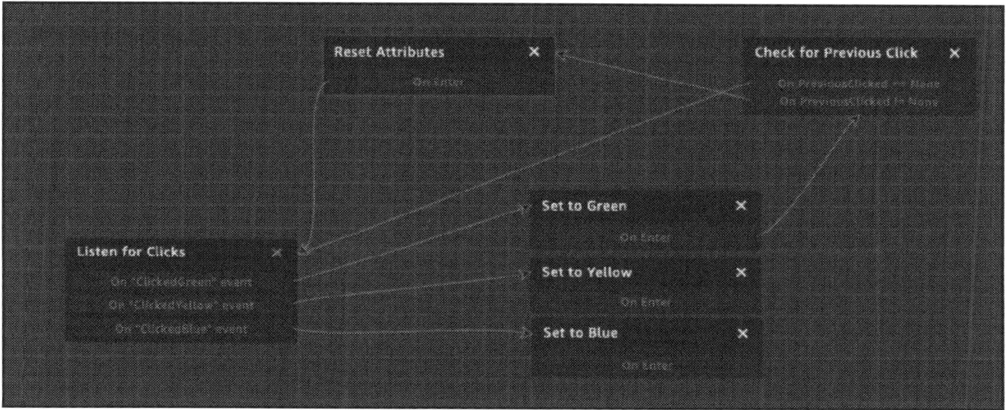

At this point, you have one color set up. Now, for the other two. They'll follow the same pattern.

Click **Add State** and name it **Check Yellow Click**. Add a **Compare String Attribute to a Constant** then set Attribute to **PreviousClicked** and Constant to **Green**.

Drag a transition from **On PreviousClicked == Green** to the **Listen for Clicks** state. Drag another transition from **On PreviousClicked != Green** to the **Reset Attributes** state. Finally, drag a transition from the **Set to Yellow** state to the **Check Yellow Click** state.

When the user clicks the yellow lamp, the behavior checks if they had previously clicked the green statue. If not, then it resets the puzzle. Otherwise, it reverts to the listening state.

> **Note**: Typically in a puzzle such as this, you'd provide additional audio clues to help the user. You will learn how to incorporate audio into your scenes in Section 2, "Building an Educational Experience."

Your behavior will look like the following:

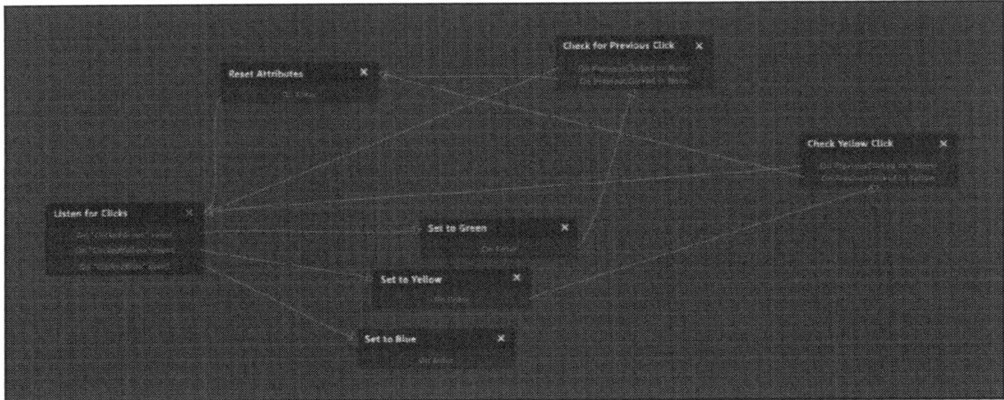

As you build out your behaviors, it helps to spread out your states so that the transitions are easy to follow versus looking at a spaghetti behavior. You want to avoid behaviors that look like this:

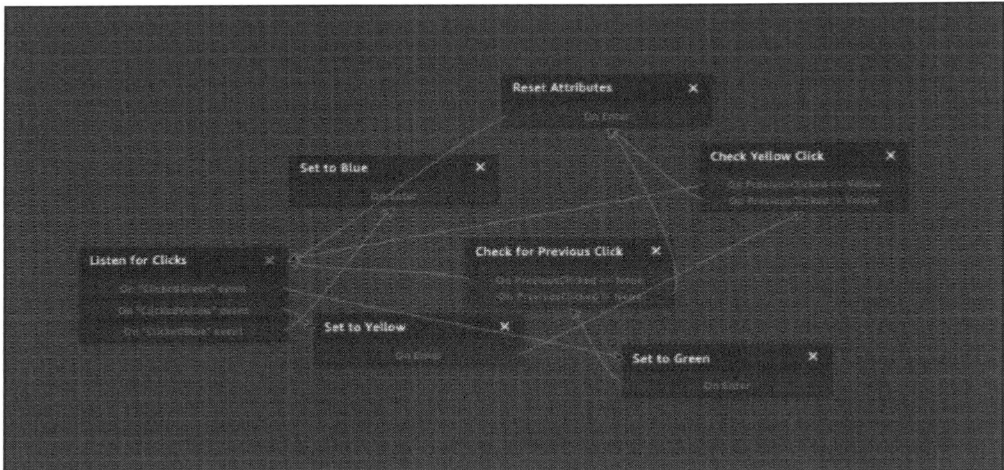

Now for the blue vase. Click **Add State** and name the new state **Check Blue Click**. Add a **Compare String Attribute to a Constant**. Set Attribute to **PreviousClicked** and Constant to **Yellow**.

Drag a transition from **On PreviousClicked != Yellow** to the **Reset Attributes** state then drag a transition from the **Set to Blue** state to the **Check Blue Click** state.

Click **Add State** and name this state **Puzzle Solved**. Add an **Emit Message** action and set Channel to **ColorPuzzleComplete**. Drag a transition from **On PreviousClicked == Yellow** to **Puzzle Solved**. For now, you won't have an entity respond to the message, but it's still important to know if the user has solved the puzzle.

With the Puzzle Solved state still selected, click **Add Action**. Select the **Misc** category, and then select and add the **Log Message** action.

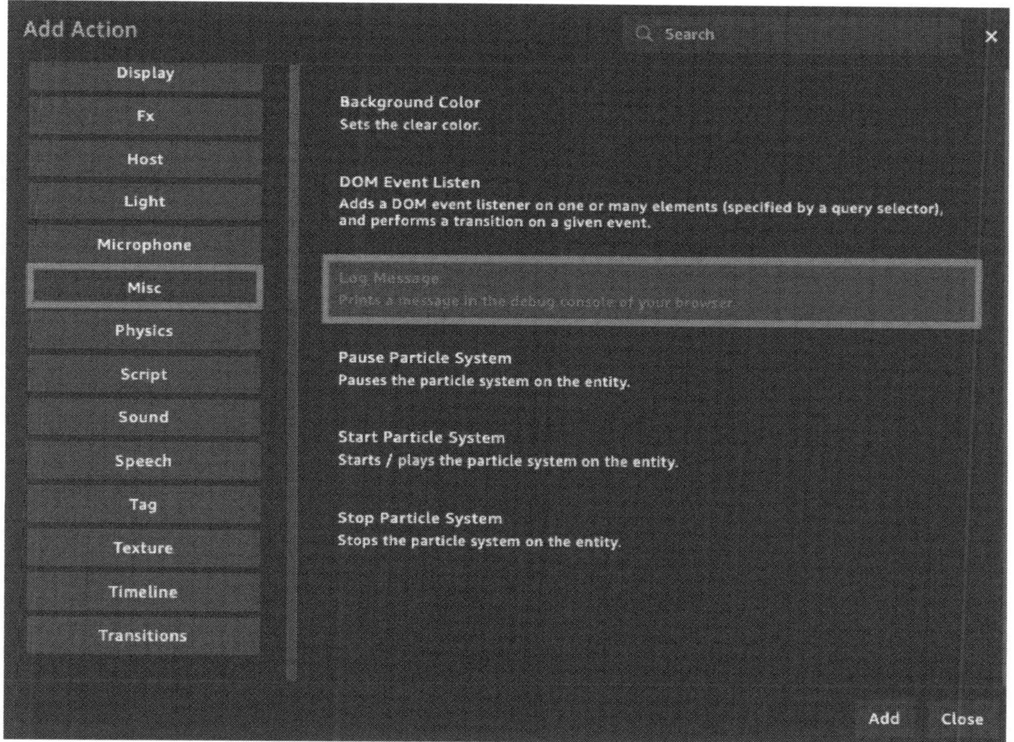

Logging the results

Logging is a way to send messages to the browser, which you can read with the developer tools. Each browser comes with its own set of tools to help diagnose, troubleshoot and develop web pages. Since Sumerian is a web-based engine, you can use these tools as well.

Each browser provides different methods to access their tools, so you'll need to look up how to access them.

This book uses Chrome as the primary browser. If you are using Chrome, simply press F12 on your keyboard. When the tools appear, make sure you've selected the **Console**.

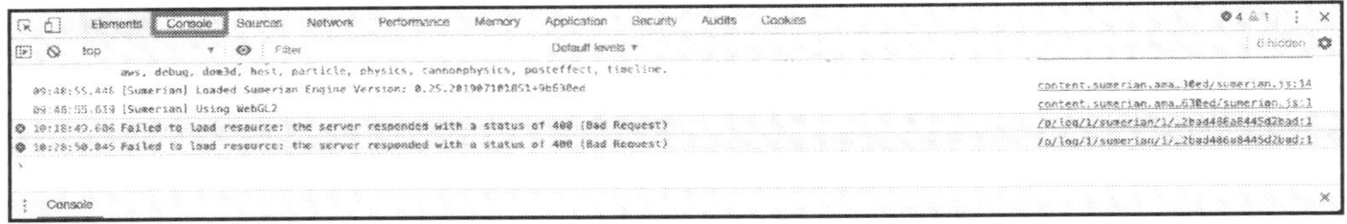

The console displays any relevant messages for the current page. It will show any errors, warnings, and messages. The console can be quite useful when troubleshooting complicated behaviors.

In the Log Message action, set the Message to **Puzzle Solved**. Next, select the **Set to Green** state and add the **Log Message** action to it. Make sure to move the **Log Message** action above the Transition action. Set Message to **Green Clicked** then do the same for **Set to Yellow** and **Set to Blue**. Also, select the **Reset Attributes** action and add a **Log Message** action. Set Message to **Puzzle Reset**. Remember to move the Log Message action above the transition or the Log Message won't run.

When you're done, your behavior will look like this:

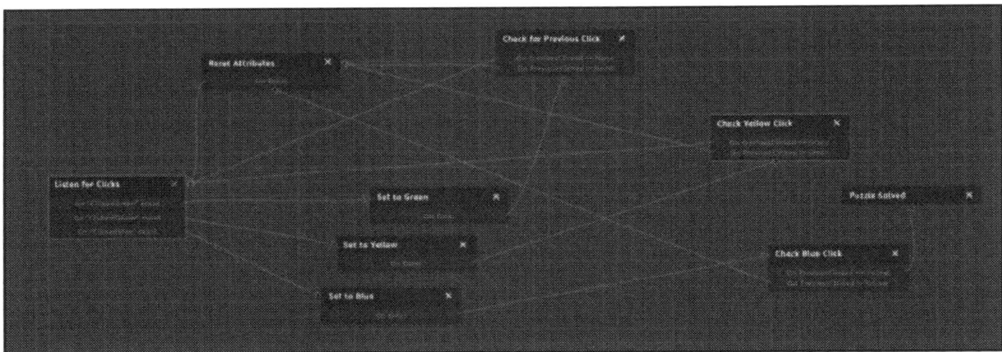

Testing your escape room

Now play your scene. Click on the **Green Statue**. Your console should display a message.

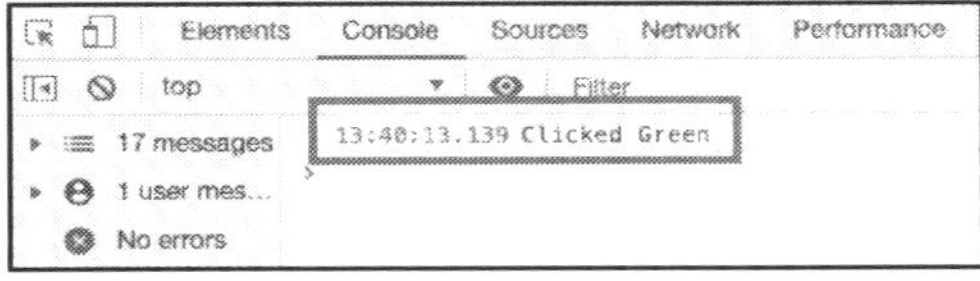

Next, click the yellow lamp then the blue vase. You'll see that you get a "puzzle complete" message.

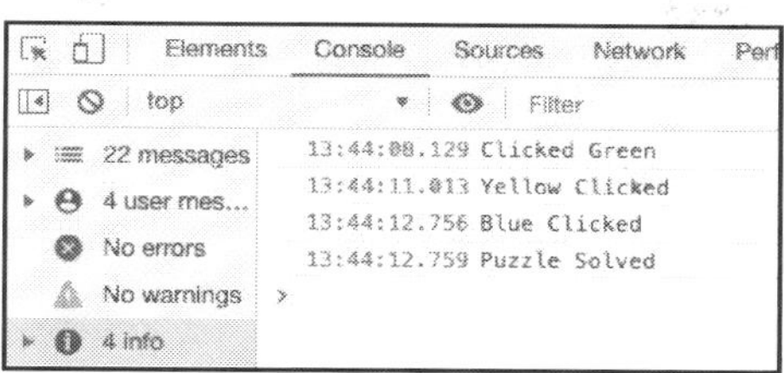

Stop and restart your scene. This time, click the **green statue** and then **blue vase**. Now, you'll get a message letting you know that the puzzle has reset.

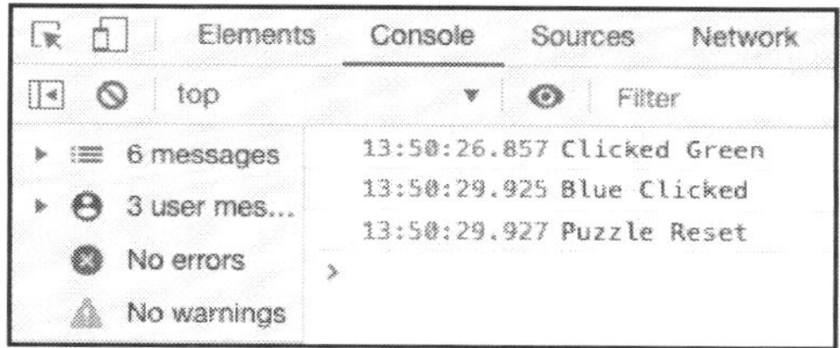

You now have a working puzzle! But there's just one problem: The user can access the puzzle at any time. You want the puzzle to only become activated under after the user clicks the light switch. So your next step is to add that functionality.

Click **Add State** and name the state **Listen for Puzzle Start**. Click **Add Action** and add a **Listen** action. Set Channel to **ActivateSwitch**. Drag a transition between your new state and the **Listen for Clicks** state. Your behavior will look like this:

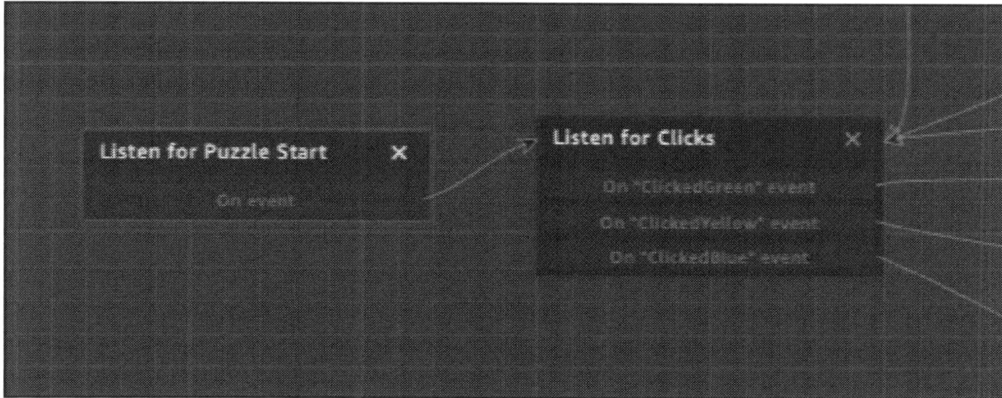

While you've added a new state and positioned it to be the first state to run, Sumerian considers it just another state – position doesn't matter.

Every behavior comes with a state that is, by default, the initial state. Thankfully, you can designate a state to be the initial state.

Select the **Listen for Puzzle Start** state and, in the Inspector, click **Set As Initial State**. Now, the behavior will wait for the `ActivateSwitch` message to broadcast. Once it does, the user will be able to perform the second puzzle.

The next puzzle will involve some physics, which you'll learn in the next chapter.

Using multiple clues

The clue for this escape room is intentionally vague; because there are no audio clues to help the user yet, the puzzle may be too hard for many people.

For your upcoming challenge, you'll update the puzzle to include three other images. When the user clicks on the green statue, the clue should update to the following:

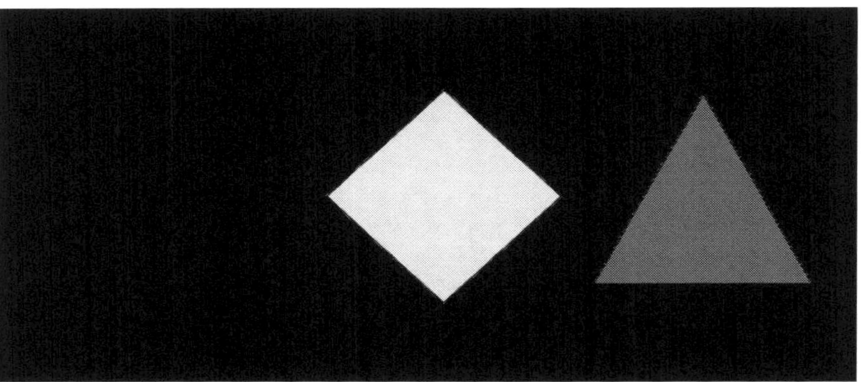

Then, when they click on the yellow lamp, the clue should use the following:

When the user completes the puzzle, the following image will appear:

If the user clicks a colored item out of sequence, the clue should revert to the three colored shapes.

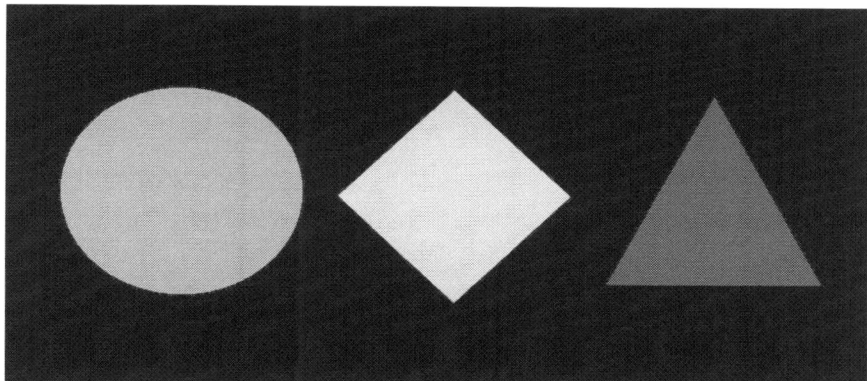

Your task is to update the **Color Puzzle Manager**. First, you need to update the project to use these new clues.

Start by importing all the clue images into your project. Do this by clicking the folder icon in the Assets panel and then selecting the images.

In the Entities panel, click the **Clue** entity. Rename it to **Clue 1**.

In the Inspector, click **Add Component** and then select **Start Machine**. In the newly-added State Machine component, click the + button to add a new behavior.

Rename the behavior to **Clue 1** and rename the first state to **Listen for Instructions**. Create **add two more states**. Rename one state to **Show Clue** and the other to **Hide Clue**.

In the Show state, click **Add Action** and, in the Display category, select the **Show** action. For the Hide state, add a **Hide** action from the Display category. Add **transitions** to both the states and create transitions from the new states to the **Listen for Instructions** state.

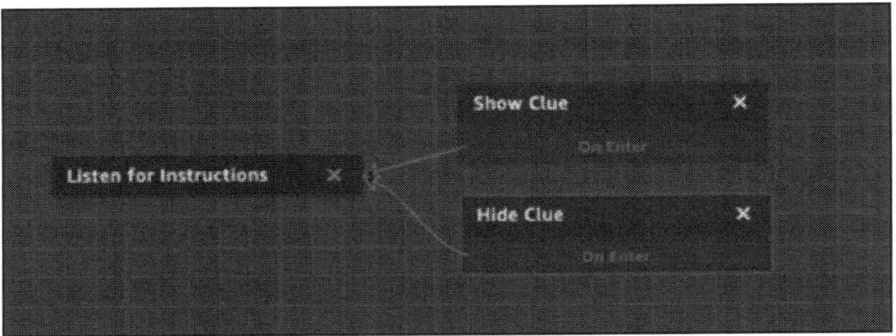

Select the **Listen for Instructions** state. Add **four Listen** actions to it. Have them listen to the following messages: **ShowClue1, ShowClue2, ShowClue3, ShowClue4**

Your behavior will look like this:

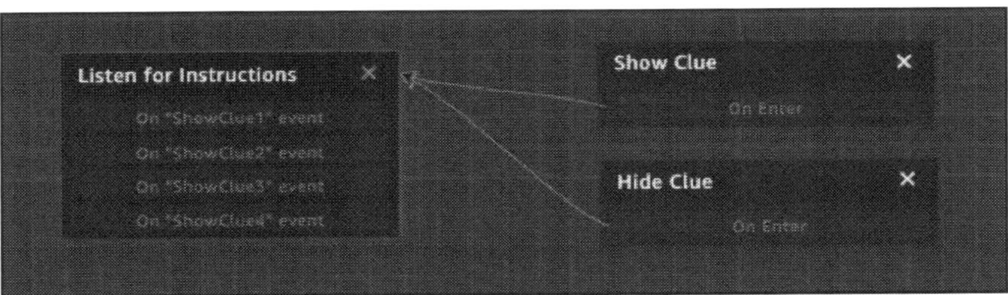

Drag a transition from the **ShowClue1** action to the **Show Clue** state. For the other listen actions, drag transitions to the **Hide Clue** state. This means when another clue displays, this clue will hide.

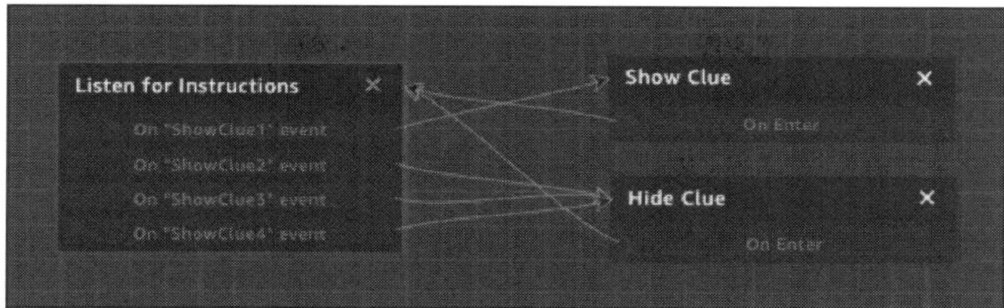

With Clue 1 selected in the Entities panel, click the **duplicate** button. This will also duplicate the behavior. Because you duplicated the entity, it's still using the Clue 1 material. In the Assets panel, switch to the Material tab and **duplicate** the Clue 1 material. Rename it **Clue 2**. Switch the Textures tab and drag **Clue2.png** to the Texture property.

Select the **Clue 2** entity, and drag the Clue 2 material to the Material component. Switch the Assets panel to the **Behaviors** tab and edit the **Clue 2** behavior.

Drag a transition from the **ON "ShowClue1" event** to the **Hide Clue** state. Drag a transition from the **ON "ShowClue2" event** to the **Show Clue** state.

Do this same process for **Clue 3** and **Clue 4**.

At this point, your scene is ready to use for your challenge.

Challenge

Challenge: Multiple clues

At this point, you have prepared four clues. They have behaviors to hide and show clues. Your challenge is to alter the **Color Puzzle Manager** behavior to use these clues.

Just a few hints: You'll need to create two additional states and then wire those states into the overall behavior. You'll also need to update two other states.

Also remember, you just need to broadcast one message. When you broadcast a message to `ShowClue1`, the other clues will hide because of the way you set up the behavior. Now give it a shot!

Solution

Hopefully, that wasn't too bad. If you got stuck, then follow along.

To get started, select the **Color Puzzle Manager** to open the State Machine editor. First, select the **Reset Attributes** state. Click **Add Action** and add an **Emit Message** action. Set Channel to **ShowClue1**. Make sure to drag the new action above the Transition action.

Now, select the **Puzzle Solved** state. Add an **Emit Message** action to it. Set Channel to **ShowClue4**.

Next, click **Add State**. Name it **Reveal Clue 2** then add an **Emit Message** and a **Transition** action. In the Emit Message action, set Channel to **ShowClue2**.

Now duplicate the state by clicking the **Duplicate State(s)** button. Rename the state to **Reveal Clue 3**. In the Emit Message action, set Channel to **ShowClue3**. At this point, it's time to hook them up.

In Check for Previous Click, drag a transition from **On PreviousClicked == None** to **Reveal Clue 2**. In Reveal Clue 2, drag a transition from the **On Enter** to **Listen for Clicks**

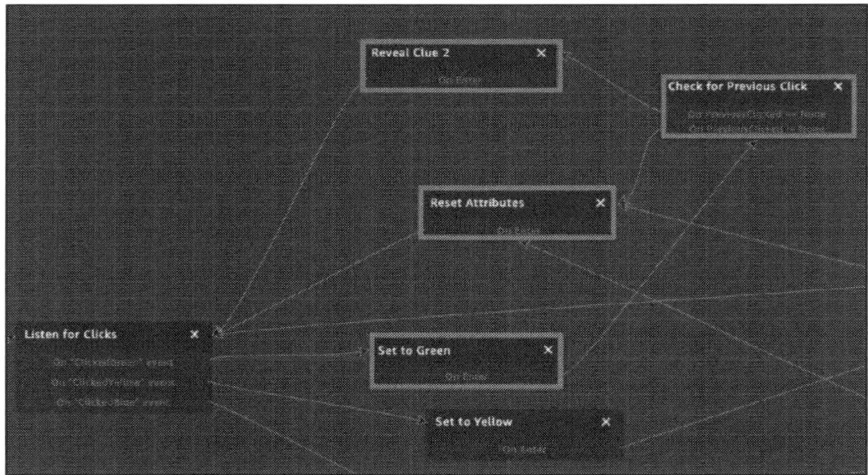

Now, do the same thing for the Reveal Clue 3 state. In Check Yellow Click, drag a transition from **On PreviousClicked == Green** to **Reveal Clue 2**. In Reveal Clue 3, drag a transition from the **On Enter** to **Listen for Clicks**

At this point, you have updated your behavior to use additional clues. Run your scene and this time, when you complete the puzzle, you'll experience a moment of inspiration.

Key points

- **Attributes** allow you to **associate data with a given entity**.
- An attribute takes both a **key** and a **value**. A key is used to look up a value much like in a dictionary, a word is used to look up its definition.
- Editor defined attributes can only be **string attributes**.
- Behavior defined attributes can be **strings, booleans and numbers**.
- Attributes can be **compared against constants** to create branching logic.
- **Logging prints messages** to the browser console.

Where to go from here?

Attributes provide an excellent mechanism for tracking the choices made by your users. You can branch choices based on them but you can also perform mathematical operations on them as well. You'll put them to work in the next section of this book.

To learn more about attributes, check out the documentation page: https://docs.aws.amazon.com/en_pv/sumerian/latest/userguide/statemachines-attributes.html

Chapter 6: Physics

By Brian Moakley

Modern graphic engines typically come with their own physics engine, and Sumerian is no different. The difference between it and an engine like Unity or Unreal is that Sumerian's physics simulation is all managed within a web browser.

Managing physics in a web browser is challenging since physics engines are computationally heavy. They must compute trajectories, determine how surfaces and gravity affect a moving object, calculate collisions and determine how those collisions affect velocity and rotation.

Those are just some of the things that a physics engine must do for you. They do a lot more, and they must do it all in a way that doesn't slow down your scene. Sumerian provides you with everything you need from a physics engine. In this tutorial, you'll learn how to use physics to make your third puzzle come to life.

> **Note**: At the time of this writing, the physics engine is slated to undergo a complete rewrite. Watch the Sumerian official documentation for any changes.

Setting up the third puzzle

When the user solved the second puzzle, they were left with a picture of a lightbulb. This clue points to a lightbulb that doesn't exist in your room... yet. You'll need to add it in a moment.

When the user completes the puzzle, the lightbulb will fall from a hanging lamp. The user will need to click the lightbulb to indicate that they have picked it up.

Next, they must throw it at the painting. They'll throw it by clicking on the red center of the painting. By hitting the red center, the walls will open and the user will be allowed to escape. (Not really, but I'm getting ahead of myself — muahahaha).

Open your scene, if it isn't already open, and click **Import Asset**. Search for the **Lamp Hanging** asset.

Select the asset and click **Add** to import it into your assets library. Once you return to the editor, drag a **lamp_hanging.fbx** onto the scene. Set its position to (**-1.586**, **3.280**, **0.436**). Rename it to **Hanging Lamp** and drag it into the **Furniture** entity.

Nice, you now have a lamp hanging in your escape room.

Next, you need to add a lightbulb to your lamp. Click **Create Entity** and select the **Sphere** entity.

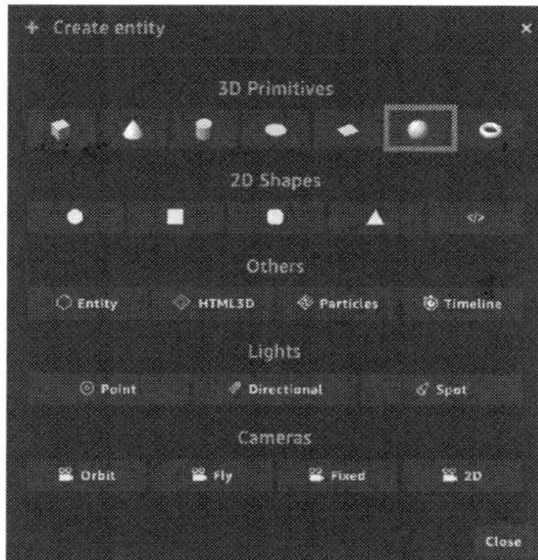

In the Inspector panel, rename the entity to **Lightbulb**. Set the position to (**-1.588**, **2.218**, **0.437**) and the scale to (**0.141**, **0.141**, **0.141**).

You now have a lightbulb inside the lamp, and you're ready for a physics puzzle.

Using Rigid Bodies

When you add a new entity to Sumerian, that entity will not respond to physics. As mentioned, physics can use a lot of your computer's resources, so an opt-in approach makes sense.

To start using physics, you need to add a Rigid Body component. This not only tells Sumerian that your entity will respond to physics, but it also allows you to set various physical properties for the entity.

Select the **Lightbulb** in your scene and click **Add Component**. From the list of options, select **Rigid Body**.

The component will show all the various options for your rigid body.

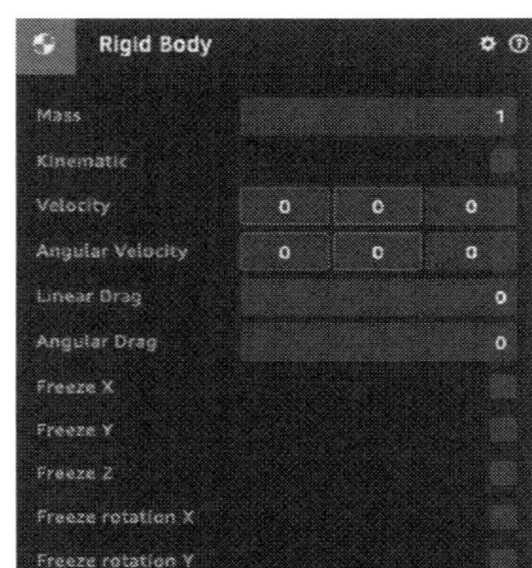

The Rigid Body component allows you to add an entity's velocity at the start of the scene as well as its angular velocity. You can also add drag to it and prevent the entity from moving or rotating on a certain axis.

Now, run the scene and look at the lamp. You'll notice that the lightbulb is gone. This happens because the lightbulb starts responding to physics once the scene starts. By the time you look, it's gone.

Where did it go? Stop the scene and look underneath the escape room. That's a long way to drop.

You'll learn why it fell through the floor in a moment. For now, you want to configure the lightbulb to fall on demand.

Select the **Lightbulb** in the Entities panel. Click **Add Component** and select the **State Machine** component. Click the + button to add a new behavior. Name it **Lightbulb**.

In the State Machine editor, select **State 1**. Name it **Click to Activate**. Later, you'll have the lightbulb fall from gravity as a result of a message. But for now, you'll have it fall with a click.

Click **Add Action** and, in the Controls category, select the **Click/Tap on entity** action, and click **Add**.

Now comes the magic. In the Entities panel, select the **Lightbulb**. You want the lightbulb to respond to physics, but not at the start of the scene. Instead, you want it to react when you click the lightbulb.

To do this, you need to set the Rigid Body to **kinematic**. When you set a rigid body to kinematic, you indicate that you are manually moving the entity via animation. This means that the Rigid Body won't respond to gravity or move due to collisions. That said, these entities can still be notified when a collision occurs, even though the entities won't react to the collision.

In the Inspector panel, check the **Kinematic** property.

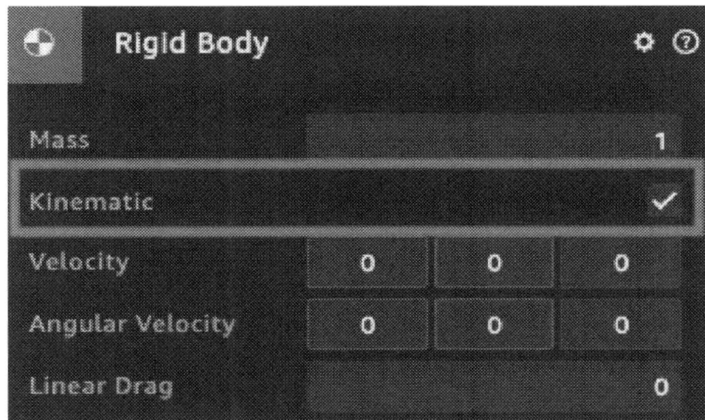

Play your scene and look at the lightbulb. You'll notice that it's fixed in place.

To make it move, you need to disable the kinematic property of the Rigid Body.

At this time, Sumerian doesn't have an action to disable a rigid body being kinematic. For that, you have to write your first bit of code.

In the Assets panel, switch to the Behaviors tab and click on the **Lightbulb** behavior to open it in the State Machine editor. Click **Add State** and name your new state **Disable Kinematic**.

Click **Add Action** and, in the Script category, select the **Execute Script Expression** action. This will run a script expression when a state is entered.

You'll notice the following dummy code:

```
ctx.entityData.example = "hello"
```

Replace the dummy code with the following:

```
ctx.entity.rigidBodyComponent.isKinematic = false
```

It should look like this:

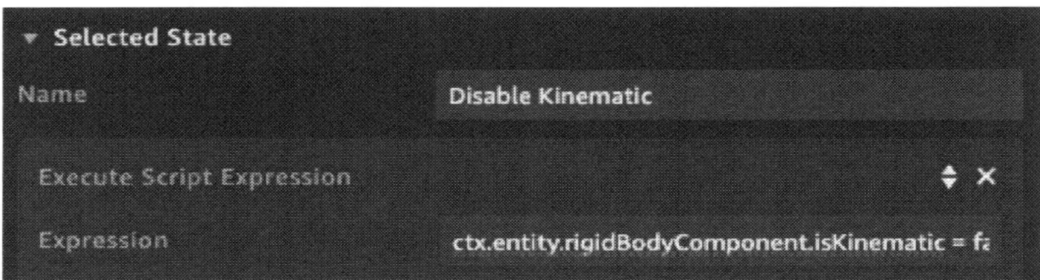

The code starts with `ctx` variable. This represents the current context, which you'll learn all about in Chapter 12, "The Sumerian API." The `entity` represents the current entity which is the Lightbulb. Next, the code accesses the current rigid body and disables the kinematic state.

If this is your first time encountering JavaScript, do not panic. You will not be tested. You'll learn all about JavaScript in Chapter 11, "Introduction to JavaScript." For now, all you need to know is that the code turns off the kinematic state.

Now, drag a transition between **Click to Activate** and **Disable Kinematic**.

Your behavior should look like the following:

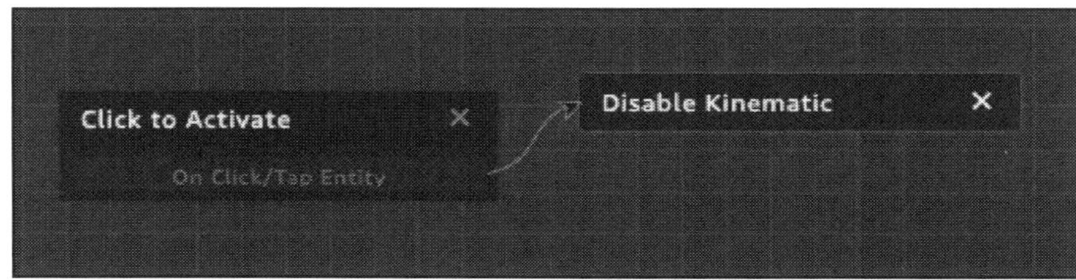

Now, run the scene and click the lightbulb. This time, you'll see your lightbulb fall, but the floor won't stop it. You'd better take care of that!

Adding colliders

As you learned, using the physics engine is an optional process and you opt your entities into it by assigning Rigid Body components.

Not surprisingly, collisions are also opt-in. By default, all objects will fly through each other. You need to add a collider to stop them.

A collider defines the shape of the entity. You have limited shapes when using colliders: You can use a Box, Cylinder, Sphere or an infinite plane.

An infinite plane is great for floors. Select the **Floor** entity and, in the Inspector panel, click **Add Component**. Add a **Collider** component.

You'll see that you have a few options. In the Shape drop-down, select **Infinite Plane**.

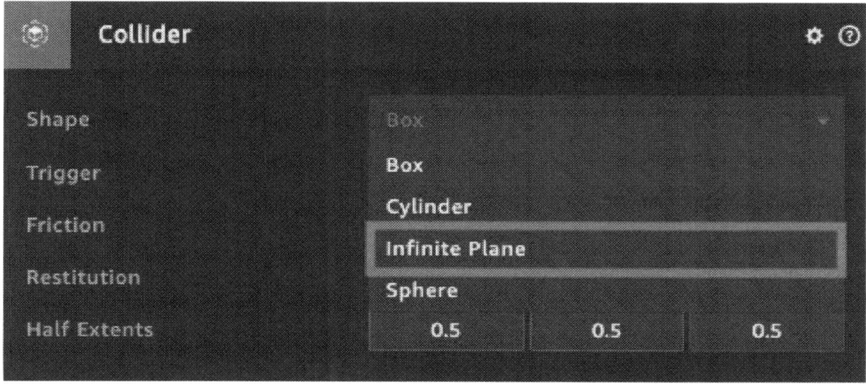

You now have a new collider plane in your scene.

Unfortunately, the plane is vertical so it's acting like a wall instead of a floor. You need to turn it into a horizontal plane, but there's no way to do that without rotating the floor. Select the **Gear** icon in your collider component, then select **Remove** to remove your collider component.

To make the collider horizontal, you'll need to make a child entity do all the work. Click **Create Entity** and select the **Entity** option from the Others section. Name it **Floor Collider**.

Drag it into the **Floor** entity to make it a child then set its position to (**0**, **0**, **0**). Now, click **Add Component** and add a **Collider** to it. In the Collider component, set it to **Infinite Plane**.

Next, set the rotation to (**-90**, **0**, **0**). Use the transform arrows to move the plane just on top of the rug.

Now, run your scene. You'll notice that the lightbulb continues to fall through the rug, even though there's a collider attached to it.

That's because the Lightbulb entity doesn't also have a collider. You need two colliders to form a collision. Select the **Lightbulb** entity and, in the Inspector panel, click **Add Component**. Select the **Collider** component. This time, set the collider to be a **Sphere**. You'll notice a green outline will encompass your sphere. The green indicates the borders of the collider.

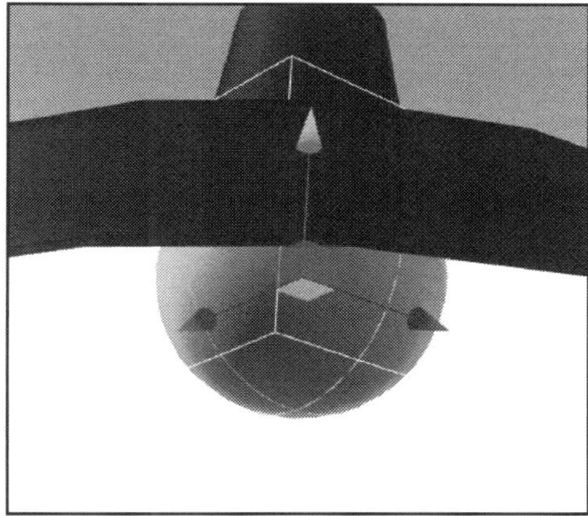

Now, when you run your scene, your lightbulb will land on the rug.

Adding velocity

At this point, you have a lightbulb on the floor, but that's not all you want to do with it. The lightbulb is a part of the puzzle, and the user needs to be able to pick it up and throw it.

Picking up the lightbulb is the easy part. When the user clicks the lightbulb, you'll simply hide it. This is a matter of adding a click action that triggers a hide action, which you'll add next.

In the Assets panel, select the **Behaviors** tab and then the **Lightbulb** behavior. You want the click action to be added *after* the lightbulb has fallen to the ground. So select the **Disable Kinematic** state then click **Add Action**. In the Transitions category, add a **Transition** state.

Add another **state**, name it **Click on the Lightbulb** and add a **Click/Tap on Entity** action. Add another **state** and name this one **Hide Lightbulb and Notify**. Then, add a **Hide** action to it. Next, add an **Emit Message** action to it and set the channel to **LightbulbTaken**.

At this point, any interested objects will know that the user is holding the lightbulb.

Finally, add a **drag transition** from the **Disable Kinematic** state to the **Click on Lightbulb** state, and from the **Click on the Lightbulb** state to the **Hide Lightbulb and Notify** state. Your behavior will look like the following:

Run your scene. Click on the lightbulb to make it drop; once it has landed, click on it again.

The lightbulb should disappear. Magic!

For the second part of the puzzle, you need to throw the lightbulb at your painting. Throwing your lightbulb means adding velocity to it, which you can handle with an action. Being that this is a 3D engine, you apply velocity on the X, Y and Z axes. Once you apply force, the object will respond to gravity as well.

To trigger the throw, the user needs to click on the red part of the painting while holding the lightbulb. In the Entities panel, select the **Red Diamond** and in the Inspector panel, click **Add Component**. Select a **State Machine** component. Click the + button to add a new behavior and name it **Red Diamond**

> **Note**: So far you've been naming your behaviors after the entity that uses them. Later, you may create entities that are used by multiple entities. In that case, it's better to name the behavior after what it does as opposed to what uses it.

Like the last behavior, this behavior is also quite linear. Rename State 1 to **Listen for Lightbulb**. Add a **Listen** action, and have it listen to the **LightbulbTaken** message.

Add another state. Name it **Click to Throw**. Add a **Click/Tap on entity** action. **Add one more state** and name it **Emit Throw Message**. Add an **Emit Message** action and set the Channel to **ThrowLightbulb**.

Now, drag a transition from **Listen for Lightbulb** to **Click to Throw** and from **Click to Throw** to **Emit Throw Message**.

At this point, you can add velocity to the lightbulb. The user will be throwing the lightbulb from a fixed position, so you'll provide different velocities for the player's position. This ensures that the lightbulb will hit the target every single time.

You first need to keep track of the user's position. In the Entities panel, select the **Lightbulb**. Add a custom attribute to it. Name it **Position** and set the value to **Right**. This indicates that the user is standing on the right comfy chair.

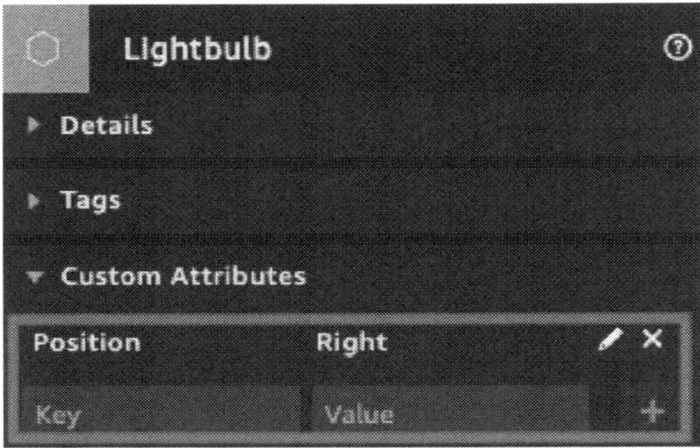

Each time the user switches between furniture, the behavior will need to track it. In the Inspector panel, click the + in the State Machine component to create a new behavior. Name it **Throw Lightbulb**.

Notice that Lightbulb is now responding to two different behaviors. This is useful to avoid complicated logic.

Select the first state and name it **Listen for User Actions**. Add **four Listen actions** and set the channels to: **MoveToLeftComfyChair, MoveToRightComfyChair, MoveToCouch and ThrowLightbulb**.

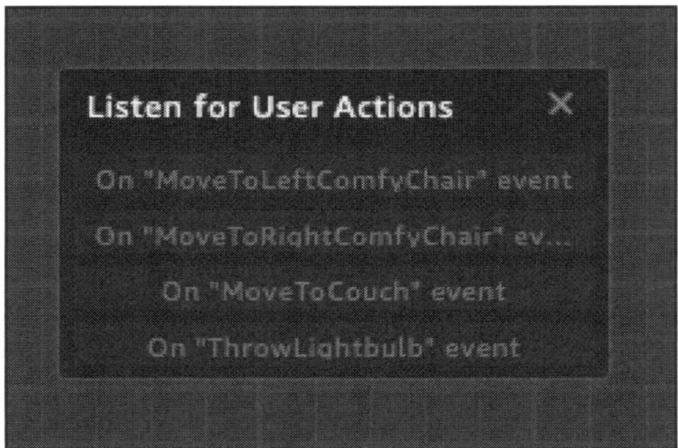

Now, **add a state**. Name it **Set to Couch** and add a **Set String Attribute** action and a **Transition** action to it. For the Set String Attribute action, set the Name to **Position** and the Value to **Couch**.

Duplicate the state, name it **Set to Left Chair** and set the String Attribute Value to **Left**. **Duplicate** your new state and name it **Set to Right Chair** and set the String Attribute Value to **Right**. The behavior will look like the following:

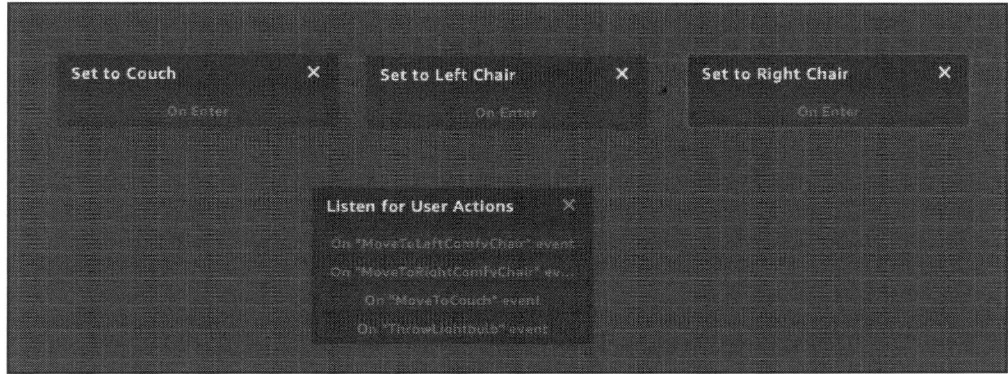

Now to setup the transitions. Drag a transition from **MoveToLeftComfyChair** to **Set to Left Chair**. Drag a transition from **MoveToRightComfyChair** to **SetToRightChair**. Then, drag a transition from **MoveToCouch** to **SetToCouch**.

Finally, drag transitions from **Set to Couch**, **Set to Left Chair** and **Set to Right Chair** back to **Listen for User Actions**. Your behavior should look like the following:

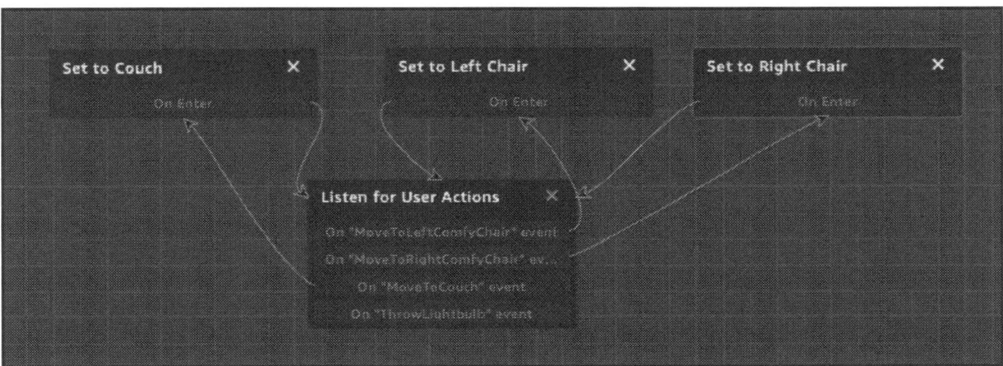

At this point, the behavior knows where the user is located. Now, for the throwing part. First, you need to show the lightbulb.

Add a new state and name it **Reveal Lightbulb**. Add a **Show** action and a **Transition** action. Drag a transition from the **ThrowLightbulb event** to the **Reveal Lightbulb** state.

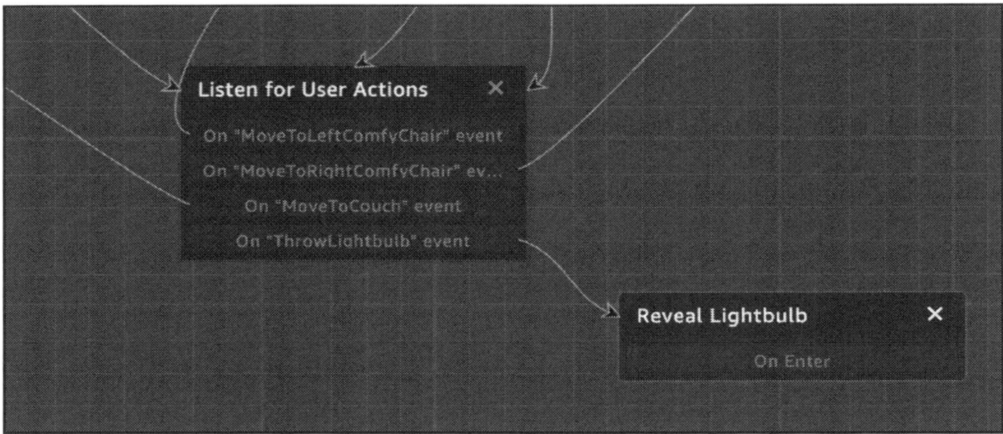

Now, you need to check for the actual position. **Add a new state** and name it **Check for Left**. This state will test if the user is standing on the right comfy chair. If not, the user must be standing on the left chair or the couch.

Click **Add Action** and in the Attribute category, add a **Compare String Attribute to a Constant** action. Set the Attribute to **Position** and the Constant to **Left**. Drag a transition from **Reveal Lightbulb** to **Check for Left**.

Duplicate the state and name it **Check for Right.** Set the attribute constant to **Right**. Drag a transition from **On Position != Left** to **Check for Right**.

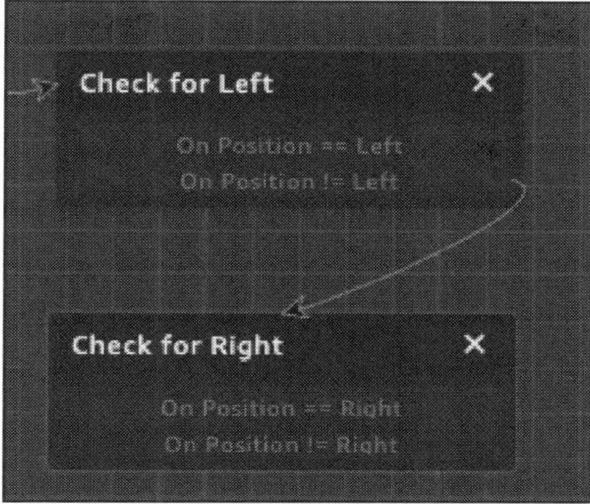

Now that you have all of the logic in place, it's time to launch the lightbulb.

Add a new state and rename it to **Launch from Left Chair**. At this point, you can launch the lightbulb. Remember, the lightbulb is on the ground. You want it to appear that the user is throwing it, so you need to change its position.

Add a **new action** and, in the Physics category, add the **Set Rigid Body Position** action. Set the position to (**-0.757**, **1.361**, **1.606**).

Click the **new action** again and, in the Physics category, add the **Set Rigid Body Velocity** action. This is where you add the velocity amount. Set the velocity to (**-10**, **2.5**, -**3**).

The first thing you did was set the Rigid Body position. Remember, the lightbulb is no longer kinematic so it responds to the physics system. This is why you set the Rigid Body position versus just moving the entity. The position is set to be from the user's perspective, so when the velocity is added, it looks like the user is throwing the lightbulb.

Drag a transition from the **Check for Left** state to the **Launch from Left Chair** state. Use the **On Position == Left** event.

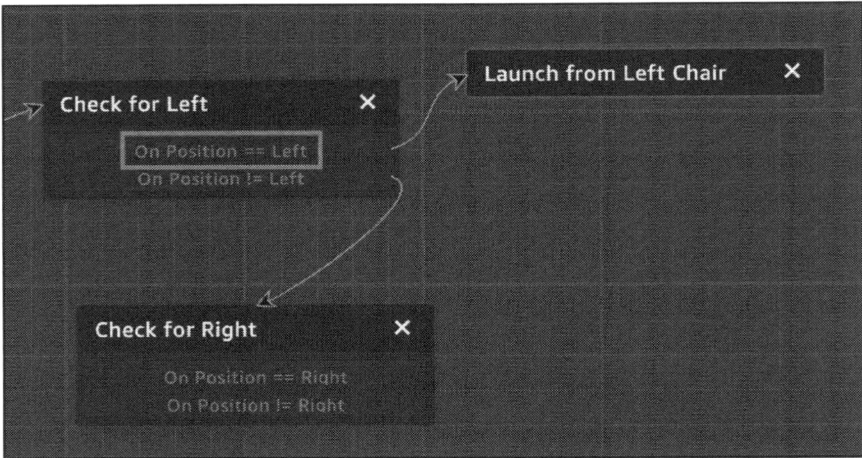

Run the scene. First, jump to the left comfy chair. Then, click the lightbulb, and when it lands on the ground, click it again. After that, click the red diamond to throw the bulb. You'll see that it goes right through the painting because the painting has no colliders attached to it.

You'll handle this in a moment. For now, you need to add the other two states. Open the **Throw Lightbulb** behavior and duplicate the **Launch from Left Chair** state. Rename it to **Launch from Right Chair**. Set the rigid body position to (**-2.896**, **1.361**, **1.606**). Set the velocity to (**-10**, **3**, **-2.5**).

Drag a transition from the **Check for Right** state to the **Launch from Right Chair** state, then drag the transition from the **On Position == Right** event.

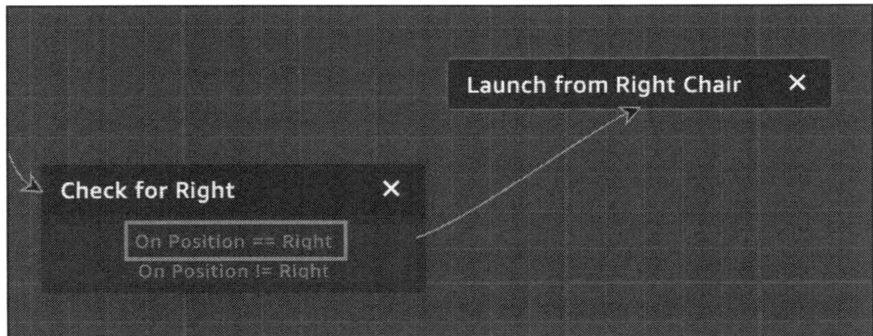

Now, run the scene and click on the painting from the right chair. You'll see how the user can now throw the lightbulb from this position.

Finally, you'll deal with throwing the lightbulb from the couch. **Duplicate the state** and rename it to **Launch from Couch**. Set the Rigid Body position to (**-1.556**, **1.361**, **-0.262**). Set the velocity to (**-23**, **2**, **4.6**). Finally, drag a transition between the **On Position != Right** and the **Launch from Couch** state.

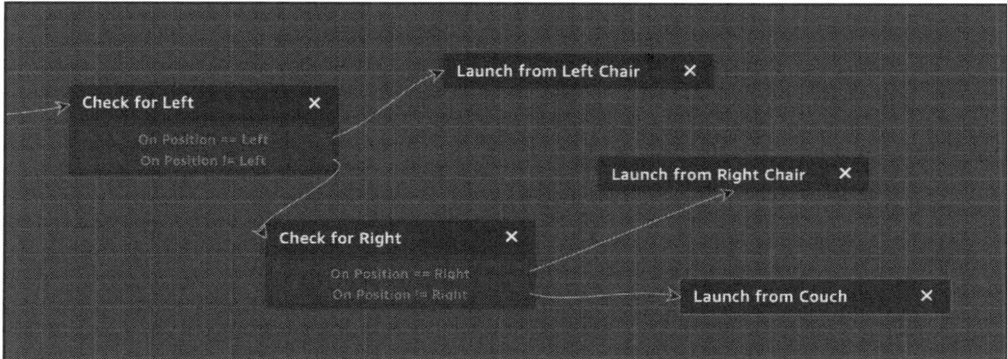

Now that you have the velocities all in place, you need to add solidity to the world. In the Entities panel, select the **Painting Background** and in the Inspector panel, click **Add Component**. Add a **Collider** to it. Now, play your scene again, and this time, the lightbulb bounces off the painting.

Time to make something happen.

Listening for collisions

Oftentimes, you'll want to know when two bodies collide. With your escape room, you want to know when the lightbulb collides with the red diamond. When that occurs, you'll open the escape room.

Begin Contact and **End Contact** actions respond to collision events like every other event. Keep in mind, when responding to collisions, your entity needs to have a collider attached to it.

In the Entities panel, select the **Red Diamond** and in the Inspector panel, click **Add Component**. Add a **Collider** to it.

In the Assets panel, open the **Red Diamond** behavior. Select the **Emit Throw Message** and add a **Transition** action to it.

Click **Add State** and name your state **Collide with Lightbulb**. In the Collision category, add a **Begin Contact** action to the state.

Click **Add State** and name it **Hide Red Diamond**. Add a **Hide** action to it. Drag a transition from the **Emit Throw Message** state to the **Collide with Lightbulb** state. Then, drag a transition from the **Collide with Lightbulb** state to the **Hide Red Diamond** state.

Your behavior will look like the following:

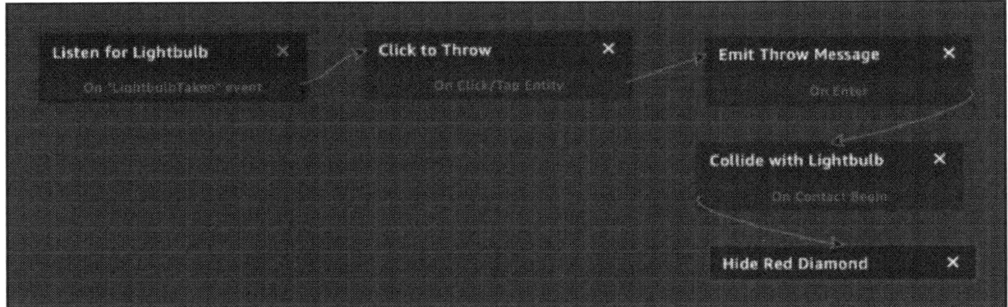

Play the scene and throw the lightbulb at the red diamond. When it collides, the diamond should disappear.

Note: As it turns out, collision detection can be very twitchy with Sumerian. If your behavior expects a collision event and that event doesn't happen, reload the page and page try again. Thankfully, the physics engine is slated for an overhaul so this behavior should go away.

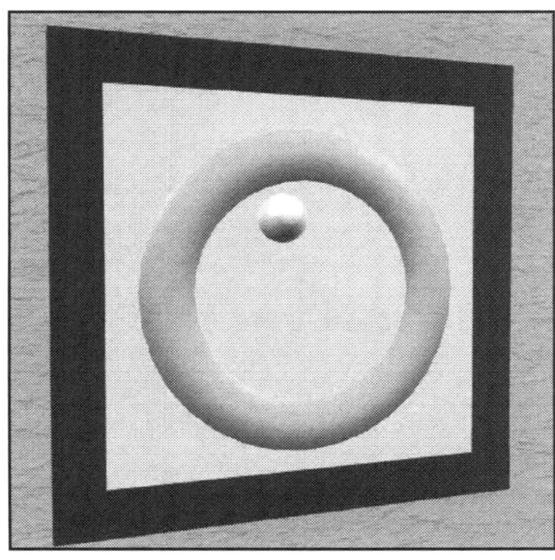

In some cases, you want a collision event but not an actual collision. For instance, imagine that you've produced a virtual art museum. When a user stands in front of the picture, your experience would then provide narration about the particular painting.

For this to work, you want to use a collider that doesn't stop motion but still gets notified when it's entered. To do this, you'll use a trigger. A trigger uses a collider to define a collision space, but it doesn't cause collisions. Entities can pass right through it.

Select the **Red Diamond** in the Entities panel, and in the Inspector panel, check the **Trigger checkbox**. Objects will be able to pass through the collider. Now, you want to extend the collider beyond the Red Diamond. Set the value of the Half Extents to (**1**, **0.5**, **0.5**). The Collider will look like this:

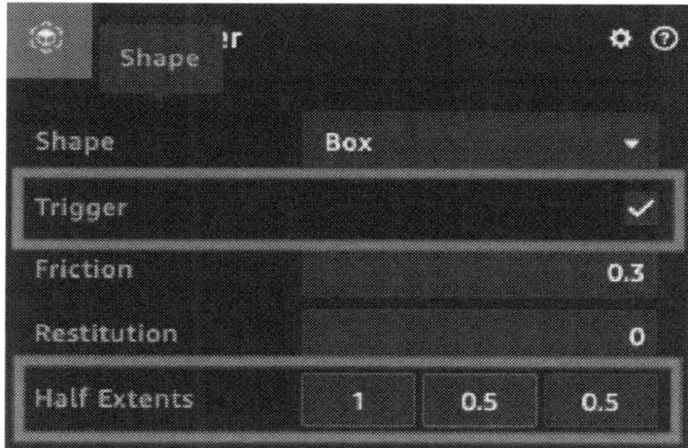

If you look at the painting, you'll notice that the collider now extends beyond the length of the red diamond.

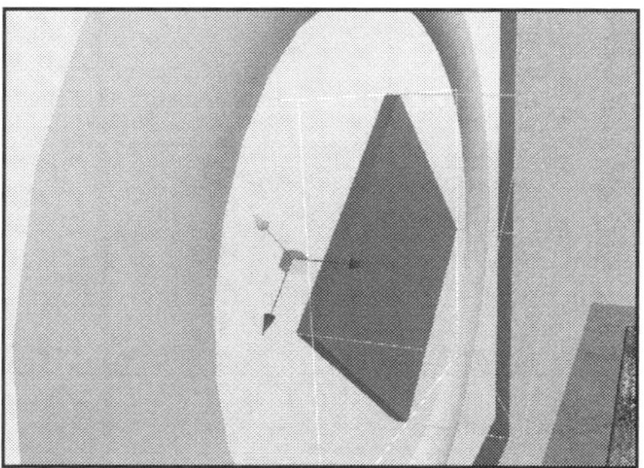

Note: You can increase how far both regular colliders and triggers extend.

Play your scene and throw the lightbulb at the red diamond. The lightbulb will pass through the collider, but you'll also notice that the diamond doesn't disappear. That's because no collision occurred. You need to listen for a trigger event instead.

Open the **Red Diamond** behavior and select the **Collide with Lightbulb** state. Remove the **Begin Contact** action and, instead, add a **Trigger Enter** from the Collision category. Drag a transition between the **On Trigger Event** event to the **Hide Red Diamond** state.

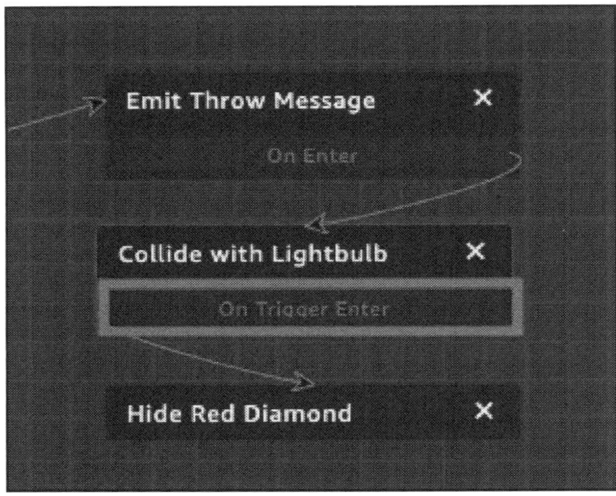

Now, when you play the scene and throw the lightbulb at the red diamond, the diamond will disappear before the lightbulb hits it. That's because the lightbulb hits the trigger first.

There's only one thing left to do, and that's to escape the escape room!

Escaping the escape room

The user solves the last puzzle by throwing a lightbulb at the painting. When this happens, the wall should open up revealing the exit.

Open the **Red Diamond** behavior and select the **Hide Red Diamond** state. Rename it to **Puzzle Complete**. Remove the **Hide** action. Now, add an **Emit Message** action. Set the Channel to **PuzzleComplete**.

Select **Wall 3**, and in the Inspector panel, add a **State Machine** component. Click the + button to add a new behavior and name it **Move Left Wall**.

In the State Machine editor, name the default state to **Listen for Puzzle Completion**. Add a **Listen** action. Set the Message channel to **PuzzleComplete**.

Next, add a **new state**. Name it **Move Left Wall**. Add a **Tween Move** action. Set the Translation to (**0**, **0**, **-1**) then **drag a transition** between the two states.

Select the **Move Left Wall** behavior in the Asset Panel and **duplicate it**. Rename it **Move Right Wall**. In the editor, select the **Move Wall** state and set the Tween Move to (**0**, **0**, **1**).

Select **Wall 4** and drag the **Move Right Wall** behavior to it.

With the walls set up, you need to provide a way for the user to escape. Click **Create Entity** and select a **Quad**. Name it **Escape Arrow**. Set the position to (**4.052**, **1.437**, **-0.663**), the rotation to (**0**, **-90**, **0**) and the scale to (**2.03**, **2.03**, **2.584**).

In the Assets panel, click the **Import files** icon.

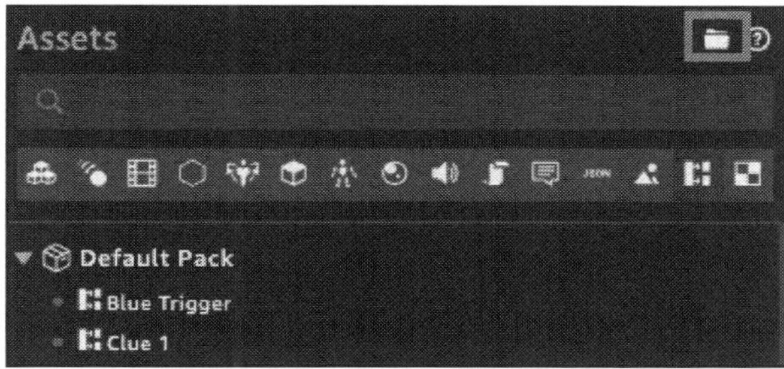

From **resource files**, select **exit.png** and import it into Sumerian.

Select the **Escape Arrow**. In the Inspector panel, expand the **Material** component. Drag **exit.png** from the Asset panel to the **Texture** property. Since this a transparent texture, you need to indicate transparency when using the Classic shader. Expand the **Opacity** category and check the **Enabled** property.

With the Escape Arrow selected, click **Add Component** and add a **State Machine**. Click the + button and name the new behavior to **Exit Arrow**.

Rename the default state to **Escape the Room**. Add a **Click/Tap** action to the state. Click the **Add State** button. Name it **Change Room**.

At this point, you'll redirect the user to a different web page. For now, you'll use Google as the target, but be sure to read the challenge to do something else.

With the Change Room state selected, click **Add Action**. In the Controls category, select the **Pick and Exit** action. In the URL, type **http://www.google.com**.

Finally, drag a transition between **Escape the Room** and **Change Room**.

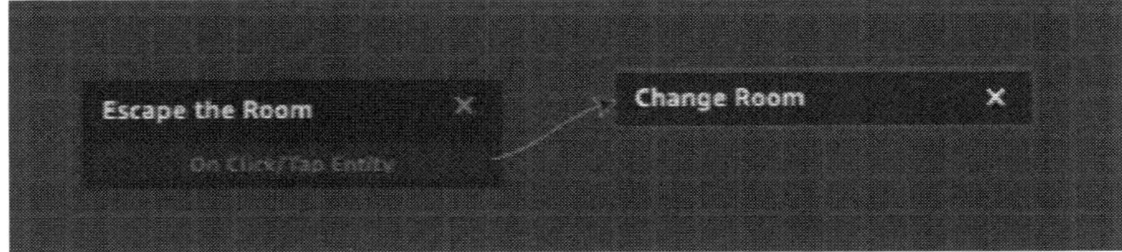

You almost have a complete working room. Right now, the lightbulb falls when the user clicks it. You did this to make it easy to work on the final puzzle without having to keep completing the first two puzzles. But now, you want it to happen only when the user has solved the second puzzle.

In the Asset panel, select the **Lightbulb behavior**. Rename the first state, Click to Activate, to **Listen for 2nd Puzzle**. Remove the **On Click/Tap** action then add a **Listen** action. Set the Message Channel to **PuzzleSolved** and drag a transition from **Listen for 2nd Puzzle** to **Disable Kinematic**.

Before you run through the escape room, make sure to reveal any entities that you may have hidden.

Now, run through your escape room from the very beginning. Work your way through the puzzles and click the escape arrow. You should see the following:

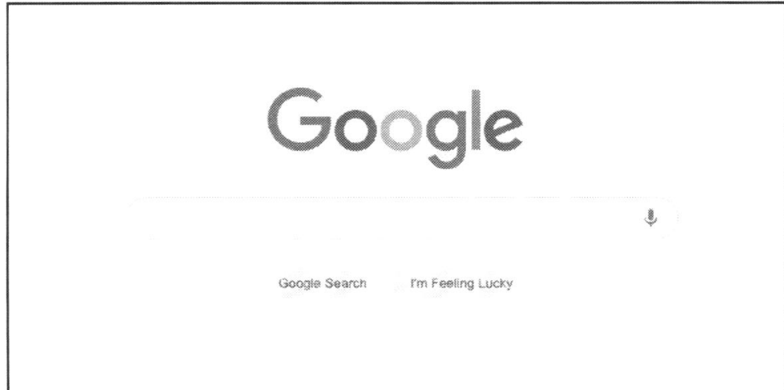

Congrats! You've escaped!

Key points

- A rigid body component indicates that the entity is going to use the physics system.
- A kinematic rigid body means the entity will not respond to collisions or gravity.
- A collider determines the boundaries for an entity.
- Colliders can be larger or smaller than the attached entities.

Where to go from here?

If you've ever been to a Swedish furniture store, you know that those stores are large and sprawling, filled with lots of different showrooms.

Your job is to create an entirely new escape room, using all of the pre-built assets included with Sumerian. Have fun with the project but also, don't make it too hard.

Before you finish your escape room, you need to link to another Swedish themed escape room. Thankfully, there's a great resource for finding escape rooms, which is the Amazon Sumerian Slack channel. To browse the channel, head over to **amazonsumerian.slack.com**.

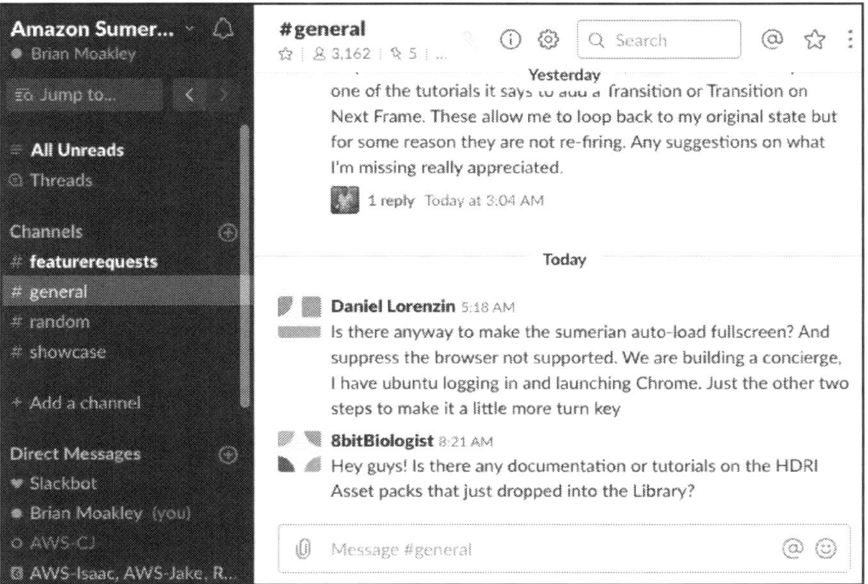

> **Note**: Slack is a free instant message platform. It's used by groups and organizations all over the world. You learn more about slack by visiting https://slack.com

Once in the Sumerian Slack, ask where to look for escape room links. There may be a dedicated channel for them. Find a published escape room and paste it in the **Pick and Exit** exit action, then publish your room.

When you publish your escape room (don't worry, you'll learn about publishing soon), paste the published game URL in the appropriate Slack channel. By linking escape rooms, you can get a true experience of being trapped in a Swedish furniture store.

Chapter 7: Virtual Reality

By Brian Moakley

Virtual Reality (VR) is a technology that aims to remove the four borders of your computer monitor and replace them with a living, albeit computer-generated, world. People have been pursuing this technology for decades, but it's only been in the past years that VR has become accessible to the average consumer.

Typical virtual reality devices rely on a headset that performs two functions. First, it blocks out the physical world so that the head-mounted display (HMD) provides the only light. The second thing it does is project computer-generated images to each eye. When you move your head, the display matches your head movement, providing an unparalleled sense of immersion. Some headsets provide controllers to match your hand movements. There are even treadmills that allow you to walk in realtime.

Of course, VR tooling is equally as important as the headsets. As more people purchase VR gear, they'll be eager to consume VR content.

Thankfully, Sumerian supports creating VR experiences. In fact, this feature has been in front of you the entire time. If you look at your canvas, you'll see that there's a button that activates virtual reality.

However, unless you set up your browser, you may run into this message:

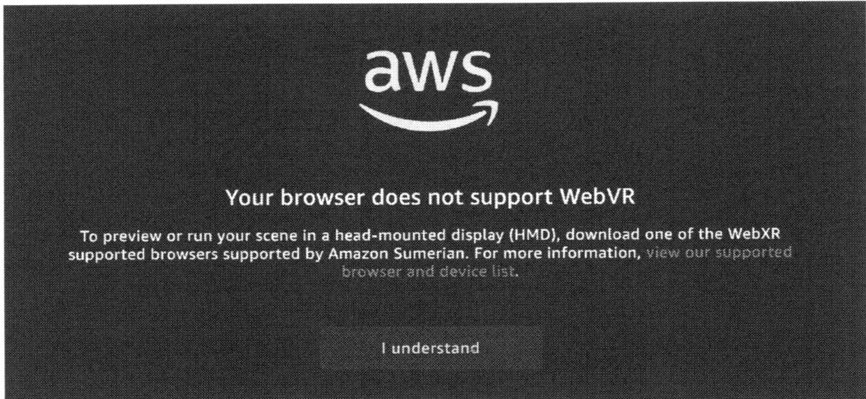

Don't worry, you'll make this message go away later on. This chapter will show you how to set up your browser to work with VR, and then give you the chance to play around with some VR features. Once you get the knack of how things work, you'll put your knowledge to work by updating the escape room to work in VR.

Configuring Sumerian to use VR

Sumerian supports a large number of VR headsets. At the time of this writing, Sumerian supports:

- Oculus Rift
- Oculus Go
- Oculus Quest
- HTC Vive
- HTC Vive Pro
- Lenovo Mirage Solo
- Samsung Gear VR
- Google Daydream

Sumerian is very proactive about supporting VR headsets. If you purchased a new VR headset and it's not on this list, then chances are that Sumerian will support it soon.

VR headsets come in two different types: Tethered and untethered. A **tethered headset** is one where the host computer generates everything that appears in the HMD. The tether may be a simple cord coming out of the back of a headset, or the actual contents may be wirelessly transmitted from the host computer. The key point is that you need a separate computer to generate the visuals and then transmit them to the HMD.

An **untethered headset** is one where the HMD generates all of the content for the user. With a focus on mobility, these headsets provide a VR experience at the expense of limited movement or graphical fidelity.

Sumerian supports both of these headset types, although how you interact with your scene will be slightly different. Sumerian uses a technology known as **WebVR**, which allows for virtual reality experiences through a common browser. WebVR launched in the spring of 2014, so it's a relatively new technology. This means support is scattered throughout a variety of browsers. Whereas Firefox supports WebVR out of the box, Safari does not. Chrome's support requires configuring and may not be available on all platforms.

Before you can do any work with VR in Sumerian, you must first prepare your headset. Each manufacturer provides specific instructions. Make sure you go through all of these instructions so that, by the time you start working with Sumerian, your headset is up and running.

If you run into issues getting your headset working, contact the device manufacturer or visit the support forums. Some headsets can be a bit tricky, but thankfully, setup is getting easier all the time.

Setting up a tethered headset

Once your headset is ready, your next step may require you to configure your browser. If you're using an untethered headset like the Oculus Go, Oculus Quest, Lenovo Mirage Solo, Samsung Gear VR and Google Daydream, you can skip to the next section, "Setting up an untethered headset".

Each browser requires a different configuration. To see if Sumerian supports your headset, head to https://webvr.rocks/.

> **Note**: If you can't get your headset to work in VR, you might find help in the Amazon Sumerian Slack channel: https://amazonsumerian.slack.com/

Here are some instructions to get WebVR up and running in Google Chrome.

First, you need to have at least version 66 of Chrome. To find out your version, **click on the three dots** on the right side of the browser. Select **Help** and then **About Google Chrome**.

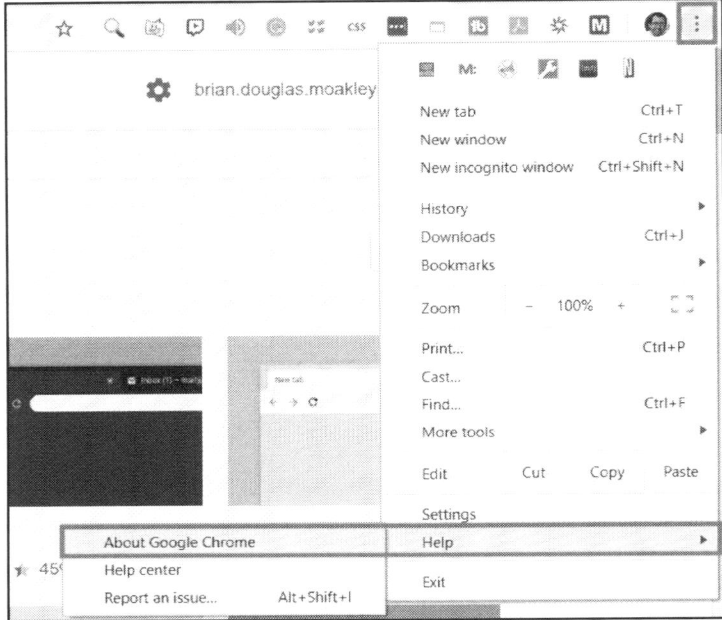

Once you've confirmed that your version of Chrome supports WebVR, you need to activate it. In the URL field, type **chrome://flags**.

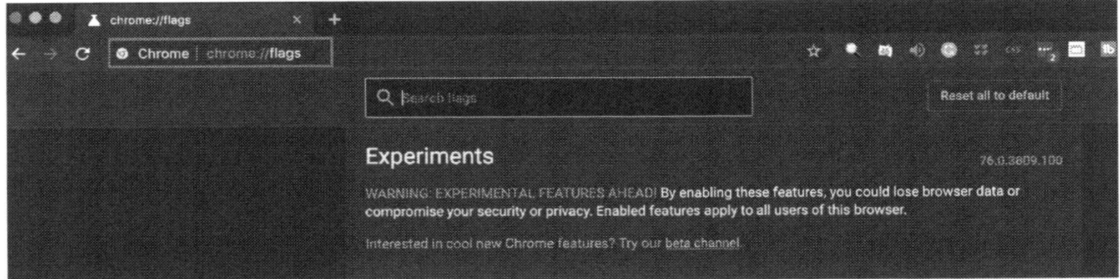

If you are using an HTC Vive headset, search for the **WebVR** and set it to **Enabled**.

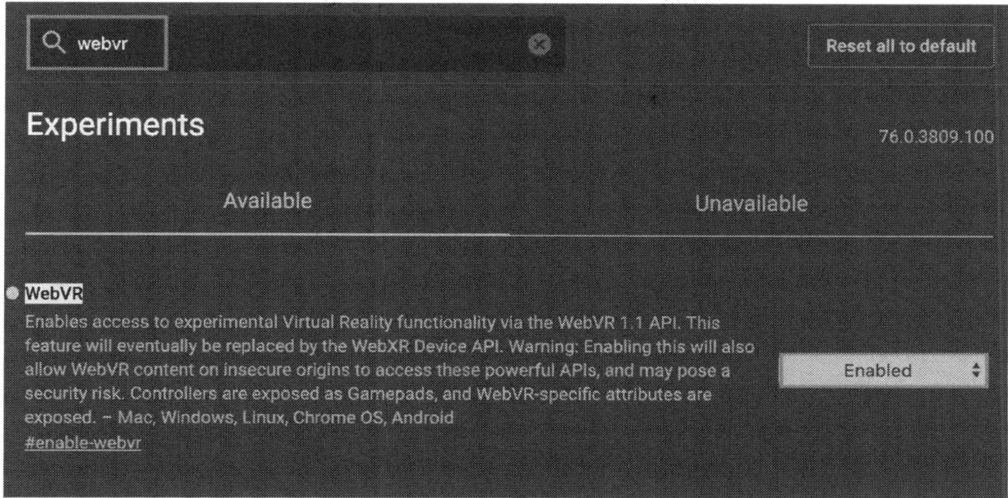

Do the same for the following properties:

- **WebXR Device API**: **Enabled**
- **WebXR Gamepad Support**: **Enabled**
- **Oculus hardware support**: **Disabled**
- **OpenVR hardware support**: **Enabled**

> **Note:** These settings are found on the Windows platform. If you don't see the options listed, your platform may not support VR. For more information, you'll need to read Chrome's documentation for your particular platform.

These properties activate the technologies that enable you to experience VR from a browser. If you have an Oculus Rift, set the following properties:

- **WebVR**: **Enabled**
- **WebXR Device API**: **Disabled**
- **WebXR Gamepad Support**: **Enabled**
- **Oculus hardware support**: **Enabled**
- **OpenVR hardware support**: **Disabled**

At this point, you need to restart the browser and turn on your headset. When you press the VR button this time, you'll preview your scene inside of your headset.

> **Note**: While working on this book, I ran into mixed results working with Google Chrome and an HTC Vive. I found Firefox to have better results since it doesn't require any configuration. Hopefully, this will change in the coming year.

With that, you should be off to the races! Remember, this technology is relatively new, so you may run into problems.

Setting up an untethered headset

If you're working with an untethered headset, you'll need to publish your scene. Once you publish your scene, you can then enter it into the device's integrated browser and view your content. Once you make a change to your scene, you'll need to republish it to see it in your headset.

To publish your scene, click **Publish** in the top-right part of the editor, then select **Create public link**.

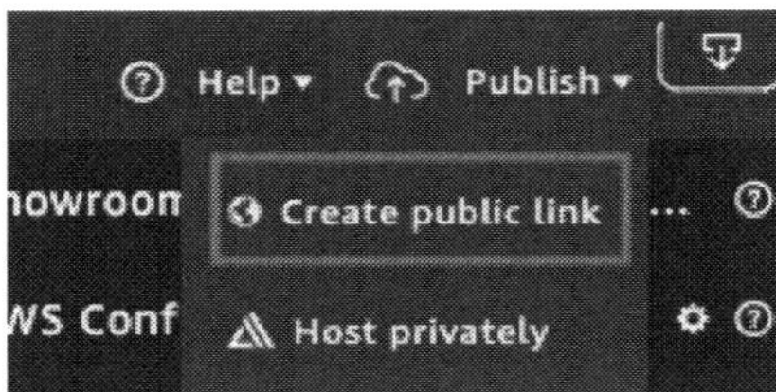

> **Note**: In the following chapter, you'll learn about additional options and how to optimize your scene for publication.

You'll receive a published link such as: https://us-east-1.sumerian.aws/7b78d519f48e4b9cb389ba0fa8a5ae34.scene. As you can imagine, that link may be a bit frustrating to type in your device's browser.

To save time, you can use a link shortener service such as bit.ly. This will convert the long link into something like bit.ly/2MhWWzO, which is far easier to type.

> **Note**: Bit.ly requires an account to shorten your links. This allows you to customize them and to track any stats. If you want a no-frills link shortening service, use cutt.ly instead.

Using the VR Asset Pack

Now that you have your headset configured to work with WebVR, your next task is to learn how to use Sumerian's VR implementation.

Open Sumerian and, instead of returning to your escape room scene, create a new scene. Once you've learned the basics, you'll incorporate them into your escape room. Oftentimes, demonstrating new concepts is easier when you start with a fresh scene.

In the Sumerian dashboard, click **Create new scene** and name it **Learning VR**.

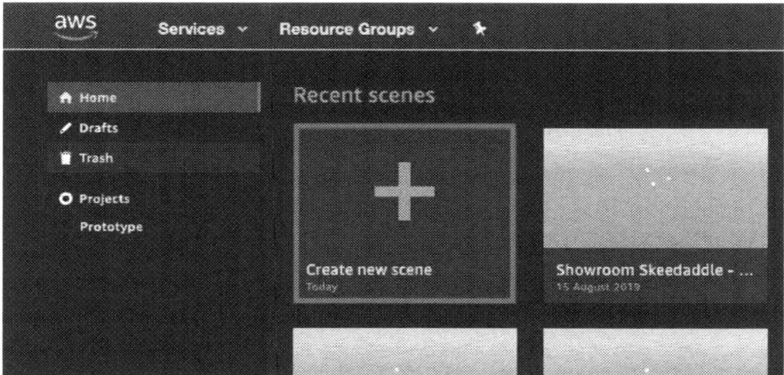

With your scene up and ready, your first step is to add VR functionality. Since not every project is going to use virtual reality, you must opt in by importing a specific asset. Click **Import Assets** and in the search field, type: **VR**

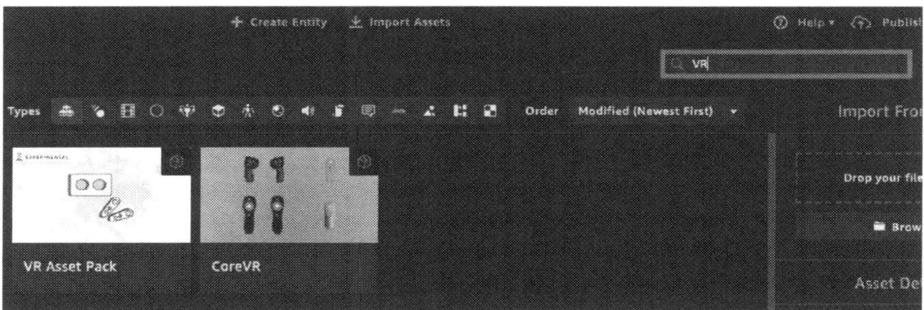

You'll notice that this returns two assets: VR Asset Pack and Core VR. Core VR was the first asset pack developed for Sumerian. However, Amazon has recently deprecated Core VR in favor of the **VR Asset Pack**. Being deprecated, Core VR may be removed at any time, so it's best not to use it in your projects.

Once you've imported the VR Asset pack, you'll notice that it has imported a lot of items in the Assets panel. With VR, you need to use a special camera. VR works by projecting an image to the left eye and an image to the right eye. Your brain does the hard work of stitching those images together. Unfortunately, the default camera doesn't provide this functionality. You need to use a special VR camera.

> **Note**: At some point in the future, Sumerian will unify the camera system so that the default camera will also work as the main VR camera. Keep an eye on project updates by visiting the following URL: https://aws.amazon.com/releasenotes/?tag=releasenotes%23keywords%23amazon-sumerian.

In the Assets panel, switch to the Entities tab and drag a **VRCameraRig** to the canvas. In the Entities panel, select the **VRCameraRig**. You'll see that you have a few options in the Inspector panel.

You can have multiple VR cameras so you need to designate this camera as the current camera. In the Inspector panel, check the **CurrentVRCameraRig** option. Since it's helpful to have the VR camera show up at the current camera's location, check the **StartAtCurrentCamera** option as well.

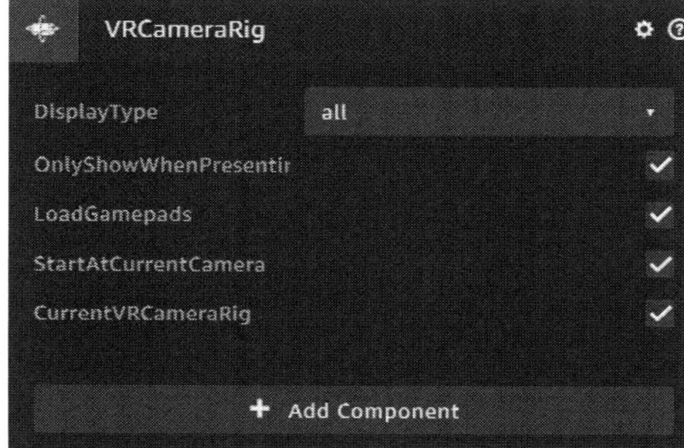

If you're using a tethered VR system, play your scene and then press the VR button on the canvas. Otherwise, publish your scene and view it in your VR browser. You'll notice that you can look around. Pretty cool stuff!

> **Note**: The rest of the chapter will instruct you to play your scene. If you're using an untethered headset, consider that shorthand for publishing your scene.

Granted, there's nothing to really see or do, but you'll take care of that soon enough.

Teleporting and movement

One of the hard facts of life with VR is that it can make you sick.

According to Jonathan Ogle-Barrington, an author of *Unity AR & VR by Tutorials*, motion sickness occurs when there is a mismatch between the vestibular system (inner ear and brain) and the oscular system (eyes and brain). Essentially, the eyes may be telling you that you are falling from a high vantage point, but your inner ear is telling you that you aren't moving at all. This conflict of information can cause sweating, fatigue, headaches and even vomiting. In a nutshell, it's not a good time.

A trick to limit motion sickness is to limit movement. That's why teleporting is an essential tool in your VR toolbox. And thankfully, this is a tool that the VR Asset Pack provides.

In your scene, click **Create Entity** and select the **Box** entity. In the Transform component, set the Scale to (**30**, **1**, **30**). In the Material component, set the Color (Diffuse) Color to **00ff00**. The color you select doesn't matter. Ideally, you want a color that contrasts with the color of the VR pointer, which makes the pointer easer to see.

Wait! Did someone mention a VR pointer? When using VR, you'll typically be using a controller represented in 3D space with a line projected from it. This line lets you know what you're pointing at. Some headsets come with multiple controllers; others don't. Sometimes, these controllers are referred to as gamepads.

In cases where your controller passes over an entity, Sumerian provides an icon that indicates that you can perform some action. In this case, you're providing a teleporting behavior, so you need a teleporting icon.

In the Assets panel, switch to the **Scripts** tab.

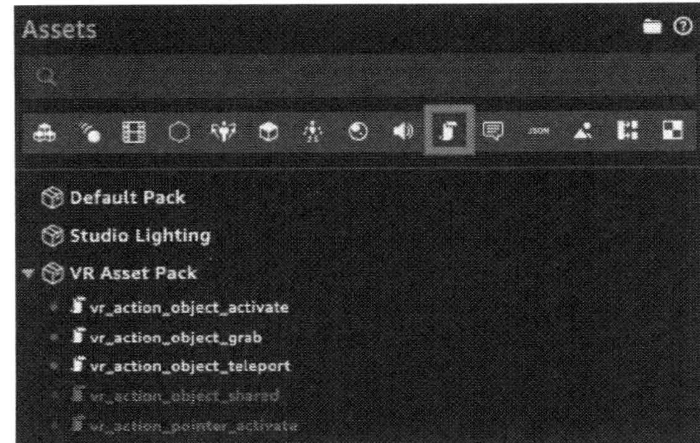

In the Scripts tab, drag the **vr_action_object_teleport** onto your **Box** entity.

Play your scene in a VR headset. Look at the green box and point one of the VR controllers at it. You'll notice a teleport icon where you point it. Clicking the controller's button will teleport you to the location.

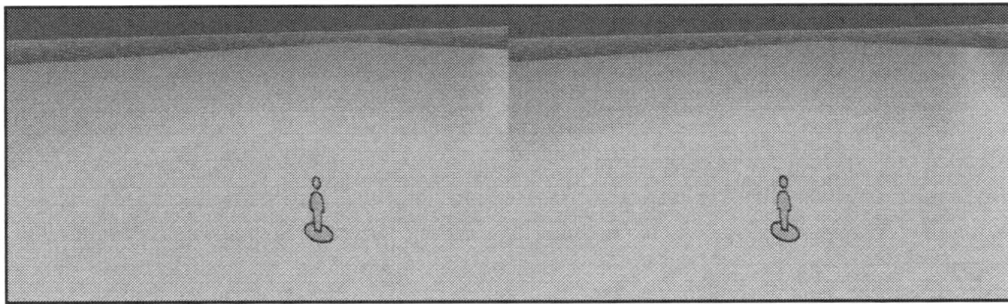

All it took was adding a script. How's that for convenience?

Grabbing entities

In VR, one of the cool things that you can do is actually grab things. This allows users to pick up entities with a press of a button. Even better, implementing this ability is as easy as adding a script to an entity.

Again, click **Create Entity** and select the **Box** entity. Set the Position to (**0.5**, **1**, **-1.5**). Select the newly-created box and, in the Assets panel, switch to the Scripts tab. Set the Material to have a **red** color.

Drag the **vr_action_object_grab** script and drop it on the box.

Now play your scene and switch to VR. Click on the box and you'll see that you can move it with your controller. You can rotate it as well.

Notice that it doesn't respond to gravity. As you learned in Chapter 6, "Physics", that's because the box doesn't have a Rigid Body component attached to it.

Stop the scene and select the red box. In the Inspector panel, click **Add Component** and add a **Rigid Body** to it. Click **Add Component** again and add a **Collider** component.

Finally, click on the green box and **add a collider** to it as well.

Now, play your scene, pick up the box and release it. You'll see that it now responds to gravity and physics.

Activating the escape room

So far, you've learned how to teleport and how to grab things. The last, and probably most important, thing is to learn how to **activate** things.

Don't worry – this won't be totally new to you. Activating is the equivalent of clicking on an entity. The big difference between a click action and a VR activation is that the click transitions to another action. When you activate an entity, that entity sends out a message instead.

To see this in action, you'll update the escape room to work in VR by using activations.

Note: At the time of this writing, some of the provided Sumerian assets are **high poly**, meaning they've been made up of lots of triangles. High poly models can affect the framerate of a scene. A variable framerate can induce motion sickness in VR. If you find yourself working on the scene and getting a little queasy, stop using VR until the queasiness passes. Motion sickness is something you can't power through. Just take a break, step aside and have a glass of water. You'll feel better for it!

To get started, return to Sumerian and start your Showroom Skeedaddle scene. Click **Import Assets** and import the **VR Asset Pack**.

In the Assets panel, drag a **VRCameraRig** to the canvas and, in the Inspector panel, **check all of the VRCameraRig component options**.

Now, when you run the scene, you can switch to VR mode and look around your escape room. Of course, you can't do anything with it yet.

Currently, your user activates all of your puzzles by clicking their mouse. Your task is to activate these puzzles from your VR controller.

You can activate an entity either by clicking on it or by hovering over it.

In the Entities panel, select the **Light Switch** entity. In the Assets panel, switch to the **Scripts** tab and drag a copy of the **vr_action_object_activate** to the light switch.

Unlike the other scripts, this one contains a few additional parameters. The Input option determines how you want to trigger the activation. The user can hover a controller over the entity or click the controller at it. In this case, select the **OnActionButtonDown** option. Next, you need to emit a message. Set Emit Message to **ActivateSwitch**.

Now, play the scene. When you hover your controller over the Light Switch, you'll see it's replaced with a pointer icon.

The activation triggers just the first puzzle. You now need to activate the three different-colored entities.

In the Entities panel, select the green **Statue** and drag the **vr_action_object_activate** to it. Set the Input to **OnActionButtonDown** and set Emit Message to **ClickedGreen**.

Do the same for Desk Lamp, setting Emit Message to **ClickedYellow**. Do the same for the Vase setting Emit Message to **ClickedBlue**.

Finally, you need the Lightbulb to be clickable. Add the**vr_action_object_activate** to it. Set the Input to **OnActionButtonDown** and set Emit Message to **LightbulbTaken**.

So far so good, but the Lightbulb responds only to clicks and not to activations. To fix this, open the **Lightbulb** behavior and in the **Click on the Lightbulb** state, click **Add Action**. Add a **Listen** action and set the channel to **LightbulbTaken**. Finally, drag a transition from the **OnLightbulbTaken** event to the **Hide Lightbulb and Notify** state.

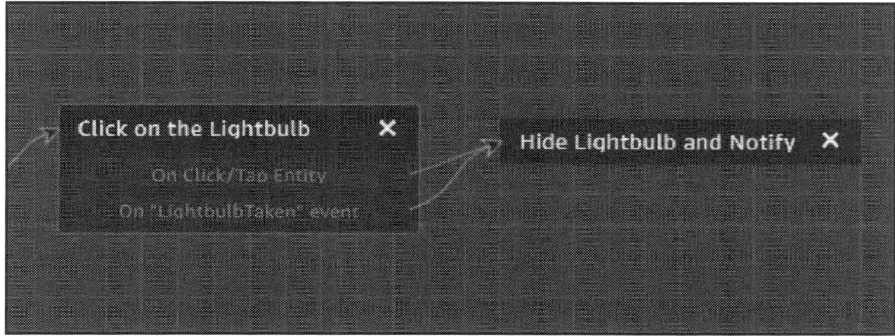

Now, play the scene. You should be able to activate the Light Switch, solve the puzzle and pick up the Light Bulb.

To add the throwing element, select the Painting in the Entities panel and drag a **vr_action_object_activate** script onto it. Set the Input to **OnActionButtonDown** and set Emit Message to **ClickedPainting**.

Now, you want it to respond to the activation. Select the **Red Diamond** behavior to edit it. In the Click the Throw state and add a **Listen** action. Set the Message Channel to **ClickedPainting** and drag a transition from the **On "Clicked Painting" event** to the **Emit Throw Message** state.

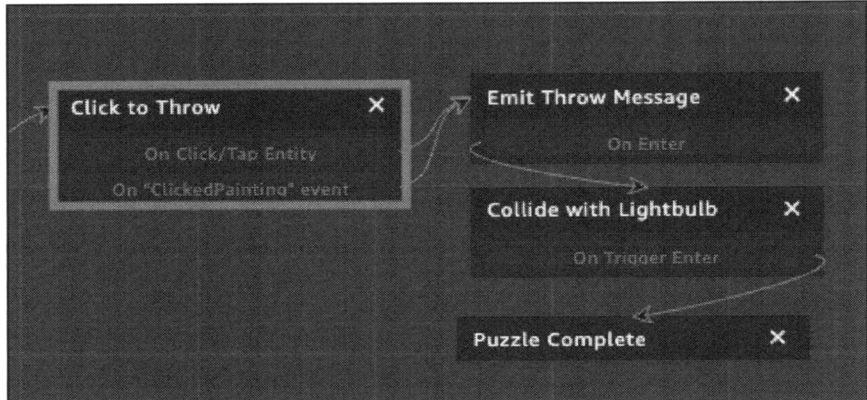

Now when you run the scene in VR, you should be able to get through all of the puzzles with a click of the controller.

At this point, you have an almost-functional escape room. The VR escape room is missing two things: A proper ending and movement.

The current ending is not VR friendly. It sends the user to another escape room, and the quick transition would be jarring. A better solution is to present a "Congratulations, you escaped!" message with a button prompt to launch another escape room. Later in the book, you'll learn how to display user interface elements. Once you learn how to create a user interface, head on back to this chapter and see if you can produce an appropriate VR-friendly ending.

Finally, there's no way to move in the scene. In the regular version, the user jumps between the pieces of furniture. You'll do this now using an activation.

Challenge

Challenge: Teleportation

Currently, users can teleport by clicking on a piece of furniture. Your task is to use this teleportation mechanism with your VR controller. This requires you to add the activate script to the couch and the comfy chairs. Of course, there are a few other things to do as well, but that's the fun of the challenge.

Here's a hint: Remember that the scene has two cameras now. One camera is for standard users and the other is for VR users. Think about what happens when a regular user clicks on a piece of furniture. Now figure out how to update the scene when a VR user clicks on that piece of furniture.

Give it a shot!

Solution

This challenge boils down to clicking on a piece of furniture and moving the camera to it. When a regular user clicks on a piece of furniture, the regular camera moves. For the challenge, you need the VRCameraRig to move.

First, you need to set up the VR click actions. Drag an instance of the **vr_action_object_activate** script onto the **Couch**, the **Left Comfy Chair** and the **Right Comfy Chair**.

For all instances of the script, set the Input to **OnActionButtonDown**.

Next comes the messages. For the couch, set Emit Message to **MoveToCouch**. For the Left Comfy Chair, use **MoveToLeftComfyChair**, and for the Right Comfy Chair, use **MoveToRightComfyChair**.

Now, you need to move the VRCameraRig. Thankfully, you don't have to do much at all. Instead of writing a new solution, you can just reuse an existing one. In the Entities panel, select the VRCameraRig and drag a **Player Camera** behavior onto it. The Player Camera behavior listens for all the events and moves the associated entity. In this case, the VRCameraRig will move just like the Player Camera.

Now you can teleport with style.

Key points

- Web VR is a new technology. You will need to research your preferred browser to learn if WebVR is supported on your platform.
- Headset support is always being updated.
- Tethered headsets can run Sumerian scenes from the editor whereas untethered headsets will need to publish the scene.
- To enable VR in your scene, you need to import the **VR Asset Pack**.
- The asset pack allows you to grab, teleport and activate entities.

Where to go from here?

At this point, you know everything you need to put together a nice interactive VR scene. Not surprisingly, there's a lot more to it. You can deactivate controllers, configure the pointers and provide velocity when you drop things.

To learn more about the various configuration options available, check out the VR Assets tutorial on the official documentation site. You can find it here: https://docs.sumerian.amazonaws.com/tutorials/create/beginner/vr-asset-pack/

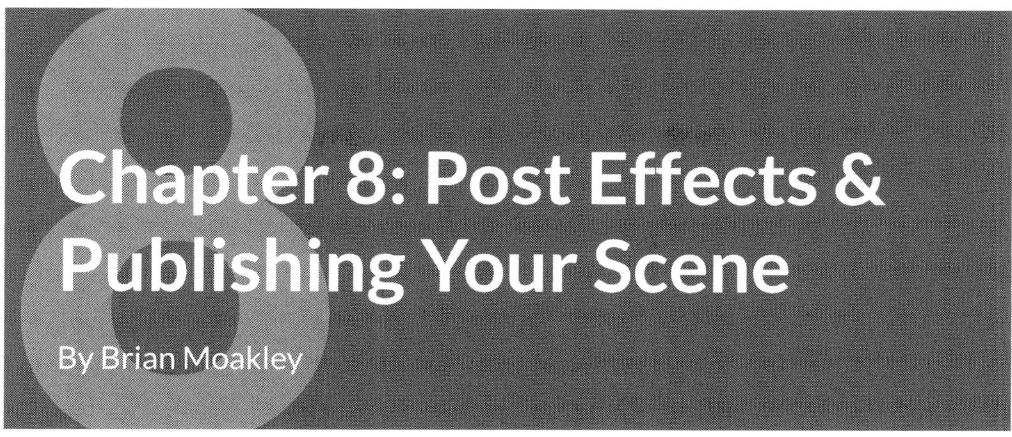

Chapter 8: Post Effects & Publishing Your Scene

By Brian Moakley

By this point in the book, you should be familiar with Sumerian. You can add entities, provide logic and even include virtual reality in your scenes. You have all the tools necessary to make some awesome experiences. Unfortunately, no one can use your scene unless you publish it. You can create an amazing experience, but it won't get any appreciation until you let other people interact with it.

Publishing is only part of the equation; you may want to optimize your scene or even add additional effects to make it great. Don't worry, this chapter will guide you through the process.

Saving snapshots

Throughout this book, you've been using the Entities panel to select entities and configure the components that are attached to them. You can also use the Entities panel to adjust various aspects of your scene.

In the Entities panel, select **Showroom Skeedaddle** and look at the Inspector panel. You'll notice that your scene has a lot of components attached to it.

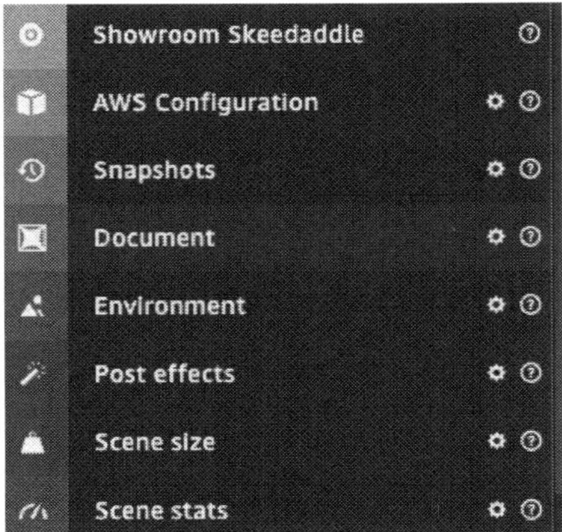

This is where you can configure your scene and add additional effects to it.

Use the **AWS Configuration** when you need to access services outside of your scene. You'll do this in later chapters.

Now, before you make any changes, expand the **Snapshots** component. This component allows you to save versions of your scene before you make any major changes. Later, you can revert any changes. This is great when you are developing a scene and you need to make some big changes. You can save a snapshot and then make your changes. If something goes wrong or the feature isn't working, you can simply restore to your saved snapshot.

You'll be making some changes, so now is a good time to save a snapshot. For the name, enter **Pre Post Effets** and click **Create**.

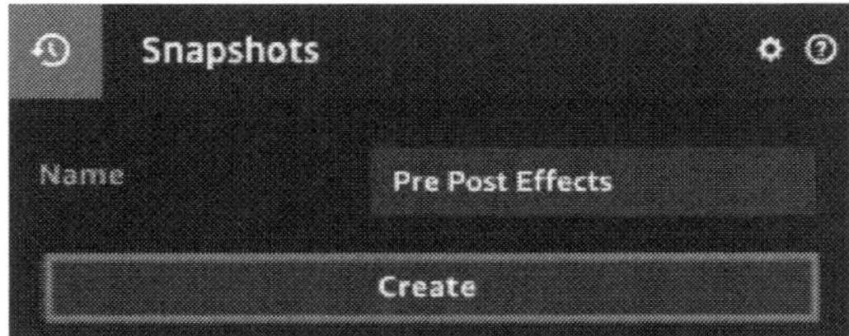

Once saved, you'll see a list of snapshots that you can restore. Simply select the snapshot you want to restore from the dropdown and click the Restore button.

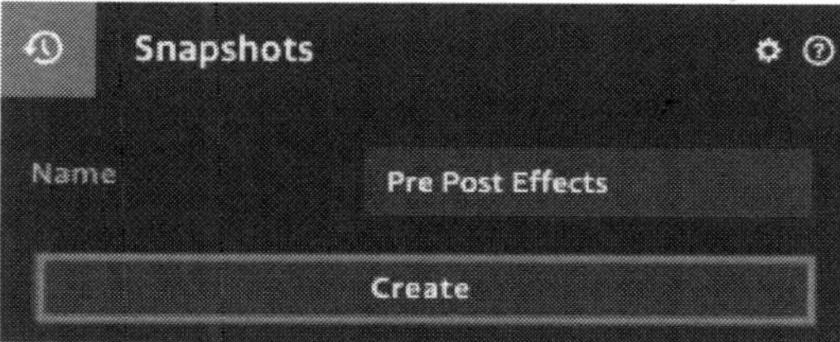

This will restore all your assets from when you made the snapshot.

Note: As you continue through the rest of the book, try saving snapshots as you make your way through the chapters. This will allow you to jump back to earlier parts of your project in case you run into issues while troubleshooting problems.

Adjust scene settings

Right now, the scene feels a little heavy. Click on the **Scene Stats** component. You should see something like this:

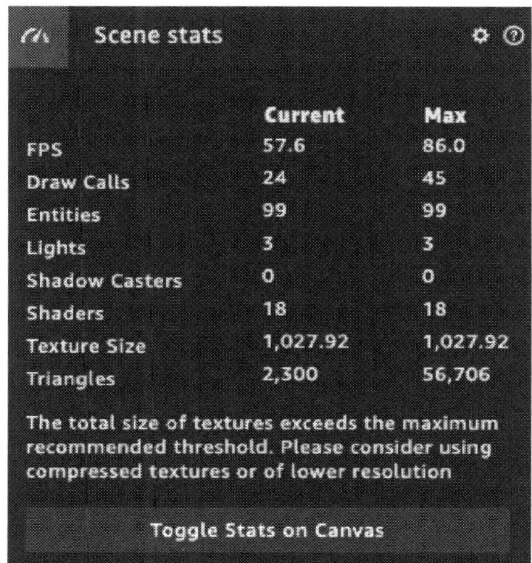

This gives you a breakdown of the "cost" of your scene at the location you're viewing it from. As you move the camera, the numbers will change depending on things like how many entities are displaying and the lighting conditions.

Ideally, you want to provide a great experience with a scene that doesn't take a lot of resources to render. Although computers are growing in power all the time, you don't want to provide an experience that can only a small percentage of your audience can enjoy.

The first category is **FPS**, or Frames per Second. A higher FPS provides a smooth experience. Lights, draw calls and all of the various entities that make up your scene all affect your FPS.

When working with VR, you want a high FPS so that you can provide a smooth visual experience for your user. Frame rates that bounce all over the place can induce motion sickness.

Draw Calls is the drawing for your scene. The more items the scene has to draw, the slower it will run. Limiting shadows and post-effects will decrease the draw calls you need.

You can also speed up your FPS by designating entities as **static**. When an entity doesn't move, you can mark it as static. Sumerian will then optimize that entity's materials to decrease the number of draw calls it needs to render the scene.

From the Entities panel, select **Wall 1** and expand the **Transform** component. Check the **Static** checkbox.

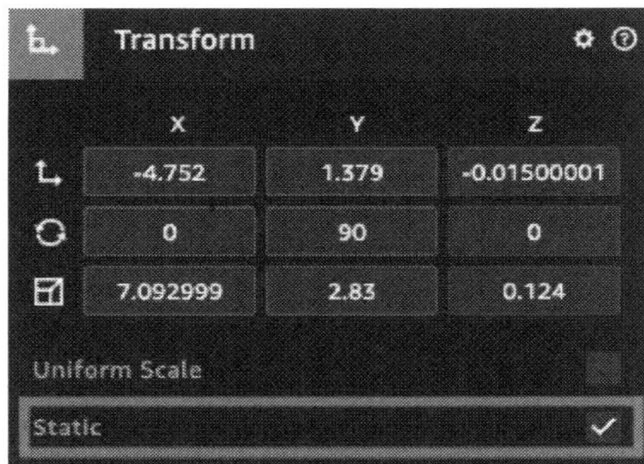

Starting at the top of the Entities panel, select each entity and, if they don't move, check the **Static** checkbox. If an entity has children, and those children don't move, then you can set the static property on the parent. When you do, Sumerian will prompt you to ask if you want to set all the children to static.

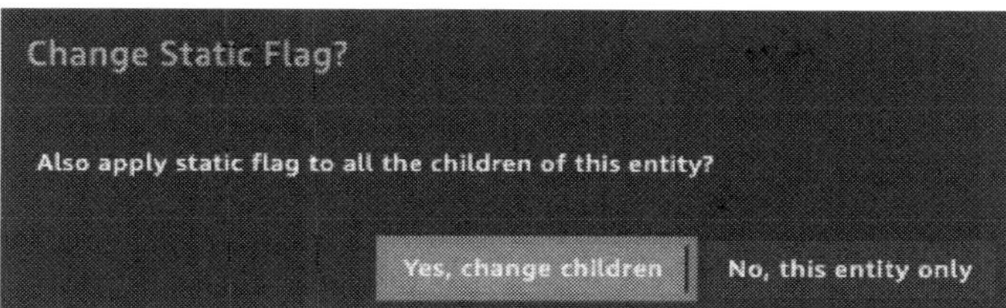

Doing so will make your scene render and perform faster. To learn about the other settings, review the Sumerian documentation.

https://docs.aws.amazon.com/sumerian/latest/userguide/scene-scenestats.html

> **Note**: Once you feel comfortable with the engine, take some time to review the Sumerian User Guide. It's a treasure trove of information and a great place to go when you have questions about the engine or its components.

Finally, if you want to see how traversing the scene directly in your canvas affects your stats, click the **Toggle Stats on Canvas**. This will display a small window with all of your stats inside.

Configuring the environment settings

So far, you've focused on configuring various options regarding the scene itself, but you can also configure your scene's environment. Select your scene and expand the **Environment** component. You'll see that you have many different options.

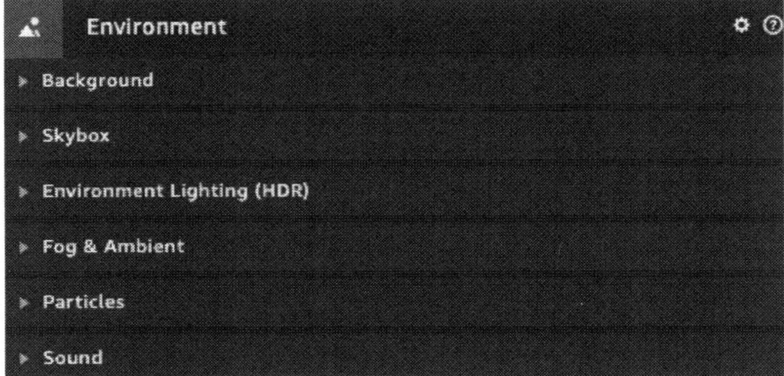

The **Background** section allows you to configure the color of your background. By default, this is configured to a grey color. If the grey color isn't to your liking, you can click the Color box to change it.

The **Skybox** section allows you to replace the dreary grey color with textures to represent the sky. A skybox is just a series of images that wrap around the entire world.

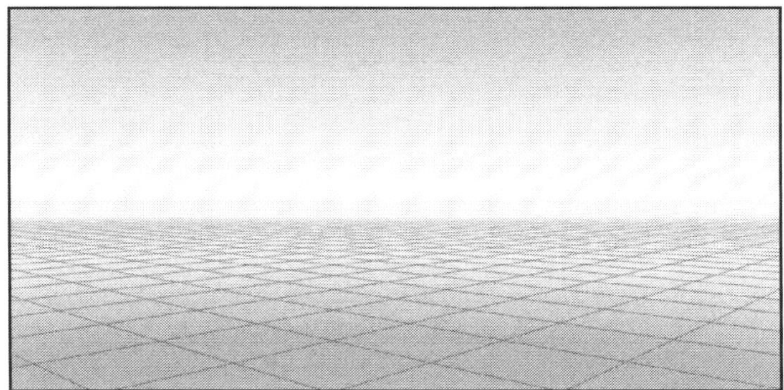

By default, all scenes are generated with an empty skybox. You can create your own skyboxes by adding textures to the component.

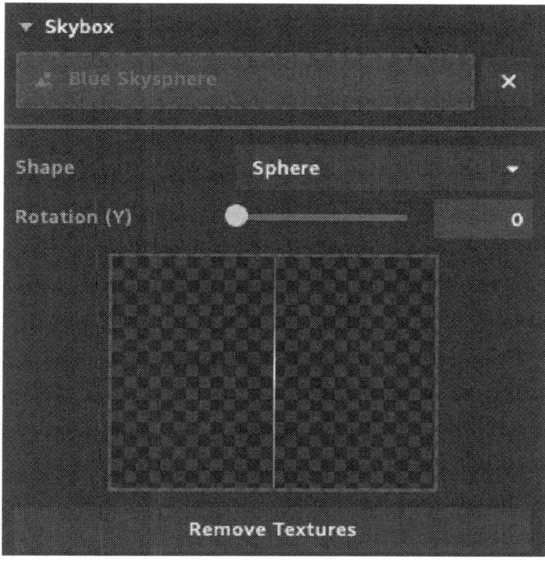

Sumerian also includes some built-in skyboxes as well. If you click **Import Assets** and then search for **skybox**, you'll see that you have many options.

When you import a skybox, it's imported into the Skybox tab in the Assets panel.

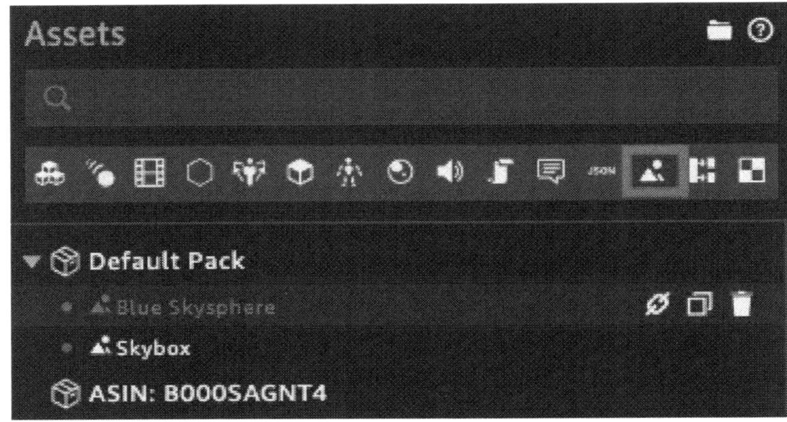

Some skybox assets just import textures instead of an actual skybox asset. In this case, you must assign the textures to your current skybox. By default, skyboxes are spherical. This means when you add a texture to it, the skybox texture will wrap around a sphere. A box skybox means you need to provide a texture for the various viewpoints.

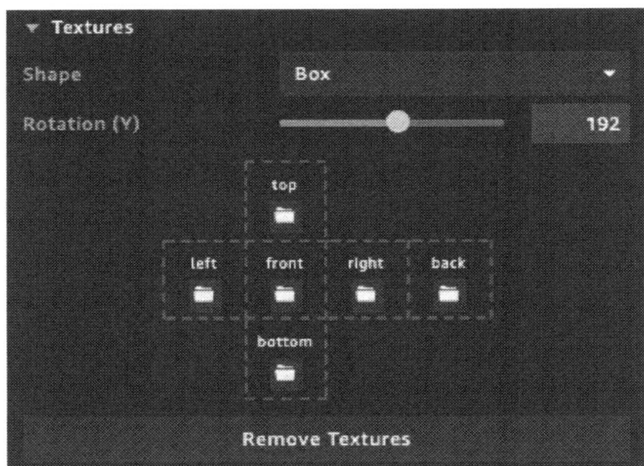

The **Environment Lighting** section allows you to set the HDR textures for your background. This is an advanced form of rendering that supports a wider range of colors. Sumerian includes several HDRI images that you can import to see this high-end feature in action.

The **Fog & Ambient** section allows you to modify the global light and to incorporate fog into your scene. The Ambient property is a color that you can apply to the light. By default, it's set to #000000. This means that you haven't applied any lighting effects. By selecting a color, you add that color to the light.

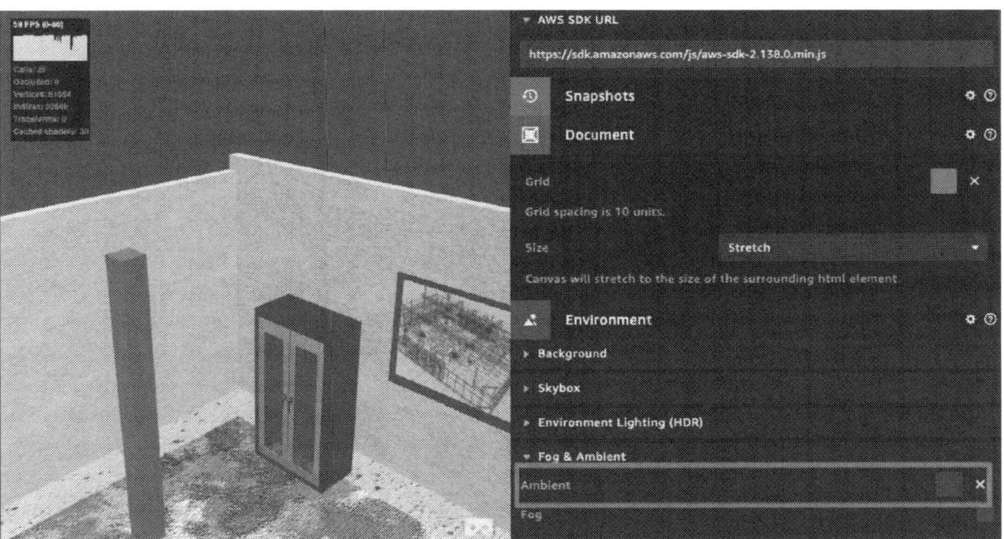

Fog essentially removes entities from the scene. If you have a scene with a large number of entities, you can use fog to hide them. This is a great way to increase performance.

When you add fog, you provide near, far and color properties. The near property indicates when you would like the fog to start to appear and the far property indicates when you can't see anything.

The **Particles** section is a global feature that allows you to add snow to your enter scene. Thankfully, Sumerian features a particle system, which you can use to simulate fire, smoke and other fun things. This is a global setting that affects the entire scene where as particle system is attached to an entity. You'll learn how to create your own particle system in Chapter 13, "Animation and Particle Systems."

Finally, the **Sound** section lets you configure the global sound settings for the scene. You'll be learning about adding sound in Chapter 9, "Custom Models and Sound."

Post effects

Post effects are where you can have a lot of fun with your scene. You can use antialiasing to smooth out jagged edges or motion blur to smooth out movements.

You can think of a post effect like an Instagram filter. The engine determines the elements it needs to display in the scene and then draws the image. Before that happens, you can apply a filter to it.

Expand the Post Effect component and you'll see there's only one button which reads, "Add Effects". **Click the button**.

You'll see a list of different post effects. Select the **Sepia** post effect and click **Add**.

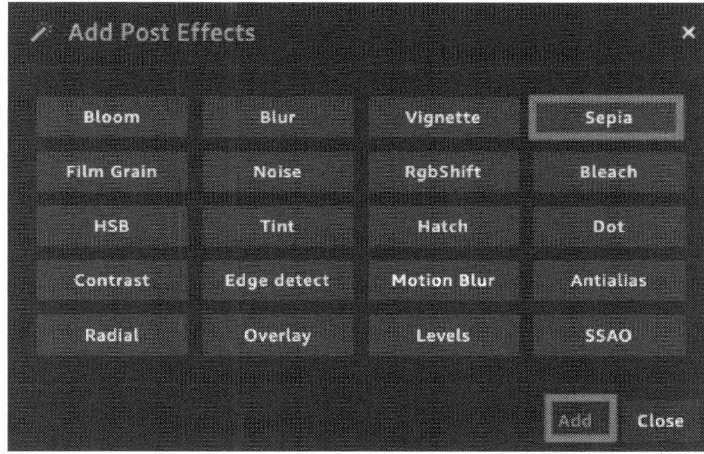

Once you add the post effect, your escape room will go all arty on you.

You can add as many post effects as you like. Sumerian applies the effects in the order that you added them.

For example, if you wanted to reproduce the look of the game *Return of the Obra Dinn*, you'd add a **Hatch** effect, and your scene would look like this:

On the Hatch effect, set the Spread to **4** and then drag the Hatch **above the Sepia**.

Now, you're left with an arty-looking room.

If you don't want to view the effects while developing your scene, you can turn them off. Click the **Post Effect** button located near the top menu bar to disable them.

This only works while you're editing. The moment you play your scene, the post effects will be applied. While the effects look cool, they do make it harder for users to solve your room. You can remove the effects by clicking the **x** button or you can jump to the Snapshots component and restore an earlier version of your scene.

Keep in mind that post effects are not free. They require processing and can increase the overhead of your scene as well. Last but not least, post effects will not work in VR.

Document settings

So far, you've been developing your scene with the assumption that your users will be on a desktop computer. But given that Sumerian is a web-based technology, a large portion of your audience will be using mobile devices. You can test your scene on various mobile devices, which is always a good idea, but you can also configure the canvas to match the resolution of the scene.

Click the **Document** component and you'll see that you have fields.

The first field, **Grid**, changes the color of the scene grid. For example, set the color to **Red**.

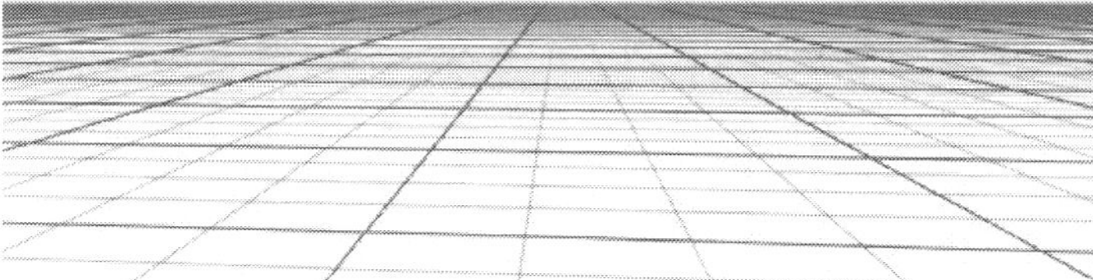

The Size field allows you to set the resolution of the canvas. You have three different options. Currently, you've set the canvas to *Stretch*. This stretches the scene across the width of the window. The `Aspect Ratio` allows you to set a target ratio. For instance, you can set a ratio to 16:9 or supply your own target ration. The `Resolution` option allows you to target a specific pixel resolution. You can select a preset your own resolution or use one of the presets.

For now, select the **Resolution** option.

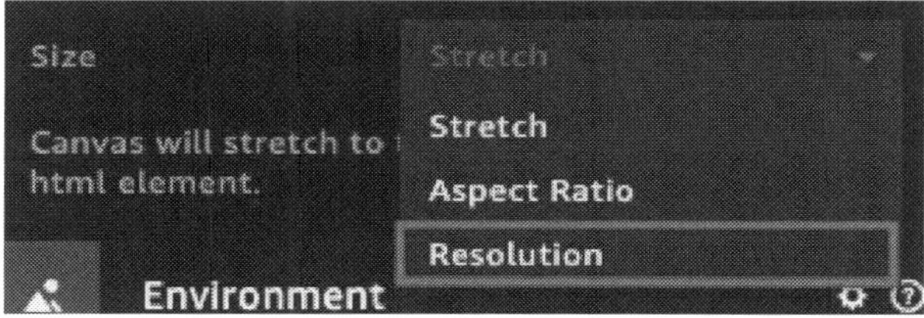

You can select one of the several presets or you can provide your own resolution.

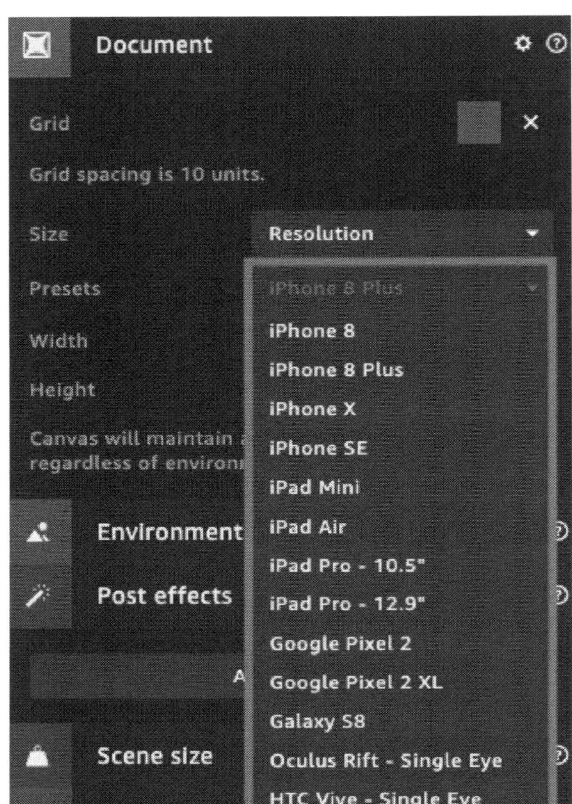

If your device isn't listed, you can find its resolution and add it manually.

Publishing

At this point, your scene runs really well. You've added some cool effects and have everything ready to go. The last thing you need to do is publish it.

You have two options when you publish: You can make your scene private or public.

Regardless of which option you choose, the scene will be hosted by Amazon Web Services. With public scenes, any person can access the scene. All they need to view your content is a link.

If you host privately, you determine who can view your scene. Unfortunately, setting up private viewing is a little complicated. It requires using Amplify and configuring your app to work with both Sumerian and Cognito. Cognito is a service that manages users.

Later in this book, you'll learn how to configure AWS to work with Sumerian so you can leverage all those excellent services. For now, you'll publish your game scene with public permissions.

> **Note:** If you're unfamiliar with AWS, JavaScript or working on the console, then you should avoid privately publishing your scene until you understand the related technologies, as they take a lot of configuring. If not, then at least have someone familiar with these technologies review your configuration to avoid exposing private scenes to unauthorized users.

Regardless of whether a scene is public or private, you can incorporate that scene into your own web apps. Amazon manages the authentication for you.

To publish your scene publicly, click **Publish** and select **Create public link**.

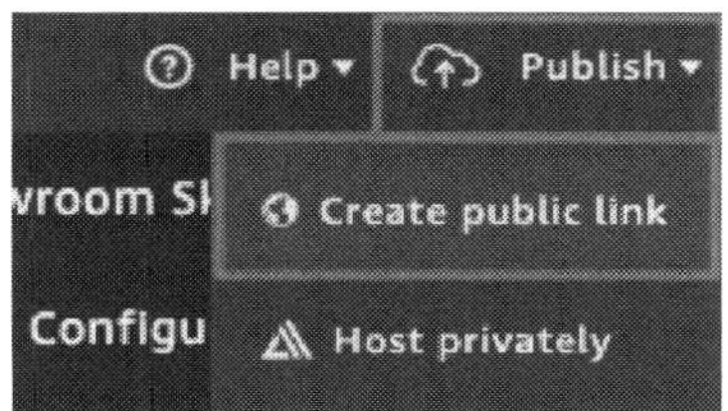

You'll see a dialog that asks you to confirm your publication, along with another **Publish** button.

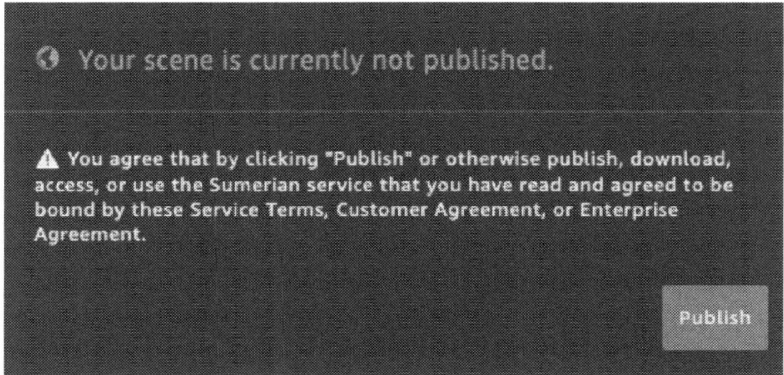

Once you do that, you'll receive a public link. You can pass the link to anyone who's interested.

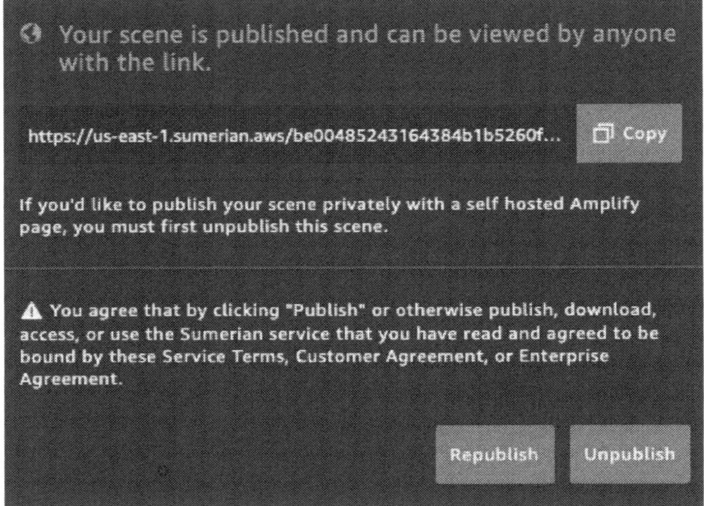

Later, you may discover a bug or mistake within your scene. Once you fix the mistake, you need to republish it. To do so, click the same publish button, and then click **Republish**.

You also have the option to unpublish a scene. You may want to unpublish a scene in cases where an event expires or you find that it uses too many AWS resources.

Key points

- **Snapshots** allows you to **save versions of your scene** during various points in development. This allows you to **restore your scene** at any later point in time.
- Setting entities to **static** is an easy optimization to make your scene run faster.
- Use the **environment settings** to configure the world around your scene such as adding **skyboxes** to applying **fog**.
- **Post effects** provide great visual effects but they can **affect your scene's performance**.
- Publishing your scene publicly allows everyone access it. With private access, you set your user access levels.

Where to go from here?

For more information about publishing your scene, check out this excellent online resource:

https://docs.sumerian.amazonaws.com/tutorials/create/intermediate/amplify-react-2/

Congratulations! You've completed your first Sumerian experience. You made an escape room that touches all aspects of the engine, but believe it or not, you're just getting started.

In the next section, you'll create an instructional experience. In the process, you'll learn about Sumerian's sound and lighting system, how to animate entities and how to leverage the power of the engine by learning Sumerian's application programming interface.

See you in the next section!

Section II: Building an Educational Experience

Building an escape room is not only fun, but it's also a great way to learn a 3D engine. But while escape rooms are entertaining to build, Sumerian can do much more. The engine can power a range of different experiences, such as virtual house tours or a digital concierge service.

In this section, you'll create an experience to educate a user. Imagine returning from the store with a new bread machine. Instead of reading the instruction manual, you scan a QR code. This opens a web browser that provides a quick-start walkthrough on how to use the device.

You'll create a walkthrough like this in the upcoming section. By doing so, you'll explore the following topics:

Chapter 9: Custom Models & Sounds: In this chapter, you'll provide your own models to create a scene and you'll incorporate sound into your experience to narrate the demo.

Chapter 10: Lights, Camera, Action: This chapter provides an overview of the camera and lighting system. You'll learn how to use cameras and lighting to direct a user's focus.

Chapter 11: Introduction to JavaScript: Being successful with Sumerian means knowing JavaScript. This chapter will get you up and running with the language. You'll learn JavaScript basics while working in the context of Sumerian.

Chapter 12: The Sumerian API: The Sumerian API allows you to take your experiences to the next level. This chapter will help you get started with the API by introducing you to its core concepts.

Chapter 13: Animation & Particle Systems: You'll learn how to tween entities, animate models and use the timeline editor. You'll also use the particle system to add some steam to your bread.

Chapter 14: Incorporating Web Content: This chapter shows you how to embed YouTube videos into your scene. You'll also learn how to provide dynamic information in a scene by using HTML, CSS, and JavaScript.

Chapter 9: Custom Models & Sound

By Brian Moakley

Imagine that you've just returned from the store, and in your hands is the new Bread Maker 6-5000, a powerhouse of a machine designed to bake the tastiest bread. Upon opening the quick start guide, you find a simple QR code. You can scan the code with a QR reader program on your phone and you find a nice little demo that shows you the basics of the machine. In the next six chapters, you'll build this demo and gain a better understanding of Sumerian and its various components in doing so. There's no better place to start than at the beginning, so get yourself a nice mug of coffee and crack those knuckles — there's some bread that needs baking!

Setting up a Sumerian project

To get started, launch the Sumerian dashboard and this time, click the **Projects** link on the left-hand side of the dashboard.

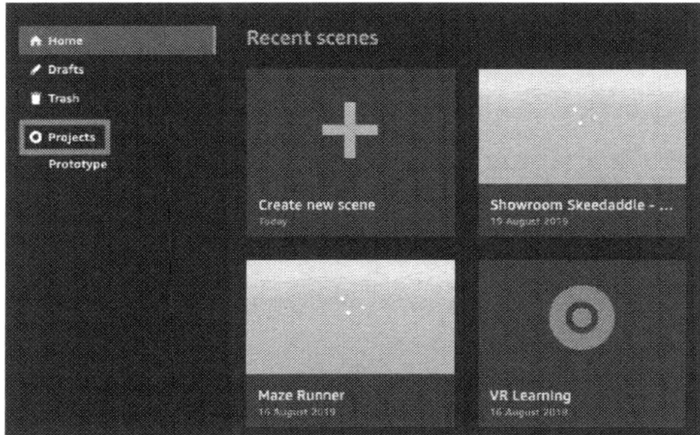

So far, you've just created scenes and saved them – but what about working on something that's composed of multiple scenes? **Sumerian projects** allow you to organize these scenes. You can think of projects as a grouping mechanism.

Click **New Project** to create a new project. Give it the name: **Bread Maker 6-500** and click **Create**.

Once you create a project, you'll be brought to the scene list. A project can contain up to a thousand scenes. You'll also notice tabs for Assets and Templates.

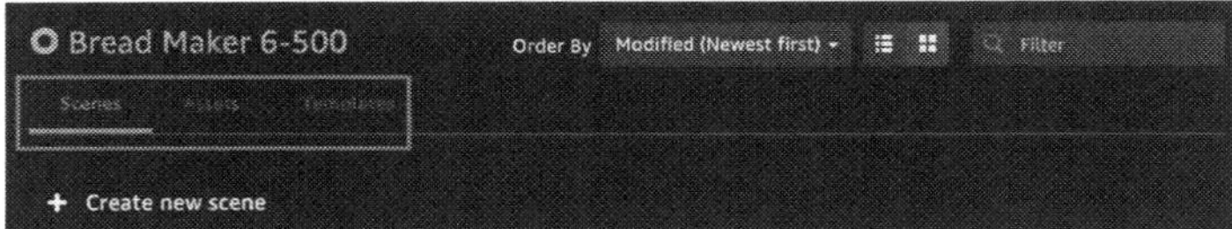

When you create a scene, you can export assets, which other scenes in your project can then import. You can find a list of those assets in the Assets tab.

Templates allow you to create starting points for scenes. For instance, imagine you're creating lots of different demo variations of the Bread Maker 6-500. You may add your models and configure your lighting, then save the results as a template. You then use that template as a starting point for any other demo. You don't have to redo the hard work of setting up your models.

Click **Create new scene**, name the scene **Quickstart** and click **Create**. This will launch an empty scene. Exit to the dashboard and select the **Bread Maker 6-500** project in the project listing.

You'll see the newly-created Quickstart scene in the scene details. **Select the scene**, but don't click on the link (the scene name); otherwise, the scene will open. You just want to select the scene by clicking on the row. Once selected, the right-hand column changes to show the Scene Details.

You can rename your scene, duplicate it and delete it, if necessary. You'll notice that the thumbnail it uses indicates the current template. By clicking on the thumbnail, you'll see the option to provide your own.

Now, open your scene. It's time to get busy.

Setting up the scene

You built an entire escape room from scratch in the last section. You needed to create the entire room because the user interacted with various facets of the room. They controlled the camera and determined where to look. In this scene, you'll build only a partial room. The scene interaction will be limited, so it doesn't make sense to construct a complete environment.

Think of your scenes like a Hollywood set. You only want to provide assets that the user will see. For instance, a mansion on a Hollywood set may look exquisite and well-detailed, but once you step through the doorway, you'll discover that the house is just the outside facade.

With your scene open, click **Create Entity** and select a **Box** entity. Set the box's Translation to (**-11.367**, **3.711**, **-7.37**). Set the Scale to (**12.428**, **0.145**, **7.19**) and name the entity **Countertop**.

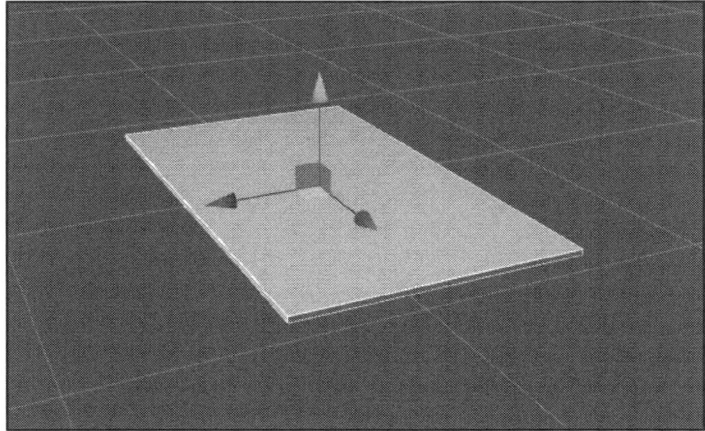

Click **Create Entity** again and select an **Empty Entity**. Name it **Kitchen Walls**. You'll use this entity to store your walls.

Once again, click **Create Entity** and this time, select another **Box** entity. Name it **Wall**. Set the Translation to (**-11.912**, **5.065**, **-3.847**). Set the Scale to (**0.179**, **9.88**, **14.555**).

You now have a wall with a countertop running through it... literally. The countertop goes right through the wall. But you don't have to worry about that since the user won't see it.

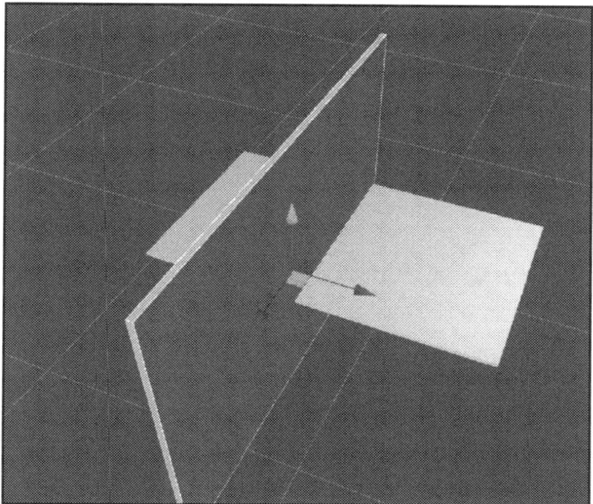

Drag your new wall into the **Kitchen Walls** entity.

Click **Create Entity** again and select another **Box** entity. Name it **Wall 2**. Set the Translation to (**6.903**, **5.064**, **-11.041**). Set the Rotation to (**0**, **90**, **0**). Set the Scale to (**0.179**, **9.88**, **34.718**). Now, drag **Wall 2** to the **Kitchen Wall** entity.

Now that's one bizarre kitchen.

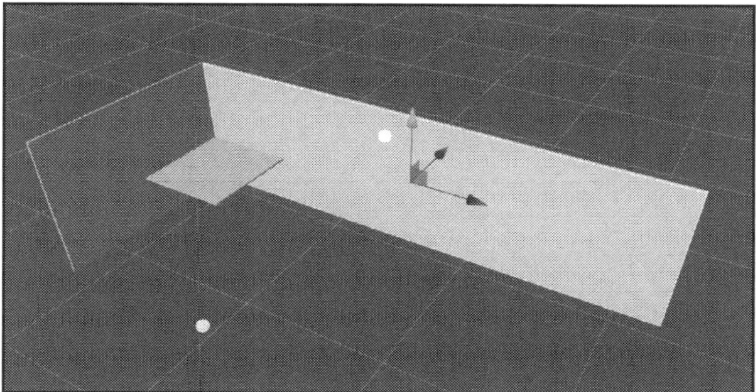

Believe it or not, that's your completed kitchen. There are no floors or ceilings, only two walls and an empty countertop. Remember, the user won't be seeing the entire kitchen. They'll only see what you want them to see.

Note: If it bothers you to see the countertop sticking through the wall, resize it so it stops against the kitchen wall. Just remember, the user won't know. In some cases, like the escape room, the geometry needs to be perfect. In others, it's okay to color outside the lines, so to speak.

Tiling textures

The kitchen is a little bare and could use some decoration. It doesn't require much; a little texture can go a long way. Thankfully, there are two textures included to decorate the walls and the countertop. These are special textures meant to be tiled.

In the Assets panel, click the **Import files from your computer** button – it looks like a folder icon. In **resources/textures**, navigate to **Textures_Tiling** and select both of the textures.

In the Assets panel, switch to the **Materials** tab and select the **Default Material**. This is your countertop. Change the name to **Countertop Material**. Next, switch to the **Textures** tab and drag the **Granite_Color.png** texture to the **COLOR (DIFFUSE)** section on your Countertop Material.

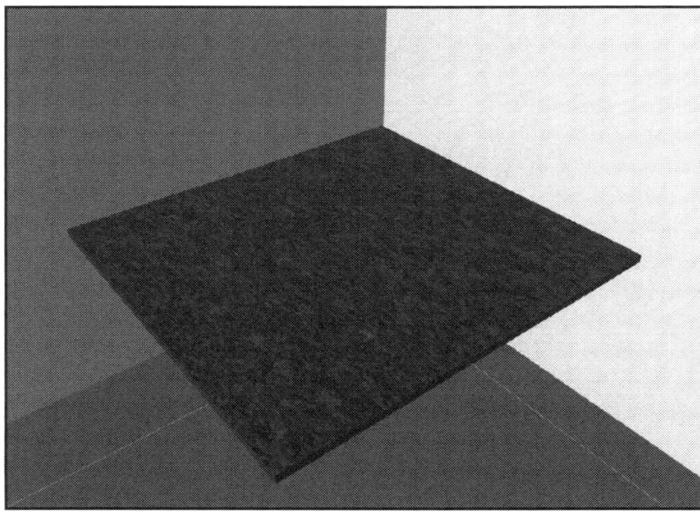

Now, you have a countertop worth looking at! If you zoom into it, you'll find the detail looks a little mushy. Since the user will be looking at the bread machine with the camera close to the counter, it'd be better to increase the tiling to make the close-up view look sharper.

In the Assets panel, select the **Texture** tab and then select the **Granite_Color.png**. The Inspector panel will display some information about the texture. Expand the **Placement** section. The placement determines how the texture maps onto a 3D surface. You define the placement by U,V coordinates. You can control how the image repeats using the **Repeat U** and **Repeat V** commands.

Increase the Repeat U and Repeat V value to **5**. This decreases the tiling size, sharpening the overall counter.

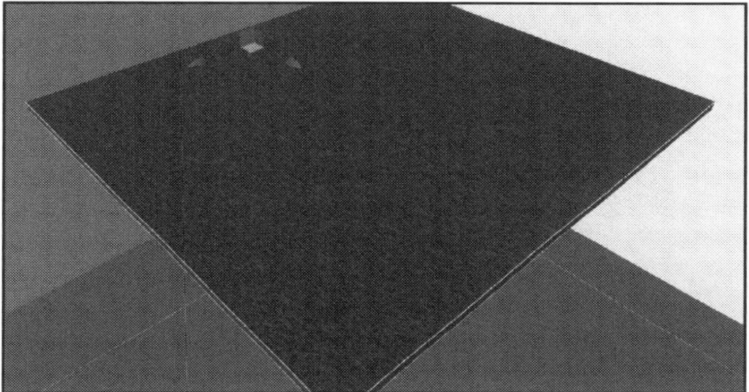

Feel free to play around with these options to see how they affect the texture. You also have a lot of advanced options to control how the textures look as well.

Now, for the wallpaper. Switch back to the **Material** tab and select **Default Material 2**. Rename it to **Wallpaper Material**.

Select the **Texture** tab and drag the **WallPaper_Color.png** texture to the **COLOR (DIFFUSE)** section. Your wallpaper will appear on one of the walls.

Now, for the other wall. In the Entities panel, select **Wall 2**. In the Assets panel, switch to the **Materials** tab. Drag the **Wallpaper Material** to the Wall 2 **Material component**.

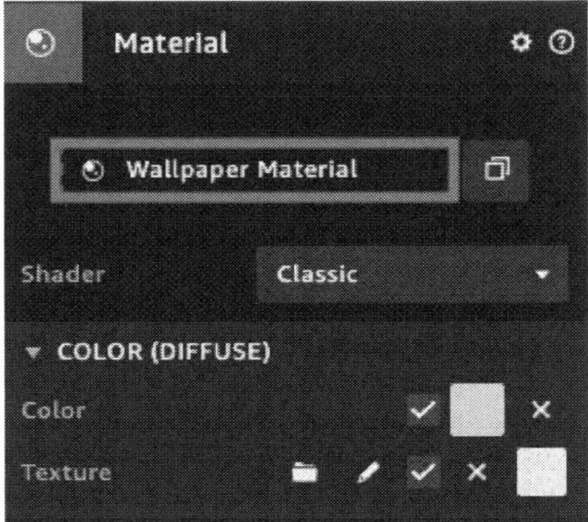

You'll notice that your wallpaper doesn't exactly match up. The flowers on the long wall are horizontally stretched.

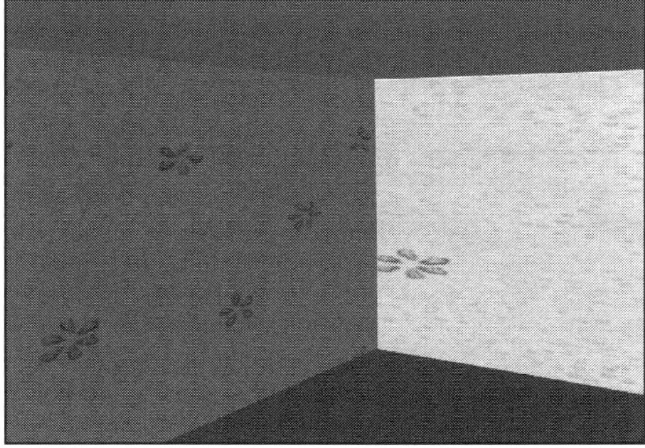

To fix this, you can increase the horizontal tiling; however, this requires creating a new texture and material. In the Assets panel, switch to the **Textures** tab and then **duplicate** the **WallPaper_Color.png** texture.

Select the duplicated texture. In the Inspector panel, set the name to **WallPaper_Color_Long.png** and, in the Placement section, set the Repeat U to **3**.

Switch back to the **Materials** tab and select the **Default Material 3**. Rename it to **Wallpaper Long** and assign the **WallPaper_Color_Long.png** to the **COLOR (DIFFUSE)** section.

Finally, in the Entities panel, select **Wall 2** and assign it the **Wallpaper Long** material.

The wallpaper now has matching-sized flowers.

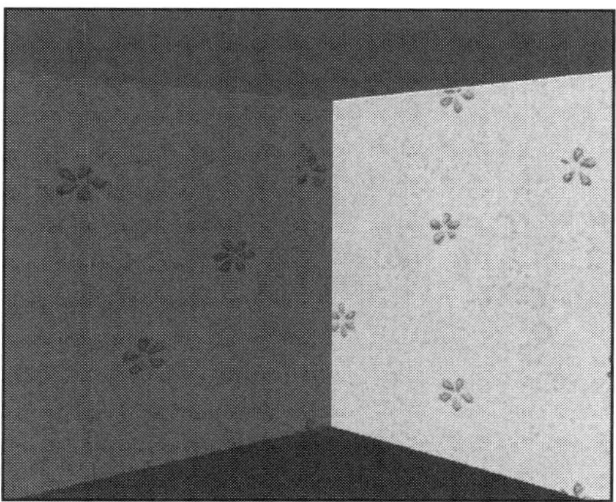

Importing and adding models

With your kitchen all set up, your next task is to import your models. Earlier, you imported the models by clicking Import Assets. In this chapter, you'll upload your own models.

> **Note**: Keep in mind that AWS charges for model storage. At the time of this writing, AWS charges six cents per gigabyte of storage. Thankfully, the models used in this chapter are relatively small.

Sumerian allows for two model formats: FilmBox (.fbx) and Wavefront OBJ (.obj). These are two industry-used formats. The max size for a model is 50 MB.

When you import a model into Sumerian, Sumerian will convert the model into an asset pack that you can incorporate into your scene. If the model contains animations, Sumerian will import those animations.

In the Assets panel, click the **Import files from your computer** button and, in **resources/models**, **shift select** all of the FBX files. It may take a moment, but when Sumerian has finished, you'll have a bunch of new entities.

Switch to the Entities tab to see your models.

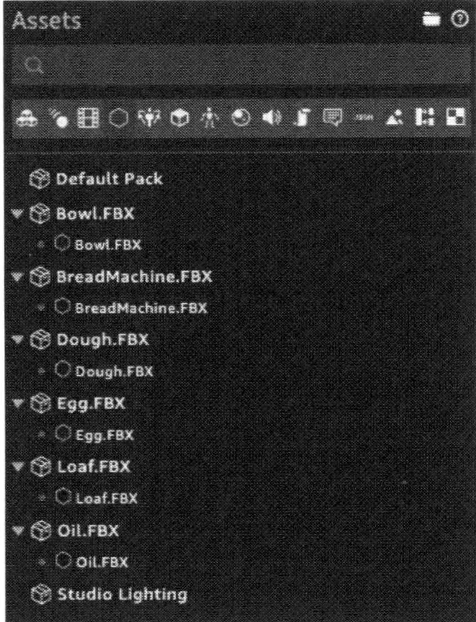

Drag the **BreadMachine.FBX** entity onto the canvas. Name it to **Bread Machine**. Set the Translation to (**-10.485**, **3.78**, **-7.01**) and the Rotation to (**0**, **180**, **0**).

Unfortunately, your bread machine looks more like a Styrofoam cooler.

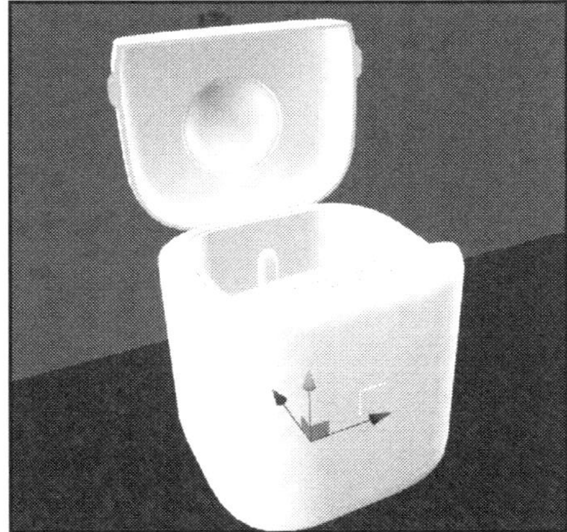

That's because Sumerian imports the textures as separate images. You'll fix this soon, but for now, you need to add the rest of the models. First, import the following models and add them to the canvas. Make sure to add three eggs to your scene. Once you have all your models in your scene, rename them according to the following table:

Asset Name	Entity Name
Oil.FBX	Oil
Bowl.FBX	Flour Bowl
Watercup.FBX	Water Cup
EGG.FBX	Egg 1
	Egg 2
	Egg 3

Set the positions of the models to the following:

Entity Name	Position X	Position Y	Position Z	Rotation X	Rotation Y	Rotation Z	Scale X	Scale Y	Scale Z
Oil	-11.093	3.841	-10.312	0	180	0	1	1	1
Flour Bowl	-11.089	3.777	-9.649	7.801	-87.005	-1.491	1	1	1
Water Cup	-10.58	3.824	-10.196	6.025	0	0	0.75	0.75	0.75
Egg 1	-10.387	3.841	-9.812	38.48	2.445	63.149	1	1	1
Egg 2	-10.285	3.841	-9.541	38.48	-60.752	63.149	1	1	1
Egg 3	-10.176	3.808	-9.684	38.48	-128.305	63.149	1	1	1

Your scene should look like the following:

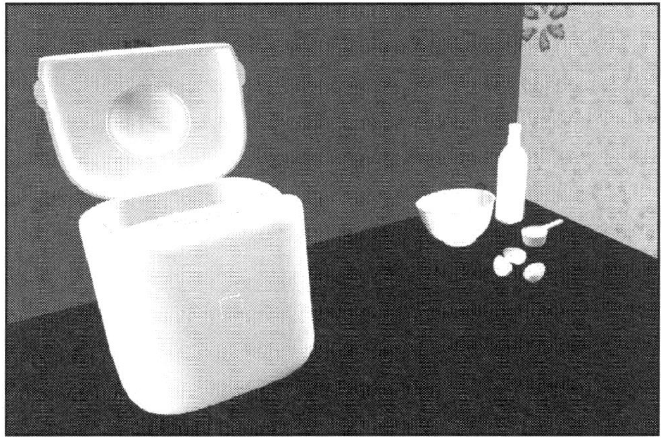

Click **Create Entity** and select an empty **Entity**. Name it **Ingredients**. Drag all of your models *except* the Bread Machine into the **Ingredients** entity.

Create a new **Empty Entity** and name it **Eggs**. Drag it to the **Ingredients** entity, then drag all the **eggs** to it. Your panel should look like the following:

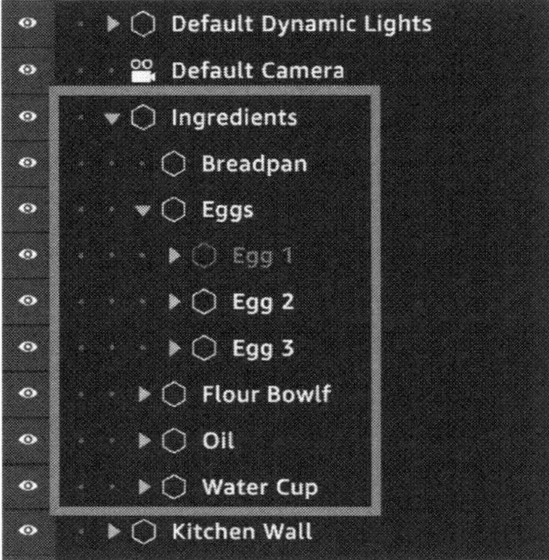

The bread pan is going to sit next to the ingredients. This is actually part of the bread machine. In the Entities panel, expand the **Bread Machine** and select the **Bucket_14_-_Default** entity. Rename it to **Breadpan**.

In the Entities panel, drag the **Breadpan** entity out of the Bread Machine and to the **Quickstart** scene.

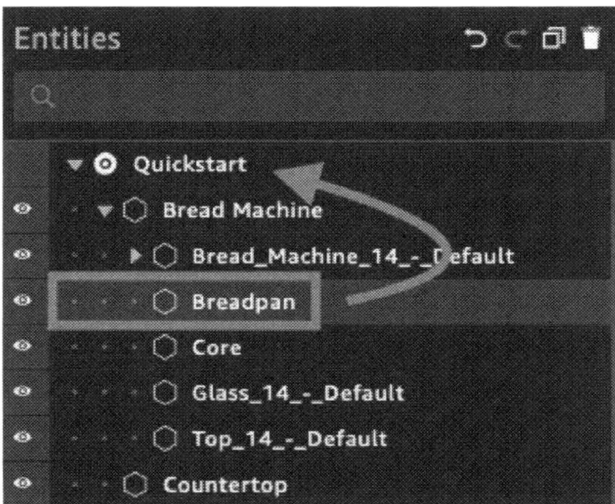

Set the Translation to (**-10.693**, **3.461**, **-8.6**).

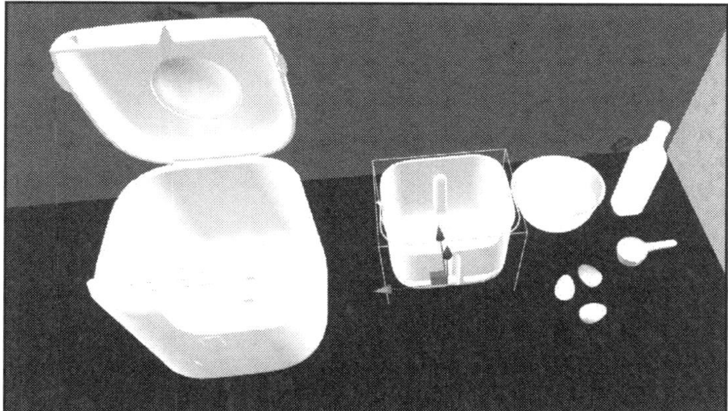

Now that you have your models, it's time to add a little color to the world.

Texturing your models

While your models may look nice, they seem to lack a bit of color. As you know, when you imported the models, Sumerian didn't include the actual textures. However, you can still see the model. Sumerian has created a material for you and assigned it a generic white color.

To add a more realistic color, click **Import files from your computer** button in the Assets panel. In the **resources** folder, navigate to **textures/Texture_BreadMachine**. **Shift-select** all of the textures and click the **Open** button.

The textures will have interesting names like **BreadMachine_AmbientOcclusion.png** and **BreadMachine_Normal.jpg**. Jake Nolt, the model artist for this book, provided these names to let you know what role the images play for your model.

These images refer to the classic shader included with Sumerian. The PBR shader uses a similar approach, but its internal methodology is different.

To get started, select the **14_-_Default** Material so that it appears in the inspector. Rename it to **Bread Machine Material**.

The first shader category is the **COLOR (DIFFUSE)** category. This provides simple colors to your model. Drag the **BreadMachine_Color.png** texture to this category. You'll see your model gain some color.

The **normal** category is next. The normal category determines how light bounces off the model. It doesn't affect actual light in a scene, but it provides greater detail on a model.

Drag the **BreadMachine_Normal.png** texture to the **NORMAL** category and look at the model update.

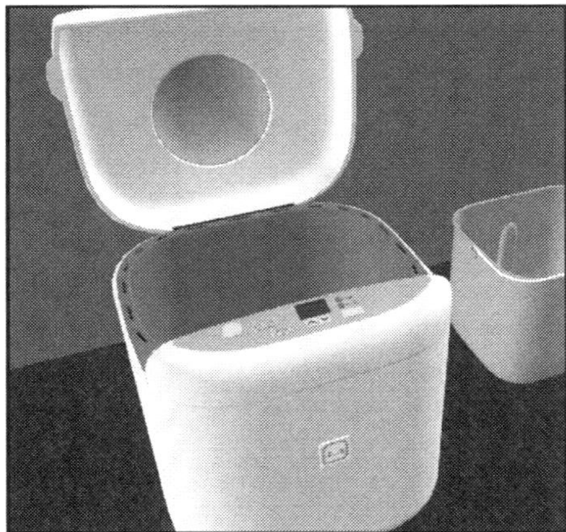

The **specular** category determines the direct reflections on an object. Drag the **BreadMachine_Specular.png** to the **SPECULAR** category.

The reflectivity defines how much light the material reflects. Drag the **BreadMachine_Reflective.png** to the **REFLECTIVITY** category.

Finally, the **Ambient** category determines the color and value of an object without considering the lighting. Drag the **BreadMachine_Ambient.png** to the **AMBIENT** category.

You've made the model look quite different now, just by adding a few additional images.

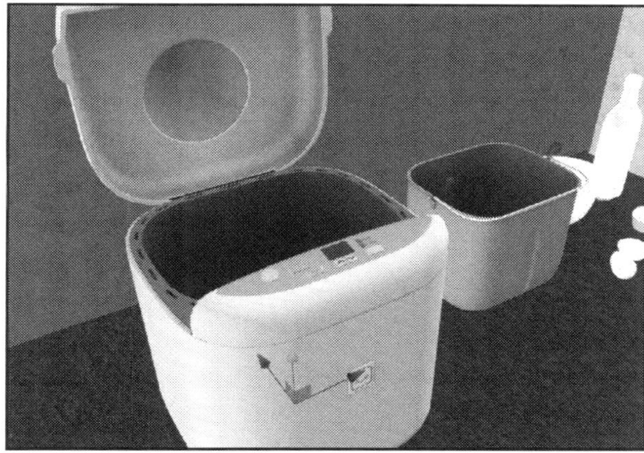

Now for the ingredients. In the Assets panel, click the **Import files from your computer** button. In **resources**, navigate to **textures/Textures_Ingredients**. Import all the textures.

All of the models contain their own material. You can use this material to texture your model or you can create new material.

Your project will contain two scenes, with only one of them being user-facing. In this case, you'll have all your models share the same material.

In the Assets panel, switch to the **Materials** tab. Click the + and select **Material**. Name it **Ingredients Material**.

Then, switch to the **Textures** tab. Drag the **Ingredients_Color** to the **COLOR (DIFFUSE)** category. Next, drag the **Ingredients_Normal.png** to the **NORMAL** category, the **Ingredients_Specular** to the **SPECULAR** category, the **Ingredients_Ambient** to the **AMBIENT** category and the **Ingredients_Reflection** to the **texture** in the **REFLECTIVITY** category.

In the Entities panel, search for **18_-_Default** to get a list of entities that all end with that phrase. Select each of these entities and set them to use the **Ingredients Material**.

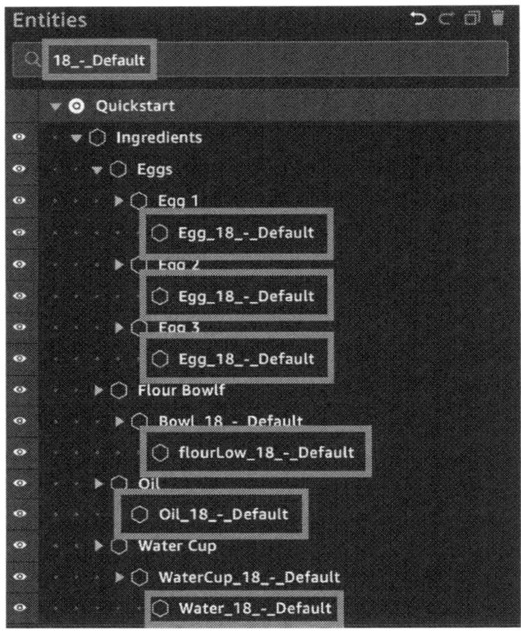

You now have textured models. Your scene is really coming together!

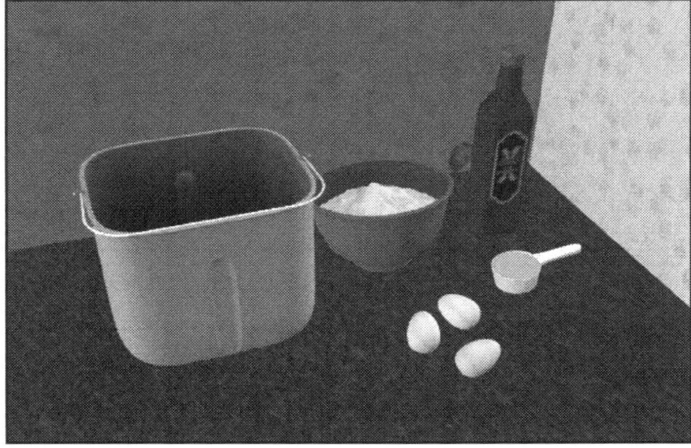

Now, you're ready to start providing instructions to your instructional scene.

Adding sound

This experience is designed to teach the user how to operate a bread machine. Usually, tutorials use pre-recorded voice-overs to handle instructions like that.

Thankfully, working with audio is not too difficult. First, you must provide your audio in a supported audio format. At the time of this writing, Sumerian supports OGG, MP3 and WAV (WAVE). The file size has a hard limit of 10 MB.

You add a sound asset much like you add all your other assets: You import it into the Assets inspector.

Open the **resources** folders and you'll see a **sounds** folder. This folder contains all the sounds necessary for this experience. The number at the start of the file name indicates the play order for the sound file.

In the Assets inspector, click the **Import files from your computer** button and import all of the sound files.

Now, to start the demonstration. In the Entities panel, select the **Bread Machine**. In the Inspector panel, click **Add Component**, and add a **State Machine**. Click the **+** to add a new behavior. Name the new behavior **Bread Machine Demo**.

Select **State 1** and rename it to **Play Introduction**. Now, click **Add Action**. Select the **Sound** category. You'll see that you have lots of different audio actions available.

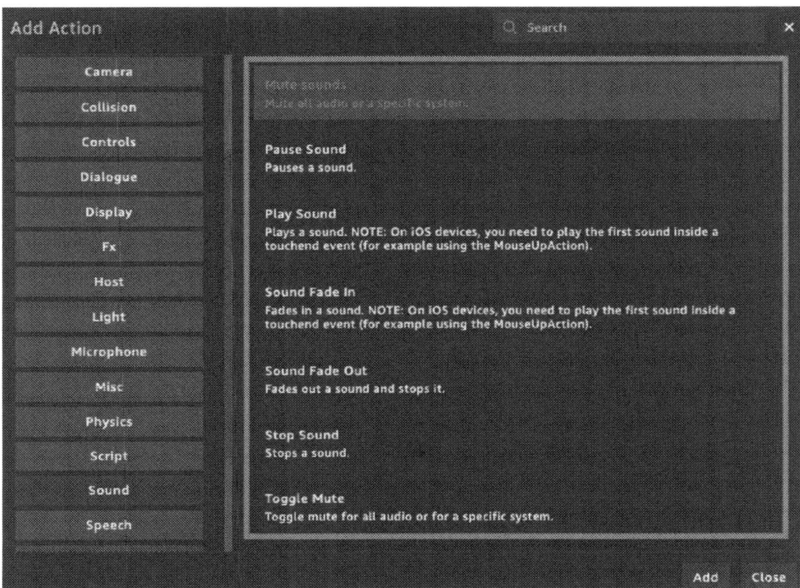

Add a **Play Sound** action. Now you might want to pick a sound to play, but unfortunately, the Play Sound action doesn't let you do that. That's because you haven't attached any sound to the entity yet. Your entity needs to have an attached Sound component before it can play your audio.

Select the Bread Machine entity and click **Add Component**. Select a **Sound** component. This component lets you set the volume and provides a field where you can drop files.

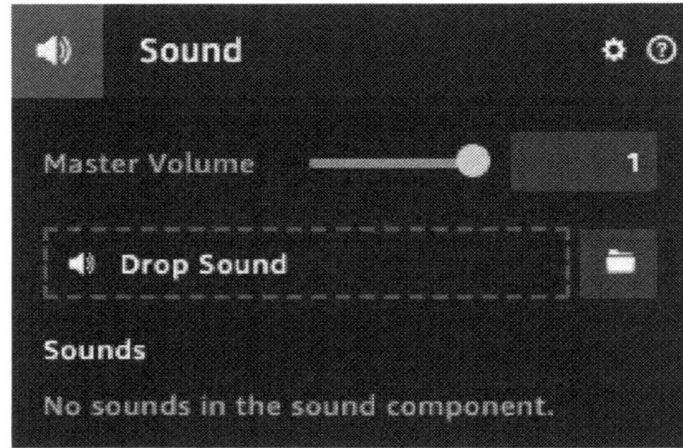

In the Assets panel, switch to the **Sounds** tab. Drag the **1_this-is-your-new-breadmaking-machine.wav** to the sound field. You now have a sound attached to your entity.

Now, open the Bread Machine Demo behavior and select the **Play Introduction** state. In the Sound action, select the **1_this-is-your-new-breadmaking-machine** from the drop-down. Now, play your scene.

You'll notice two things have happened. First, your sound played right on start as expected. Second, the Bread Machine closed without you touching it. Don't worry, there are no ghosts in this kitchen.

Next, you'll stop that unwanted animation. Select the **Bread Machine** and, in the inspector, you'll see there's an animation component attached to it. Some models include animations.

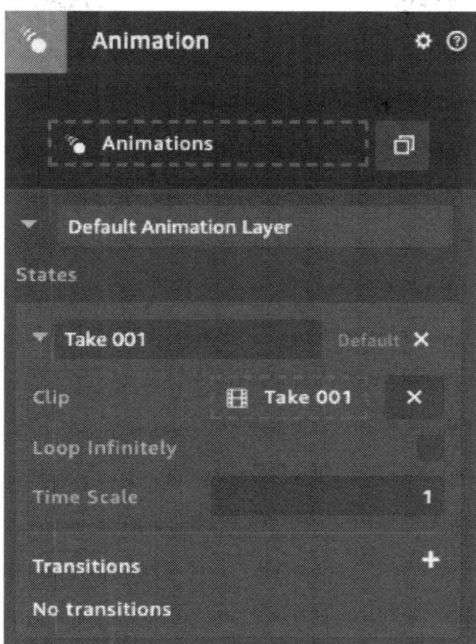

You'll be playing with animation in Chapter 13, "Animation and Particle Systems." For now, remove the **Animation component** from the Bread Machine.

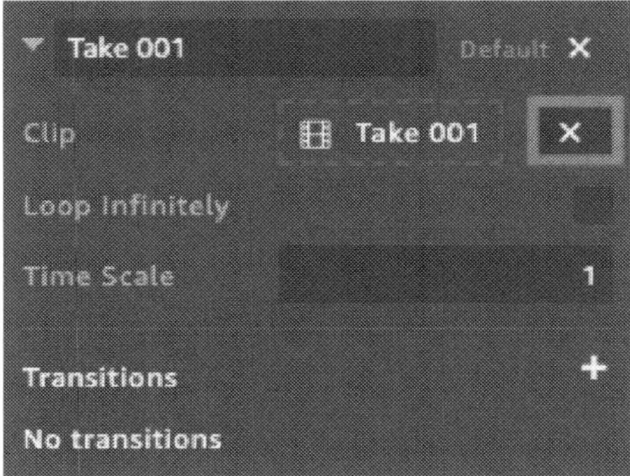

Now, in edit mode, **zoom far away** from the Bread Machine. Play your scene. The sound will be distant and slightly hard to hear because you are working with 3D sounds.

When you assign a sound to an entity, that entity is the audio source. As you move away from the sound, the sound will lower in volume. If you position the camera to the right of the sound, the sound will play through the right speaker. This creates a sense of "reality" in your scene. Your audio source has a physical location in the world.

For other sounds, like music or narration, this arrangement isn't ideal. For example, when providing narration, you don't care about the audio source location. You want the audio to play at the same volume, regardless of its position to the camera.

You accomplish this using 2D sound. 2D sound disregards location during playback.

In the Assets panel, switch to the **Sounds** tab and select the **1_this-is-your-new-breadmaking-machine** sound.

You'll notice that you have a few options. You'll also notice that 3D audio is checked by default. **Uncheck 3D audio**.

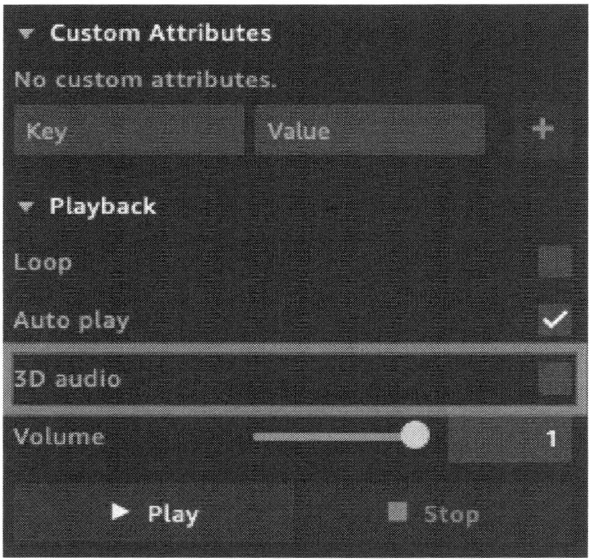

Now play your scene and zoom out. As expected, the audio will play at a consistent volume.

Adding the rest of the sounds

At this point, you're ready to add the rest of the narration. Select the Bread Machine and **drag the rest of the sound files to the Sound component**. By the time you're done, you'll have accumulated quite a large list of files.

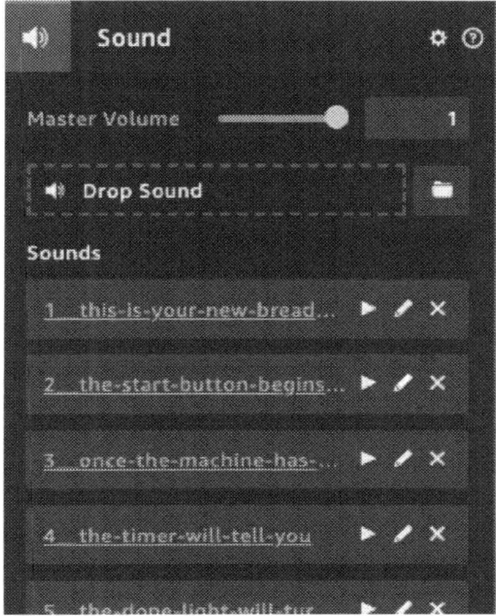

Now, play your scene. You will hear what sounds like a demon incantation. Oops! By default, Sumerian sets all sounds to play at start, so all of your sounds are playing at once. Fix this by going to the Assets panel, selecting the **1_this-is-your-new-breadmaking-machine** sound, and unchecking **Auto play**.

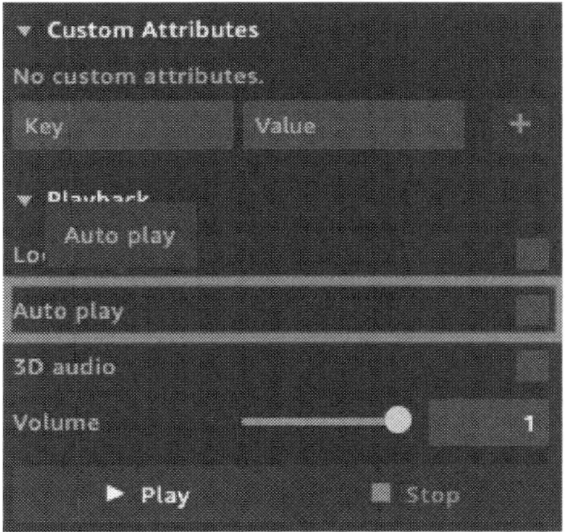

Select each sound and **uncheck both 3D Sound and Auto play**.

Now, open the **Bread Machine Demo** behavior. Add a **new state** and name it **Start Button Description**. Add a **Sound** action and set it to use the **2_the-start-button-begins-the-baking-process** sound. Drag a transition from the **Play Introduction** to the **Start Button Description**.

Notice that the event is *On Sound End*. This transition occurs once the sound finishes playing.

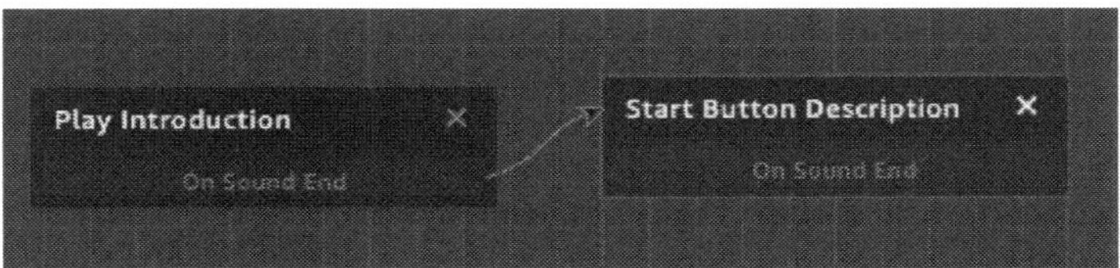

Add a new state. Name it **Pause**. Click **Add Action**. In the Animation category, add a **Wait** action. Set the time to **1**.

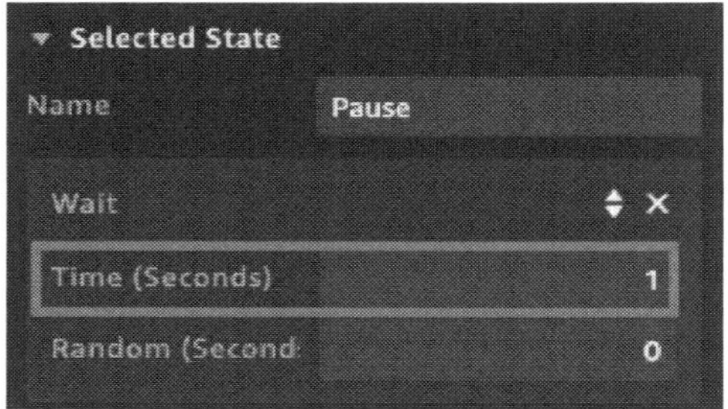

The wait action is useful whenever you need your behavior to take a short break.

Drag a transition from **Play Introduction** to **Pause** and from **Pause** to **Start Button Description**.

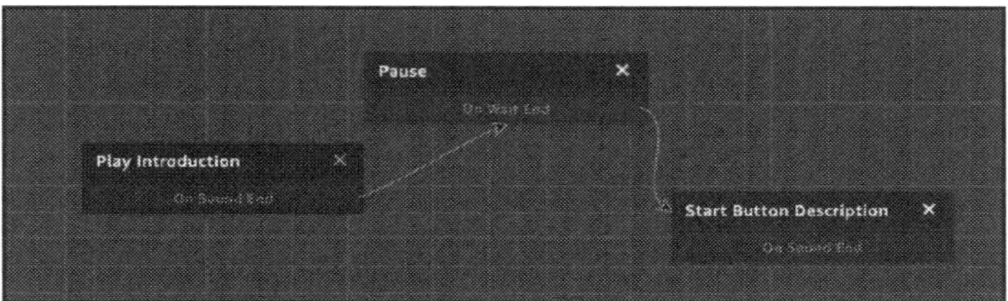

Play the scene and notice how the audio sounds much better.

Now, for the rest of the audio. Your behavior will expand in size as it cycles through all the audio. At the start of the behavior, there will be narration followed by a pause. Later, there will be no pauses as there will be various instructions for the user to do.

Now, create the following states:

State Name	Action	Transition From:
Pause 2	Wait 0.5 seconds	Start Button Description
In Use Description	Sound 03_once-the-machine-has-started	Pause 2
Pause 3	Wait 1.0 seconds	In Use Description
Timer Description	Sound 4__the-timer-will-tell-you	Pause 3
Done Button Description	Sound 5__the-done-light-will-turn-green	Timer Description
Open Button Description	Sound 6__press-the-open-close-button	Done Button Description
See Machine in Action	Sound 7__now-lets-see-our-machine-action	Open Button Description
Simple Recipe	Sound 8__were-making-a-simple-recipe	See Machine in Action
Click Ingredients	Sound 9__click-on-each-ingredient	Simple Recipe
Click on Pan	Sound 0__now-were-ready-start	Click Ingredients
Press Start Button	Sound 11__press-the-start-button	Click on Pan
Baking Is Done	Sound 12__the-baking-is-done	Press Start Button
Loaf of Bread	Sound 13__and-look-at-that	Baking Is Done

When you have all of your starts in place, your behavior should look like the following:

Congratulations! You have the beginning of an educational experience. Unfortunately, it's not very good... yet.

When you start the scene, the narration starts without orientating the user. When the narration speaks about various functions, there's no annotation on the machine to direct the user's eye. There's also no way to move the camera.

As you can see, you're just getting started with the experience. In the next chapter, you'll improve the experience by managing multiple cameras, leveraging the lighting engine and adding interactivity.

Key points

- When developing scenes, focus on just the elements that will be visible to the end user.
- Texture tiling can be adjusted by adjusting the textures Repeat U and Repeat V values.
- Sumerian converts models into asset packs. The model is broken down into entities.
- Models are imported without their textures. You will need to import textures and add them to models by way of materials.
- Sumerian supports OGG, MP3, and WAV sound formats.
- Sounds are imported to 3D sounds and will auto play by default.

Where to go from here?

Models and sounds are the key ingredients in creating compelling scenes. Once you import your model, it's just a matter of dragging it into your canvas and then incorporating it into your scene. You can learn more about models by reviewing the Sumerian official documentation found here: https://docs.aws.amazon.com/en_pv/sumerian/latest/userguide/assets-models.html

Sound is also a critical aspect when working with Sumerian. In this tutorial, you used sound to drive a demo but you can also add music and sound effects. You can learn more about sound from the following tutorial: https://docs.sumerian.amazonaws.com/tutorials/create/beginner/music-and-sound/

Chapter 10: Lights, Camera, Action

By Brian Moakley

Throughout this book, you've been creating scenes that use both the lights and cameras. You've been passively using these items. You've been using lights to illuminate everything in the scene while the user has controlled the cameras.

You can also use these items to illustrate important parts of your scene as well as control the user's perspective. For instance, in the current bread machine demo, there's narration, but that narration is divorced from the elements of the scene. At one point, the narration details the various buttons. However, that narration is lost if the user is pointing the camera at a wall or looking at the ingredients.

In this chapter, you'll use both the lights and camera to focus the user's attention and, in the process, learn how those systems work inside of Sumerian. You'll also add a little interactivity as well.

In Hollywood, you typically hear the expression, “Lights! Camera! Action!” but for this chapter, we'll switch things up to “Camera! Lights! Action!” Granted, you wouldn't want to run cameras without light, but hey, we're not using expensive 35mm film stock so we can afford the change.

Working with cameras

Every new scene comes with a camera, and this camera does a couple of things. You use this camera to navigate through 3D space so that you can place and manipulate 3D objects. Yet once you press the play button, this editor camera becomes the main camera. This is a locked-down camera. You can look around and even move the location.

By holding down the middle mouse button, you can move this camera even while the scene is playing. For your current scene, this isn't a good idea. You've built this scene like a Hollywood set. The user just needs to look up or down to discover that they aren't in a real kitchen.

This setup poses another issue. By using the camera as both an editor camera and a scene camera, you will need to set up the camera in its starting position every time you start a scene. This is just needless busywork because you can use multiple cameras.

When you use multiple cameras, only one camera can be the active camera. Then, as your scene plays, you can switch between those cameras much like a live television show.

Open your Quickstart scene and click **Create Entity**. At the bottom of the dialog, you'll notice that you have four camera options.

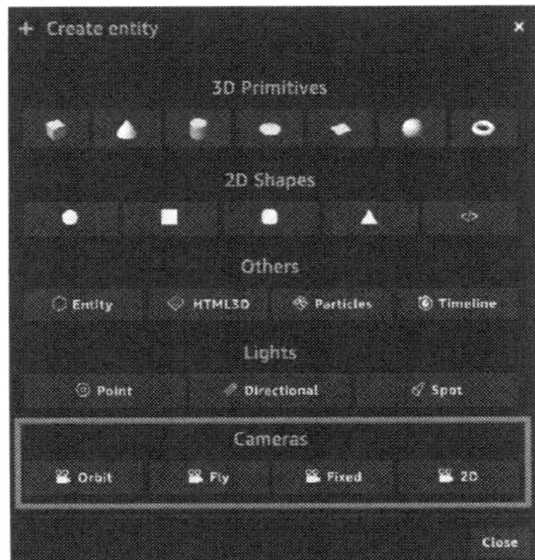

The **Orbit** camera is the default camera selection. This is the type of camera that you've been using throughout this book. The camera is great for orbiting an entity, but you can also move around the scene.

This option creates an entity, attaches a camera component, and also adds a script to it that controls the camera. The script contains lots of options that you can configure.

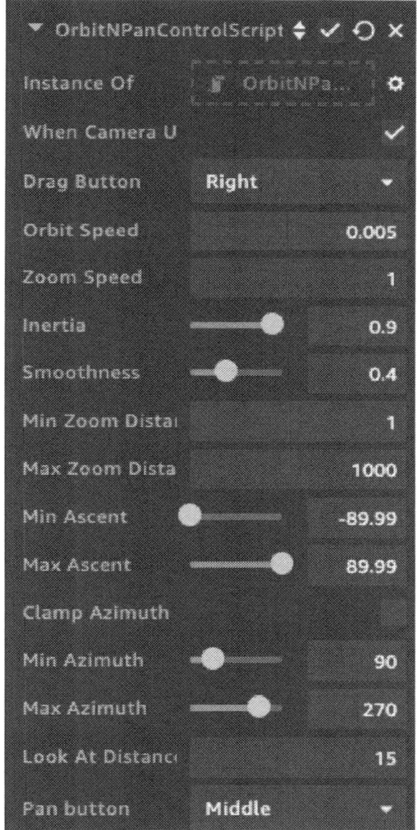

Using the Sumerian API, you can write your own control scheme. You'll learn about the API in Chapter 12, "The Sumerian API."

The **Fly** camera works using typical first-person controls. To move around a scene, you use the **WASD** keys. Looking is managed by pressing the left mouse button. It also contains a lot of configuration options.

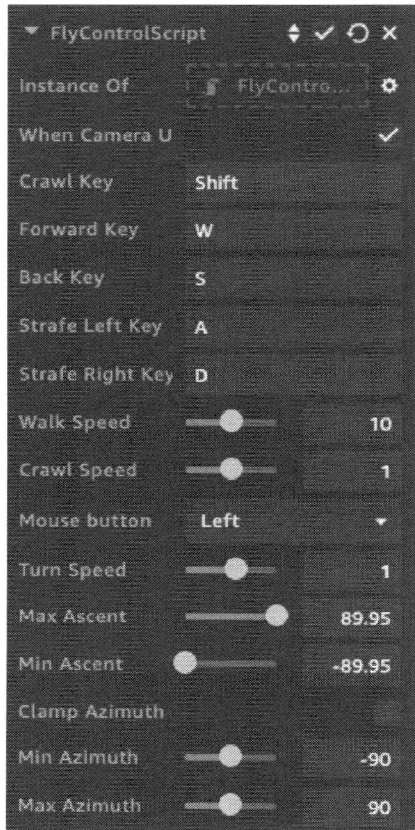

The **Fixed** camera is just an entity with a camera component attached to it. The camera is locked at a specific translation and rotation. The user can't manipulate it at all.

The **2D** camera is much like the Orbit camera, except it's best used to work with 2D elements. This camera flattens depth which makes it ideal for using images instead of models.

Understanding the 2D, and by extension the 3D camera as well, you need to understand two important concepts: Frustum and projection.

Projecting your frustum

After a long moment of silence, the psychiatrist exhales a long sigh and turns to the depressed camera. “The root of the problem,” she says, “is that you have a tendency to project your frustum onto others.”

Cameras like to project. This isn't a problem. It's why we like having cameras around. Yet, it's how cameras project that determines the look of your scene.

By default, cameras work very much like our eyes. As entities move closer to the camera, they will increase in size. Conversely, as they move back, they shrink as well. However, if they move too close or too far, they disappear.

This is the result of the frustum. A frustum is a pyramid with the top cut off. This frustum extends from the camera and projects into the scene. The frustum displays any objects that enter its view to the user.

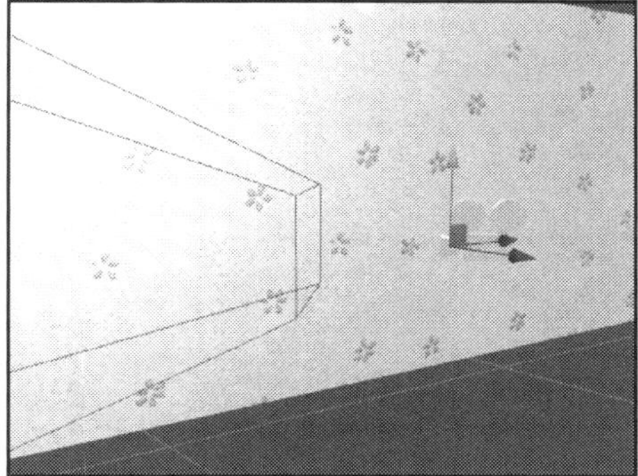

When you select a camera, Sumerian provides a preview of what will be displayed.

You run into issues when a model extends beyond the top of the frustum. When this happens, the part of the model that passes through the frustum is gone.

For example, if the camera was moved right against the bread machine, the console area is cut off.

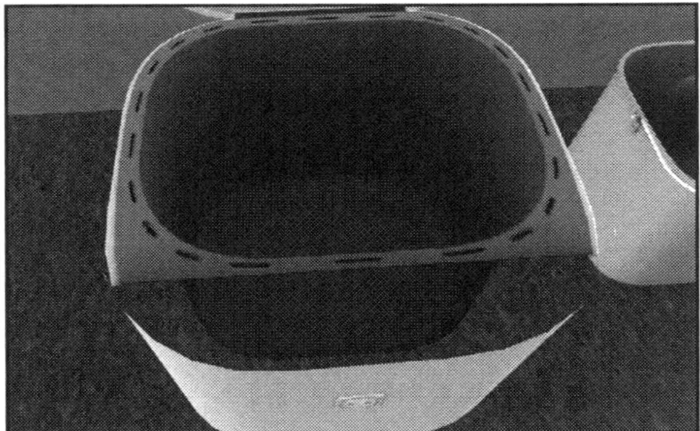

There are a few ways to fix this. First, you could move the camera away from the model. You could also move the model away from the camera. Finally, you can change the size of the frustum.

The camera component contains a section called Clipping Planes which determines the size of the frustum.

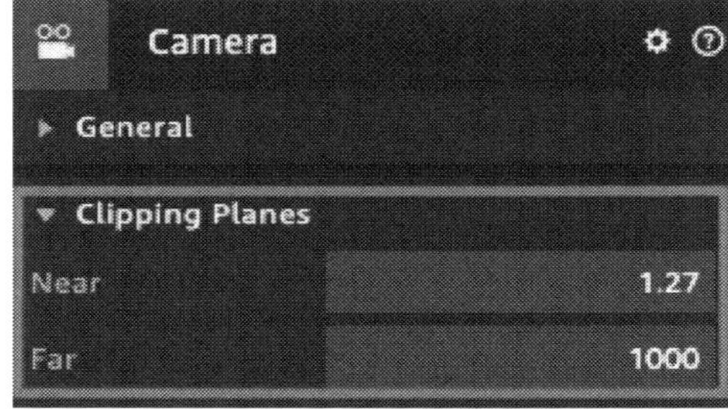

Decreasing the Near value decreases the space between the top of the frustum to the camera.

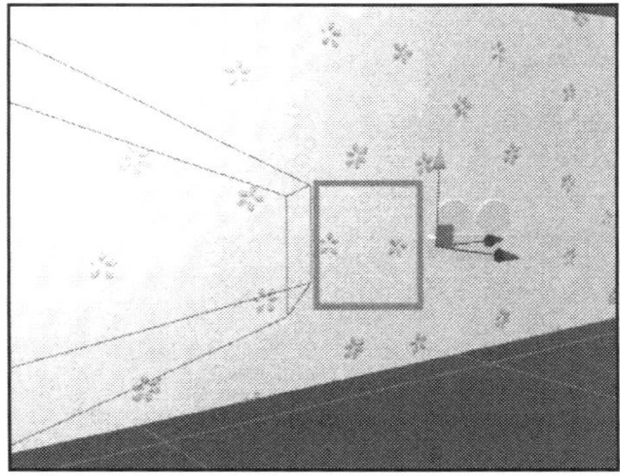

This shows more of the model, but it also may impact the performance of your scene. The Far value determines the overall size of the frustum. A larger size means that more objects will be rendered.

Like all things, you must weigh the pros and cons of the scene performance against what you are trying to do with the scene and how you are trying to do it.

Working with 2D

With 2D, things are a little different. With 2D, depth doesn't matter, yet you are still working in a 3D engine. To remove depth, you must change the camera's projection.

Switching the camera to a parallel projection changes how your scene will appear.

For example, the following screenshot contains cubes of equal size. The cube that is closer to the camera appears larger, whereas the cube further away looks to be smaller.

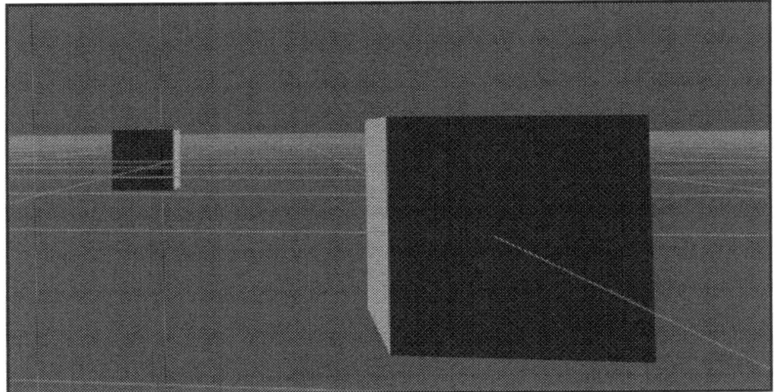

Switching to a parallel projection removes the depth from the scene. Now, both cubes are the same size regardless of distance and appear next to each other.

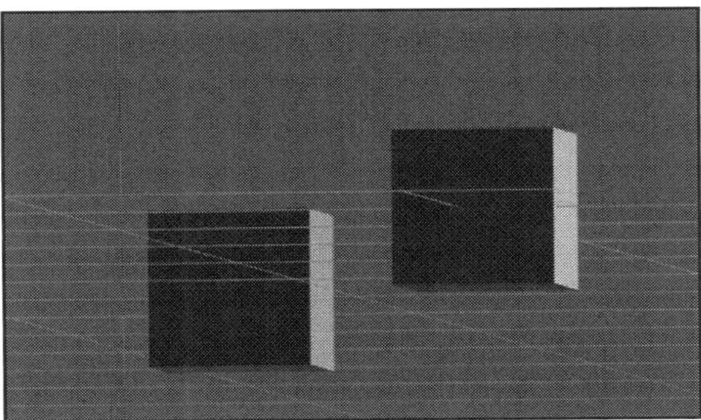

When you look at the camera, it is no longer projecting a frustum. It projects a long rectangle.

The parallel project does contain clipping planes like the frustum, but it also has a size to determine the size of the projection.

In summation, if you do anything with 2D, use the parallel projection.

Setting up cameras

Now that you understand cameras; it's time to put them to use. The first thing to do is to create a starting point.

Right now, the demo just starts, which can be disorientating. The user should initiate an action to begin the demo.

This isn't just a good strategy, it's a requirement for iOS devices. Apple requires that a Mouse Up/Touch end event fires before any sound is played.

> **Note**: Why a touch end versus a touch start? A touch end means that the user-initiated a complete touch. The user pressed down on the screen, and then lifted their finger off the screen. This indicates compliance. A canceled touch is when a user touches on an element, then slides the touching finger off of it. This indicates non-compliance.

Click **Create Entity** and select **Entity**. Rename it to **Cameras**. Now to create your cameras.

Click **Create Entity** again, and this time select a **Fixed Camera**. Name it **Demo Start Camera**. Set the Translation to (**5.446**, **4.73**, **-3.945**) and drag it into the **Cameras** entity.

This is how the scene will start; looking at some empty wallpaper.

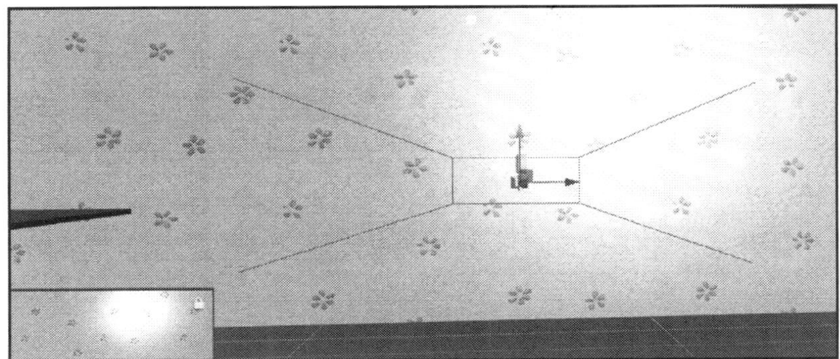

There is a hotspot due to the lighting, but you'll take care of that in a moment.

Of course, if you play the scene, the scene will start from the editor camera's position. This is because the editor camera is designated at the *Main Camera*. You can think of the Main Camera as the entry point to the scene.

There can only be one Main Camera, and you cannot delete a Main Camera. Every scene is required to have one. You can designate another camera to be the camera, and then delete the current camera.

Select the **Demo Start Camera**, and in the Camera component, check the **Main Camera checkbox**.

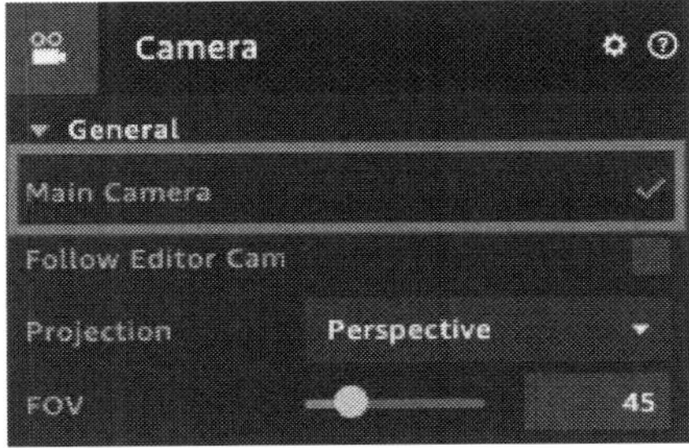

Now when you play the scene, you'll see your wallpaper in all its blazing glory. The narration also starts.

Click **Create Entity** and select a **Quad**. Name it **Start Button**. Set the Translation to (**5.356**, **4.391**, **-10.931**). Set the Scale to (**3.454**, **1**, **1**).

In the Assets panel, click **Import Assets**. Navigate to **resources/textures** and select **press-to-start.png**. Switch to the **Materials** tab and select the **Default Material**. Rename it to **Start Button Material**.

In the Inspector panel, set the **press-to-start.png** to the **COLOR (DIFFUSE)** category.

Your wall will look like this:

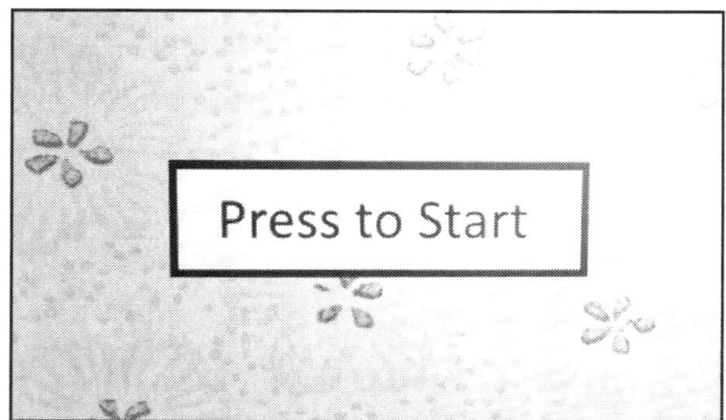

In the Entities panel, select the **Start Button**. Click **Add Component** and select **State Machine**. Click the + button to create a new behavior. Name it **Demo Start Button**.

Rename the first state to **Click to Start**. Click **Add Action** and in the Controls category, add a **Click/Tap on entity** acton.

Click **Add State** and name it **Switch Camera**. Drag transitions from the **Click to Start** state to the **Switch Camera** state.

Before you can switch cameras, you need to add a few more cameras.

Click **Create Entity** and select a **Fixed Camera**. Rename it to **Bread Machine Camera**.

Duplicate the camera and name the new camera **Bread Machine Closeup Camera**.

Duplicate your last camera and rename it to **Ingredients Camera**.

Now you have three cameras that cover different parts of the scene. Select the **Bread Machine Camera**. You want the camera to take a medium shot of the bread machine. First, set the Translation to (**-9.206**, **6.167**, **-7.077**). Set the Rotation to (**-46**, **90**, **0**).

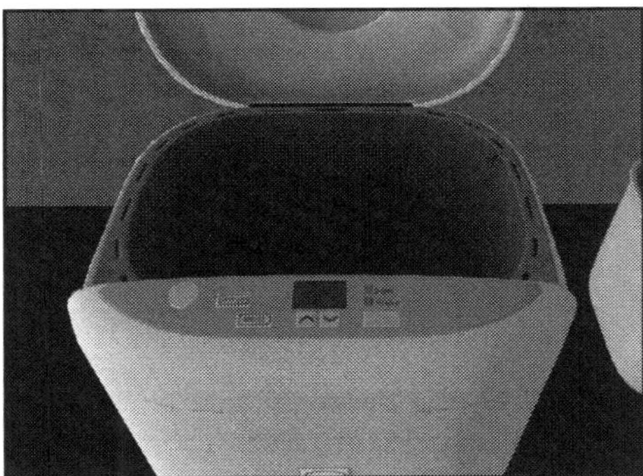

The camera is a little close to the bread machine. You can move the camera back, but you can also change the camera's field of vision (FOV). Lower numbers get closer to the subject whereas larger numbers move further away. This means you can perform an extreme closeup of a model without having the model break the frustum.

Set the FOV to **57** and now you'll get a fuller view of the machine.

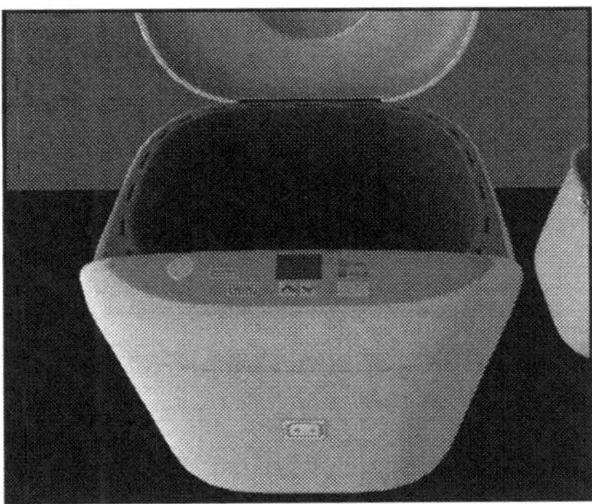

Note: When setting up a camera, it's helpful to set that camera to temporarily be the Main Camera. That way, you can play the scene and immediately see your adjustments.

Now that you are finished with the camera drag the **Bread Machine Camera** into the **Cameras** entity.

Select the **Bread Machine Closeup Camera**. Set the Translation to (**-9.217**, **6.007**, **-6.918**). Set the Rotation to (**-46**, **90**, **0**). Set the FOV to **23**. Drag the camera into the **Cameras** entity.

Now you get nice a close up of the console.

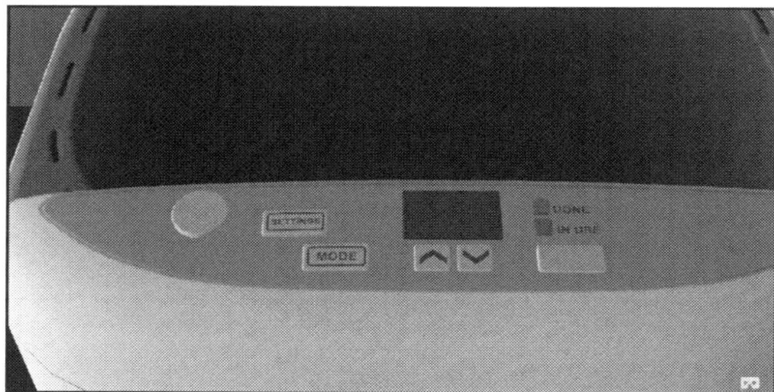

Select the **Ingredients Camera**. Set the Translation to (**-9.222**, **5.97**, **-9.12**). Set the Rotation to (**-46**, **90**, **0**). Set the FOV to **58**. Drag the camera into the **Cameras** entity.

You now have a nice view of all your ingredients.

As you can see, fixed cameras work great with "incomplete" sets. You don't need to build an entire kitchen if the user doesn't view it.

Switching between cameras

Now that you have your cameras all set up, you need to switch between them. A simple Switch Camera action handles this. This means adding additional states and making adjustments to your behaviors.

Open the **Demo Start Button** behavior and select the **Switch to Camera** state. Click **Add Action** and, in the Camera category, select the **Switch Camera** state.

Your new action will contain a drop-down of all the cameras in the scene. Select the **Bread Machine Camera**.

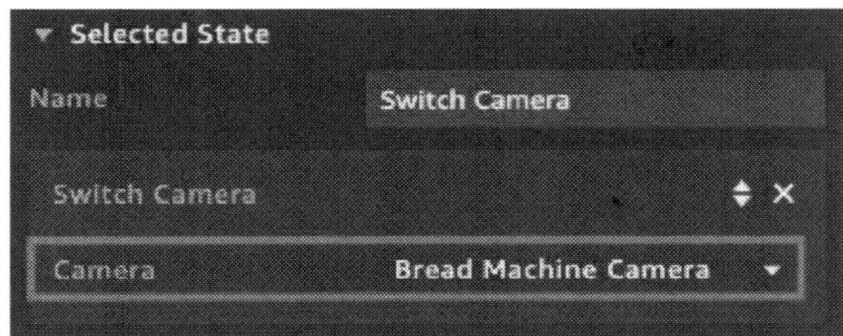

Click **Add Action** again and add an **Emit Message** action. Set the channel to **StartDemo**. You want the demo start before the switch action, so **drag** the Emit Message **above the Switch Camera**.

Open the **Bread Machine Demo** behavior. Click **Add State** and name it **Listen for Demo Start**. Add a **Listen** action to it and set the message channel to **StartDemo**. Drag a transition from **Listen for Demo Start** to **Play Introduction**. Finally, click **Set As Initial State**.

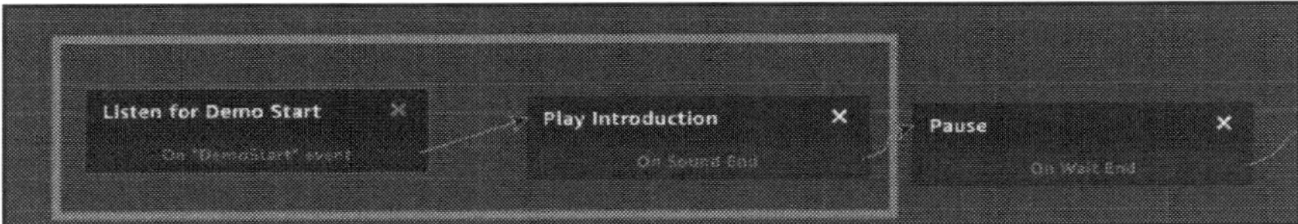

Now play your scene.

The scene is looking better. Now's a good time to incorporate your other cameras.

Select the **Bread Machine Demo** behavior and in the State Machine editor, select the **Pause** state. Rename it to **Switch to Closeup and Pause**. Click **Add Action** and in the Cameras category, add a **Switch Camera** action. Set the cameras to the **Bread Machine Closeup Camera** and drag it **above the Wait action**.

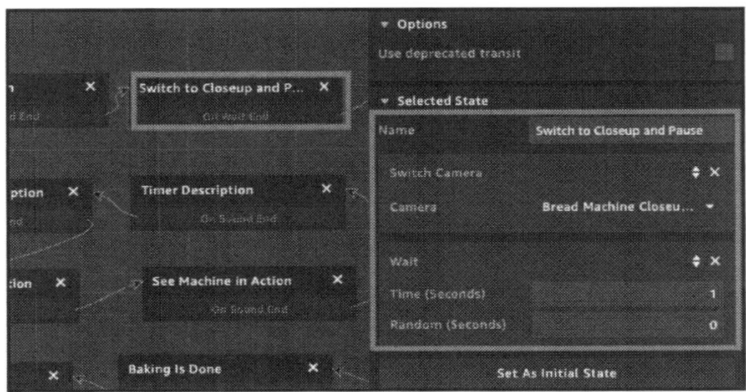

Select the **Simple Recipe** state. Rename it to **Simple Recipe and Switch Camera**. Add a **Switch Camera** action and set the action to use the **Ingredients Camera**. Drag the Switch Camera above the Play Sound action.

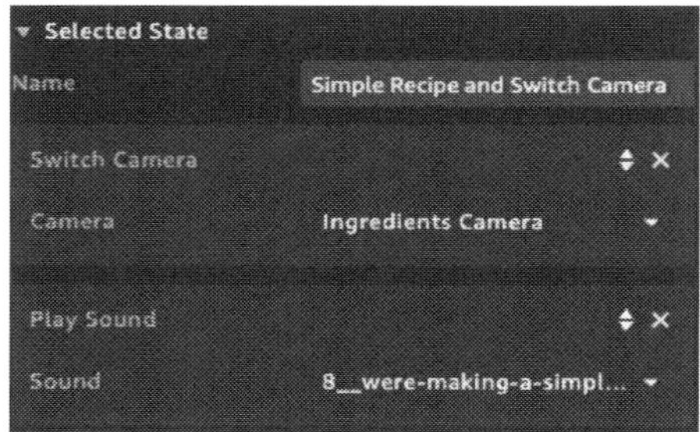

Select the **Press Start Button** state. Rename it to **Press Start and Switch Camera**. Add a **Switch Camera** action and set the action to use the **Bread Machine Camera**.

Now, play your scene, and you'll see it's coming together. As you can see, by directing the user where to look, it's now a focused experience.

Lights!

Providing scene content requires a camera and lights. These items are so important that Sumerian provides them with every new scene. This is why you haven't had to worry about them. But like cameras, lighting can be used to illustrate important aspects of your scene. You can use lights to direct attention which you'll do later in this chapter.

Sumerian provides three types of lights that you can use in your scene. Click **Create Entity** and look at the **Lights** category.

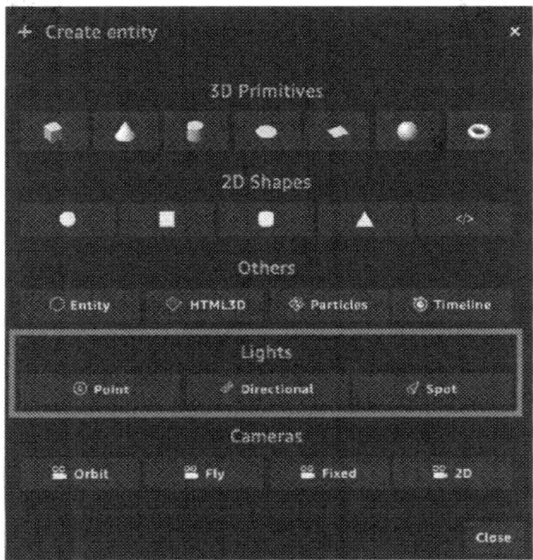

Clicking on one of these light options will create a light, but remember at the end of the day, a light is just an entity with a specialized component attached. Any entity can become a light by attaching a Light component to it.

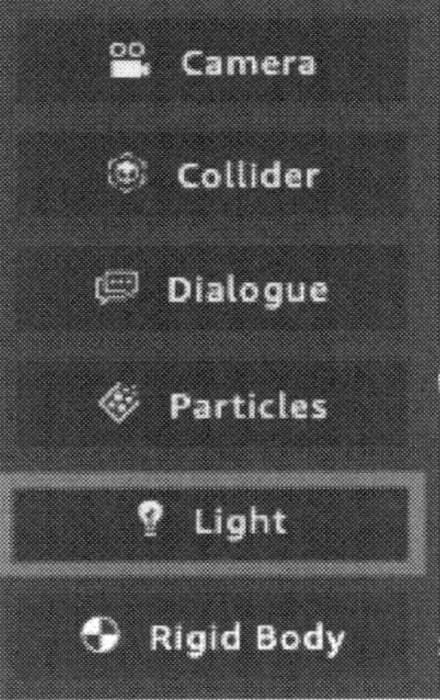

All lights come with three properties: Color, Intensity, and Specular. Color is the light color. By default, all lights use white light. Intensity determines the brightness of the light. Specular determines the brightness in the center of the light. You can think of a specular light as being very powerful in the center and gradually fading away.

Here's a light with low intensity (0.24) but a high specular setting (10):

Here's the same kind of light with a lower specular setting (2.77):

The three kinds of light available are a Directional light, a Point light, and Spotlight.

A **Directional** light acts like the sun. It lights your entire scene. Distance doesn't matter to a directional light.

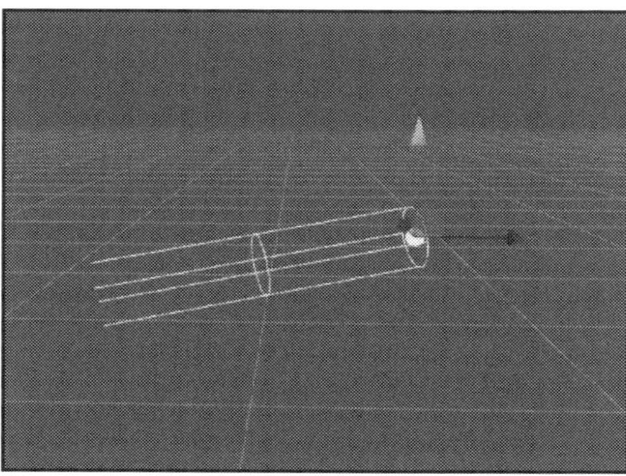

Directional lights do have a direction and can be rotated.

A **Point** light acts like a light bulb. The light provides a circular range around it, and anything within that range will be illuminated. The center of the sphere is a source, so it's the most powerful. The light grows less powerful towards the edge of the sphere.

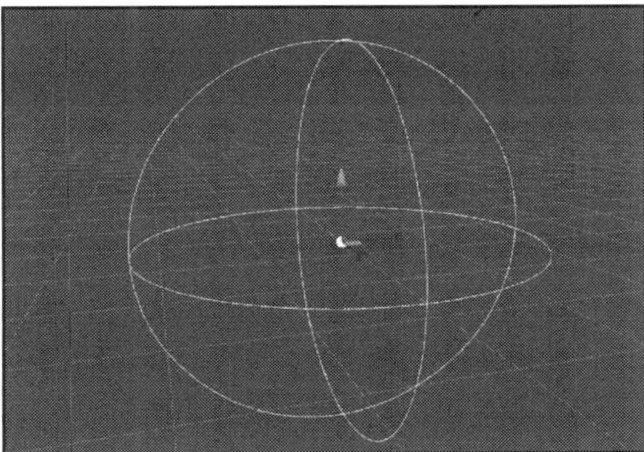

A **Spot** light is a powerful light that can be directed in a certain direction. The light is emitted in a cone that you can adjust.

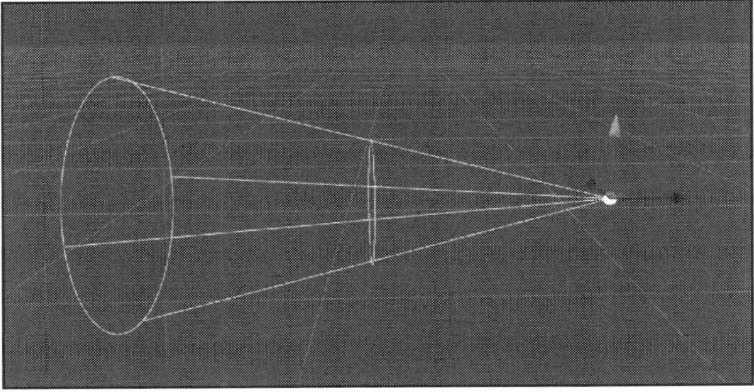

With lights, you get shadows. Because shadows take resources, you must opt-in to use them.

Every scene comes with two directional lights. In the Entities panel, select the **Key - Directional** light, which is located inside the Default Dynamic Lights entity. This is the light that is creating a hot spot. Hide the light by clicking the eyeball next to the light's name. You'll notice the entire scene goes dark.

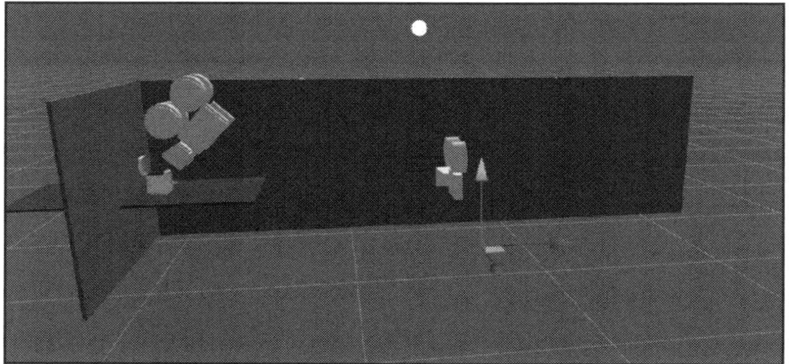

Show the light, and this time rotate it. You'll notice that the hotspot will move along the wall.

Once you are done rotating the light, revert it to its original location using the undo option.

Another way to remove the hotspot is to change the specular value. With **Key - Directional** still selected, set the Specular value to **0.21**. Now the hotspot goes away.

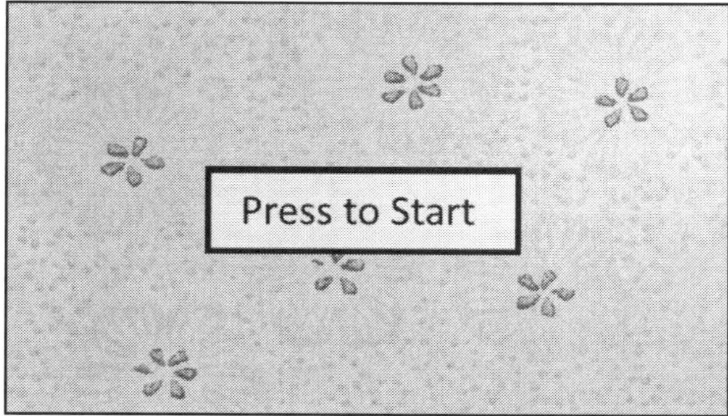

Lighting callouts

Throughout the experience, the narration describes important features of the Bread Machine's console. During this part of the experience, you switch to a close up of the console, but the user will still need help finding the appropriate button.

This is a great use for the spotlight. You can place a light over the button. When the appropriate button is mentioned, the light will turn off. When the discussion moves on to another feature, the light will turn off.

For this, you'll create five spotlights. Each spotlight will have a behavior associated with it.

> **Note**: Some buttons are missing their textures like the Open button and the Start button. You'll add these in an upcoming section.

Create the following spot lights and set their position and location according to the table:

Entity Name	Position X	Position Y	Position Z	Rotation X	Rotation Y	Rotation Z
Console Light	-10.024	5.374	-7.01	-90	-4	-1.59
Open Light	-10.028	5.374	-6.72	-90	-4	-1.59
Start Light	-9.964	5.374	-7.14	-90	-4	-1.59
Done Light	-10.036	5.262	-7.113	-90	-4	-1.59
In Use Light	-10.006	5.26	-7.113	0.540	90	0.055

Next, set the light properties of all the lights according to the table:

Entity Name	Color	Intensity	Specular	Cone Angle	Penumbra	Range
Console Light	#ffffff	2.77	2.22	35	5	0.63
Open Light	#ffffff	1.4	2.22	27	5	0.63
Start Light	#ffffff	1.45	2.22	21	5	0.63
Done Light	#00ff00	10	2.22	12	5	0.63
In Use Light	#ff9900	10	2.22	12	5	0.63

Your console will look like this:

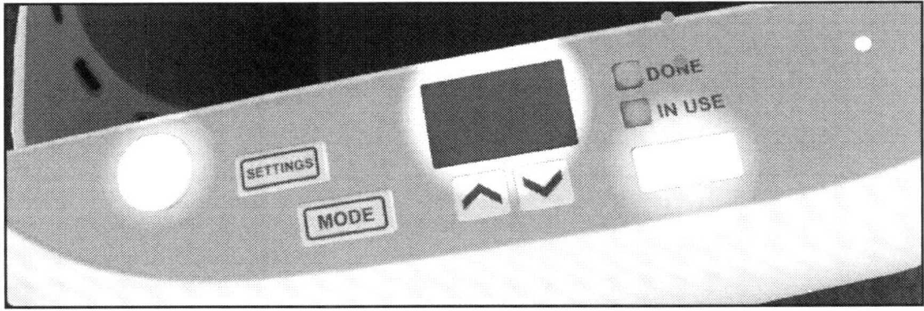

Hide your new lights and **Drag them** into the **Default Dynamic Lights** entity.

Each light must be able to turn on and turn off. To do this, you'll create five behaviors.

In the Assets panel, click the + button in the Default Pack and select **Behavior**. Name it **In Use Light**. Rename the default state to **Listen**.

Add two Listen actions. In the first listen action, set the message channel to **TurnOnInUse**. For the second action, set it to **TurnOffInUse**.

Click **Add State** and name your new state to **Turn On**. Add a **Show Action** and a **Transition Action** to it.

Click **Add State** again and name your new state to **Turn Off**. Add a **Hide Action** and a **Transition Action** to it.

Drag a transition from the **ON "TurnOnInUse"** event to the **Turn On** state. Drag another transition from the **ON "TurnOffInUse"** event to the **Turn Off** state.

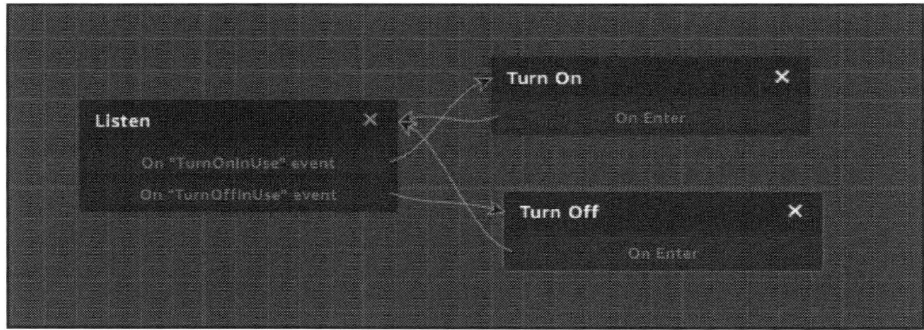

Duplicate this behavior four more times. Update it for each light and **assign each behavior to the appropriate light**. When you finished, you should have the following behaviors: **In Use Light, Done Light, Console Light, Open Light and Start light**

> **Note**: Sumerian also includes an option to change the values of a light. In this case, it's easier to just hide a light. Also, in Chapter 12, "The Sumerian API," you'll learn how to leverage the API to get rid of all these duplicate behaviors and control the lights from one entity.

Integrating the lights

At this point, all you need to do to integrate the lights is to send out messages. The behaviors will take care of the rest.

Open the **Bread Machine Demo** behavior. Select the **Start Button Description** state. Add an **Emit Message** state and set the channel to **TurnOnStart**.

Next, select the **In Use Description** state. Add an **Emit Message** state and set the channel to **TurnOffStart**. Add a **Wait** action to it and set it to **2**. **Remove** the transition from the **On Sound End**. Create a transition from **On Wait End** to **Pause 3**.

Select the **Pause 3** state. Rename it to **Turn on In Use and Pause**. Add an **Emit Message** action and set it to **TurnOnInUse**. Change the time for the Wait action to **2.75**.

Select the **Timer Description** state. **Add two Emit Message actions**. Set one channel to **TurnOffInUse** and set the other to **TurnOnConsole**.

Select the **Done Button Description** state. **Add two Emit Message actions**. Set one channel to **TurnOffConsole** and set the other to **TurnOnDone**.

Select the **Open Button Description** state. **Add two Emit Message actions**. Set one channel to **TurnOffDone** and set the other to **TurnOnOpen**.

Finally, select the **See Machine in Action** state. Add an **Emit Message** action and set the channel to **TurnOffOpen**.

Now, play your scene. Now you all the various aspects of the machine are illustrated with light.

ACTION!

You've set up your cameras, and you've positioned your lights. Now, you need a little action to the scene. Your console contains two buttons that drive the demo forward. Both of these buttons are blank.

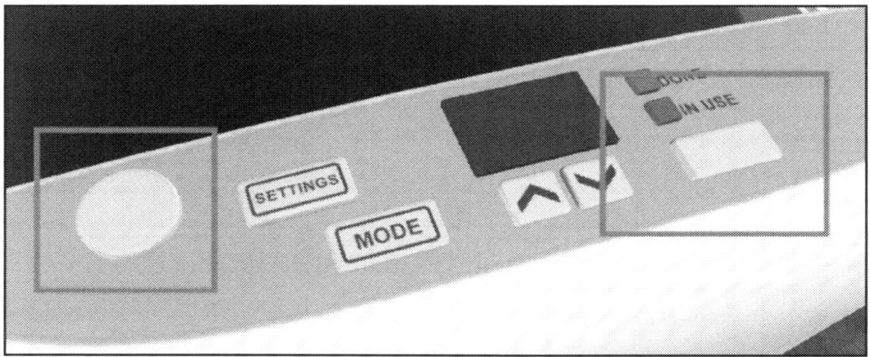

This was very much intentional. When the user clicks or taps the button, an action should occur. You could add a behavior on the Bread Machine, but this means the entire machine would respond to the action as opposed to just the button.

To make a part of the model intractable, you need to add it as a separate entity. In your case, you'll use quads for entities. By adding images onto the quads and placing the quads on the bread machine, it appears that the user is pressing a button.

The Start button

Once the user has added all the ingredients to the bread machine, they start the baking process by pressing the start button. The Start button is a quad with texture added to it.

To get started, click **Create Entity** and select the **Quad**. Name it **Baking Start Button**.

Set the Translation to (**-9.963**, **5.141**, **-7.142**). Set the Rotation to (**-75.991**, **91**, **-1.991**). Set the Scale to (**0.073**, **0.031**, **7.109**).

Next, in the Assets panel, click the **Import files from your computer** button. Look in **resources/textures** and select **But-Start.png**. Once it's imported, switch to the **Materials** tab. Select the **Default Material** and rename it **Baking Start Button Material**. Next, switch to the **Textures** tab and drag **But-Start.png** to the **COLOR (DIFFUSE)** category.

Next, in the Material component, expand the **OPACITY** and check the **Enabled** checkbox.

Congrats! You now have a new start button!

With the Start Button still selected, click the **Add Component** button. Add a **State Machine** and click the + button to add a new behavior. Name it **Baking Start Button**.

Rename the first state to **Listen for Button Activation**. Add a **Listen** action and set the message channel to **ActivateStartButton**.

Click the **Add State** button and rename it to **Click Button**. Add a **Click** action to it.

Create one more state and name it **Emit Message to Start Cooking**. Add an **Emit Message** action and set the channel to **StartCooking**.

Now for the transitions. Drag a transition from the **Listen for Closed Lid** event to the **Click Button** state. Next drag a transition from the **Click Button** state to the **Emit Message to Start Cooking** state.

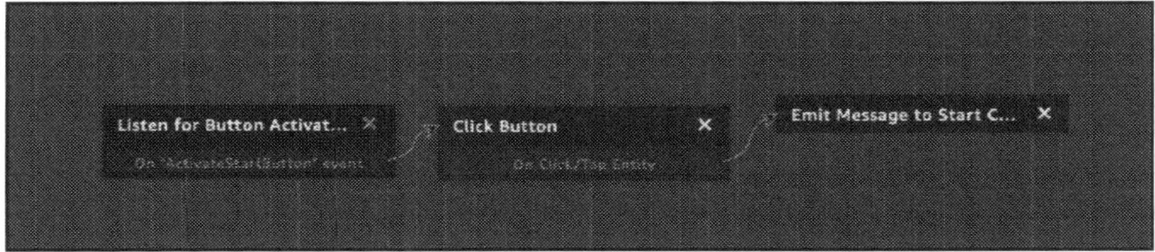

Now to integrate it with the rest of the scene. Open the **Bread Machine Demo** behavior.

Click **Add State** and name your state to **Activate Start Button**. Add an **Emit Message** and set the channel to **ActivateStartButton**. Also, add a **Transition** action to it as well.

You'll need a state for when the bread is cooking. Click **Add State** and name the new state **Start Cooking**. Add a **Listen** action to it. Have the state listen to the **StartCooking** channel. Later, you'll produce a custom countdown, but for now, you'll just transition it to another state.

Drag a transition from the **Press Start Button and Switch Camera** state to the **Activate Start Button** state then drag a transition from the **Activate Start Button** to the **Start Cooking** state. Finally, add a transition from the **Start Cooking** state to the **Baking Is Done** state.

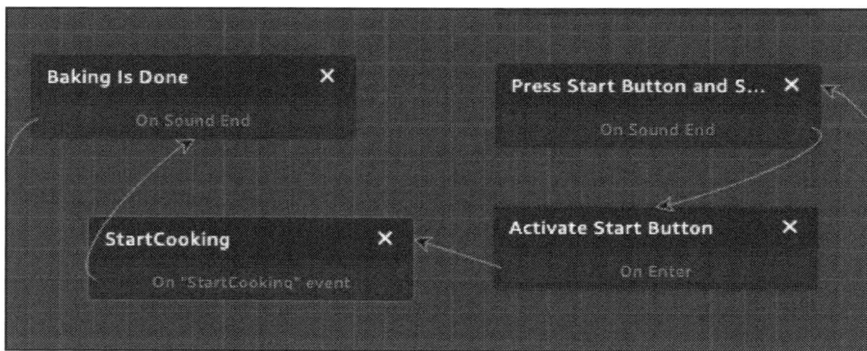

Now, your demo will wait for the user to press the start button. Next comes the open button.

The Open button

This button pretty much replicates the start button.

Click **Create Entity** and select the **Quad**. Name it **Open Button**. Set the Translation to (**-10.028**, **5.147**, **-6.721**). Set the Rotation to (**-80.484**, **89.999**, **3.819**). Set the Scale to (**0.061**, **0.059**, **0.347**).

Next, in the Assets panel, select **Import files from your computer** icon. Look in **resources/textures** and select **But-OpenClose.png**. Once imported, switch to the **Materials** tab. Select the **Default Material** and name **Open Material**. Switch to the **Textures** tab. Drag the **But-OpenClose.png** texture to the **COLOR (DIFFUSE)** category. Next, expand the **OPACITY** and check the **Enabled** checkbox.

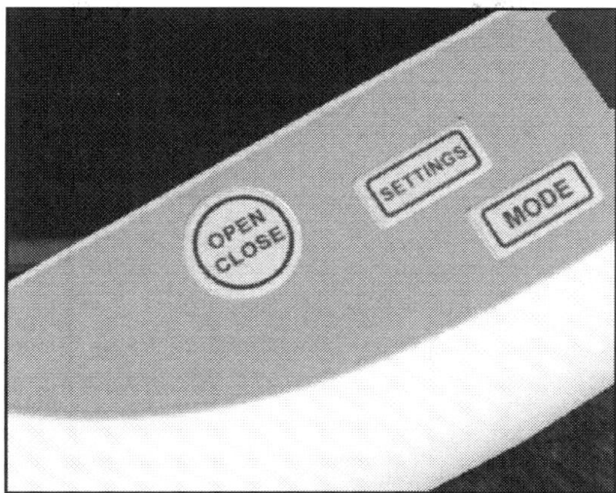

With the Open Button still selected, click **Add Component**. Add a **State Machine** and click the + button to add a new behavior. Name it **Open Button**.

Rename the first state to **Listen for Activation**. Add a **Listen** action and set the message channel to **ActivateOpenButton**.

Click the **Add State** button and rename it to **Click Button**. Add a **Click** action to it.

Create one more state and name it **Emit Message to Open Lid**. Add an **Emit Message** action and set the channel to **OpenLid**.

Now for the transitions. Drag a transition from the **Listen for Activation** event to the **Click Button** state. Next, drag a transition from **Click Button** to the **Emit Message to Open Lid** state.

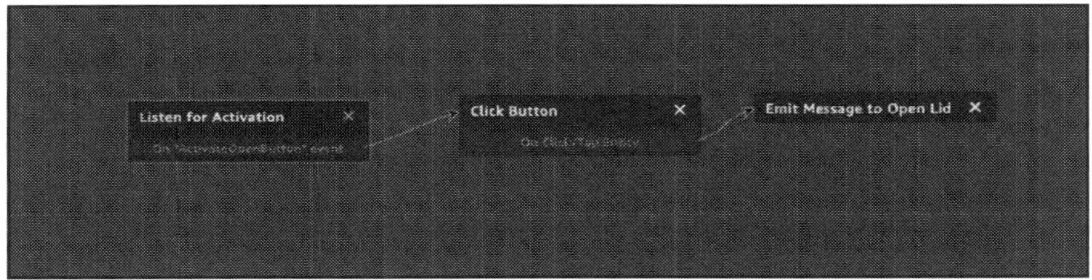

With the button ready to go, you need to integrate it with the rest of the demo.

Now, open the **Bread Machine Demo** behavior. Click **Add State** and name it **Activate Open Button**. Add an **Emit** and **Transition** action to it. Set the Emit action to use the **ActivateOpenButton** channel. This will allow the user to press the button.

Click **Add State** and name the state to **Wait for Open Button Press**. Add a **Listen** action. In the Listen action, set the channel to **OpenLid**.

Drag a transition from the **Baking is Done** state to the **Activate Open Button** state. Then drag a transition from the **Activate Open Button** state to the **Wait for Open Button Press**. Then from the **Wait for Open Button Press** state to the **Fresh Loaf of Bread** state.

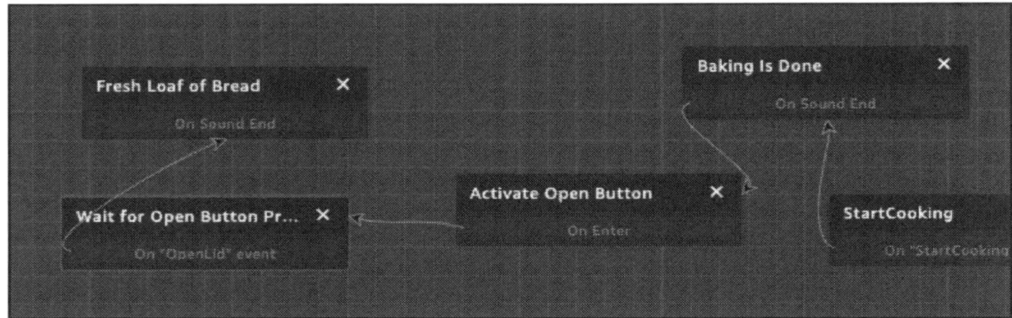

Now, run your scene from beginning to end. Your scene plays out, but the demo will stop to prompt the user to press the start button and then the open button.

As you can see, the demo is coming together. There is a lot of behavior duplication occurring, and it would be nice to add some additional interactivity. Thankfully, you do this with the Sumerian API, but before you learn the API, you first must understand JavaScript, which is the topic of the upcoming chapter.

Key points

- Sumerian provides many different camera types such as the **Fly, Fixed, and 2D camera**.
- If you need a specific camera type that doesn't exist, **you can always write your own**.
- Cameras project a frustum. Only the **objects inside the frustum will be rendered**.
- The projection determines how the entities will appear. A **perspective projection adds depth** whereas a **parallel projection removes depth**.
- Change the clipping panes to increase or decrease the frustum.
- Sumerian provides three light types: a directional, point and spot.
- A **directional** light **globally illuminates** the scene.

- A **spot** light is a **powerful light emitted in a cone**.
- A **point** light is emitted in a **circular range**.

Where to go from here?

Lighting and cameras determine what the end-user will ultimately see. To learn more about lighting and cameras, check out this tutorial on both of the systems: https://docs.sumerian.amazonaws.com/tutorials/create/getting-started/camera-light/}

Chapter 11: Introduction to JavaScript

By Brian Moakley

Sumerian is a 3D engine built using web technologies such as HTML, CSS, and JavaScript. When you build web pages, you use both HTML and CSS to provide the look of the page, whereas JavaScript provides interactivity.

So far, you've been able to add interactivity in your scenes by using behaviors, but behaviors will only take you so far. For example, you may want to leverage AWS to provide live chatting or to search a database. For this work, you need to use JavaScript.

Now, some of you may be thinking, "I don't plan on using external services, so I don't need to know JavaScript." Learning JavaScript also means saving time in the editor.

In the current scene, you created five lights that activate and deactivate based on messages sent to their behaviors. You created a behavior for each light. Imagine you were working on a complicated scene and were employing a hundred different lights. If you used only behaviors, you'd need to maintain a hundred different behaviors, each one identical except for its listening channel. Using JavaScript, you only need to write two scripts, which you'll do in Chapter 12, "The Sumerian API."

That said, learning a language can be difficult, especially if you've never written code. This chapter will give you a quick introduction to working with JavaScript. It will give you enough knowledge to follow the rest of the book.

If you want to dive deep with the language, you'll need to spend some time learning it. After all, there are entire books that cover what this single chapter aims to do. Thankfully, there are lots of free resources on the web to help you along.

Getting started

JavaScript is a web technology that you use to provide interactivity. Sumerian is built in a way to leverage JavaScript It's a great tool to learn and play around with the language.

Launch the Sumerian dashboard and select the **Bread Maker 6-500** project. Click **Create new scene** and name the new scene **Learning JavaScript**.

To get started, click **Create Entity** and select a **Box** entity. This will be your test subject.

When you write a script, you attach it to entities by way of components. Entities can have lots of scripts.

Click **Add Component** and select the **Script**. This adds an empty script component. Click the + button to add a new script.

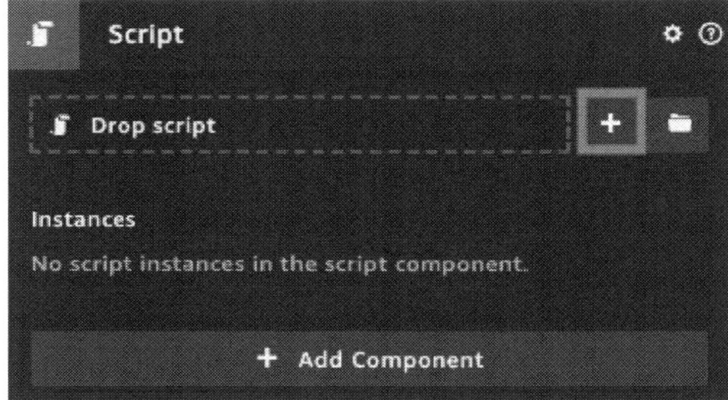

After you click the button, you're presented with different prebuilt scripts. These scripts provide various behaviors for your game, such as flying, WASD controls and even adding lens flares.

Since you're learning JavaScript, you'll select a custom script. At the time of this writing, you can choose either the Preview Format or the Legacy Format. The Preview Format is the future of Sumerian, so select **Custom (Preview Format)**.

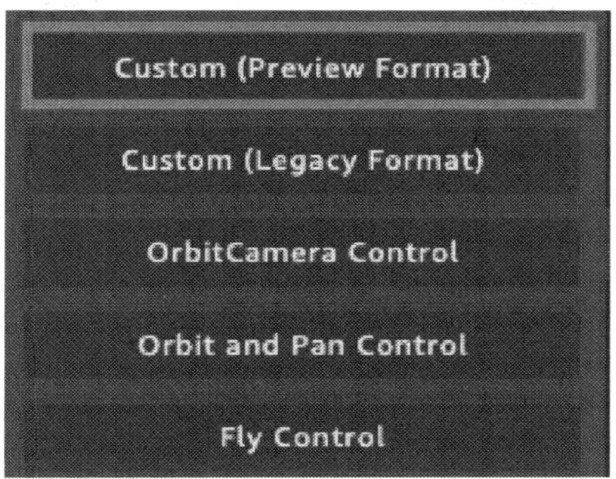

When you add a script, you get a script instance listed in the Script component. With some scripts, you can provide additional customization much like any other component. You'll learn how to do this in Chapter 12, "The Sumerian API."

Your scripts are also shown in the Assets panel. In the Assets panel, select the **Script** tab and you'll see that it appears like any other asset. Select your **Script**. You'll see it has details, tags and custom attributes. Rename this script to **Hello JavaScript**. To edit the script, click **Edit in Text Editor**.

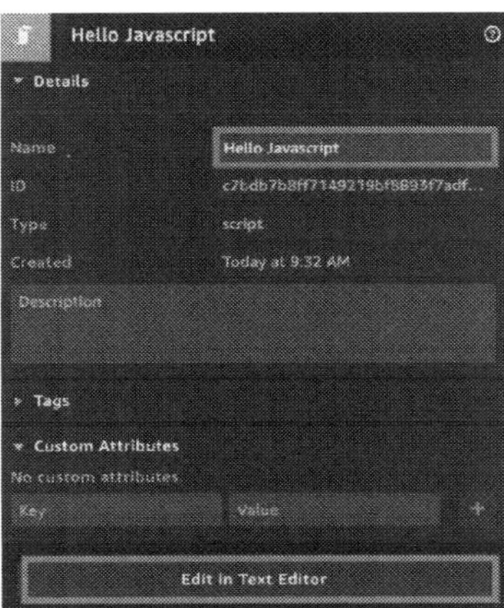

The text editor is where you write all your scripts. This editor acts as a mini Integrated Developer Environment (IDE). It performs code completion, has integrated documentation and allows you to switch between all your scripts.

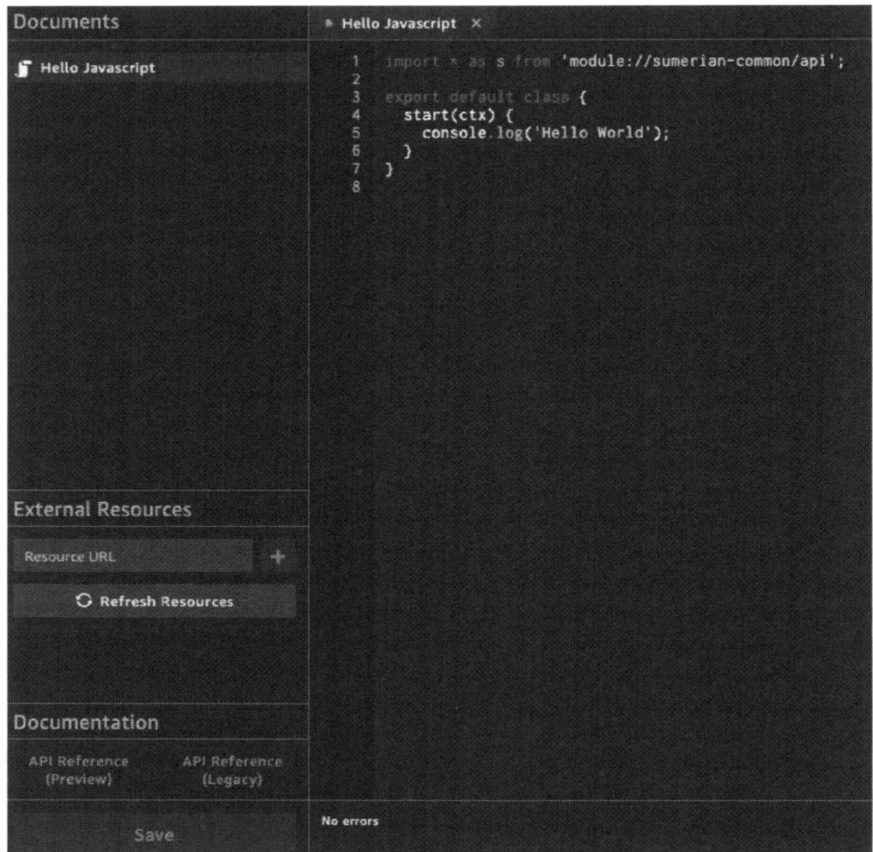

> **Note**: While the text editor does a fine job at editing scripts, there are plans to allow external editors to work with Sumerian. However, there's no estimated delivery date yet.

Now comes the fun part: Writing JavaScript!

Java vs JavaScript

JavaScript is often confused with Java. While the names are similar, JavaScript and Java are quite different in both syntax and execution. It's important to understand this because as you start writing in JavaScript, it's natural to ask for help.

Asking a Java programmer for help with your JavaScript project is the equivalent of asking a Mandarin speaker to help with your Japanese. At best, you can expect an exaggerated eye roll served with a long, "Why do I even bother?" sigh. This isn't your fault.

You can trace the confusion between Java and JavaScript back to the 90s, with the release of the Java programming language. The language made waves with its release. It promised a "write once, run everywhere" approach to coding. This meant your Java programs could run on any platform that supported the Java environment.

During this time, Netscape Communications was competing for market share on the web. Netscape produced the popular Netscape browser. The company needed a language to produce dynamic web pages. They created a language called LiveScript. Being that Java was incredibly popular at the time, Netscape renamed LiveScript to JavaScript, thus seeding confusion for decades to come.

Believe it or not, the confusion doesn't end there: JavaScript isn't even the official name. When Netscape submitted JavaScript for standardization, there was a lot of arguing over the name, so the standards body (ECMA) named it after itself. JavaScript's true name is ECMAScript.

Thus, you'll often see the language version stated as ES6, which stands for ECMAScript 6 which is JavaScript version 6. In short, if you aren't confused, consider yourself one of the lucky few! :]

Your first script

In almost every textbook about programming, your first task is to print out some text. This book is no exception. With the Sumerian text editor open, **erase the existing code**.

Write the following exactly as you see it. Capitalization and punctuation matter. A computer requires precise code:

```
console.log("Hello Sumerian");
```

If this is your first line of code, congrats! Welcome to a brave, new, exciting world. You'll notice that `Hello Sumerian` is just text, otherwise known as a **string**.

The semicolon at the end of the statement indicates the end of the line of code. The semicolon acts as a period in code. If you forget a semicolon, JavaScript will add one for you. There are cases where this may cause problems, so it's a good habit to always provide your own semicolons.

Click **Save** and close the text editor. To see your results, you need to open your browser's developer tools.

For a browser like Chrome or Firefox, simply press **F12**. For other browsers, you'll need to look up how to enable the developer tools.

Most developer tools contain a tab named Console. This is where you'll find messages from the current web page. These messages can be helpful when debugging web page issues.

Click on the **Console** tab and you'll see a bunch of text followed by your own message: "Hello Sumerian".

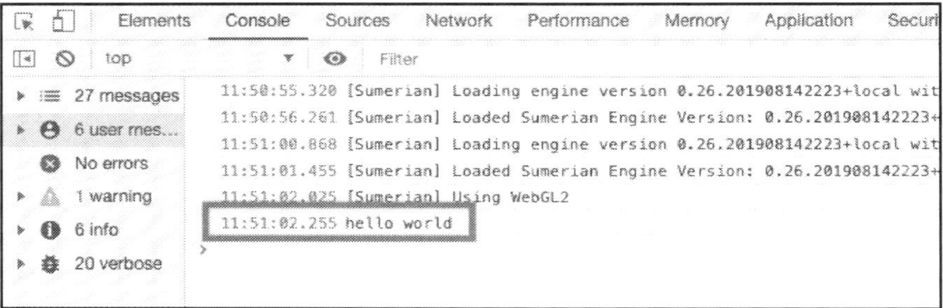

> **Note**: Some consoles print out a lot of unimportant text. Some of these consoles will let you filter the text.

If you made a typo, then you'll see a message like the following:

```
11:51:02.025 [Sumerian] Using WebGL2                                          Capabilities.js:63
11:51:02.255 hello world                                 sumerian-custom-scri…b3.script.js?v=1:17
11:52:48.914 ▸ [Sumerian] An error occurred at line 1 when loading the "Hello Javascript"   ScriptProxy.js:407
             script. SyntaxError: Invalid or unexpected token
               ErrorEvent {isTrusted: true, message: "Uncaught SyntaxError: Invalid or unexpected token", filenam
             ▸ e: "sumerian-custom-scripts/c7bdb7b8ff7149219bf8893f7adf8cb3.script.js?v=2", lineno: 17, colno: 19
               , …}
```

While the errors will point to the line, the descriptions can be a bit vague. Over time, you'll understand the meaning of these cryptic messages. For now, just compare your code with the code in the book. Remember, you must copy the code **exactly**.

When you add the code and save the file, the message prints to the console. Typically, code will only run when you play your scene. Later, you'll designate when the code runs. For now, keep checking the console after you save a file.

JavaScript variables

When working with programs, you'll often create variables to store data. If you've done any Algebra, variables should be old hat to you.

For example:

```
x = 5
y = 10
z = x + y
```

Can you guess the value of `z`? The answer is 15. To perform that equation, you substituted the numbers for the letters. So the following equation:

```
z = x + y
```

Is evaluated, like so:

```
z = 5 + 10
```

You do the same with JavaScript, except you can use different kinds of data. In `Hello JavaScript`, add the following:

```
var name = "Ray";
var tutorialsWritten = 300
var likesSumerian = true;
```

You've defined three variables. You define a variable by using the `var` keyword. Keywords are special words determined by the language. These words are reserved, meaning you can't create a variable named `var`. In this case, `var` creates a variable for you.

As you can see, you write `var`, provide the variable name and then assign a value.

You write variable names in lowercase. Variables can't contain spaces, so if you want a variable name to have multiple words in it, you capitalize subsequent words. Thus, you express "tutorials written" as `tutorialsWritten`.

You use = to assign a value, not to test equality. You'll learn about equality momentarily.

Finally, when you assign a value, it must conform to a certain type. To create a `string` (text), you must put your text between quotes. To create a number, you can just write it as a regular number. In JavaScript, a number can be an integer or it can contain floating point values (`3.14159`). You can also create Boolean variables, which are either `true` or `false`.

You can always change the variables you created above. If you want a variable to be fixed and unchanging, you create a constant, like this:

```
const daysInYear = 365;
```

The `daysInYear` variable is now fixed to `365`. Changing it produces an error.

Trying this:

```
daysInYear = 10;
```

Will result in this:

```
15:29:21.926 ▸ [Sumerian] An error occurred at line 8 when loading the "Hello Javascript" script. Assignment to constant variable. TypeError: Assignment to constant variable.
    at window._sumerianScriptFactories.c7bdb7b8ff7149219bf8893f7adf8cb3.script (sumerian-custom-scri…3.script.js?v=36:24)
    at ScriptProxy_ScriptProxy._getCustomScriptObject (ScriptProxy.js:175)
    at ScriptProxy_ScriptProxy._updateCustomScriptObject (ScriptProxy.js:89)
    at ScriptProxy.js:55
```

Even the editor will let you know there's a problem.

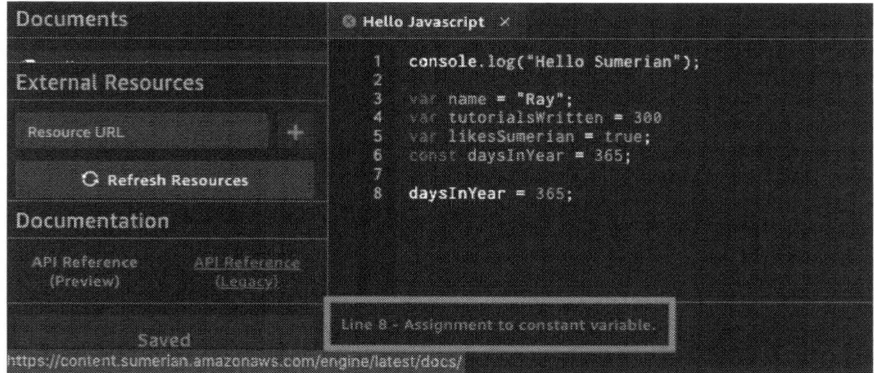

Now delete the line and add the following code:

```
console.log(name + " has written over " + tutorialsWritten + "
tutorials.");
```

Save the code and switch back to Sumerian. You'll see the following in the console:

```
Ray has written over 300 tutorials.
```

Here, you combined various strings to produce a new string. Notice that when you add a number to a string, you produce a new string.

Using + is a great way to add items. What if you wanted to increase the number of `tutorialsWritten` by one?

Add the following:

```
tutorialsWritten = tutorialsWritten + 1;
console.log(tutorialsWritten);
```

Here, you increase the number of `tutorialsWritten` by one and then assign the result back to `tutorialsWritten`. This results in 301.

This is such a common operation, you can also write it like so:

```
tutorialsWritten += 1;
```

This is the shorthand method of increasing items. Believe it or not, you can even further shorten it to:

```
tutorialsWritten++;
```

> **Note**: You'll see this last approach used in a lot of loops (as it's the convention), but it's a good rule of thumb to avoid it when you can as it can introduce subtle errors. In fact, the operation is so prone to subtle bugs that some modern languages like Swift have removed it. If you're interested in more information, just search for `increment operation danger`.

Arrays

Oftentimes, you'll work with related variables. Imagine that you want to track quiz results for a class. You could write variables like the following:

```
var quiz1 = 85;
var quiz2 = 92;
var quiz3 = 65;
var quiz4 = 89;
```

This becomes a headache as you add more quizzes. With arrays, you can group multiple values. Add the following:

```
var quizzes = [85, 92, 65, 89];
```

Your quizzes variable now contains multiple values. The brackets always indicate an array. When you add items, you put commas between them. You can add as many items as you want.

To access them, you need to specify an index. An index is basically saying, "give me a quiz at the following location."

The index is zero-based, which means the first item in the array is at the `0` index. So, for example, to print out the third quiz, add the following:

```
console.log(quizzes[2]);
```

The following will print out:

```
65
```

A common error is to forget that you start counting with zero. In these cases, a person may try to get the fourth element by writing the following:

```
console.log(quizzes[4]);
```

While the programmer thinks they're accessing the fourth element, they are actually accessing the fifth element. Unfortunately, the fifth element doesn't exist.

Try running the code. You'll get the following:

```
undefined
```

In a programming language like Java, the entire app would crash. With JavaScript, the browser just lets you know that there is no value in the fifth index.

An array is a type of object, and objects can contain properties. If you want to know the number of elements in an array, write the following:

```
console.log(quizzes.length);
```

When you save, you'll the result printed to the console.

```
4
```

This is useful when you are looping through arrays as you'll see in a moment.

JavaScript allows arrays to contain different types of variables. For example, add the following:

```
var chris = ["Editor in Chief", 240, true];
```

You'll make use of mixed-typed arrays when working with Sumerian.

Using `const`, you can fetch the data in a way that makes sense. Try the following:

```
const companyTitle = 0;
const publishedTutorials = 1;
const enjoysSumerian = 2;

console.log("Chris is the " + chris[companyTitle]);
console.log("Chris has written " + chris[publishedTutorials] + "
tutorials.");
console.log("Does Chris like Sumerian? " +
chris[enjoysSumerian]);
```

Looking through the code, the meaning of the array index is clear. At glance, it's easier to infer the meaning of `chris[companyTitle]` from code such as `chris[0]`.

When in doubt, write your code in favor of readability and clarity.

> **Note**: When using `const` variables, you must create new variable names. You can't reuse existing variables as constants.

Looping through values

You've defined an array of quiz results and now you want to average all the results. Add the following:

```
var average = (quizzes[0] + quizzes[1] + quizzes[2] +
quizzes[3]) / 4;
console.log(average);
```

Here you've added all the quiz results together. Notice that you put the addition in parentheses. JavaScript adheres to the order of operations, meaning certain math operations occur first. Because of this, division has higher precedence so JavaScript will try to divide first, which won't return the result you're expecting. By using parentheses, you specify that you want to evaluate the addition before the division.

If you're confused about the order of operations, do a web search for **PEMDAS**.

When you run the code, you get the following result:

```
82.75
```

What happens if you add more quizzes? You would have to update your calculation for every new quiz. Remember, you write code to save time.

Thankfully, loops are a great tool to use. Loops automate the grunt work for you. In the next example, you'll create a `for` loop. A `for` loop will run a predetermined amount of time defined by you.

Add the following:

```
var gradeTotal = 0; // 1
for (var i = 0; i < quizzes.length; i++) { // 2
    gradeTotal += quizzes[i]; // 3
} // 4
```

There's a lot going on here. Time to break it down:

1. This line creates a new variable to store your grade total. Notice the // at the end. That indicates a JavaScript comment. JavaScript will ignore any code or text after the //. Comments are a great way to write notes in your code.
2. This is the actual loop. It starts with the `for` keyword followed by a parenthesis. There are three statements in the parentheses: The first creates an `i` variable that manages the duration of the loop. The `i` starts at zero, which is the first element of the array. The next statement determines how many times the loop will run. In this case, the loop will run while `i` **is less than** the number of quizzes. The length is four and the loop will run while `i` is less than four. Finally, the last statement will run after each loop. In this case, the `i` variable is being increased by 1. You'll notice an opening brace. This is the start of the loop body.
3. This is the body of the loop that will run with each iteration of the loop. This statement gets the quiz for the current loop iteration and adds it to the `gradeTotal`.
4. The closing brace indicates the end of a loop. All the code between the braces will run. Remember that when you have an opening brace, you must have a closing brace.

Now, add the following after the loop:

```
var averageTotal = gradeTotal / quizzes.length;
console.log(averageTotal);
```

This calculates the average based on the length of the array. Now, you can add as many items as you want to the array and you'll always get the correct average.

Save the script and check out the console:

```
82.75
```

Now, add the following **before** the loop.

```
quizzes.push(39, 97, 56);
```

This allows you to add three more quiz results to the array. **Save** the array, and you'll see a different average.

```
74.71428571428571
```

There are a few other arrays you'll see in this book, such as the `while` loop and the `forEach` loop. Both work by looping through a collection of items and running code on each item. Don't worry, we'll walk you through how they work when the time's right.

Branching logic

As you acquire data in your programs, you'll need to make choices based on that data. These choices distill to true or false questions.

Is the player out of life? Does the current student's average exceed 80? Did the user enter a valid email?

You create branches based on these questions. These branches allow for different outcomes. For instance, if the email is valid you can send the user to the login page otherwise, you would present an error.

Add the following:

```
if (likesSumerian == true) {
    console.log("Ray likes Sumerian");
}
```

The `if` keyword indicates the start of your branching logic. You ask the actual question inside of the parentheses. The statement must always evaluate to `true` or `false`. This question is referred to as an expression.

Notice the expression uses ==. This tests for equality. In this case, you are testing if `likesSumerian` is equal to `true`. The result of this expression is either `true` or `false`.

To test for inequality, use != instead. For example, this code:

```
if (likesSummerian != true) {
    console.log("Ray does not like Sumerian");
}
```

Is the same as this code:

```
if (likesSummerian == false) {
    console.log("Ray does not like Sumerian");
}
```

You can also use greater than (>) or less than (<) as well as greater than or equals (>=) or less than or equals (<=).

Following the expression is an opening brace. This shows that all the code afterward will be executed if the expression evaluates to `true`.

When you save, you'll see the following:

```
Ray likes Sumerian
```

The `likesSumerian` variable is a `boolean`. This means it is either `true` or `false`, so you can write an `if` statement as following:

```
if (likesSummerian) {
    console.log("Ray likes Sumerian");
}
```

You can also provide an `else` clause for when the expression results to `false`. Update your `if` statement to this:

```
if (likesSumerian) {
    console.log("Ray likes Sumerian");
} else {
    console.log("Ray does not like Sumerian. He needs more
coffee. :]");
}
```

Now set the `likesSumerian` to false and save the file, and you'll see the following:

```
Ray does not like Sumerian. He needs more coffee. :]
```

You can have multiple `else` statements that evaluate expressions.

```
if (averageTotal > 80) {
    console.log("Keep up the good work!");
}  else if (averageTotal > 65) {
    console.log("Try harder!");
} else {
    console.log("Stop watching YouTube!");
}
```

You'll see the following:

```
Try harder!
```

Notice that the `else` is last. This is acting as a catch-all. If both of the `if` statements evaluated to `false`, then the `else` clause is evaluated.

Unfortunately, your `if` code is prone to error. Reorder it to the following:

```
averageTotal = 90;
if (averageTotal > 65) {
    console.log("Try harder!");
}  else if (averageTotal > 80) {
    console.log("Keep up the good work!");
} else {
    console.log("Stop watching YouTube!");
}
```

Now when you run it, the console produces:

```
Try harder!
```

This occurs even though your average is now set to 90, because of the way you structured the if-block. You should state the `try harder` condition within a range of values.

Thankfully, you can create compound expressions. You can add additional expressions using &&. In shorthand, this means **and**, as in the coordinating conjunction.

Alter the first line of the if-statement to this:

```
if (averageTotal > 65 && averageTotal < 80) {
```

Here, you are joining two expressions. **Both** expressions must evaluate to `true` for the overall expression to be `true`.

Now when you save, you get the correct result:

```
Keep up the good work!
```

You also have an **or** operator, which you indicate by using `||`. By using an or operator, this means only one condition must be true for an expression to be true.

Change the first line of the `if` statement to this:

```
if (averageTotal > 65 || averageTotal < 80) {
```

Now when you save, the following prints:

```
Try harder!
```

The expression checks to see if the `averageTotal` is higher than 65. This evaluates to `true`. This indicates the entire expression is `true`. Since the first expression is true, the second expression isn't even evaluated. This is known as **short-circuiting**.

Functions

JavaScript allows you to write functions. A function is just a way to encapsulate code and then call that code on demand. In your current script, you've written some code to average some quiz scores. You've used it once. What if you wanted to use it again?

You could simply copy and paste that previous code, but that's a bad idea. It creates needless work. Instead, use a function.

A function takes a name and parameters. Parameters are simply variables that you pass into the function so you can use them. You can define your own variables in the function as well.

Add the following:

```
function averageQuizScores(quizScores) {
}
```

Here, you have a function named `averageQuizScores` and it takes in a parameter named `quizScores`. The `quizScores` parameter can be anything. JavaScript is not a strongly-typed language, so the callee can pass in an array or string.

Now, you'll put your average calculating code in the function and print out the result. Change the code to use **quizScores** instead of **quizzes**.

It should look like the following:

```
function averageQuizScores(quizScores) {
    var gradeTotal = 0;
    for (var i = 0; i < quizScores.length; i++) {
        gradeTotal += quizScores[i];
    }
    var averageTotal = gradeTotal / quizScores.length;
    console.log("the average is " + averageTotal);
}
```

Underneath the function, add the following code to call the function:

```
averageQuizScores(quizzes);
```

Save the file and you'll get the following:

```
the average is 74.71428571428571
```

Functions can also return values. In the `averageQuizScroes` function, replace the log statement with the following:

```
return averageTotal;
```

Now, update the call to the function:

```
console.log(averageQuizScores(quizzes));
```

This now prints out the following:

```
74.71428571428571
```

In JavaScript, functions are considered **first-class citizens**. This means you can store functions in variables and pass them to other functions.

```
var averages = averageQuizScores;
console.log(averages(quizzes));
```

As you can see functions are pretty cool.

Hoisting variables

One thing JavaScript does differently than other languages is that it hoists variables. Add this function:

```
function averageQuizScoresHoist(quizScores) {
    var gradeTotal = 0;
    for (var i = 0; i < quizScores.length; i++) {
        gradeTotal += quizScores[i];
        var currentScore = quizScores[i];
    }
    console.log("current score: " + currentScore);
    var averageTotal = gradeTotal / quizScores.length;
}
```

The `for loop` declares a variable called `currentScore`. In a typical language, that variable would only be accessible inside of the `for` loop.

Add the following after the function and save:

```
averageQuizScoresHoist(quizzes);
```

In a typical language, this would produce an error, but with JavaScript, the following prints:

```
56
```

This may be confusing, but it's working like it's supposed to. JavaScript employs a technique called hoisting. JavaScript hoists all of your variables to the top of a function.

This is how JavaScript sees your function:

```
function averageQuizScoresHoist(quizScores) {
    var gradeTotal = 0;
    var currentScore;
    for (var i = 0; i < quizScores.length; i++) {
        gradeTotal += quizScores[i];
        ccurrentScore = quizScores[i];
    }
    console.log("current score: " + currentScore);
    var averageTotal = gradeTotal / quizScores.length;
}
```

When you declare a variable with the `var` keyword in a function, JavaScript's hoisting mechanism moves that variable to the top of the function. If you want the variable to only exist in the `for` loop, you need to define the variable with `let`. The `let` keyword indicates that the variable will only exist in the current block – that is, between the current set of braces.

In the `for` loop, change the `currentScore` line to the following:

```
let currentScore = quizScores[i];
```

Now **save**. This time, you get an error.

```
16:11:43.547 ▸ [Sumerian] An error occurred at line 61 when loading the "Hello Javascript" script.
          currentScore is not defined ReferenceError: currentScore is not defined
              at averageQuizScoresHoist (sumerian-custom-scri…3.script.js?v=44:77)
              at window._sumerianScriptFactories.c7bdb7b8ff7149219bf8893f7adf8cb3.script (sumeria
          pt.js?v=44:82)
              at ScriptProxy_ScriptProxy._getCustomScriptObject (ScriptProxy.js:175)
              at ScriptProxy_ScriptProxy._updateCustomScriptObject (ScriptProxy.js:89)
              at ScriptProxy.js:55
```

Before moving on to the next section, **switch `currentScore` back to a var**:

```
var currentScore = quizScores[i];
```

Arrow functions

An arrow function is just a regular function that has undergone a starvation diet. That is, it does the same thing as a function except it is much slimmer.

There are lots of times in JavaScript that you'll need a quick and dirty function to get the job done. Arrow functions are short and concise so you aren't declaring functions all over the place.

You can use arrow functions wherever you call regular functions.

Add the following:

```
var quizAverage = () =>  {
}
```

This is the skeleton of an arrow function. It's the equivalent of:

```
var quizAverage = function() {
}
```

The parenthesis takes in any parameters. In this case, you'll provide `quizScores` as that variable. Update your code, like so:

```
var quizAverage = (quizScores) =>  {

}
```

Next, you'll provide the function body, which goes after the curly braces. Update your code so it matches this:

```
var quizAverage = (quizScores) =>  {
    var gradeTotal = 0; // 1
    for (var i = 0; i < quizScores.length; i++) {
        gradeTotal += quizScores[i];
    }

    var averageTotal = gradeTotal / quizScores.length;
    return averageTotal;
}
```

And now, it works just like before. Add the following:

```
console.log(quizAverage(quizzes));
```

Now **save**, and you'll see the following in the console:

`74.71428571428571`

Arrow functions can become really concise. Add the following:

```
var square = (x) => {
    return x * x;
}
console.log(square(10));
```

Save and view the console. It reads:

`100`

As there's only one parameter, you no longer need the parentheses. Also, being there's only one line, you don't need a `return` statement or even braces.

Update your code to the following:

```
var square = x => x * x;
console.log(square(10));
```

When you save now, you'll get the same result, but the arrow function makes it much easier to read.

Objects

JavaScript is an object-oriented language. This means you can use objects to group variables together. You can pass these objects around your code.

There are many ways to create objects in JavaScript, but the easiest way is to use the object **literal**. These are two braces against each other: {}

Add the following to your script:

```
var bestFriend = {};
```

Right now, your object doesn't do much. It'd be nice for your object to contain some properties. These are variables associated with the object.

Update your code:

```
var bestFriend = {
    firstName: "Jeremy",
    lastName: "Patterson"
}
```

You've defined a very simple object with a `firstName` and `lastName`. The object variables are known as properties. You define them by giving them a name as a variable, then adding a colon after it. Following the colon, you provide a value. If you have multiple properties, you separate them with a comma.

To access a value, add the following:

```
console.log(bestFriend.firstName);
```

This prints out the following:

```
Jeremy
```

As you can see, you access the properties by way of the period. Some properties can contain other objects. Update the object to the following:

```
var bestFriend = {
    firstName: "Jeremy",
    lastName: "Patterson",
    address: {
        street: "Main Street",
        number: "26"
    }
}
```

Now add the following:

```
console.log(bestFriend.address.street);
```

This prints out the following:

```
Main Street
```

Objects can also contain functions. This allows your object to act on its own data. Update your object so it looks like this:

```
var bestFriend = {
    firstName: "Jeremy",
    lastName: "Patterson",
    address: {
        street: "Main Street",
        number: "26"
    },
    speak: function() {
        console.log("hello, my name is " + this.firstName);
    }
}
```

You'll notice that the function refers to its own properties using `this`. This keyword stands in place of the current object.

> **Note**: The `this` keyword can be confusing and complicated, depending on the context. It changes depending on where the keyword is used. If you're new to JavaScript, make sure to look up all the pitfalls you may encounter when using `this`.

Now call `speak` by adding the following code:

```
bestFriend.speak();
```

Now, you'll see the following in the console.

```
hello, my name is Jeremy
```

Congratulations! You're cooking with objects!

Key points

- Sumerian is a great tool to learn and use the JavaScript language.
- JavaScript is officially named **ECMAScript** and has **no connection to the Java programming language**.
- **Variables store data**.
- **Arrays group related data** as one variable.
- **Loops repeat instructions** or cycle through all the elements in an array.
- Use **if statements** to **perform branching logic**.
- **Functions encapsulate code** and can be called on-demand.
- **Arrow functions condense** regular functions.
- **JavaScript hoists variables** to the top of a function.
- **Objects group** variables and functions.

Where to go from here?

You've just scratched the surface of JavaScript. As you can probably tell, the language goes very deep. What started as a simple language to interact with web pages has transformed into a tool with a variety of applications.

This chapter has introduced you to JavaScript in the context of Sumerian, but you can use it for many things like creating games, building web pages and even writing server applications.

One chapter alone doesn't do justice to the language. A great place to learn more is the Kahn Academy. Kahn Academy provides free online video tutorials that will quickly get you up to speed.

Mozilla – the creator of the Firefox browser – also produces free learning materials. Check out the Mozilla Developer Network and search for the JavaScript Learning Path. This is a free online guide that will introduce you to the language from the ground up.

Chapter 12: The Sumerian API

By Brian Moakley

When it comes to learning a programming language, oftentimes the language itself is the easiest part to learn. It's the application programming interfaces (APIs) that take the most time to get down. A language uses an API to achieve tasks in the desired framework.

For example, every browser has an API, which allows JavaScript to dynamically change a web page. The browser is a collection of multiple APIs. There's an API to create 3D graphics called WebGL. This is the framework that Sumerian uses to render 3D objects. WebVR is another API that provides virtual reality on a web page. There are so many APIs that it could take years to get to know them all.

Sumerian includes its API as well. A major difficulty in learning an API is learning how to think in that API. Each API is like a fingerprint. While some APIs copy the methodology of others, at the end of the day, each implementation is unique to the task at hand.

If you've been following this book, then congratulations! You've already learned the hard part: How to think in Sumerian. You've learned to pass messages between objects. You've learned to create interactivity by creating behaviors from a series of states, which are composed of individual actions. This is also how the Sumerian API works: You need to think in actions.

To get started, you'll create your own custom actions.

Creating custom actions

Throughout this book, you've been adding actions to states. These actions have all been pre-built. To get started with this chapter, you'll create your very first action. You'll then create some interactivity with your ingredients. When the user clicks on an ingredient, that ingredient will disappear.

> **Note**: If you skipped over the previous chapter and don't know how to create custom scripts, head back to Chapter 11, "Introduction to JavaScript" and read the first section.

Before you start, think about how you'd do the same thing with a behavior. You might create a behavior that listens to click actions. Then, when the user clicks on the item, you'd transition to a hide action followed by an emit message.

From the Sumerian dashboard, open the **Quickstart** scene. In the Assets panel, switch to the **Scripts** tab, mouse over the **Default Pack** and click the **+** button. Select **Script (Preview)**.

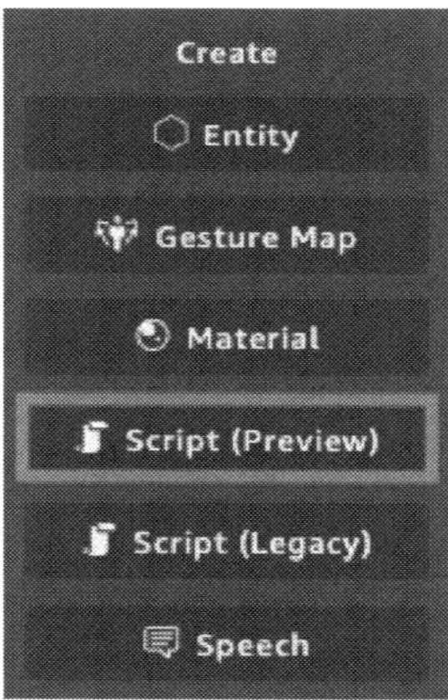

Rename the script to **Ingredients** and, in the Inspector panel, click **Edit in Text Editor**. Sumerian provides some default code.

Delete the default function.

```
1  import * as s from 'module://sumerian-common/api';
2
3  export default function(ctx) {
4      ctx.start(
5          [ s.rotation.RotateAction, { rotation: [100, 100, 100] } ]
6      );
7  }
```

This leaves you with an `import` statement, which is responsible for importing the Sumerian API. The statement imports the framework under the letter **s**, so whenever you need to access an object from the framework, you always start with **s**.

Start by typing the following below `import`:

```
export default function IngredientClickAction(ctx) {
}
```

A lot is going on in this little bit of code. Here's the breakdown:

- **`export default`**: When you write a Sumerian script, you're creating what's known as a module. Sumerian has to import your code into the engine, and you must define one function as the default export. In this case, it's your first action. You must do this once per script. This will be the default action attached to the entity.
- **`function IngredientClickAction`**: This is the name of your custom action. It starts with a capital letter and it's very clear what it's supposed to do.
- **`(ctx)`**: Your action takes only one parameter and this parameter is known as the `context`. You can think of the `context` as the heart of the framework. To do anything with the framework, you need a `context` object. The `context` allows you to run actions and can also contain data, much like attributes.

At this point, you have an empty action, which doesn't do much at all. For the demo, you want it to respond to click actions. Each context has a `start()` function, which takes in actions.

Add the following to your action, placing it between the curly braces:

```
ctx.start();
```

At this point, you provide your actions. Each action is passed into an array, which takes two objects. The first is the action type and the second object is the configuration properties.

To see the available actions, you must check out the documentation, which you can find here: https://content.sumerian.amazonaws.com/engine/latest/doc/.

This document contains a lot of information, but it has everything you need to know to be successful with the API. You're interested in the available action, so click on **module://sumerian-common/api** link.

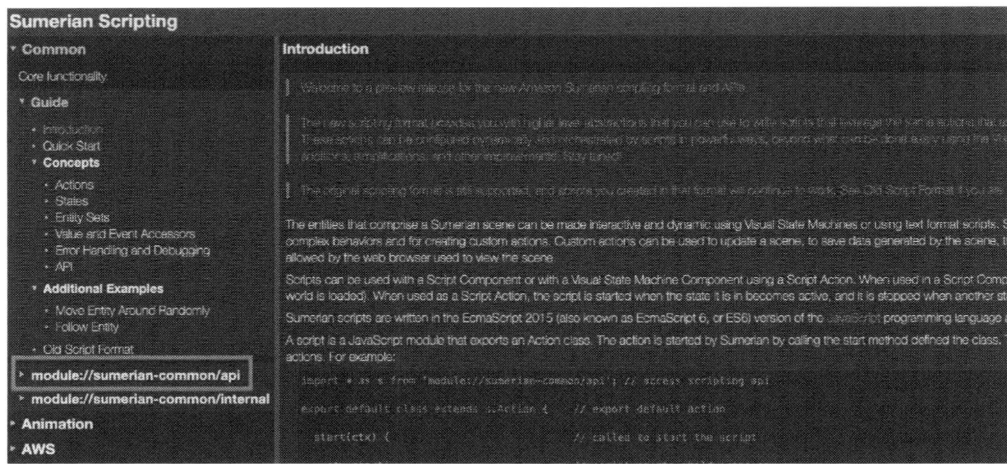

> **Note**: This is a living document with regular updates, so the document will likely look different when you visit it.

When you expand the common API, you'll see a list of the core objects. This is where you can find more information and learn about the various functions available. You'll also see action categories. Expand the **input** category.

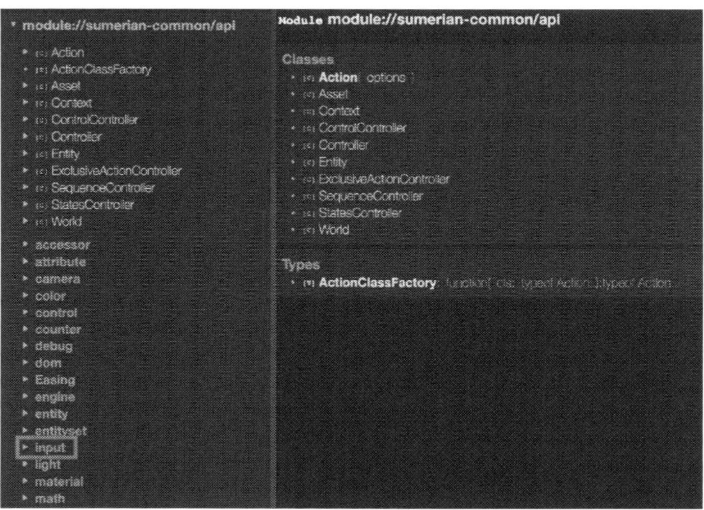

Expanding the list provides several actions related to the input. Click on **ClickAction**. The documentation will give a brief description of the action. You want to create a new action, so click on **constructor**.

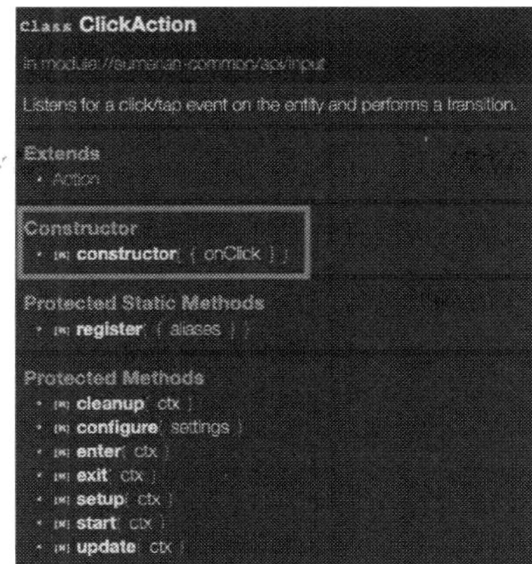

A constructor will let you know how to create an action. For instance, a Listen action requires that you pass a channel into it. In your case, you're creating a `ClickAction`. This action needs to know what happens when the user performs the click.

The constructor lists all the various properties that it will take. You'll see that it contains an `options.onClick`. This takes a function and is optional. The description reads: `Callback invoked when entity is clicked.`

This means that when the user clicks the button, the provided function will execute.

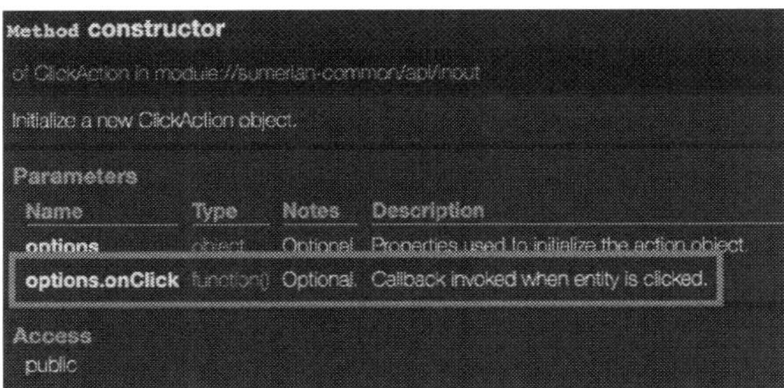

Now, you want to add your action. Update your action to the following:

```
ctx.start(
    [s.input.ClickAction, {}]
);
```

Here, you've defined an array that contains an action and an empty object. The `s.input` tells Sumerian where to find the action. The empty object `{}` is what contains the options.

Now, update it to the following:

```
ctx.start(
    [s.input.ClickAction, { onClick: function() {

    }}]
);
```

Now you've added a function to handle the click event. Whenever the user clicks on an ingredient, this function will be called.

Two things need to happen: The entity needs to disappear and you need to send out a message. You do this via your context. The parent action contains your context, so you can just use that.

Update the code to the following:

```
ctx.start(
    [s.input.ClickAction, { onClick: function() {
        ctx.start(
            [s.entity.HideAction],
            [s.message.SendAction, {
                channel: "ClickedOnIngredient"
            }]
        );
    }}]
)
```

Now, two actions will run once the user clicks on an ingredient. You'll notice that `HideAction` has no options. In this case, you don't need to provide an additional object.

`SendAction` works the same way as it does in a behavior, but it also provides another option that allows you to pass data. You'll use this later in the chapter.

Finally, you'll update your code to use an arrow function instead of a function. Update `ClickAction` to the following:

```
ctx.start(
    [s.input.ClickAction, { onClick: () => {
        ctx.start(
            [s.entity.HideAction],
            [s.message.SendAction, {
                channel: "ClickedOnIngredient"
            }]
        );
    }}]
)
```

You'll be using arrow functions throughout the rest of the book.

Now, **save** your script and switch back to the engine.

In the Entities panel, select the **Oil** entity. Drag the **Ingredients** script onto it. To test this, you'll need to make a quick alteration to your scene. Select the **Default Camera** and in the Inspector panel, check the **Main Camera** option.

Now, run your scene and click on the oil. It disappears! Voila! You're a code magician.

Working with entity sets

Congratulations on creating your first custom action. Unfortunately, it's not very convenient. It works pretty much as a behavior.

A better approach is to add the action to multiple ingredients at once. You do this by way of an entity set, which is a collection of entities. You can search through those entities or even attach actions to them.

You fetch an entity set from the `world` object. This object is accessible from a `context` object. You can get a set via a regular expression, attributes, and tags.

In the Entities panel, select the **Oil** entity and in the Inspector panel, expand the **Oil** component, which is the main component at the top of the list. Expand the **Tags** section, located above the Custom Attributes.

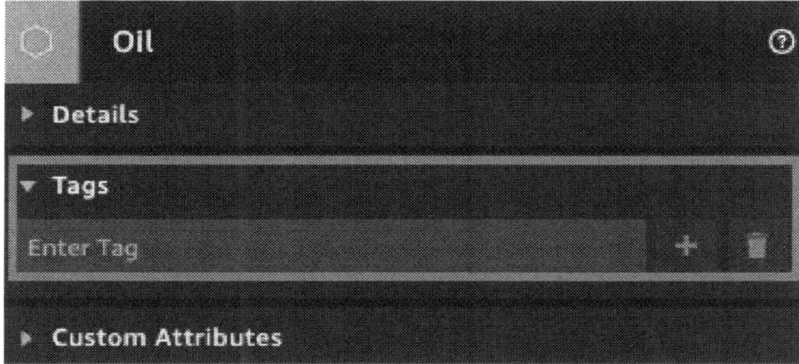

Add the tag **ingredient** and click the + button. Add this tag to the following entities: **Egg 1**, **Egg 2**, **Egg 3**, **Flour Bowl** and **Water Cup**.

Return to editing your Ingredients script. Add the following:

```
export default function IngredientsSelector(ctx) {
}
```

Remember, you can only export one action as the default, so change the header of your `IngredientsClickAction` to the following:

```
function IngredientClickAction(ctx) {
```

Now, to get your ingredient entities. In `IngredientsSelector`, add the following:

```
const ingredients = ctx.world.entitiesWithTags("ingredient");
```

This simple code takes all of your entities and bundles them up as an entity set for you.

> **Note**: If you've worked with sets in other programming languages, you'll be happy to know you can perform set operations as well, such as `intersect`, `union` and `substract`. See the documentation for more details.

Now add the following:

```
ingredients.maintain(ctx, [IngredientClickAction])
```

`maintain` allows you to start actions on the entire set. It will also stop actions when entities are removed from the set. If you don't care about actions stopping, you can use `start` instead.

Your new action should look like the following:

```
function IngredientClickAction(ctx) {
    ctx.start(
        [s.input.ClickAction, { onClick: () => {
            ctx.start(
                [s.entity.HideAction],
                [s.message.SendAction, {
                    channel: "ClickedOnIngredient"
                }]
            )
        }}]
    );
}
```

```
export default function IngredientClickAction(ctx) {
    const ingredients =
        ctx.world.entitiesWithTags("ingredient");
    ingredients.maintain(ctx, [IngredientClickAction])
}
```

Save your script and switch back to the Scene editor. Since you're batch-updating your ingredients, you can remove the script from the oil. Keep in mind, you still need to attach the script to an entity for it to function.

In the Entities panel, select the **Oil** entity and remove the script component. Select the **Ingredients** and drag the **Ingredients** script to it.

> **Note**: For the script to work, it needs to be attached to *any* entity. In your current scene, you attached the script to the Ingredients entity. This entity is the parent of all the affected entities. Having a script on a parent is inconsequential to how the script functions. You could just as easily create an unrelated entity named ScriptManager and add your script to that. It would work just the same.

Now, run your scene and click on the various ingredients. They all disappear, and it only required a few lines of code.

Attributes and values

Throughout this book, you've been keeping track of certain states with attributes. You've done this by creating attribute actions and then running comparison actions.

When working with the Sumerian API, you can also use values. Values allow you to save information like you can with attributes, but there are some differences.

First, you can choose to save data on an entity or you can save data to the world. By saving data to the world, any entity can access the value.

In your current scene, you want to keep track of when the user clicks an ingredient. When the user has clicked all the ingredients, it'd be nice to see the raw dough in the bread pan.

To get started, click the **Import files from your computer** folder in the Assets panel. In the **resources/models** folder, select the **Dough.FBX** file. This is a model of your raw dough.

Drag the **Dough.FBX** entity onto the canvas and rename it **Raw Dough**. Set the Translation to (**-10.768**, **4.26**, **-8.631**). Set the Rotation to (**-5.552**, **-1.505**, **7.016**). Set the Scale to (**1.253**, **1.529**, **1.396**).

In the Assets panel, switch to the **Materials** tab. Look for the Dough.FBX pack and select the **12_-_Default**. Switch to the **Textures** tab.

Click the **Import files from your computer** folder and, in the **resources/textures**, import all of the bread textures.

Drag the **Bread_Color.png** texture to the **COLOR (DIFFUSE)** category. Drag the **Bread_Normal.png** texture to the **NORMAL** category. Finally, drag the **Bread_Ambient.png** texture to the **AMBIENT** category.

Select the **Raw Dough** and click **Add Component**, then add a **State Machine**. Click the **+** button to add a new behavior and name it **Raw Dough**.

This will create a simple behavior. Name the first state to **Listen for Messages** and add two **Listen** actions.

Set the first channel to **ShowRawDough** and the other channel to **CookingDone**. Add two more states. Name one state **Show** and the other **Hide**.

Add a **Show** action to the Show state and a **Hide** action to the Hide state. Add **Transition** actions to both states.

Drag a transition from the **ShowRawDough** event to the **Show** state and then back to the **Raw Dough** state. Drag another transition from the **ShowRawDough** event to the **Hide** state and then back to the **Raw Dough** state.

Your behavior should look like the following:

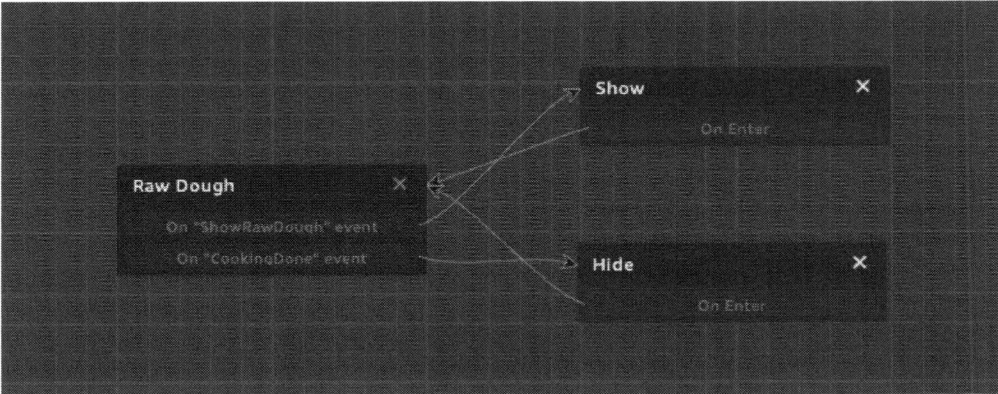

Now drag the Raw Dough to the **Breadpan**. **Hide** the Raw Dough.

This allows your dough to appear and disappear by receiving a message, which you've done throughout the book so far. This is quite useful and, since you've done it so often, it's a great candidate for a script.

Open your **Ingredients** script. The first thing you need to do is track the total ingredients.

In `IngredientsSelector`, add the following underneath `const ingredients = ctx.world.entitiesWithTags("ingredient");`:

```
ctx.world.value("ingredientCount", ingredients.size);
ctx.world.value("ingredientClicked", 0);
```

Those two lines set up your values. You've assigned them to `world`, so any script can access them. If you wanted only the entity to be able to access the values, you could write: `ctx.entity.value` instead.

The first line keeps track of the number of ingredients and the second line keeps track of the number of clicks.

At the top of `IngredientClickAction`, add the following:

```
const totalIngredients = ctx.world.value("ingredientCount");
const clickTotal = ctx.world.value("ingredientClicked");
```

This fetches the value objects that you created in the set-up action and stores them as variables.

> **Note**: If you are new to JavaScript, the use of `const` here may be confusing. After all, when you set a number to `const`, you can't change the value. Remember, an object is a collection of values. By declaring the object as a `const`, you can't change the actual object, but you can still alter the object's properties. If you tried something like this: `clickedTotal = {};`, you'd get an error.

First, you need to increment the click value. A property named `current` stores this value. Inside the `ClickAction`, add the following above `ctx.start()`:

```
clickTotal.current += 1;
```

This increments the click count. Once the click count equals the total amount of ingredients, then it's a good time to show the dough.

In your click action, add the following underneath `ctx.start()`:

```
if (clickTotal.current == totalIngredients.current) {
    ctx.start(
        [s.message.SendAction, { channel: "ShowRawDough" }]
    );
}
```

And that's it! Run your scene, and click on all the ingredients. When they all disappear, your raw dough will appear. Magic!

Values also provide an advantage over attributes that you can monitor when a value has changed. By using `monitor` on a value, you can run code every time there's a change.

Rewrite `IngredientsSelector` to do all the hard work:

```
export default function IngredientsSelector(ctx) {
    const ingredients =
        ctx.world.entitiesWithTags("ingredient");
    ingredients.maintain(ctx, [IngredientClickAction]);

    // 1
    const totalIngredients =
        ctx.world.value("ingredientCount", ingredients.size);
    const clickTotal = ctx.world.value("ingredientClicked", 0);

    // 2
    clickTotal.monitor(ctx, () => {
        if (clickTotal.current == totalIngredients.current) {
                ctx.start(
                    [s.message.SendAction, {
                        channel: "ShowRawDough"
                    }]
                );
        }
    });
}
```

Here's how it works:

1. In this action, you set up both of the values and keep references to the variables.
2. This sets up the value monitoring by calling `monitor`. It takes an active context, after which, you provide a function. This function runs every time the value changes.

This requires a small change to `IngredientsClickAction`. Replace `IngredientClickAction` with the following:

```
function IngredientClickAction(ctx) {

    const clickTotal = ctx.world.value("ingredientClicked");
    ctx.start(
        [s.input.ClickAction, { onClick: () => {
            clickTotal.current += 1;
            ctx.start(
                [s.entity.HideAction],
                [s.message.SendAction, {
                    channel: "ClickedOnIngredient"
                }]
```

```
            )
        }}]
    )
}
```

All this does is increment the value. The action is much simpler now.

Signals

One of the drawbacks of using behaviors in the Scene editor is that complexity can quickly grow out of hand. It's easy to get lost in a tangled mess of states. Using the API, you can essentially compartmentalize complexity and have it represented as a single state.

In this case, you have the user's click on the ingredients. You've already written a bunch of code to handle that. You'll wrap that up in action and add it to your behavior.

You could use a message to signal the end of your action, but you can also use — drum roll please — signals.

A signal is a way to indicate the completion of a state.

To get started, create a new custom preview script. Rename it **Mix Ingredients**. Open the newly-created script in the Text editor.

This is going to be a simple action. It'll wait until the `ShowRawDough` message broadcasts.

Replace the default function with the following:

```
export default function MixIngredients(ctx) {
    ctx.start(
        [s.message.ReceiveAction, {
            channel: "ShowRawDough" onReceive: () => {

            }
        }]
    );
}
```

This message receives an action, but it doesn't do anything yet.

Now, you must define your signal. At the time of this writing, Sumerian only supports `onSuccess` and `onFailure` signals, but there's a plan to support custom signals in the future.

Implement signals by adding the following above your function:

```
export const SIGNALS = {
    onSuccess: {
      description: 'success when user adds all ingredients'
    }
}
```

Here, you define your signal. You must always call your constant `SIGNALS`; this is defined by the engine.

To use it, your action must import the options object. This object contains a variety of possibilities including properties that you set up (which you'll do in a moment) or signals.

Alter your function declaration to the following:

```
export default function MixIngredients(ctx, options) {
```

Using this object, you can trigger your success signal.

Update the `MixIngredients` action to call the signal inside `ReceiveAction`:

```
export default function MixIngredients(ctx, options) {
    ctx.start(
        [s.message.ReceiveAction, {
            channel: "ShowRawDough", onReceived: () => {
                ctx.signal(options.onSuccess);
            }
        }]
    );
}
```

Now to use it. Save your script and return to the Scene editor. Open the **Bread Machine Demo**. Click **Add a new state**, name it **Mix Ingredients** and add an **Execute** action to it. Attach the **Mix Ingredients** script to it.

Drag a transition from the **Click Ingredients** state to the **Mix Ingredients** state. Then drag a transition from the **On Mix Ingredients Success** event to the **Click on Pan** event.

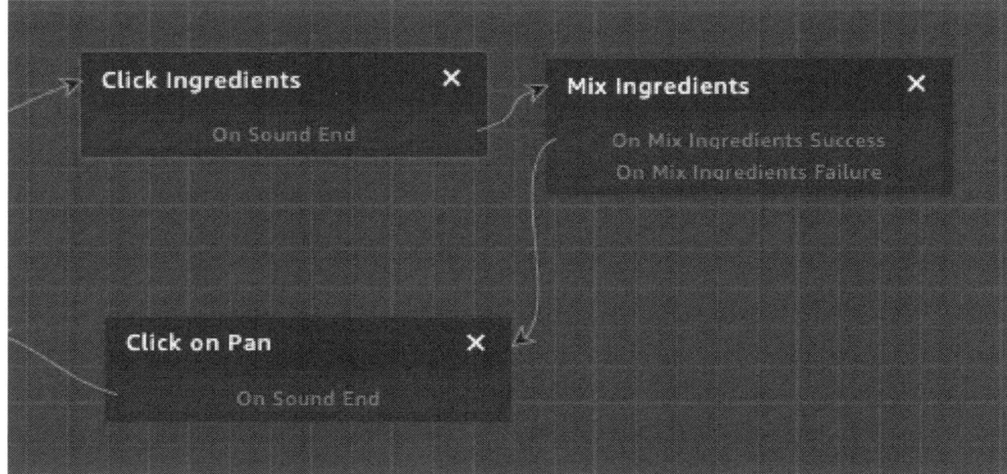

Finally, select the **Demo Start Camera** and set it as the **Main Camera**.

Now, run your scene and the demonstration will wait until the user has added all the ingredients.

Action controllers

There will be times when you have an entity with multiple different actions. Sometimes, you'll want to cycle through the actions; other times, you may want to designate a particular action state. Sumerian comes to the rescue with the concept of controllers.

Controllers allow you to group actions. After you do that, you switch between the controller states. You can either run this sequentially, define state names or even have different states run at the same time.

Sumerian defines several types of controllers. A **regular controller** allows you to run one or more actions at the same time. A **sequence controller** allows you to run actions in order. The **states controller** allows you to run one action at a time, in any order. Finally, you have a **control controller** that allows you to start and stop actions independently.

In this case, you'll be defining animation actions and you'll cycle between various states. A sequence controller is a good fit for this purpose.

You want some simple animation, and you'll use a controller do it. With your scene open, click the **Ingredients** entity. In the Inspector panel, find the Script component and click the + button to add a new script. Make sure to select a **Custom (Preview Format)**. Rename this new script to **Ingredients Animation**. Open it in the Text editor.

You want the ingredients to bounce when a particular message broadcasts. You'll handle the message broadcast a little bit later. For now, you need to set up the animation.

Replace the default action with the following:

```
export default function IngredientsAnimation(ctx) {
    ctx.start(
        [BounceAction]
    );
}
```

This creates a new action and then calls another action. Later, you'll call this action from a `ReceiveAction`. For now, add the following to create `BounceAction`:

```
function BounceAction(ctx) {
    var bounceCount = 0;
    const totalBounces = 2;
}
```

This defines the length of bounces for the ingredients. Now for the animation. At this point, you can define a state controller or a sequence controller. With the state controller, you can arbitrarily jump between states, whereas a sequence runs states in order.

First, you'll define a state controller. Add the following underneath the variables.

```
const controller = ctx.sequence();
```

This defines a sequence, which takes a series of actions. Creating a sequence returns a controller. Here, you store the controller in a variable that you can access later. Add the following in the `sequence()`:

```
const controller = ctx.sequence(
    [s.position.TweenMoveAction, {
        seconds: .5,
        relative: true,
```

```
        position: [0, 0.10, 0],
        onComplete: () => {
            controller.next;
        }
    }],
```

This defines a `TweenMoveAction`. You'll see that it takes a few parameters. You want to set the item to move upwards relative to its current position. When the animation completes, you switch to the next action in the sequence.

Now, add the following for the down state:

```
[s.position.TweenMoveAction, {
    seconds: .5,
    relative: true,
    position: [0, -0.10, 0],
    onComplete: () => {
        bounceCount += 1;
    }
}]);
```

This performs another animation, with the difference that it's moving the ingredients downwards. When the animation completes, the `bounceCount` increases. You'll add more to this in a moment.

After the `controller`, add the following:

```
controller.loop = true;
```

By setting the controller to loop, you don't need to move on to the next action. Once the action completes, the next action will fire.

You only want two bounces. Update the `onComplete` function in your second tween action to the following:

```
if (bounceCount >= totalBounces) {
    controller.loop = false;
}
```

Set the Default Camera as the **Main Camera**. Run the scene. Your ingredients will bounce two times, then stop. With sequences, you can also restart sequences and do a variety of other things.

You want the animation to run once a message is received. Update the `IngredientsAnimation` action to the following:

```
ctx.start(
    [s.message.ReceiveAction, {
        channel: "AnimateIngredients", onReceived: (data) => {
            ctx.start([BounceAction])
        }
    }]
);
```

This creates a Listen action. You set the channel and `onReceived` handles what happens when a message is received. You'll notice that the message is receiving a `data` object. With the Sumerian API, you can use messages to pass data to other entities, which you'll do in a moment.

For now, save your script and switch back to the Scene editor. Open the **Bead Machine Demo** behavior. Select the **Click Ingredients** action and add an **Emit Message** action to it. Set the channel to **AnimateIngredients**. Now, select the **Demo Start Camera** and set it as the **Main Camera**. Now run your scene and you'll see your ingredients animate in time with the demonstration.

Script properties

One of the coolest parts about working with scripts is the ability to integrate them with the rest of the Scene editor. For instance, when you add an `Orbit and Pan Control` script, you'll see a list of options. This allows you to configure the script right in the Scene editor, versus switching to the Text editor to make any changes.

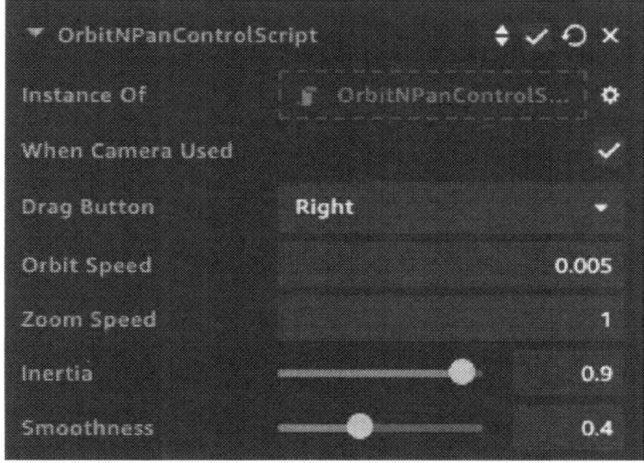

These are known as script properties. When defining the property, you must provide at least a property type, which indicates the actual data type of the property. For example, if you wanted the user to provide text, the property would be a string type.

You can find the various types available to you in the `type` section of the documentation.

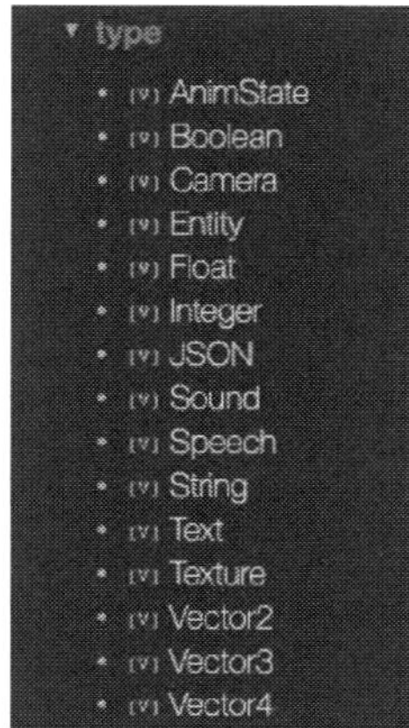

You can also set the default value of the property, add a user interface control and even set the order.

In this case, you'll use properties to configure your lights. In the current demo, you emit messages to turn on a light. Using properties, you'll set the light from a drop-down instead.

With the Scene editor open, create a new script and name it **Lighting Control**. Open the Text editor and delete the default action.

You'll allow the user to configure two properties: One property will select the light, while the other sets the state.

First, add the following:

```
export const PROPERTIES = {
}
```

The object's name lets Sumerian know that you're setting up properties for the script. Like Signals, you must do this every time you create properties.

Now, between the curly braces, add the property for the light.

```
light: {
    type: s.type.String,
    control: s.control.Select,
    options:
        ["Console Light", "Done Light", "In Use Light",
         "Open Light", "Start Light"],
    default: 3,
    order:0
},
```

This code creates a drop-down for the user to select a light. The `type` sets the value to be a string (text). The `control` sets the option to be a drop-down box. The `options` provide the name of the light. You've set the options to match the entity's name, and you'll use this name in a moment. The `default` sets the default value of the drop-down. Finally, `order` determines the order of the control in the panel.

Now add the following:

```
active: {
    type: s.type.String,
    control:  s.control.Select,
    options: ["On", "Off"],
    order: 1
}
```

This creates another drop-down, where you can set the light to be either `On` or `Off`.

Before you can see the options, you need to define an action to use them. Typically, you define your actions with a context. To use option values, you'll need to define another parameter that stores the options.

Add the following:

```
export default function LightNotifier(ctx, options) {

}
```

Now, save your file and return to the Sumerian editor. Open the **Bread Machine Demo** behavior.

Select the **Start Button Description**. Add an **Execute Script** action and drag your **Lighting Control** to it.

Now, you'll be able to set both the light and its state. Set the Light property to **Start Light** and the Action property to **On**.

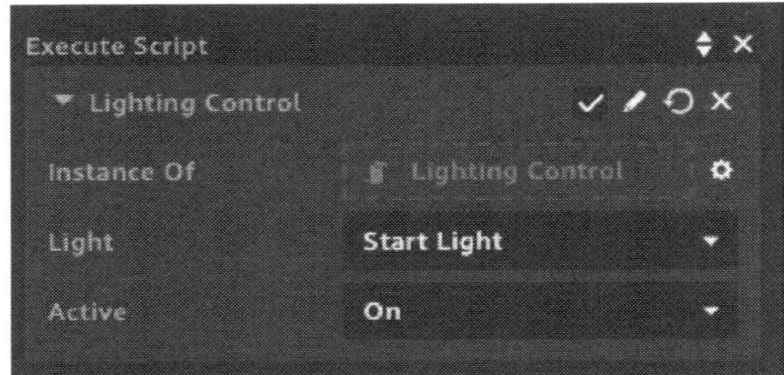

Sending data

You've created some properties that allow you to configure your lights, but they don't do anything.

Currently, the lights have behaviors attached to them. To make your lights work, you need to do two things: Remove the behaviors and tag the entities as lights.

Select the **Console Light** entity and remove the **State Machine** component. Then add a **Light** tag to the entity. Do this to the **Done Light**, **In Use Light**, **Open Light** and **Start Light**.

You've now removed all of the light behaviors. If you run the scene, the lights won't activate.

Switch back to your **Lighting Control** script. You'll use this script to send data in a `SendAction`. In the `Light Notifier`, add the following:

```
ctx.start(
    [s.message.SendAction, { channel: "ManageLight", data: {

    }}]
)
```

Using the `SendAction`, you send both the channel and some data. The channel is just some text, just as you've used throughout this book. The data is an object. You can add whatever data you want to it.

In your case, you'll declare two variables: `light` and `status`. You'll set properties based on `options` object. The `options` object contains your predefined values of `light` and `active`.

Add the following to the data object:

```
light: options.light,
status: options.active
```

When you're done, the completed action will look like this:

```
export default function LightNotifier(ctx, options) {
    ctx.start(
        [s.message.SendAction, {
            channel: "ManageLight", data: {
                light: options.light,
                status: options.active
            }
        }]
    );
}
```

You've defined two properties to contain your property data. Now, you need to read that data. Save and go back to the editor.

Click **Create Entity** and select the empty **Entity**. Give it the name **Lighting Manager** and drag it into the **Default Dynamic Lights**.

Next, create a new custom preview script. Rename it **Lighting Manager**. Add the script to the **Lighting Manager** entity.

Open your **Lighting Manager** script in the Text editor.

This time, you'll use the default action. Delete everything in the braces.

First, you'll fetch all of the lights into an entity set by adding the following to the top of the function:

```
const lights = ctx.world.entitiesWithTags("Light");
```

Now, you need to listen for the `ManageLight` action. Add the following:

```
ctx.start(
    [ s.message.ReceiveAction, {
        channel: "ManageLight", onReceived: (data) => {

        }
    }]
);
```

The script starts by listening for messages. When it receives a message, it receives the data object. You can use this object to activate and deactivate the lights.

First, you need to check if you have a valid data object. Add the following:

```
if (data) {

}
```

Now, loop through all your lights:

```
lights.forEach((item) => {

});
```

A `forEach` loop iterates through the entire collection with the `item` variable referencing the current item in the collection.

Now, add the following in the `forEach` loop:

```
if (item.name == data.light) {

}
```

Each entity has a name, which you set in the inspector. You used the same names in the property. If the names match, you have the affected light.

Now, add the following in the braces:

```
if (data.status == "On") {
    item.show();
} else {
    item.hide();
}
```

If the status is equal to `On`, then you'll call the `show()` method which shows the entity. Otherwise, you'll hide it from view.

Save your file. Open the **Bread Machine Demo** and replace all your light messages with the **Lighting Control** script. Set the correct light and the correct state (on or off).

Your behavior should look like this:

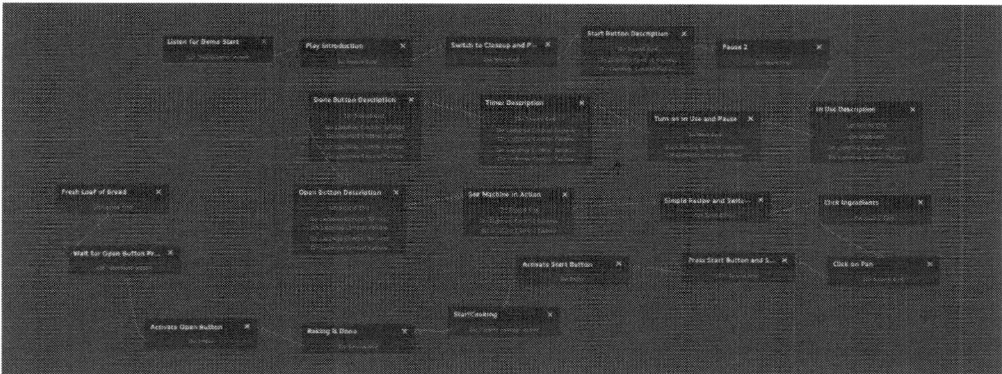

Things are just getting interesting, and you haven't touched animation yet. But don't worry, that comes next!

Key points

- Using the Sumerian API, you **create your own actions**. These actions can call other actions as well.
- Every action takes a **context**. The context is a reference to the **Sumerian engine**.
- Sumerian actions reside in categories. These **categories are documented in the API documentation**.
- Each action has its own constructor. When using a Sumerian action, always look up the **constructor requirements**.
- **Entity sets are groups of entities.** You can group entities by assigning tags to them and calling `entitiesWithTags()`.
- Data can also be saved and retrieved by entity values. Unlike attributes, **entity values can be monitored for changes**.
- **Signals send messages to states** when an action succeeds or fails.
- **Controllers provide for action states**. You can switch between these states to run different actions.

- Properties provide for script configuration in a behavior state or in the Inspector panel.
- Messages sent from actions can contain data that can be accessed from other scripts.

Where to go from here?

The Sumerian API is expansive, and using it unlocks the power of the engine. Keep in mind, the API isn't meant to replace behaviors. The Visual State Machine editor is a great tool to see the entire structure of your experience. That said, the API allows you to group actions and extend the engine.

The best place to learn more about the API is in the documentation. The documentation contains detailed information about each topic with lots of examples:

https://content.sumerian.amazonaws.com/engine/latest/doc/

The documentation contains information about debugging, working with events and a deep overview of controllers. The documentation also contains a section for those users coming from the legacy API.

By all means, dive deep into the documentation.

Chapter 13: Animation & Particle Systems

By Brian Moakley

As you've seen in this book, adding animation make scenes both interesting and dynamic. Animation adds life to a scene. It not only captures your user's attention, but it also highlights interactive elements.

Sumerian provides several methods to perform animations. You can create a tween action, you can import animation with the model or you can create your animation with the timeline component.

In this chapter, you'll be performing all of these animation types and, in the process, breathing some life into your scene. After that, you'll dabble with Sumerian's particle system to add some "steamy" effects.

Tweening the night away

So far, you've already played around with a bit of animation by attaching tween actions to entities. You first did this in Chapter 4, "Adding Interactivity with Behaviors."

The word "tween" is shorthand for between. When creating a tween, you set a start point and provide an endpoint. You then provide a length of time for the animation to play.

Using this information, Sumerian generates each frame of animation for the entity. You can tween movement, scale, rotation and even make entities look at each other.

You'll get to tweening in a moment, but before you do, you need to cook some bread. And here you thought only a bread machine could bake bread!

Open the Sumerian dashboard and then open your Quickstart project.

In the Assets panel, click on the **Import files from your computer** folder button. Navigate to **resources** and select the **Loaf.FBX** model. Drag an instance of **Loaf.FBX** onto the canvas. It'll look like a block of Styrofoam.

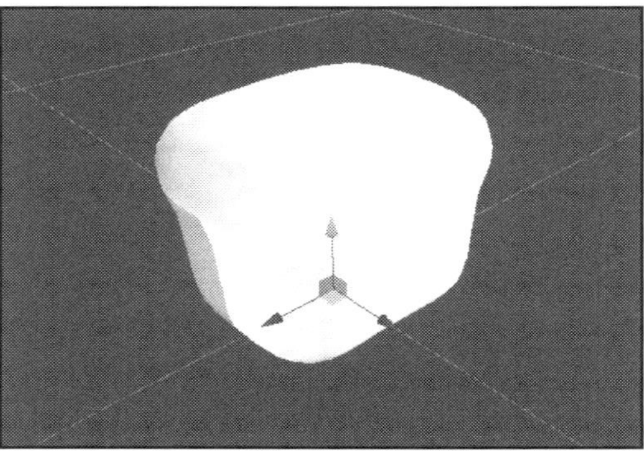

In the Assets panel, switch to the **Materials** tab. Find the **Loaf.FBX** pack and select the **12_-_Default** material. Switch to the **Textures** tab.

With the Material component in the Inspector, drag the **Bread_Color** texture to the **COLOR (DIFFUSE)** category. Next, drag **Bread_Normal** to the **NORMAL** category. Finally, drag **Bread_Ambient** to the **AMBIENT** category.

You now have a nice-looking loaf of cooked bread.

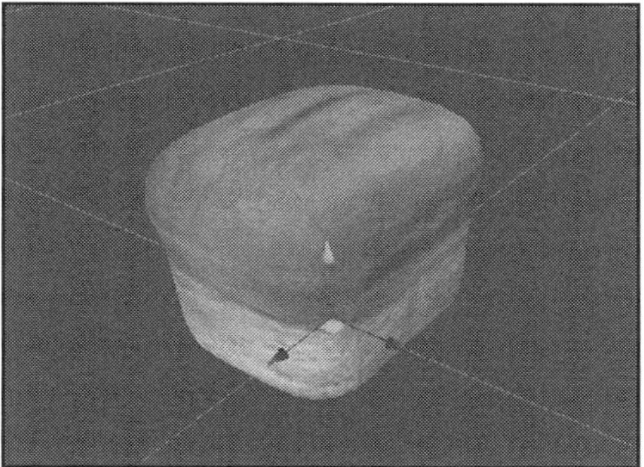

You may have noticed that you used the same texture for both the raw dough and the cooked dough. Look at the Bread_Color texture and you'll see that it contains the imagery for the cooked dough and raw dough.

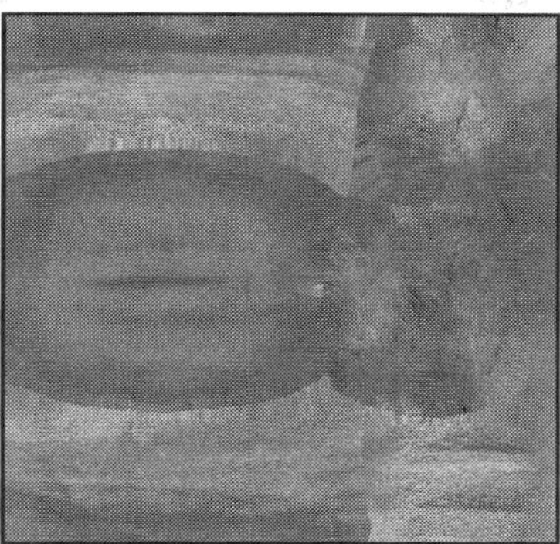

This is another way to increase the performance of your game. By sharing the same texture, the scene takes less memory and requires fewer draw calls. This will make for a better, more efficient scene.

Select the **Loaf.FBX** entity and rename it to **Cooked Bread**. Set the Translation to (**-10.794, 4.02, -8.6**). You now have some cooked bread in the bread pan.

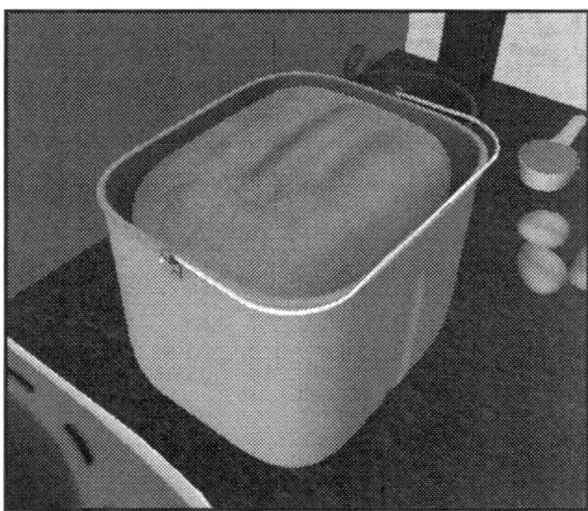

Drag the Cooked Bread entity into the **Breadpan** entity. You're ready to get tweening!

Tweening options

You've already played with the Tween actions, but so far, you only configured the options. This section provides an overview of the various options.

With the Cooked Bread entity still selected, click **Add Component**. Add a **State Machine** to it. Click the + button to add a new behavior and name it **Cooked Bread**.

Rename the first state to **Animate Bread**. Click **Add Action** and, in the Animation category, select the **Tween Move** action.

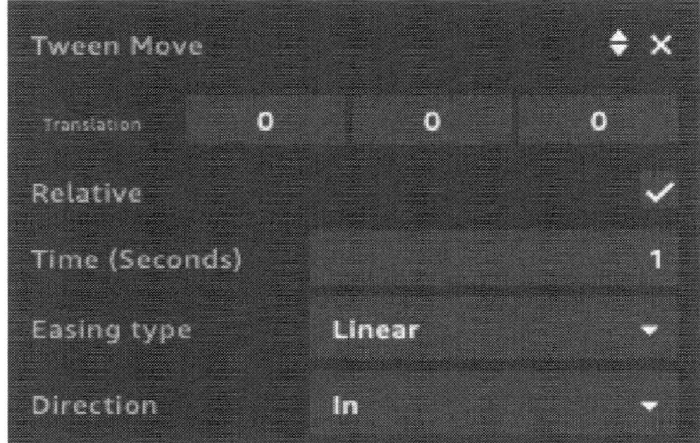

By default, all tweening is relative. This means when you provide a movement, you're providing the movement in the current entity's location.

By unchecking the Relative box, you're tweening to the absolute position according to the parent entity.

Remember, when you parent one entity to another, the zero position is the location of the parent entity.

To see this in action, do a little experimentation. First, make sure your tween's Translation property is set to (**0**, **0**, **0**). Next, check the Relative checkbox.

Next, select the Default Camera and set it as the **Main Camera**. Zoom out so you can see your scene at a glance.

Now, play your scene. Nothing happens, because you're translating the bread by zero according to its relative location.

Now, uncheck the Relative checkbox and play the scene again. This time, the bread sinks into the counter.

The Breadpan entity is the parent of the Cooked Bread entity. Breadpan's center point is lower than Cooked Bread, so the Cooked Bread entity lowers toward the counter.

Now, drag the Cooked Bread entity out of Breadpan. Do this by dragging the entity name to the scene name (Quickstart). This time, Cooked Bread has no parent at all. The zero location points toward the center of the scene.

Run the scene again, and this time, the bread animates to the center of the entire scene.

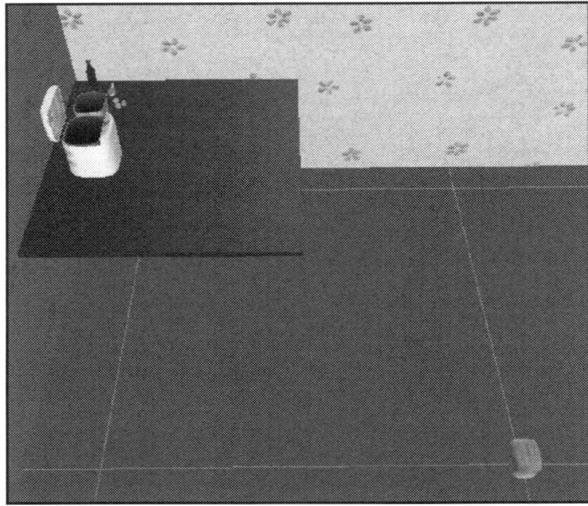

As you can see, parents make a big difference, especially when animating.

Drag the Cooked Bread entity back to the Breadpan entity and return to the Animate Bread state. There's more to do.

You just learned how to tween move an entity. You can also change the timing of the animation by altering the Time property.

The tween action contains two other properties, named **Easing type** and **Direction**. These determine how the animation plays out.

By default, a tween animation runs at the same speed from start to finish. This is called **linear animation**, and it doesn't tend to happen in real life. For example, you may roll a ball fast, but it will eventually slow to a stop. Other objects may gradually get up to speed then gradually slow down again. By changing the easing, your animations become more interesting and dynamic.

By selecting an easing type, you tell Sumerian how you want it to apply the velocity. Here's an example of a linear animation:

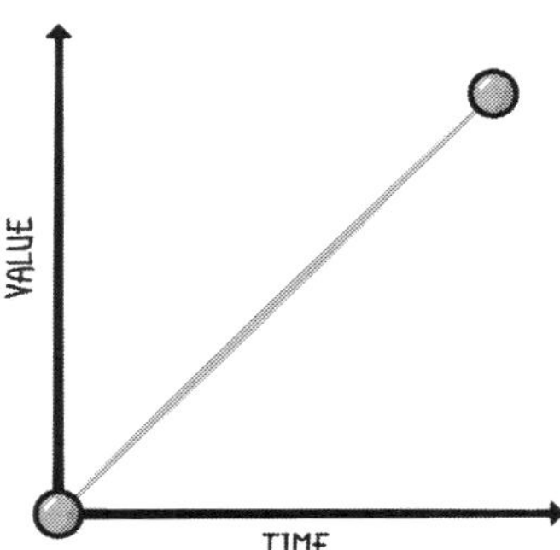

This shows your entity moving at the same speed over a period of time.

The **Direction** property lets you indicate where you want to apply the Easing type. You have three options: In, Out and InOut.

Quadratic easing allows you to slow your animation. For example, you may want your entity to lose speed as it completes its animation. In this case, you'd set the Direction to Out. This type of animation would look like the following:

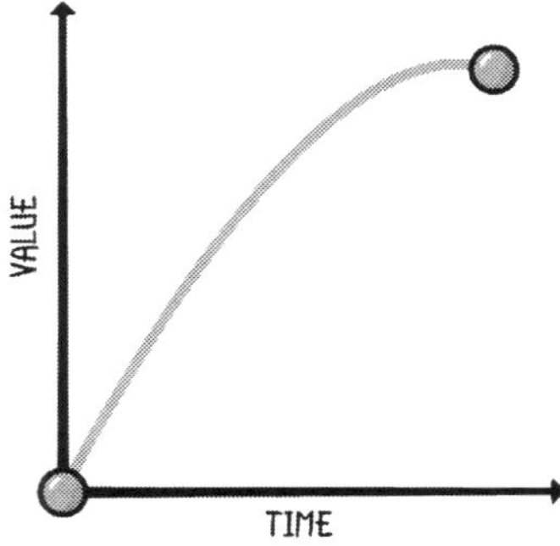

Quadratic easing that uses InOut looks like this:

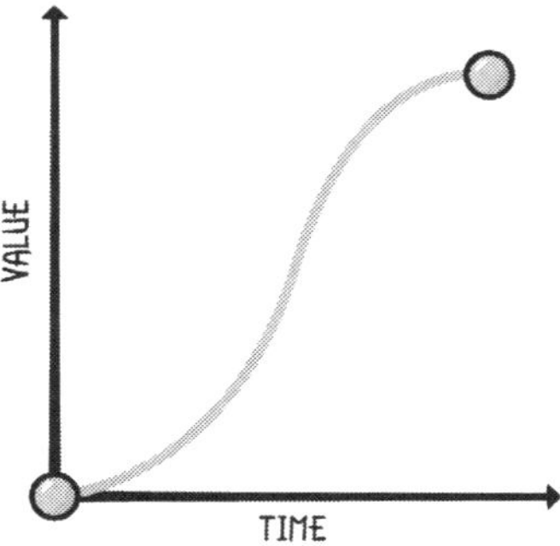

Note: You'll learn the different easing types as you use them. If you want a handy reference, visit https://easings.net/en, which provides illustrations that show how the various easing types perform.

Set the easing type to **Quadratic** and set the Direction to InOut. Set the Translation to (**0**, **0**, **7**) and the Time (Seconds) to **3**.

You're ready to present your bread, but it needs some additional setup. Open the Cooked Bread behavior. Click **Add State** and name the new state **Listen for Cooking Done**. Add a **Listen** action to it and set the channel to **CookingDone**. Click **Set As Initial State**.

Click **Add State** again. Name it **Prepare to Reveal** and add a **Show** and **Listen** action. Then set the Listen Message channel to **LidOpened**.

Drag a transition from **Listen for Cooking Done** to **Prepare to Reveal**. Drag another transition from **Prepare to Reveal** to **Animate Bread**.

The behavior should look like the following:

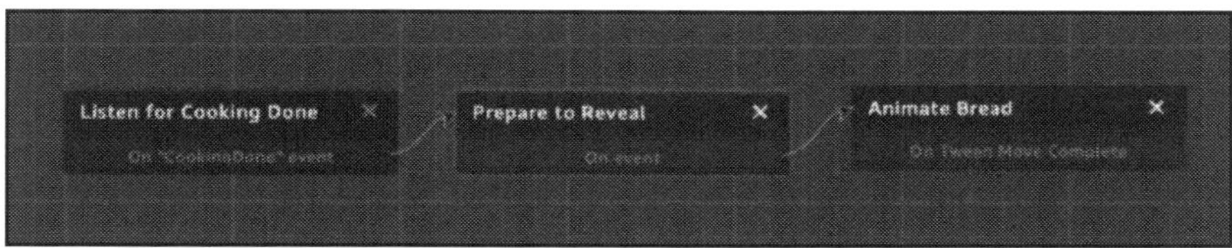

Finally, in the Entities panel, hide the Cooked Bread entity.

Tween rotating

There are many different types of tweening. One type you'll frequently use is **tween rotation**. For example, in your demo, you want the lid to rotate open and rotate closed.

Click **Create Entity**. Select the empty **Entity** and name it **Lid**. Drag it into the Bread Machine entity. Next, drag the **Glass_14_-_Default** and the **Top_14_-_Default** entity into it. Your lid should look like this:

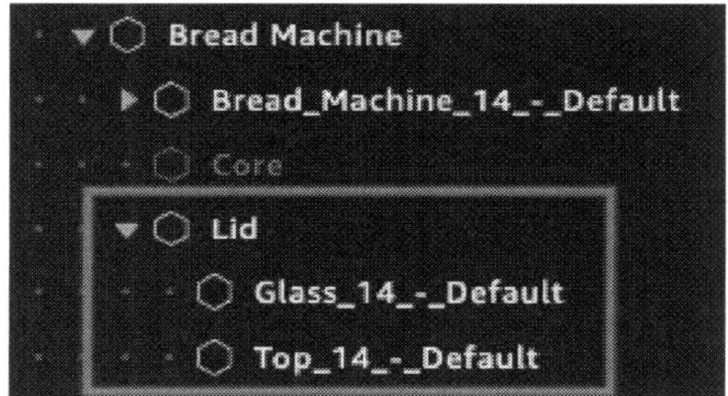

Select the Lid entity and try changing the rotation values. The lid leaves the machine and rotates in a large circle. When you created the lid entity, its default Translation was set to (0, 0, 0). This is the center point of the rotation, which is the center of the scene.

Remove the entities from the lid. Set the Translation to (**0**,**0**, **0**). You'll see the entity is positioned at the base of the machine.

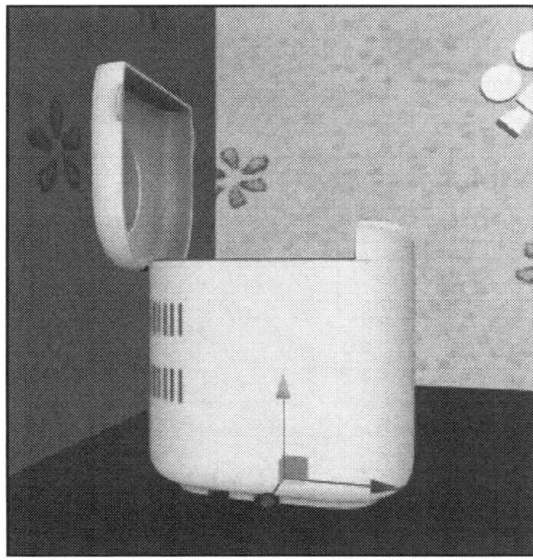

Using the transform arrows, position the entity in the center of the lid hinge. This is your rotation point.

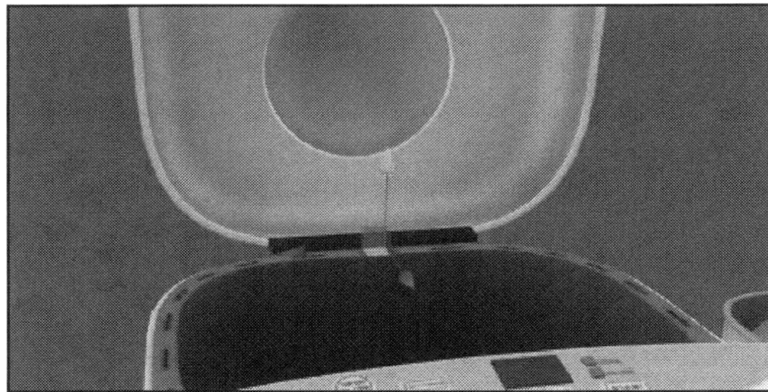

Now drag the **Glass_14_-_Default** and the **Top_14_-_Default** back into the Lid entity. Set the Lid entity's Rotation to (**0**,**-180**, **-90**).

This will close your lid. Chances are the lid clips through the rest of the model.

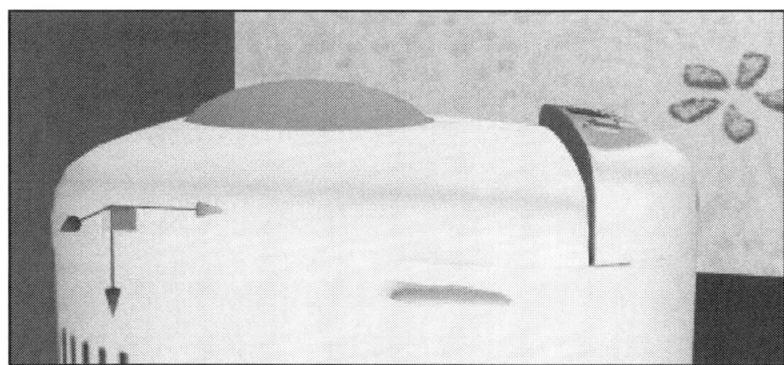

You can use the Transform arrows to position it flush against the machine and then set the Rotation back to (**0**,**-180**, **0**). Now, you can add your tween.

Click **Add Component** and select **State Machine**. Click the **+** button to add new behavior. Name the new behavior **Lid**.

This behavior will have four states: One state listens for messages, two more perform animations, and the final state sends a notification that the animation is complete.

Select the current state, name it **Listen** and add two Listen actions. Name one channel to **OpenLid** and the other to **CloseLid**.

Click **Add State** and name it **Open Lid**. Add a **Tween Rotate** and set the Rotation to (**0**, **0**, **90**).

Duplicate the state and name it **Close Lid**. Set the Rotation to (**0**, **0**, **-90**).

Click **Add State** and name the new state **Emit Completed Message**. Add an **Emit Message** to it and set the channel to **LidAnimated**.

Finally, drag a transition from the OpenLid event to the Open Lid state. Drag another transition from the CloseLid event to the Close Lid state. Then, drag a transition from the Open Lid state to the Emit Completed Message state. Do the same for the Close Lid. Finally, drag a transition from the Emit Completed Message to the Listen state.

Your behavior should look like the following:

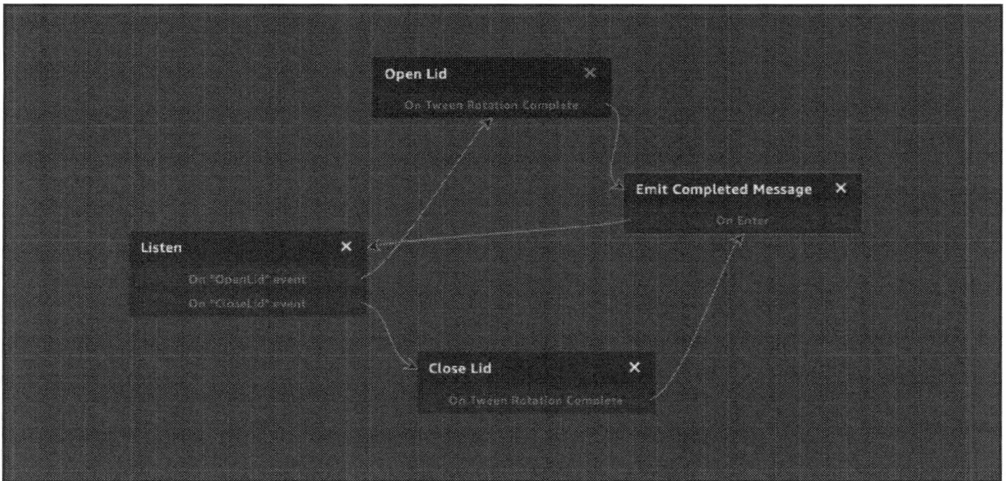

You'll integrate this with the demo soon – but first, you'll dive into other animation methods.

Using animated models

When you import models into Sumerian, those models may contain their animations. 3D modeling programs contain animating tools. Each animation is stored as a separate clip.

When creating animations, artists will sometimes rig a model. This means creating an internal skeleton so that moving one part of the model will affect the "bones" that connect to other parts.

It's natural to think of human skeletons, but these rigs can also be for animals or even inanimate objects.

When you import a model, Sumerian will create separate assets for the model, skeleton and the actual animation clips. You can use these animation clips within a behavior, which means you can trigger your animations based on clicks, messages and so forth.

Click **Import Assets** and search for the **Kyro Toaster**. Click **Add** to add it to your scene. Set the Translation to (**-10.436**, **3.711**, **-4.911**). Set the Rotation to (**0**, **90**, **0**). Set the Scale to (**5**, **5**, **5**), then rename it to **Toaster**.

Congrats! You've added a new appliance to your scene.

If you look at the toaster's Animation component, you'll notice that you have lots of different animation clips attached to it.

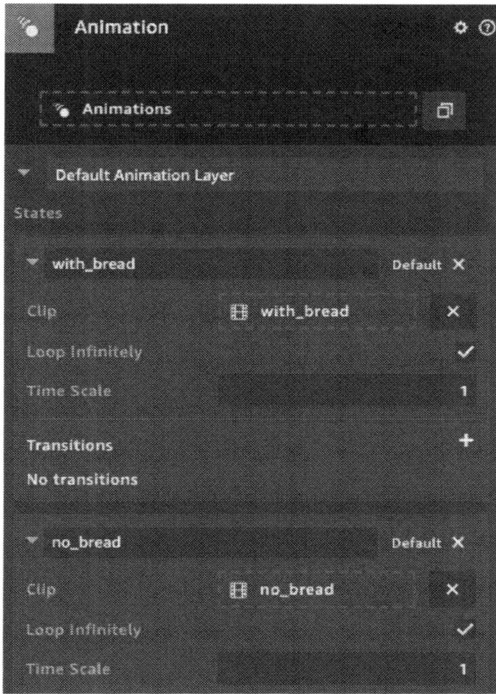

Animation clips are run on animation layers. Each layer can only play one clip at a time, but you can provide multiple layers at once.

Play the scene and you'll see two pieces of bread dropped into the toaster. This is because the "add_bread" clip is the default animation clip.

Scroll down to the "complete" clip and click **Default**. After you click this button, it'll turn blue, indicating this animation is now the default clip.

The “complete” clip looks similar to “add_bread”, so check the **Loop Infinitely** checkbox.

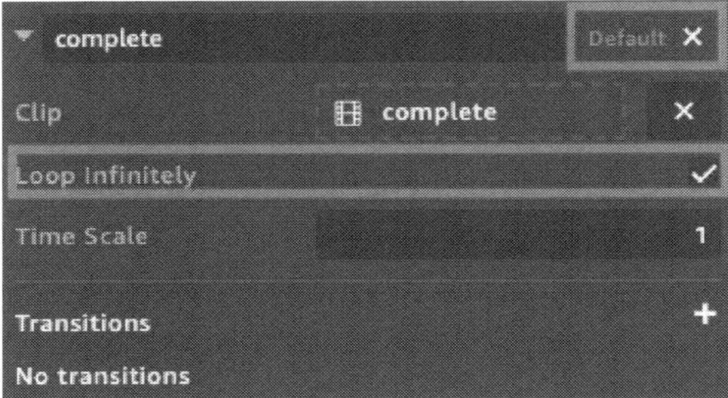

Now when you run the scene, you’ll get dancing bread.

The **Time Scale** property determines the speed of the animation. A speed of 1 means that the animation plays at the clip’s animation rate. Anything higher increases the speed, so a scale of 2 doubles the animation speed. A scale of .5 runs the animation at half-speed. This works the same in reverse, as you’ll see.

The **Transitions** property determines how clips will transition into one other. You can signify the length of the transition and the transition type.

For instance, you may have an animated model waving, then the animation transitions to another clip of the model scratching their head. Transitions determine how the animations blend.

By default, animations will blend into each other. This is useful when you have animations that have similar motions. A **SyncFade** will try and synchronize the target animation to the initial animation clip's start time. Finally, you can provide a **Frozen** transition that freezes the starting state at its current position and blends it into the target position.

The key thing to remember is that these transitions govern blending – they do not trigger an animation transition. For that, you need a state machine.

With the toaster selected, click **Add Component**. Add a **State Machine** component. Click the **+** to add a new behavior and name it **Toaster**.

Don't worry about naming the states here. You have a number of steps to complete, now.

- In the first state, add a **Click/Tap** action. Click **Add State** and, in the Animation category, create a **Set Animation** action.
- Set the animation to **add_bread**. You'll notice that you can transition from an animation completion.
- Duplicate the state. Set the animation to **activate**. Add a **Wait** action and set the Random property to **5**.
- Duplicate the state, remove the Wait action and set the animation to **complete**.
- Duplicate the state one more time. Set the animation to **no_bread**.
- Starting with State 1, drag transitions to the states in order.
- When making a dragging a transition from a state that has a Wait action, use the **On Wait End** event.
- When you reach the last transition, drag a transition back to the first transition.

It should be one circular behavior, like this:

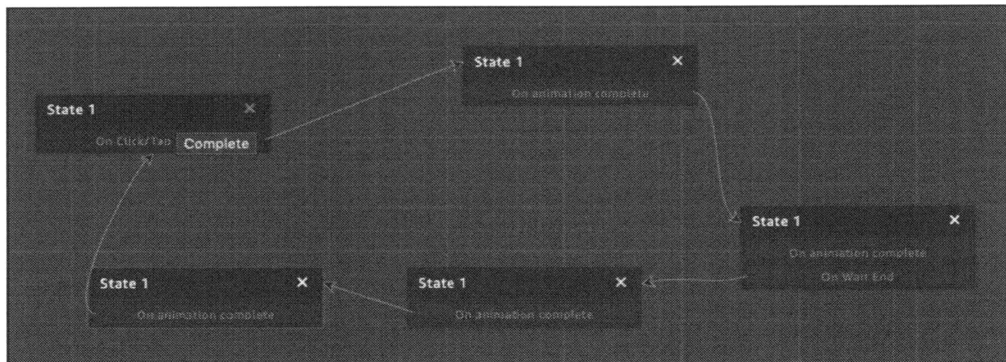

Now, play the scene and tap on the toaster. Now you'll get a complete animation cycle that you can restart by tapping it again.

Animating with the timeline component

Sumerian offers a third way of adding animation to your scene and that's by using the **timeline** component. The timeline allows you to animate translation, rotation, and scaling by using keyframes. Where a tween action allows you to animate to a certain point, a timeline allows you to animate multiple entities to several points. The timeline also works well with events and behaviors.

There are two ways to create a timeline: You can click **Create Entity** and select a Timeline object, or you can simply add a Timeline component to an existing entity.

There's a point in the demo where the narration asks the user to click on the bread pan. When the user clicks on the bread pan, the pan should animate into the bread machine.

You can add the timeline component to any entity *except* the entity you plan to animate. Since you're animating the bread pan, you can't add the timeline to it.

First, delete the toaster from your scene. You won't be toasting bread, you'll be baking it.

Now, click **Create Entity** and select **Timeline**.

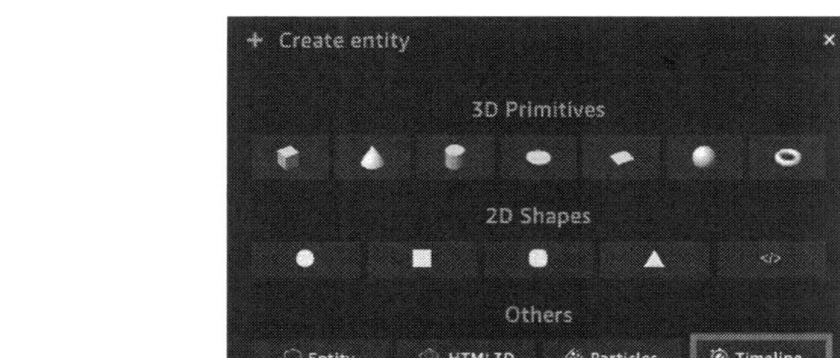

Rename the timeline to **Breadpan Timeline**. Your new entity comes with a Timeline component attached to it. The Timeline component allows you to set the duration, loop the animation and have it play on start.

Click **Toggle Timeline**.

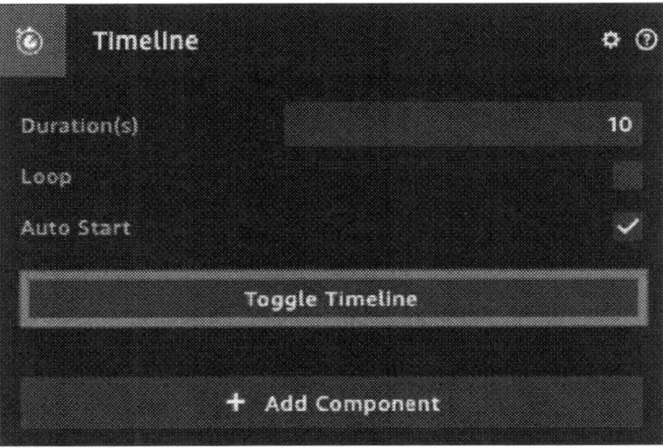

The Timeline editor is where you design your animation. It works very much like a video editor. You have a scrubber and a toolbar to play keyframes.

> **Note**: A keyframe marks the start or end of a transition. For instance, if you create a movement animation, one keyframe designates the start position and another keyframe designates the end position. The computer will then generate all the frames between those positions.

To start animating, drag the Breadpan entity into the Entity field in the timeline. When you drop it, the timeline will populate with the entity.

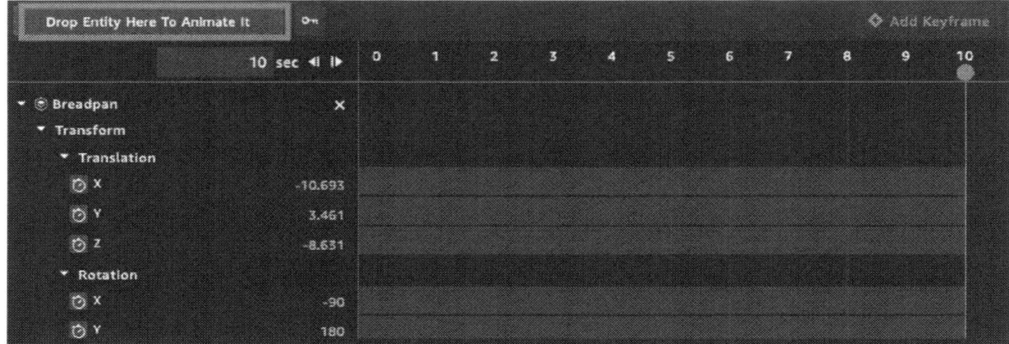

The timeline shows the Translation, Rotation and Scale properties. If you don't see all of the properties, scroll down. If you add additional entities, they will stack on top of each other. It's also useful to collapse properties that you aren't using. You won't be animating the Rotation or Scale, so collapse them by pressing the collapse arrows.

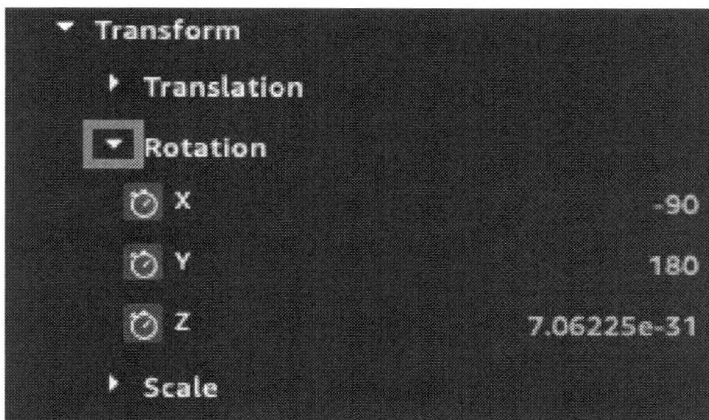

The green bars indicate the timespan. This is where you add your keyframes.

The numbers at the top of the timeframe indicate the seconds, and the blue circle is the scrubber. By moving the scrubber back and forth, you can preview the animation.

Move the scrubber to 0.

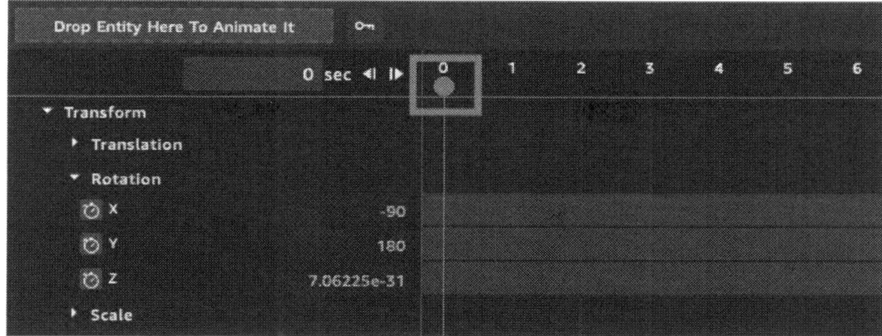

With the scrubber at the 0-second mark, click the **watch icon** that's to the left of the Y coordinate. This automatically adds a keyframe on this axis.

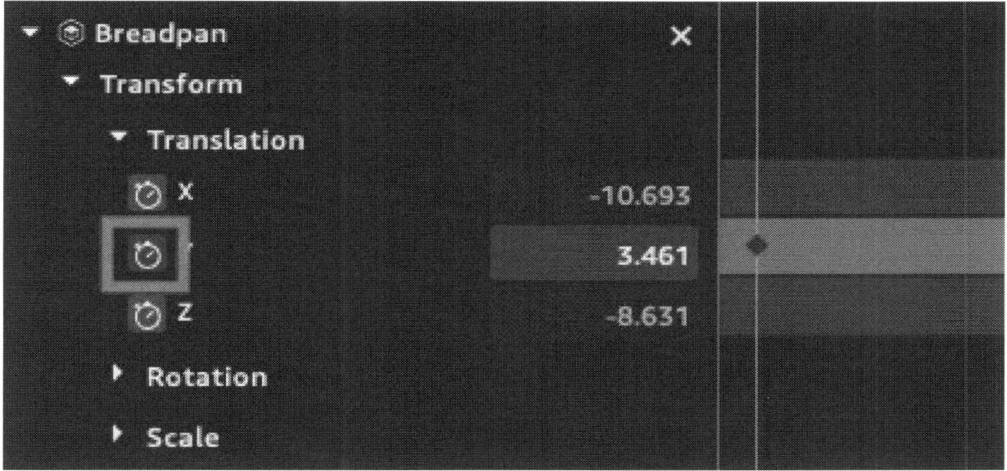

Move the scrubber to the 2-second mark. Now, set the Y coordinate to **4.781**. This also automatically adds a keyframe. Your timeline should look like the following:

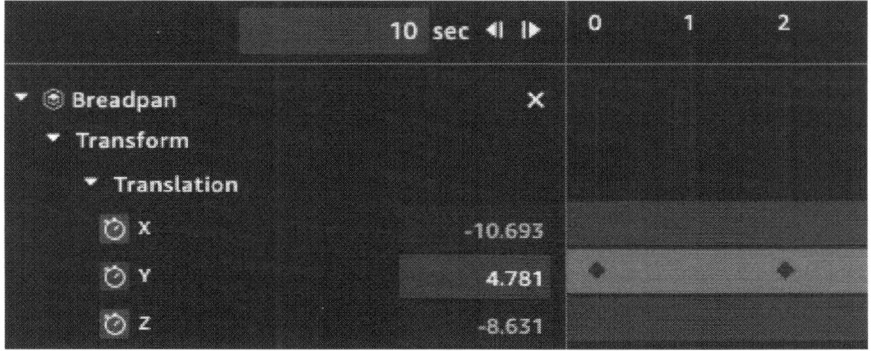

Scrub the timeline scrubber. You'll see the bread pan lift. If you move the scrubber back and forth, you'll see the pan raise and fall again.

Now, to add animations for the X and Z coordinates. Enable both of them by clicking the **watch** icon next to each one.

Select the X timeline and move the scrubber to the 2-second mark. An easy way to do this is by manually entering **2** into the seconds' field.

In the X row, click on the **green bar** to select it. Click **Add Keyframe**. This adds a keyframe for the current position, which is your start location.

Do the same for the Z coordinate. Your timeline should look like this:

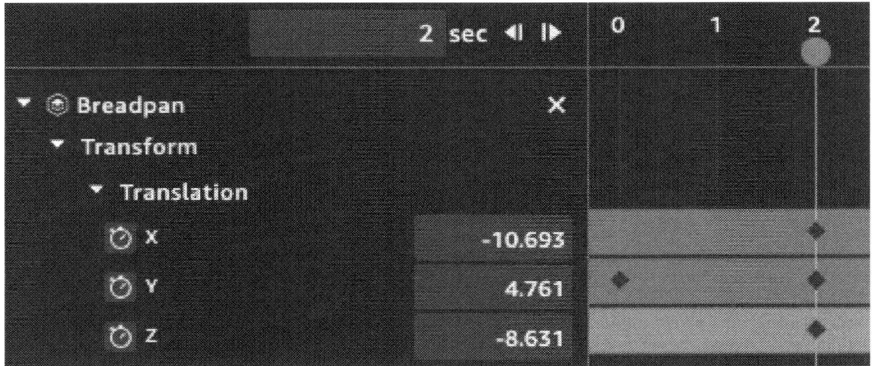

In the X, Y and Z rows, add keyframes at the 4-second mark. Set the X value to **-10.478** and the Z value to **-6.993**. You can click on a keyframe and then enter the value.

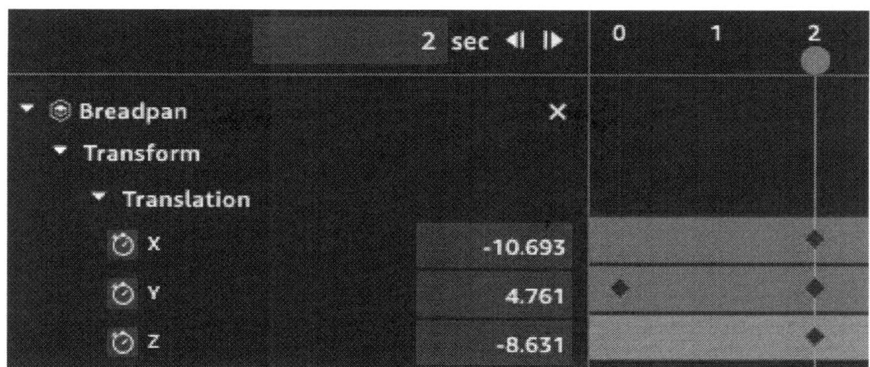

You may have keyframes at the very end of your timeline, which will mess up your animation. Select each keyframe by clicking on it and then pressing **Remove Keyframe**.

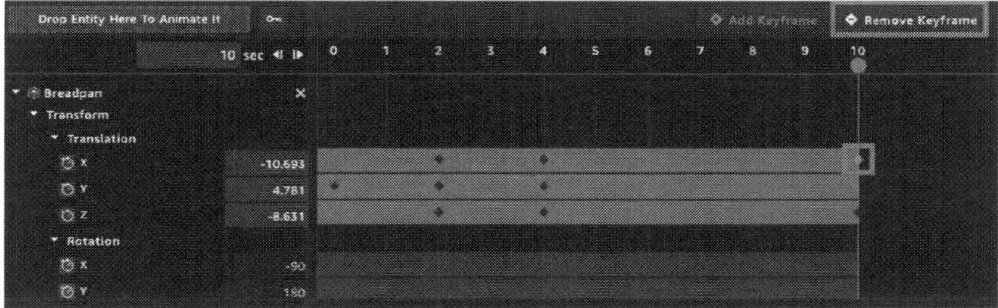

Do this for the other keyframe at the 10-second mark, if it's present.

Move the scrubber to the 6-second mark and add a keyframe in the **Y** row. Set the value to **3.7**.

Now, you have a complete animation of the bread pan rising off the counter, moving to the bread machine and lowering into it.

The animation duration is a little too long. In the Inspector panel, change the Duration to **6**. This will remove the extra part of the timeline.

Now, play your scene and you'll get a smoothly-moving bread pan.

All timelines are linear by default. If you want to use other types of animation, double-click on a keyframe and you'll get a pop-up dialog.

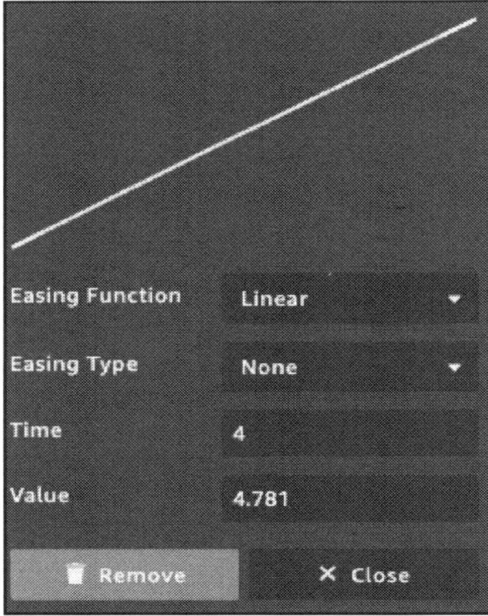

At this point, you can change your easing type. You'll even get a preview of the animation easing, which is really helpful.

Using the timeline with behaviors

Timelines are useful to encapsulate animation, but they also make it easy to animate multiple entities at the same time. You can play timeline animation directly from a behavior.

You'll do this using messages. First, your timeline is set to play on start. Select the Breadpan Timeline, and **uncheck the Auto Start** property.

First, activate your timeline when it receives a message. With the Breadpan Timeline entity still selected, click **Add Component** and select **State Machine**. Next, click the **+** button to add a new behavior. Name it **Breadpan Timeline**.

Rename your first state to **Listen for Click**. Add a **Listen** action to it and have it listen to the **ClickedBreadpan** channel.

Click **Add State** and name your new state to **Play Timeline**. Click **Add Action** and, in the Timeline category, select the **Start Timeline** action.

Drag a transition from the **Listen for Click** state to the **Play Timeline** state.

Your behavior should look like the following:

As you see, it's not hard to activate the timeline. Now, you need the Breadpan entity to fire the message.

Select **Breadpan** and add a State Machine, then create a new behavior. Name it **Breadpan**.

Name the first state to **Wait for Activation** and add a **Listen** action to it. Have it listen to the **ActivateBreadpan** channel.

Add a new state. Name it **Click to Animate**. Add a **Click** action to it.

Add a final state and name it **Send Animate Message**. Add an **Emit Message** action and set the message to **ClickedBreadpan**.

Drag a transition from **Wait for Activation** to **Click to Animate** and then from **Click to Animate** to **Send Animate Message**.

Your behavior should look as follows:

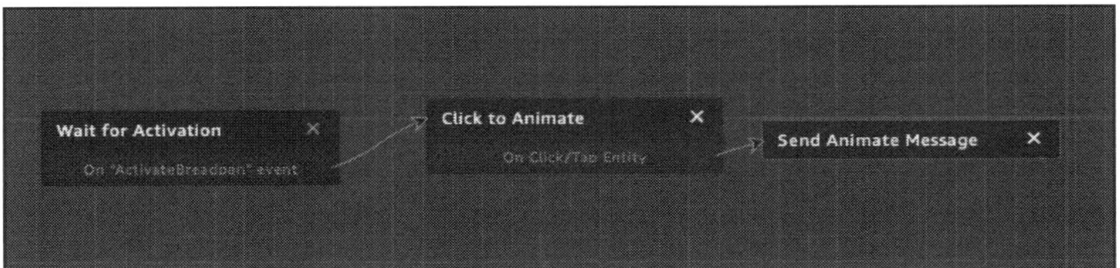

Next, you need to integrate your animation into the demo. Open the **Bread Machine Demo** and click **Add State**. Rename it to **Activate Breadpan**. Click **Add Action** and add an **Emit Action**. Set the channel to **ActivateBreadpan**.

Drag a transition from the **Click on Pan** state to the **Activate Breadpan** state. Your behavior should look like the following:

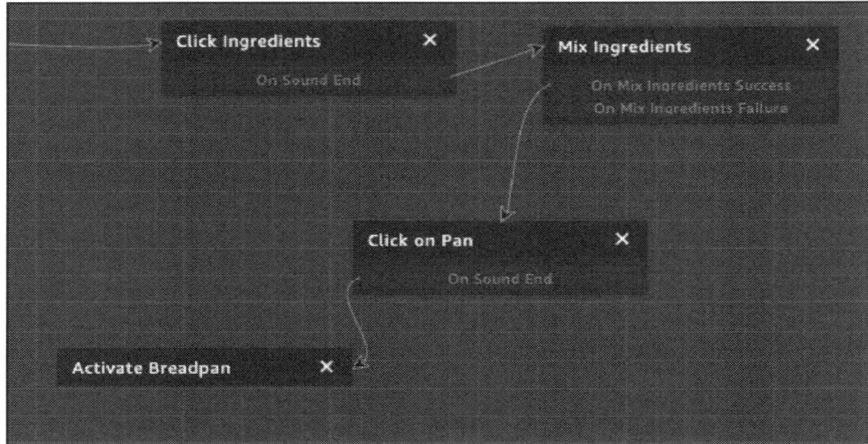

The Activate Breadpan state currently doesn't link to the rest of the states. Don't worry about that, you'll fix it in a moment.

To run the demo, select the **Demo Start Camera** and set it as the **Main Camera**. Now, play your scene.

At this point, you're stuck looking at the empty counter. Ideally, when the pan animates far enough, the scene should switch to another camera. Then, the bread machine's lid should close.

You use events to do this.

Timeline events

Timeline events work like keyframes, except you don't animate anything. An event is just a message that's broadcast once the animation reaches a specific point in the animation.

Select the **Breadpan Timeline** and click **Toggle Timeline**. If you scroll down the timeline, you'll see a section titled **Event channels**. Click the + button.

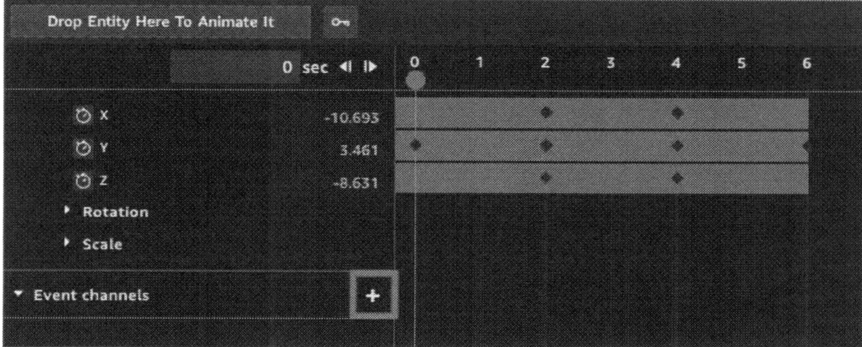

This creates your event. Name it **SwitchToBreadMachine**. Move the scrubber to **3** and click **Add Keyframe**.

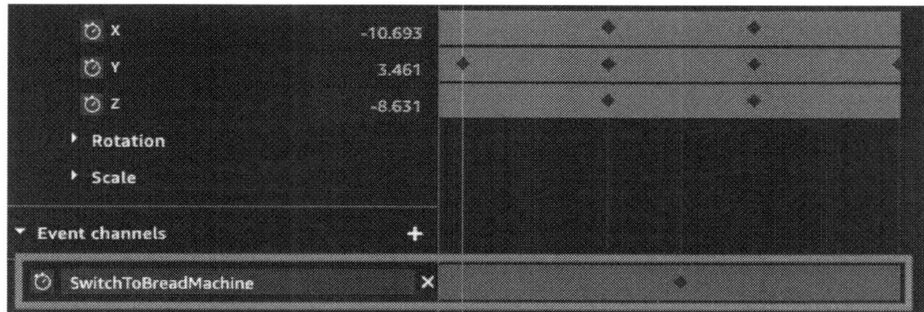

Add another event and name it **CloseLid**. Move the scrubber to **6** and add a keyframe. Your channels should look like the following:

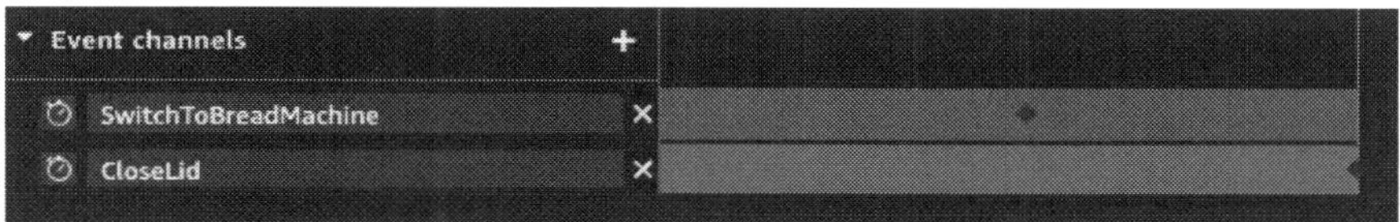

Open the **Bead Machine Demo** behavior and select the **Activate Breadpan** state. Add a **Listen** action to it and set the channel to **SwitchToBreadMachine**.

Click **Add State** and name it **Switch Camera**. Add a **Switch Camera** action and set the camera to **Bread Machine Camera**. Add a **Listen** action and set the channel to **LidAnimated**.

Drag a transition from **Activate Breadpan** to the **Switch Camera** state and then from **Switch Camera** to **Press Start Button and Switch Camera**. Finally, select the **Press Start Button and Switch Camera** and rename it to **Press Start Button**.

Your behavior should look like this:

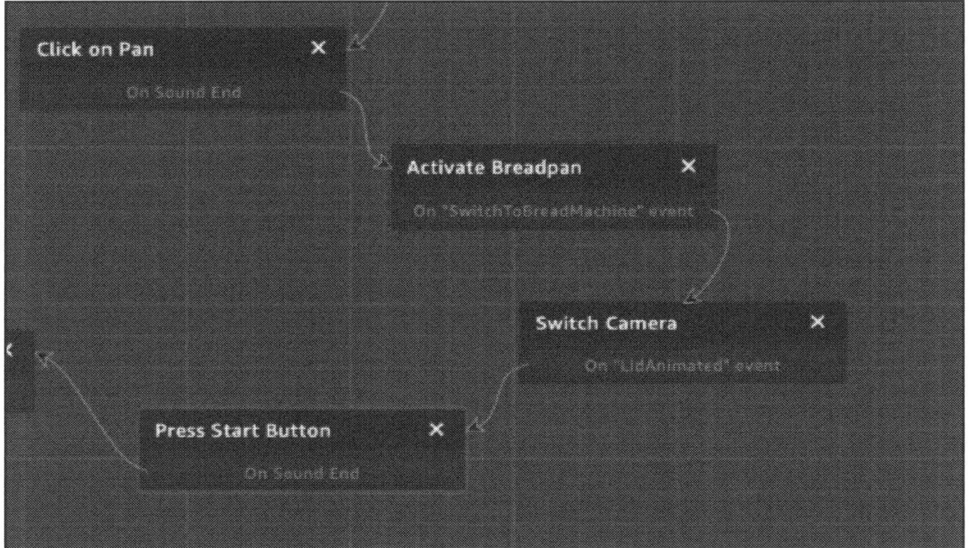

Now, play your scene. Everything plays through. Your buttons work... although when the lid opens, you get raw dough. Don't worry, you'll fix that soon.

There's also some clipping as the bread machine passes the camera. Select the Bread Machine Camera and set the Near Clipping Plane to **.5**. Now everything should run perfectly. All it needs is a little pizazz.

Sumerian particle systems

Almost every modern 3D engine provides a way to produce particles, and Sumerian is no exception. Particles are small, 3D objects that render in large quantities. You can use these systems to create snow, fire, fog and a variety of other cool effects.

For example, when a wizard launches a dazzling fireball at an enemy, what you're seeing is several particle systems in motion.

Using particle systems to create a specific effect is both an art and a science. In this section, you'll create a small misting effect. When the bread machine opens, a nice waft of steam will exit the machine.

To get started, click **Create Entity** and select **Particles**.

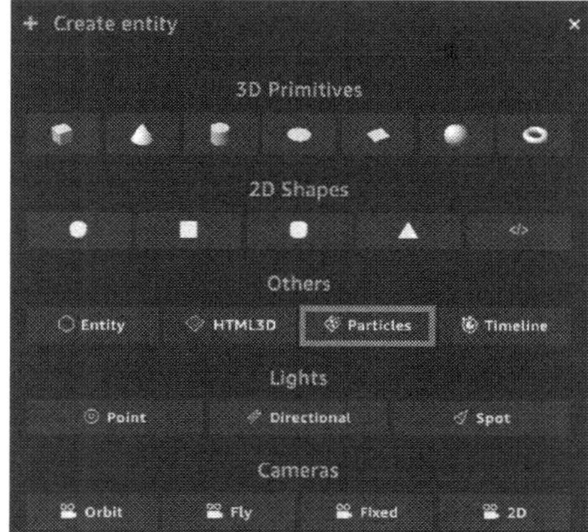

Rename the new entity to **Steam**. Set the Translation to (**-10.569**, **4.466**, **-6.944**). When you select a particle system, you'll see a green wireframe. This wireframe is the shape of the system.

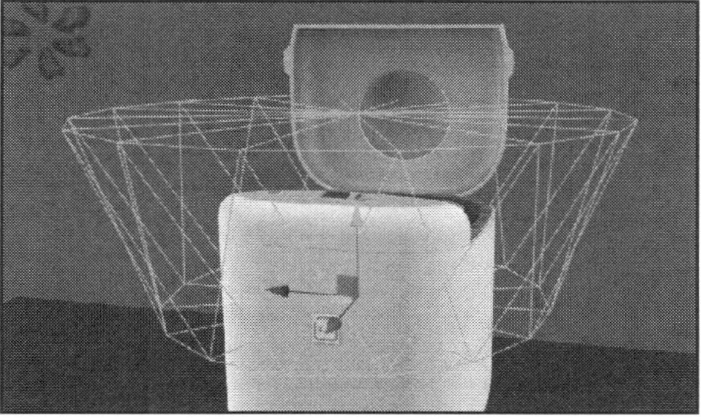

Particles emit at the bottom of the cone and they'll expire past the top of the cone. Set the Default Camera as the **Main Camera** and your particle system will emit.

The particles are a little too large to look like steam. It's time to get to work configuring.

When you examine the Particles component in the Inspector panel, you'll see that you have a lot of different options.

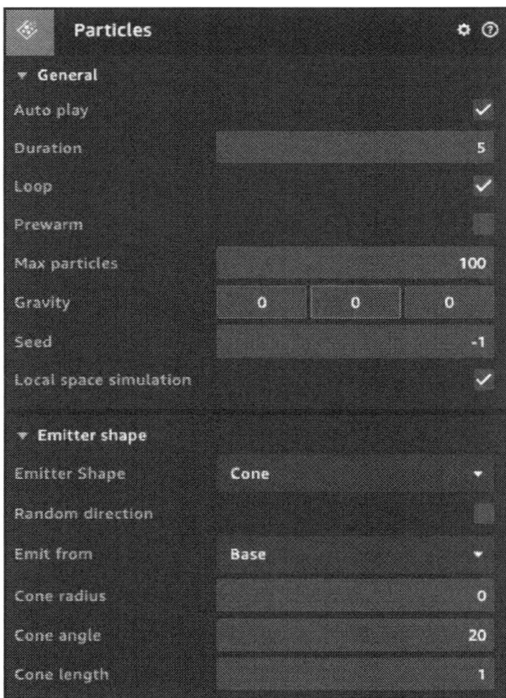

Each section in the particle component allows you to customize various aspects of the particle system. You'll start at the top and work your way down. This section won't cover every single property of the particle emitter, just the ones that you'll adjust for your demo.

Note: If you're interested in learning about all the properties, check out the Particle System documentation in the Sumerian User Guide. You can access it here: https://docs.aws.amazon.com/en_pv/sumerian/latest/userguide/entities-particlesystem.html.

General section

The properties in this section determine the very basic behavior of the emitter. By default, the emitter is set to Auto Play. This is useful for testing your system.

By default, the particle system will last for 5 seconds. Change the Duration to **2** seconds.

The **Prewarm** property loads your particles before the system starts to play. Otherwise, it will take a bit of time for it to start emitting particles. **Check** the Prewarm property.

The Loop property is useful for testing. You'll leave this checked for now, but later, you'll uncheck it.

You'll need lots of particles to simulate your mist. Currently, your system is set to emit a max of 100 particles. Change Max particles to **1500**. This doesn't affect how many particles emit; rather, it determines how many particles can be shown at once.

Finally, the Local space simulation property is set to emit particles only inside the parent entity's boundaries. **Uncheck** this property.

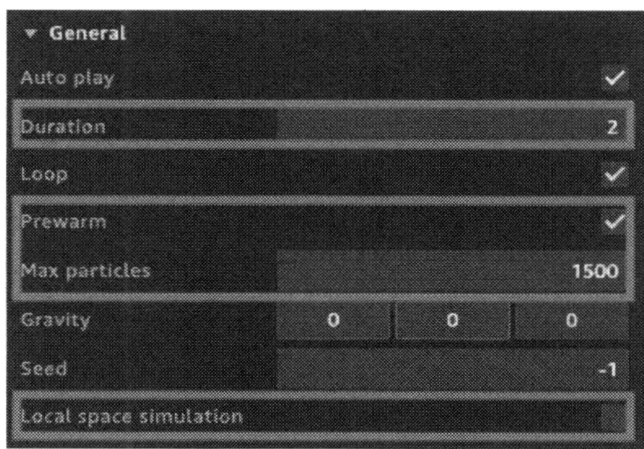

If you play the scene, it looks the same.

Emitter shape

The shape determines how the particles are emitted. You're emitting your particles from a cone, but other shapes are available. You're using a wide code, which will emit particles from the sides of the machine. It's time to make some adjustments.

Now, you want to change the shape of the cone. First, make sure the particles are set to emit from its volume. Do this by setting the Emit from property to **Volume**. This allows the particles to spawn throughout the cone.

Next, set the Cone radius to **0.3**, the Cone angle to **16** and the Cone length to **1.2**.

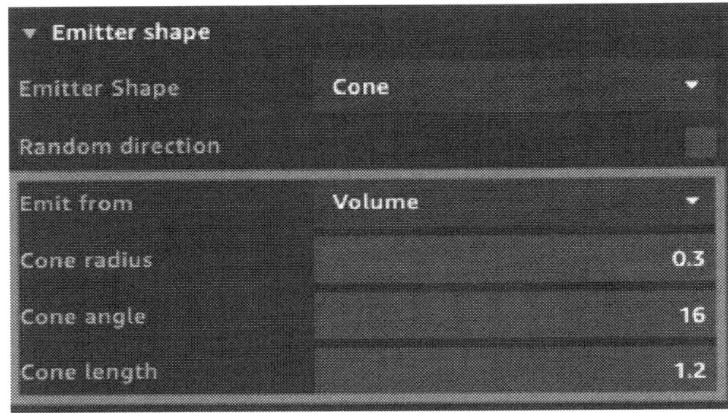

While this won't change the look of the particles, it will affect the system's shape.

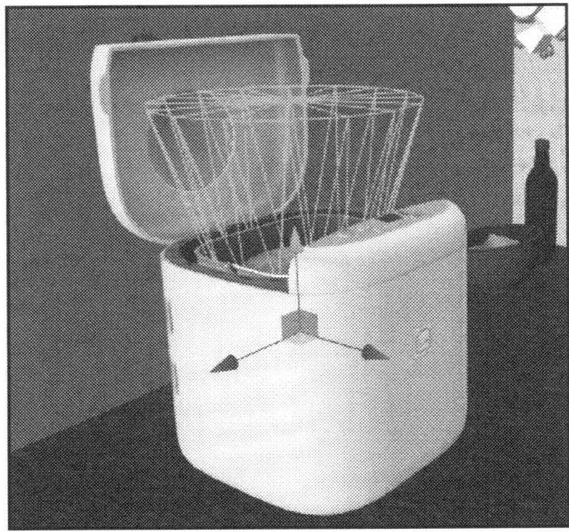

Over duration properties

This is where things get interesting since this section affects the actual particles. These are applied with each loop of the animation. You can provide constants, linear values or random values.

The **Emission rate** determines how many particles should be emitted per cycle. Set the value to **200**. This causes your bread machine to vomit a pillar of mist.

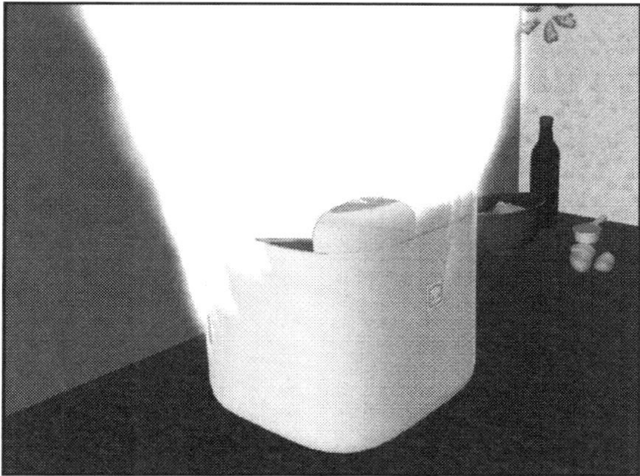

By default, the steam is moving fast. Set the Start speed to **0.5**.

The **Start size** determines the size of the particles. Instead of using Constant, select **Random Between Two Constants**. Set the value between **0.4** or **1**.

Next, you want to affect the **Start color** of the particles. The effect doesn't need to be too strong. Set the value to **Random Between Two Colors**.

For the first color, set the RGBA values to (**0.60**, **0.60**, **0.60**, **0.378**). The first three values determine the color, while the last value is transparency.

For the second color, set it to (**1.00**, **1.00**, **1.00**, **0.00**).

Finally, set the **Start lifetime** to **1**. This means that each particle will only last one second.

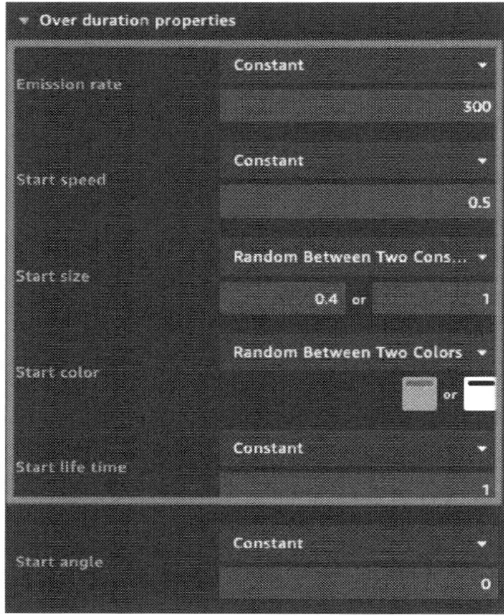

Over lifetime properties

Over lifetime properties are properties that apply to the entire lifetime of the particle emitter.

First, you want to add some colors. You'll change between back and white. Set the Color to **Random Between Two Colors**. Leave the first color as-is and set the second color to **000000**.

For the **Size** property, select **Random Between Two Constants** and set the values to **0.4** and **1**.

For the **Rotation speed**, select **Random Between Two Constants** and set the values to **-100** and **100**.

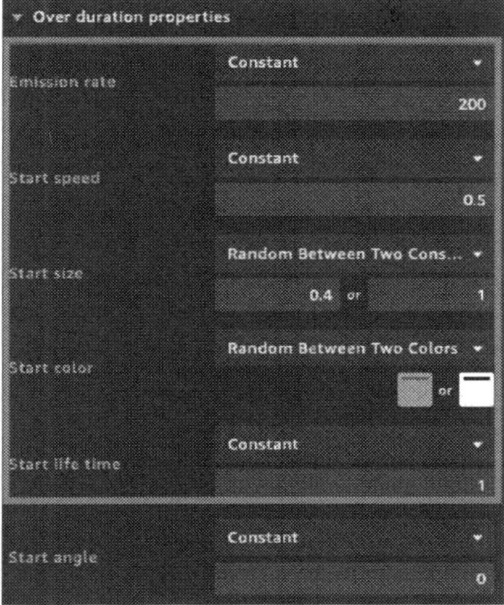

Now, run your scene and you'll see steam emit from the bread machine.

As you can see, you've created some simple steam. In the General settings, **Uncheck** the loop. When you run it, the steam starts strong, then dissipates. Can you smell the fresh bread?

Finally, uncheck the **particles auto play** property. You'll use the particles on demand.

Integrating the particles

With your steam ready to go, your next task is to have it play in your scene. Drag `Steam` into the **Bread Machine**.

With `Steam` still selected, click **Add Component**. Add a **State Machine** and create a new behavior. Name it **Steam**.

Rename the first state to **Listen for Open Lid**. Add a **Listen** action and listen to the **OpenLid** channel.

Add a new state. Name it **Show Steam**. Click **Add Action** and, in the Misc category, select the **Start Particles** action.

Drag a transition from the **Listen for Open Lid** state to the **Play Particle System** state.

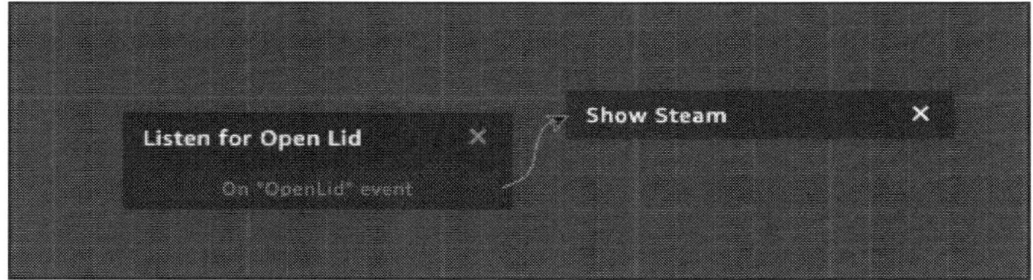

Now, to add it all together! Select the **Bread Machine Demo** behavior and select the **Baking Is Done** state. Add an **Emit Message** action and set the channel to **CookingDone**.

This message does a few things. First, it hides the raw dough and then it shows the cooked bread. This primes the bread to appear. When the user clicks on the open button, the OpenLid message is sent.

This message starts the particle system, animates the opening of the lid and plays the final narration.

Run your scene and you should see a loaf of freshly-cooked bread rising out of a machine.

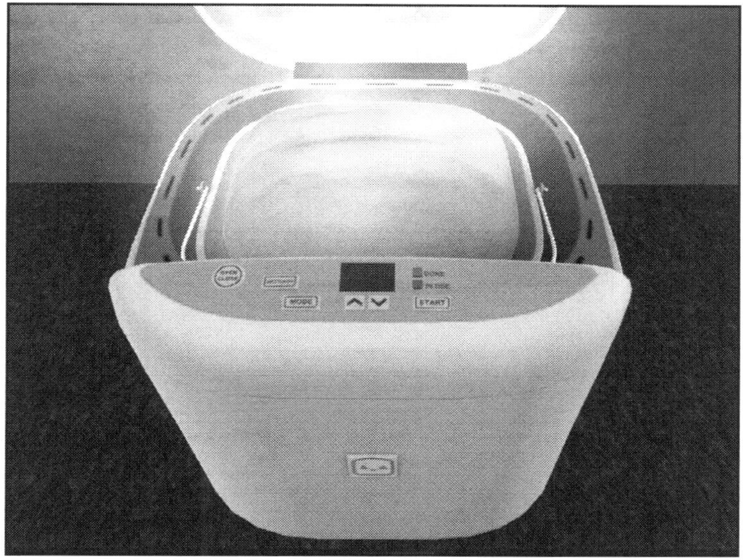

Key points

- A **tween is an animation between two points** designated to happen over a period of time.
- An **easing type** determines how the **speed of the animation** plays out over time.
- Some models contain their own animation clips.
- **Animation clips** can be **integrated into behaviors** allowing the animations to play on demand.
- The **timeline** allows you to **develop your own animations** inside of the editor.
- **Animation timelines can send messages** at certain points of the animation.
- A particle system is series of animated particles emitted from a source.
- Particles are manipulated from a variety of properties and can be used to produce a variety of effects.

Where to go from here?

Both animation and particle systems can take a static scene and bring it to life. You can use them to highlight important points or just to make the scene interesting and dynamic. To learn more about animation, check out this tutorial: https://docs.sumerian.amazonaws.com/tutorials/create/intermediate/animation-component-using-fbx/}

You can also learn about particle systems by following this tutorial as well: https://docs.sumerian.amazonaws.com/tutorials/create/beginner/campfire-particles/

Chapter 14: Incorporating Web Content

By Brian Moakley

Sumerian is built for modern web technologies using HTML, CSS, and JavaScript. Using a web-centric engine means it's very easy to incorporate web-based content.

For example, if you want to highlight a website redesign in your 3D scene, you have a few interesting options. You can take a screenshot of the website and use it as a texture. Or, you can embed the site into the actual scene. This means that users will not only be able to view your site, they'll also be able to interact with it.

This is very cool, especially when you're incorporating web content into a 3D space.

Getting started with the HTML entity

When you start your bread machine demo, the user sees a simple start button, but no other context. They'll have no idea what to expect from the experience. An introduction provides a great way to set the user's expectations of the experience. In this case, you'll incorporate a simple video to describe the experience.

There are lots of ways to create videos and lots of different hosting providers. For this demo, you'll incorporate an existing video hosted on YouTube.

To get started, open your Quickstart scene. The first thing you need to do is to make space for the video. You'll put it at the start of the scene and place the start button underneath it.

In the Entities panel, select the **Start Button** and change the Translation to (**5.356**, **2.624**, **-10.931**).

This lowers the button, making room for the video.

To add the video, you need to add a special HTML element. Click **Create Entity** then, in the Others category, select **HTML3D**.

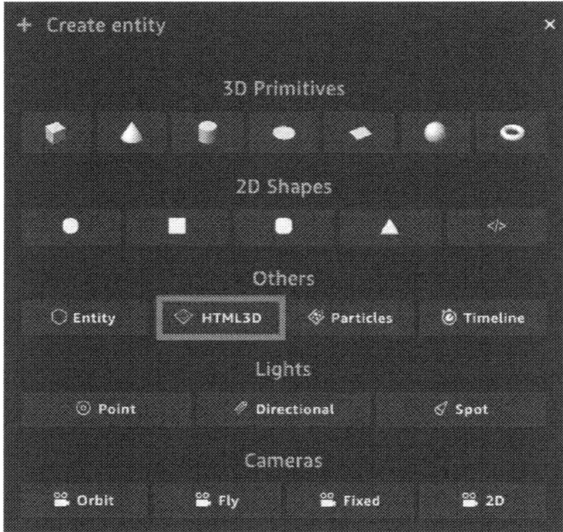

Right away, you'll see a 3D webpage in your scene.

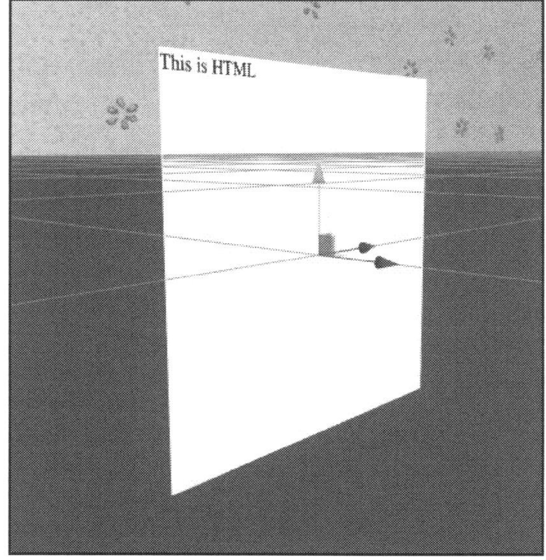

This is a 3D HTML element. You can position the element like any other piece of 3D geometry. Set the element's Translation to (**1**, **2**, **0**).

Sumerian offers another HTML element as well. Click **Create Entity** and this time, in the 2D Shapes category, select **</>**.

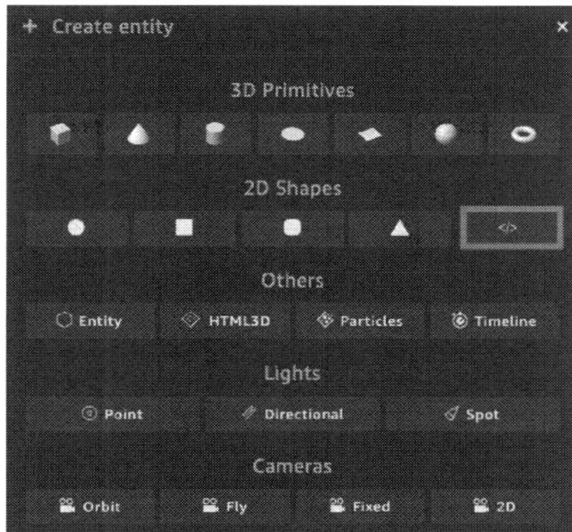

This creates a 2D HTML element. While you can rotate the camera around a 3D HTML element, a 2D HTML element will always point toward the camera.

The 2D HTML element is great for user interface elements. You'll be using it for that purpose in the next section.

Both the 3D and 2D HTML entities have similar properties. The first is that HTML entities can't be transparent – transparency renders as black. This means HTML entities are opaque.

Next, 2D HTML entities will not render in virtual reality. These entities will just appear as black boxes.

Finally, HTML content integrates with the rest of the web page. This means you can interact with it using JavaScript and the DOM API. You'll do this later in the chapter.

For now, delete the 2D HTML element and select the **HTML3d Entity**. Rename it to **Introduction Video**.

When you select the entity, you'll see that it contains an HTML 3D component. This component allows you to change the width. You can also open the element in the Text editor.

Click **Open in Editor**. Clicking the button opens the same Text editor that you used to edit JavaScript.

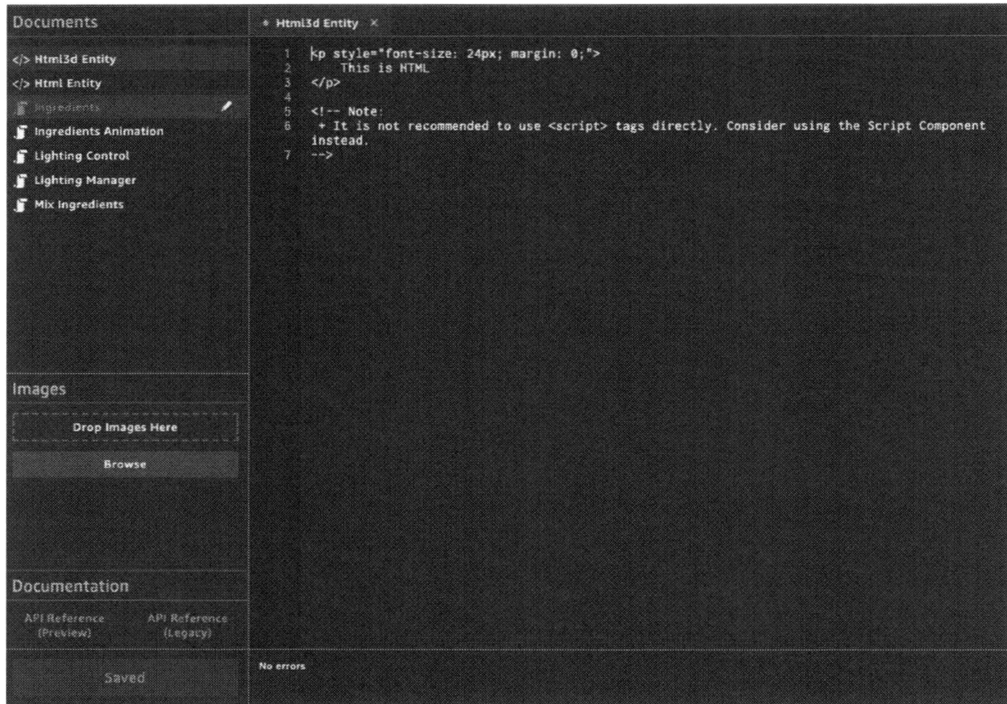

All you need to do now is write some HTML.

Quick web primer

Before you start playing with web content in your scene, it helps to understand how web content works. If you already have a good understanding, feel free to jump to the next section.

There are lots of different technologies employed in creating web pages, with entire books written about each of them. Needless to say, think of this chapter as a very brief overview.

As mentioned, you build web pages with HTML, CSS, and JavaScript. HTML provides the structure of the page, CSS determines the look of the page and JavaScript allows for interactivity.

When building a page, you start with HTML, which is an abbreviation for Hypertext Markup Language. It defines how you lay your page out.

For comparison, think of a letter. A letter starts with a header section. The header contains your address, your correspondent's address, and the date. The letter then contains a body that's broken into sections composed of paragraphs. Finally, you have a closing section.

Web pages use a similar pattern, except that HTML uses tags to separate sections.

In the Text editor, add the following:

```
<html>
    <head>
        <title>My Web Page</title>
    </head>
    <body>
        <p>This is a web page</p>
    </body>
</htmL>
```

Here, you've made a simple web page that prints out the text: "This is a web page". It isn't the most exciting page, but it's the foundation of the web.

As you can see, each element is composed of two tags. There is an opening tag () and a closing tag (). The page contains a title that will appear in the browser bar.

The body of the page contains a simple paragraph that prints text.

You use CSS to style the pages. CSS stands for Cascading Style Sheets. This is a technology where you declare presentation rules. For instance, you could make a rule that states: All paragraphs designated as `critical` will be red and bolded.

In the header, you create a class and then assign rules. Add the following after the `<title></title>` tags but still between the `<head></head>` tags.

```
<style>
    .critical {
        color:red;
        font-weight:bold;
    }
</style>
```

This defines a CSS class called critical that makes text appear red and bolded. Each line contains a key and value, which are defined by CSS and separated by semi-colons.

You define your class in the HTML style element and you apply it using an HTML attribute. Update the paragraph tag to the following:

```
<p class="critical">This is a web page</p>
```

There are lots of HTML attributes that affect elements in different ways. In this case, the class attribute is applying your critical rule. You can also apply the style directly like so:

```
<p style="color:red;font-weight:bold;">This is a web page</p>
```

That's a very brief overview. You'll learn more about the rest when you need it.

Embedding video content

At this point, you're ready to embed your video. Now that you know how to edit HTML, the rest just requires copying and pasting. You'll be copying some HTML code that embeds a video into a web page. This same code can be used to embed a video into a Sumerian scene.

Head over to the following URL: https://www.youtube.com/watch?v=mcFmPonEPZU&feature=youtu.be

On the YouTube page, click **Share**.

This presents a share dialog with lots of options. Select the **Embed** option.

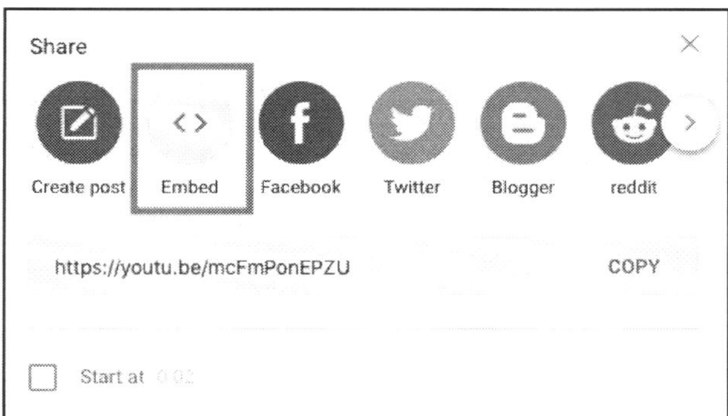

This presents another dialog that provides a preview of the video as well as the HTML it needs to display. Select the HTML code and click **COPY**.

Return to Sumerian and, with the HTML editor open, delete all of the existing code and paste the embedded code into it. Click **Save** and return to your scene.

When you return to the scene, you'll see your video, but it doesn't match the height of the embedded window.

The video matches the width, but the height is a little too much. Thankfully, you can scale the entity to a smaller height. Set the Scale to (**1**, **0.62**, **1**). Now set the Translation to (**5.365**, **5.27**, **-10.93**). While the video looks great, it's kind of small.

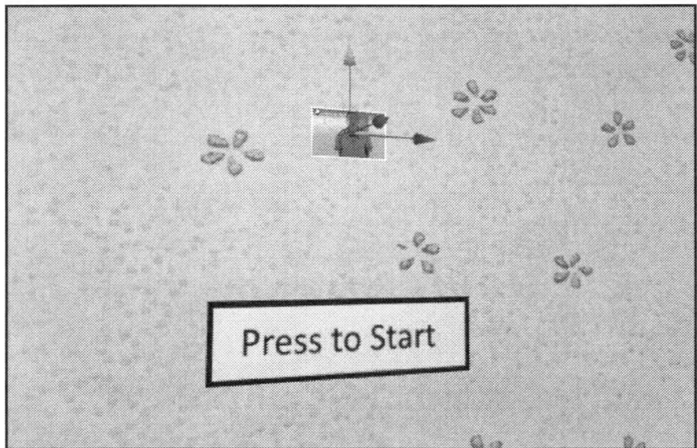

You can play around with the sizes, but an easier method is to select the entity and, in the Transform component, check the **Uniform Scale** option.

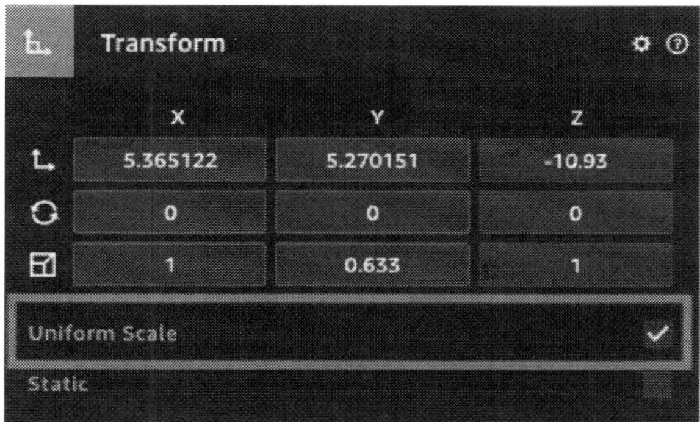

In the Scale row, select the **X** coordinate and scroll up to **5.8**. When you finish, you'll have a video with the correct translation and scale.

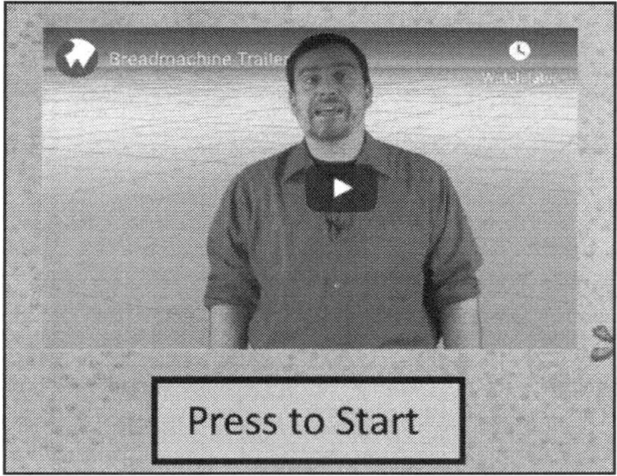

Creating a cooking time counter

Part of the bread machine demo simulates cooking time. At the moment, when the user starts cooking, the baking immediately ends.

A better experience is to provide a timing countdown. The countdown should integrate into the bread machine itself. This is a great case for using an HTML 3D entity.

This feature will contain many different components. First, you'll have the web counter. Next, you'll create a script that will allow the user to set the cooking time. Finally, you'll need to count down the remaining seconds and update the timer.

Adding the counter

To get started, click **Create Entity** and add another **HTML 3D** entity. Rename this one to **Cook Time Counter**. Set the Translation to (**-10.024**, **5.152**, **-7.01**). Set the Rotation to (**-80.498**, **89.522**, **1.014**). Finally, set the Scale to (**0.101**, **0.061**, **0.455**).

Your counter should now look like the following:

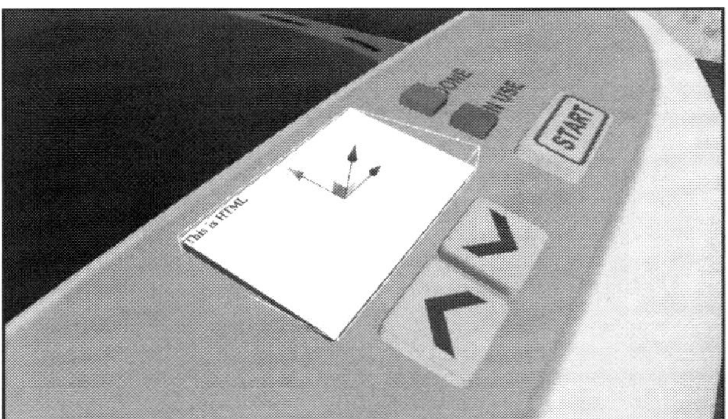

The first thing you need to do is change the background color of the console. Open the **Cook Time Counter** entity in the Text editor. Replace the existing code with the following:

```
<style>
    body {
        background-color: #d24dff;
    }
</style>
```

Here, you've created a style that applies to the `<body>` tag. This sets the background to a darker color. In CSS, you can define your colors in hexadecimal.

If you do a google search for **CSS Color Picker**, you'll find a simple tool that shows the hexadecimal equivalent of any color you select.

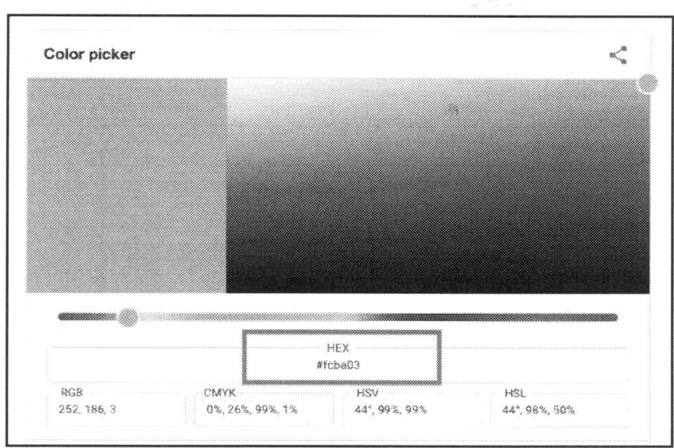

Now, add the following:

```
<p id="timer" style="font-size: 150px; text-
align:center;margin:0;height:100%; width:100%; padding-
top:55px;background-color:#000000; color:#ffffff" >00:10</p>
```

This creates a paragraph tag using an inline style. First, the tag has an ID, which is useful when working with JavaScript.

Next, you added a style that set the counter to be the entire size of the web view. It also uses a large white font so the text is easier to see.

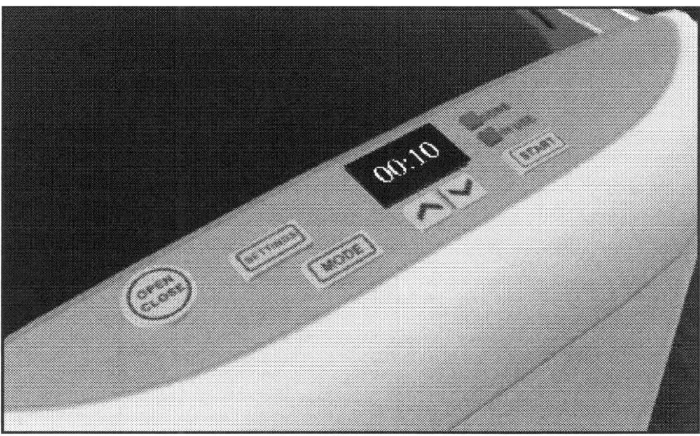

By default, the counter should be empty. In the HTML, replace `00:10` with ` `. This is a special HTML character for a non-breaking space. This space serves as a place holder.

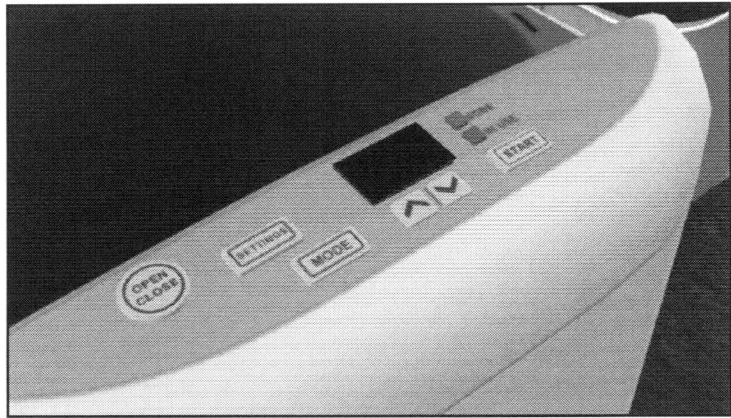

You now have an empty counter, ready to go.

Setting the cooking time

By default, the cooking time should be five seconds. You can set this directly into the scene, but a better option is to allow the user to configure this time from within a behavior.

Select the **Cook Time Counter** and click **Add Component**. Add a **Script** and click the + button. Make sure to add a **Custom (Preview Format)** script.

In the Assets panel, select the **Scripts** tab and then select the **Script** script and rename it to **Counter**. Open the script in the Text editor.

First, you need to define a property. This will allow the user to set the time amount.

Delete the default function. Add the following:

```
export const PROPERTIES = {
  countdownAmount: {
    type: s.type.Integer,
    default: 5,
    order: 0
  }
}
```

This creates `countdownAmount`, an integer set to a default of five seconds.

Now for the actual function. Add the following:

```
export default function CountdownTimerAction(ctx, options) {
    var currentTime = options.countdownAmount;
    ctx.start(
        [s.message.ReceiveAction, {
            channel: "StartCooking", onReceived: (data) => {
                // Do nothing ... for now
            }
        }]
    );
}
```

This function first gets `countdownAmount` and stores it in a variable named `currentTime`. Next... the action doesn't do anything. You'll write the code for the receive action in just a bit.

When you select **Cook Time Counter**, you'll see that you have a counter that defaults to five seconds.

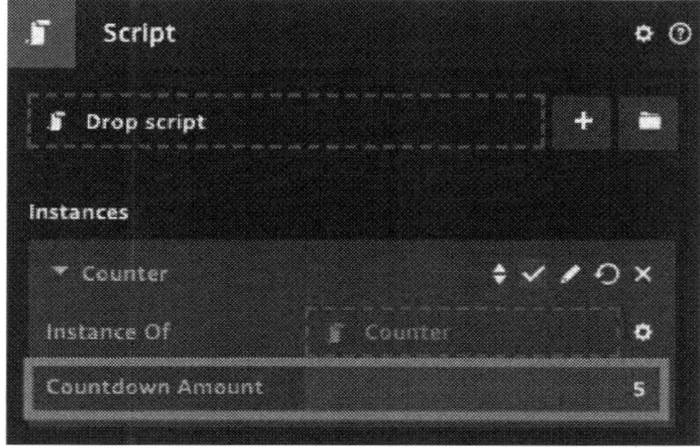

At this point, you need to make a slight alteration to the overall demo behavior. Select the **Bread Machine Demo** behavior and open it in the State Machine editor.

Select the **Start Cooking** state and change the Listen channel to **CookingDone**. And that's it! Now you are ready to code.

Writing the countdown code

Next, you're going to write code that does three different things: First, when the countdown starts, you'll turn on the In Use button. Then, you'll do the actual countdown. When the countdown ends, you'll need to turn on the Done light and send a "cooking complete" message.

First, you'll turn on the In Use light. Open the **Counter** script. In `CountdownTimerAction`, add the following to the `onReceived` callback.

```
ctx.start(
    [s.message.SendAction, {
        channel: "ManageLight",
        data: {
            light: "In Use Light", status: "On"
        }
    }],
);
```

This sends a message to the Lighting Manager to activate the light for you. Next, you need to define a countdown action.

Add the following function definition:

```
function CountdownAction(ctx, timeLeft) {

}
```

This function is recursive, which means the function will call itself passing in the remaining time left to count. Once the `timeLeft` reaches 0, then the function will end.

Add the following between the braces:

```
if (timeLeft.count > -1) {
    ctx.start(
        [s.time.WaitAction, {
            waitSeconds: 1, onTimeUp: () => {
                ctx.start([CountdownAction, {
                    count: timeLeft.count - 1
                }]);
            }
        }]
    );
}
```

If the countdown is greater than zero, then the countdown is active. If this is the case, a `WaitAction` is called. The wait runs for one second, after which the `CountdownAction` runs again, minus one second.

> **Note**: If you don't decrement the time, then the `CountdownAction` turns into an infinite loop.

Now, for the case when the timer expires. Add the `else` clause to your `if` statement:

```
} else {
    ctx.start(
        [s.message.SendAction, {
            channel: "ManageLight",
            data: {
                light: "In Use Light",
                status: "Off"
            }
        }],
        [s.message.SendAction, {
            channel: "ManageLight",
            data: {
                light: "Done Light",
                status: "On"
            }
        }],
        [s.message.SendAction, { channel: "CookingDone" }]
    );
}
```

All this does is send messages. It turns off the In Use light, turns on the Done light and then lets the bread machine behavior know that the cooking is done.

Your complete action should look like the following:

```
function CountdownAction(ctx, timeLeft) {
    if (timeLeft.count > -1) {
        ctx.start(
            [s.time.WaitAction, {
                waitSeconds: 1, onTimeUp: () => {
                    ctx.start([CountdownAction,
                        {
                            count: timeLeft.count - 1
                        }
                    ]);
                }
            }]
        );
    } else {
        ctx.start(
            [s.message.SendAction, {
                channel: "ManageLight",
                data: {
                    light: "In Use Light",
                    status: "Off"
                }
            }],
            [s.message.SendAction, {
                channel: "ManageLight",
                data: {
```

```
                    light: "Done Light",
                    status: "On"
                }
            }],
            [s.message.SendAction, {
                channel: "CookingDone"
            }]
        );
    }
}
```

While looking good, you still have more work to do.

Updating the web counter

One of the cool things about using Sumerian is that you can use the **Document Object Model (DOM)** to update it. The DOM takes a web page and breaks it down into a tree structure. Using this tree structure, you can add elements, remove elements and move things around. In short, you use it to add interactivity to your page.

To update your page, you need to get the paragraph tag and change its contents. Add the following underneath `CountdownAction`:

```
function updateTime(timeRemaining) {

}
```

This is just a regular function, you're not defining an action to run on a context. You can think of this as a helper function.

To update an element, you need to get a reference to it. Add the following:

```
const timer = document.getElementById("timer");
```

Here, you define a variable named `timer` that stores a reference to an element. You start by accessing the `document` object, which represents the current page and contains the actual structure. By calling `getElementById`, you're querying the document object for an element with an ID of `timer`. This is the <p> tag you defined in the Cook Time Counter.

Now, add the following `if` statements:

```
if (timer) {
    if (timeRemaining > 9) {

    }
}
```

The code first checks to see if you have a valid element. If the element is valid, then you check to see how much time is left. This determines how you'll format the timer. In the inner braces, add the following:

```
timer.innerHTML = = "00:" + timeRemaining;
```

The `innerHTML` property allows you to dynamically add HTML to your elements. In this case, you're adding the timer. Now, provide an `else` block:

```
if (timeRemaining > 9) {
    timer.innerHTML = = "00:" + timeRemaining;
} else {
    timer.innerHTML = = "00:0" + timeRemaining;
}
```

The `else` block just adds a zero before the countdown, which makes the countdown look nice. Your complete function should look like the following:

```
function updateTime(timeRemaining) {
    const timer = document.getElementById("timer");
    if (timer) {
        if (timeRemaining > 9) {
            timer.innerHTML = "00:" + timeRemaining;
        } else {
            timer.innerHTML = "00:0" + timeRemaining;
        }
    }
}
```

Now that you have the helper function setup, you need to add it to `CountdownAction`. Add the following after `if (timeLeft.count > -1) {`:

```
updateTime(timeLeft.count);
```

The last thing you need to do is call `CountdownTimerAction`. Update `ctx.start` to the following:

```
ctx.start(
    [s.message.SendAction, {
        channel: "ManageLight",
        data: {
            light: "In Use Light",
            status: "On"
        }
    }],
    [CountdownAction, { count: currentTime }]
);
```

Now, run your scene and you'll get your countdown. What's nice about this approach is that you can change the countdown from five seconds to ten seconds and everything will work as before.

Key points

- An HTML3D entity is used to embed HTML directly into a scene.
- These entities **cannot** be transparent.
- AN HTML2D entity always faces the camera.
- To embed a YouTube video into a scene, you **copy the share code and paste** it into the HTML editor.
- **Use the DOM** to update your HTML elements.

Where to go from here?

By embedding web pages into your scene, you can take your scenes to the next level. You've seen how you can add embed videos as well as add additional interactivity. Thankfully, technologies such as HTML and CSS have a ton of online resources written about them. One of the best places to learn is the Kahn Academy. Their "Intro to HTML/CSS" course gives you all the tools you need to build interactive experiences inside of Sumerian. Best of all, it's free.

Of course, keep reading. In the next section, you'll learn about a technology called Augmented Reality and how you can create these experiences inside of Sumerian. See you then!

Section III: Creating an Augmented Reality Experience

Augmented Reality (AR) is a technology that combines virtual reality with the real world. While virtual reality aims to create a new world, augmented reality takes the existing world and projects elements of a virtual world onto it.

For instance, in fighter jets, a pilot's heads-up display is projected into their helmet to display incoming threats or important aircraft information. In American football broadcasts, the field is often annotated with lines to show the first down, the line of scrimmage and other information. Game developers have also used augmented reality to turn the world into a virtual playground, where users "virtually" collect items and "battle" each other in real-world locations.

Sumerian provides all the necessary tools to incorporate AR experiences in your scenes. In this section, you'll create a virtual shoe store where you'll be able to try on new pairs of shoes without leaving your home. This section is composed of the following:

Chapter 15: Preparing Your Mobile Development Environment: Creating an AR experience means running your Sumerian scene on a device. This chapter walks you through the process of creating a mobile app in iOS and Android.

Chapter 16: Augmented Reality in Sumerian: This chapter introduces you to the basics of building AR scenes in Sumerian. You'll add a virtual shoe and have it appear on demand.

Chapter 17: Fetching Data from Dynamo DB: Here, you'll start to leverage the power of AWS. You'll store information about your shoes outside of Sumerian in a database and then display that data in your scene. In doing so, you'll create custom a user interface to display that information.

Chapter 18: Completing the Augmented Reality App: In this final chapter, you'll complete your shoe store by adding additional shoes and allowing users to change a shoe's size to match their feet.

Chapter 15: Preparing Your Mobile Development Environment

By Gur Raunaq Singh

Augmented Reality is an upcoming technology that lets you use an app to integrate audio/visual content into the user's real-world environment. A common example is Pokémon GO, a hugely popular mobile app that lets you find virtual creatures hidden in the real world.

In this series of four chapters, you'll build an augmented reality app that will let you view three 3D models of shoes in the real world, tap a button to fetch information about them from a database, and add buttons to manipulate the shoes' sizes.

You'll use Amazon Sumerian to build this app. You might expect to use the Unity game engine instead since it's one of the most popular ways to build augmented reality apps.

However, Unity requires a powerful computer to run efficiently, and it has a learning curve that not everyone wants to tackle. In comparison, Amazon Sumerian provides a user-friendly web-based interface that allows you to learn about, build and experiment with AR apps in a fun and easy way.

You'll see how it works by building this app step-by-step across the next four chapters. Time to get started!

Overview

Before jumping in and start building the app, you need to know about the components that make up the AR app you're going to build.

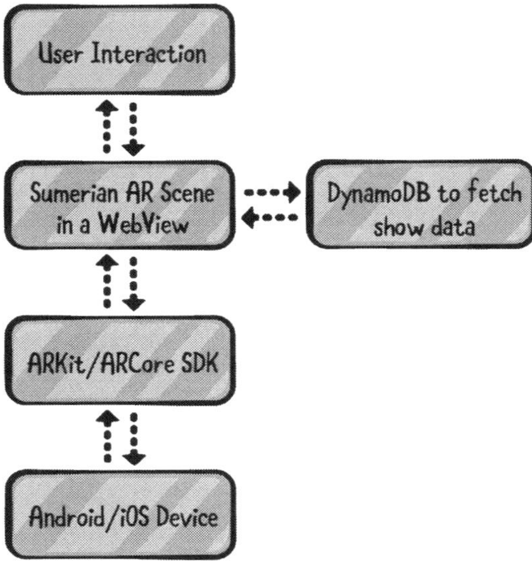

Here's what the different components do:

- At the bottom layer, you have your hardware: The Android or iOS device. This section provides a starter project written in the native programming language for each platform. The starter project contains all the libraries and SDK you'll need to build your scene, particularly ARKit for iOS and ARCore for Android.
- Next, you have a mobile app, which can run Sumerian and support the functionality you need to build augmented reality experiences.
- The Sumerian scene that you'll build in the next three chapters runs on top of the mobile app in a web view, just like a website runs on a web browser. You'll understand how this works as you build the scene.
- In addition to tracking how and where objects will display in AR, the scene also communicates with the DynamoDB database, a service from AWS. You'll learn about that in Chapter 17, "Fetching Data from DynamoDB."

You might be wondering why there's a complete chapter dedicated to setting up your development environment.

To understand this, you need to know how the apps on your mobile device work.

Creating mobile apps

To build a mobile app, you need an IDE (Integrated Development Environment). You won't be able to build a mobile app unless you've installed this software on your computer, along with some additional packages. In this case, the starter project for this chapter contains a pre-built project that you just have to build and run on your device.

The software you need to build apps on iOS is called **XCode** and the one for Android is called **Android Studio**. These are both free to download and install.

For iOS devices, you can download Xcode from the Mac App Store: https://apps.apple.com/us/app/xcode/id497799835?mt=12. You can find Android Studio at https://developer.android.com/studio.

Both contain additional frameworks. When you finally build and launch the development environments, you'll need to download additional components.

Thankfully, to build an augmented reality app with Amazon Sumerian, you don't need to know all the components of mobile development for Android or iOS. You just need to do build the scene in the Sumerian editor, then use the public link of the scene to build and run an app on your mobile device.

Think of it this way: To view a website, you use a piece of software called a web browser, like Chrome, Safari, etc. In this case, your Sumerian scene acts as the website, and the app that you'll download and build on your mobile device acts as a special web browser that runs your scene.

The Sumerian environment handles all the hard work of talking to the hardware. You just need to know enough to publish your scene to your device. Thankfully, this chapter has you covered.

Importing the augmented reality template

Your first step is to create a published Sumerian scene with a public URL to run on the app that you'll install on your mobile device. Here's how you do it.

Open the Sumerian dashboard.

In the **Home** section of the Dashboard, find **Create a scene from template**. This section contains pre-built templates from the Sumerian team, which already have some of the entities and scripts you need to build a basic scene.

Since you'll be making an AR app, select the **Augmented Reality** template. In the pop-up window, enter **Shoes in AR** as the name and click **Create**.

Once the scene loads, you'll notice that there are already a few new entities, such as **ARAnchor**, which aren't in an empty Sumerian scene. You'll learn more about what these entities are and what they do in the next chapter. For now, all you need is a published scene with a public link.

To publish the scene, go to the Sumerian editor and, in the top-right corner, click **Publish**.

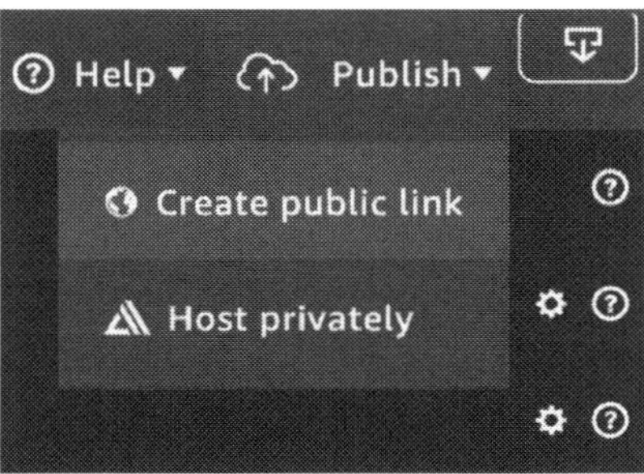

From the drop-down menu, select **Create Public Link**, read the agreement and click **Publish**. It will take a few seconds to complete, then you'll be able to see the public link of your scene. To copy the URL, click **Copy**. You'll use this link later when you publish your app.

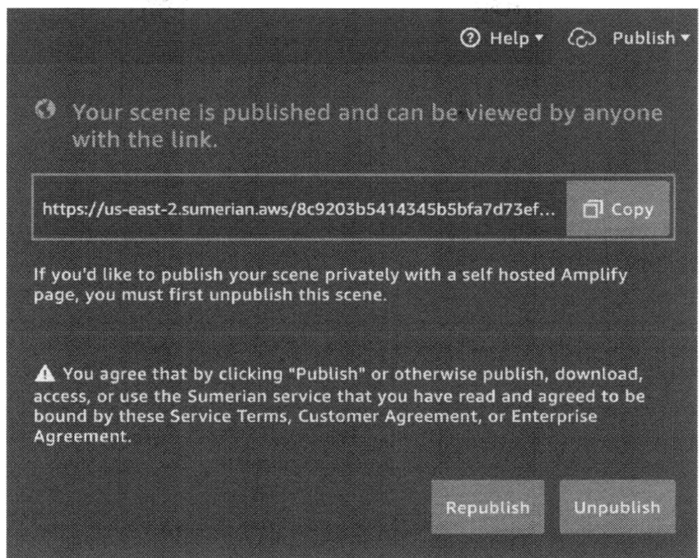

Setting up your computer

Here's what you need to do to install the mobile app that will run your Sumerian scene:

- Download a .zip file containing the starter project with all the necessary files needed to build the mobile app.
- Download or set up the IDE, depending on whether you're going to build your app on Android or iOS.
- Download and install any necessary additional packages.

Follow the instructions in the next subsection if you're planning to run your app on an iOS device. You can skip to the subsequent section for instructions on running your app on an Android device.

> **Note**: The following sections cover Xcode on macOS and Android Studio on Windows. If you're using a different setup, you'll need to research the requirements for each platform and/or IDE.

Setting up the app on iOS

Before you start setting up, make sure you have the required hardware: A computer running macOS.

Next, make sure that you have an ARKit-capable iOS device. You can view the list of compatible devices here: https://developer.apple.com/library/archive/documentation/DeviceInformation/Reference/iOSDeviceCompatibility/DeviceCompatibilityMatrix/DeviceCompatibilityMatrix.html.

> **Note**: While macOS does include an iOS simulator, you can only test augmented reality scenes on an actual device.

Once you've prepared the necessary devices, you can start by setting up your macOS device.

Creating an Apple Developer account

The first step to test on an iOS device is to create an Apple Developer account. If you already have a developer account, feel free to skip to the next section.

An Apple Developer account is separate from your existing iCloud account; you need it to build apps that run on an iOS device. You can sign up for free, but you need to pay an annual fee if you want to publish your app on the Apple App Store. Since this project will only test and build the app on your iOS device, you don't need to pay anything for now.

Go to the Apple Developer website at https://developer.apple.com/programs/enroll/ and click **Start Your Enrollment** at the bottom of the page. Follow the on-screen instructions to create a developer account using either your existing Apple ID or a new one.

Downloading the starter project

Once you have your Apple Developer account ready to go, your next task is to download the Sumerian project files, which are different from your scene. The scene contains everything you build using Sumerian and the project files have all the code that you need for your scene to talk to ARKit.

ARKit is Apple's augmented reality development platform for iOS mobile devices. It allows developers to build high-detail AR experiences for iPad and iPhone. The starter project that you'll download next contains all the necessary packages that will communicate with the ARKit SDK on your iOS device.

You can download the AWS Sumerian ARKit starter project page at https://github.com/aws-samples/amazon-sumerian-arkit-starter-app/tree/dedf5c85e9e6f117f5b11ca73f1dac70283a8a50.

Download the project as a .zip file by clicking on the green **Clone or Download** button. When prompted, select **Download ZIP**.

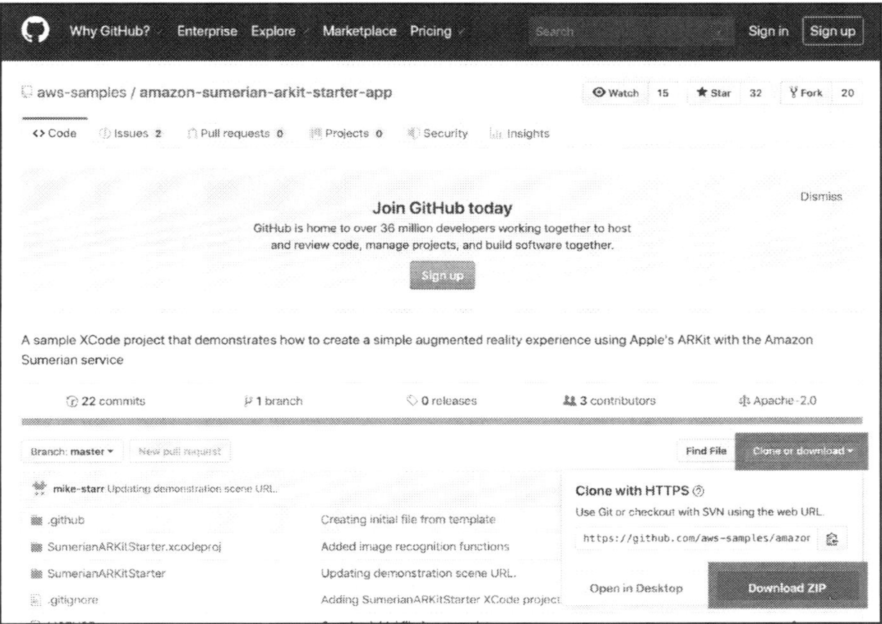

Once the download completes, double-click the file to extract its contents to a folder.

Setting up Xcode

It's all coming together! The next step is to run the Sumerian project on a device.

Download and install the latest version of Xcode from https://apps.apple.com/ca/app/xcode/id497799835?mt=12 or the App Store on your macOS device.

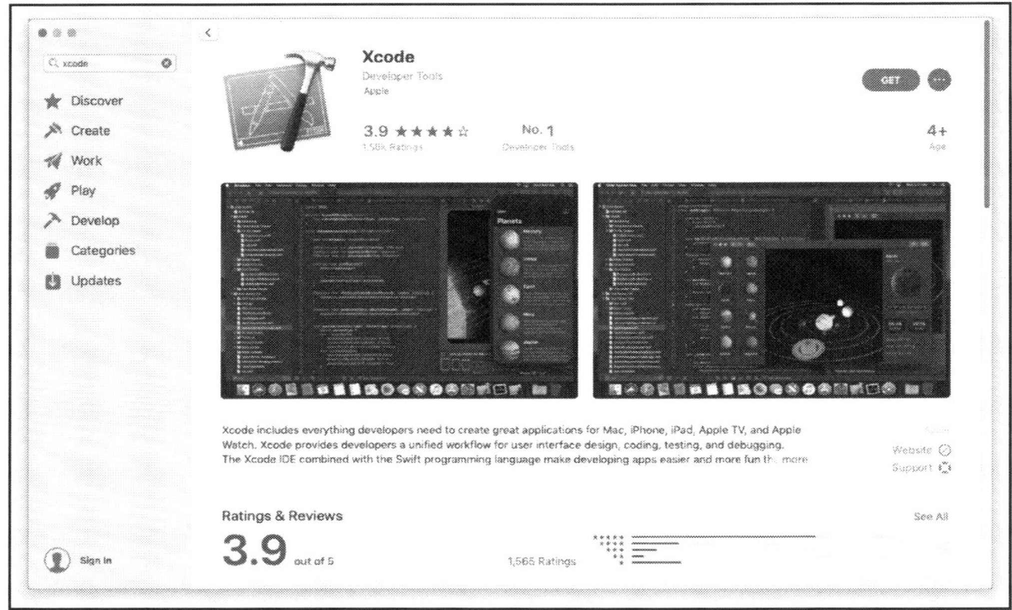

> **Note**: When you first open Xcode, you may see an **Installing Components** window. Make sure you're connected to the internet so that it can download and install the necessary files.

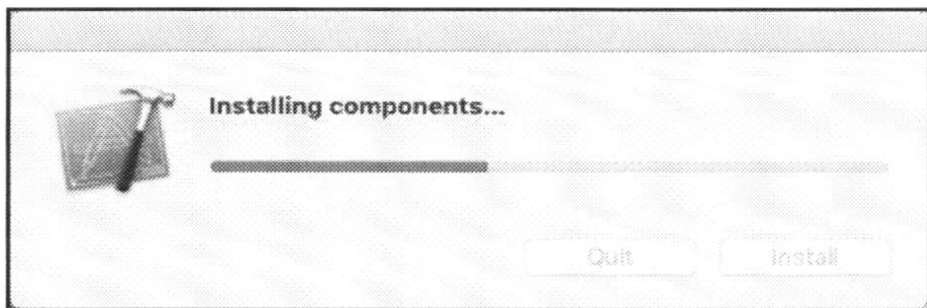

Once your download has finished, open Xcode and choose **Open** from the **File** menu. Then navigate to the directory where you downloaded the Sumerian ARKit starter project and select **SumerianARKitStarter.xcodeproj** to open it.

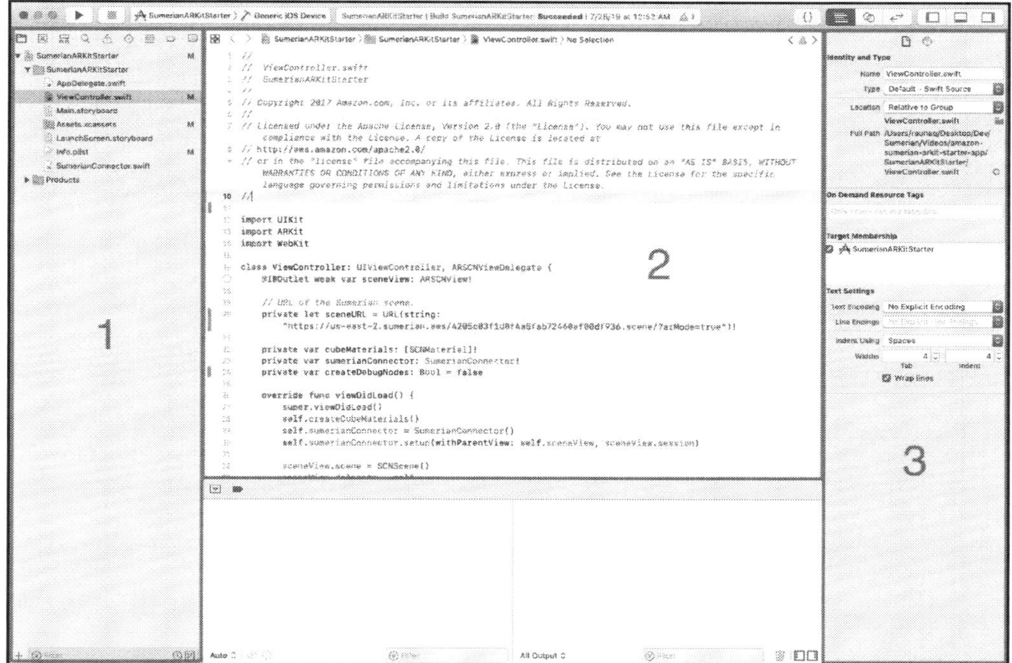

There are three key sections of the Xcode editor:

1. **Navigator**: Use this section to navigate to the different parts of a project.
2. **Editor**: When you click on a file to select it from the Navigator, its contents will open in this area so you can edit them.
3. **Utility**: The Xcode utility area is mainly used for the Inspector pane, which displays the properties of a selected file.

There is much more to learn about the Xcode editor, but for now, all you need to know is how to navigate around the project and where to make changes in those files.

In the Navigator area, select **ViewController.swift**. This will display the file's contents in the editor.

```
import UIKit
import ARKit
import WebKit

class ViewController: UIViewController, ARSCNViewDelegate {
    @IBOutlet weak var sceneView: ARSCNView!

    // URL of the Sumerian scene.
    private let sceneURL = URL(string:
        "https://us-west-2.sumerian.aws/5e69e695363248d5b3573baad3ab992a.scene#arMode")!

    private var cubeMaterials: [SCNMaterial]!
    private var sumerianConnector: SumerianConnector!
    private var createDebugNodes: Bool = true

    override func viewDidLoad() {
        super.viewDidLoad()
        self.createCubeMaterials()
        self.sumerianConnector = SumerianConnector()
        self.sumerianConnector.setup(withParentView: self.sceneView, sceneView.session)
```

Then, change the value of `sceneURL` to point to the URL of your published scene, which you created earlier, and append `/?arMode=true` to the URL.

```
class ViewController: UIViewController, ARSCNViewDelegate {
    @IBOutlet weak var sceneView: ARSCNView!

    // URL of the Sumerian scene.
    private let sceneURL = URL(string:
        "https://us-west-2.sumerian.aws/5e69e695363248d5b3573baad3ab992a.scene/?arMode=true")!

    private var cubeMaterials: [SCNMaterial]!
    private var sumerianConnector: SumerianConnector!
    private var createDebugNodes: Bool = true
```

The default configuration of the starter project displays digital cubes in the augmented reality scene, which you don't need for this project. To disable them, change the value of `createDebugNodes` to `false`.

```
class ViewController: UIViewController, ARSCNViewDelegate {
    @IBOutlet weak var sceneView: ARSCNView!

    // URL of the Sumerian scene.
    private let sceneURL = URL(string:
        "https://us-west-2.sumerian.aws/5e69e695363248d5b3573baad3ab992a.scene/?arMode=true")!

    private var cubeMaterials: [SCNMaterial]!
    private var sumerianConnector: SumerianConnector!
    private var createDebugNodes: Bool = false
```

As you learned earlier, the starter project already contains all the necessary files and packages to run a Sumerian augmented reality scene. All you had to do was change the project's default URL to the public link of your Sumerian scene.

Configuring the starter project

You need to go through three stages to get from writing code to have a running app on a mobile device:

- **Build**: During the build stage, the IDE (Xcode, in this case) takes the different files present in your project and creates from them a single package file called a **binary**. This helps secure the app. It also reduces its size by holding only the necessary files it needs to run.
- **Install**: Once the build stage completes successfully, you compile the final binary file from the computer to the mobile device and install it on the device.
- **Run**: Before you can sideload an app – that is, install it from a source other than the official App Store – to your device, you need to add your Developer account needs as a Trusted Developer on your device.

Once you've done this, you can install and run the app.

Now, it's time to start with the build process for your app.

Building your app

Connect your compatible iOS device to your computer and make sure you've unlocked your iOS device's screen.

You might see a prompt on your device showing **Trust this Computer?**.

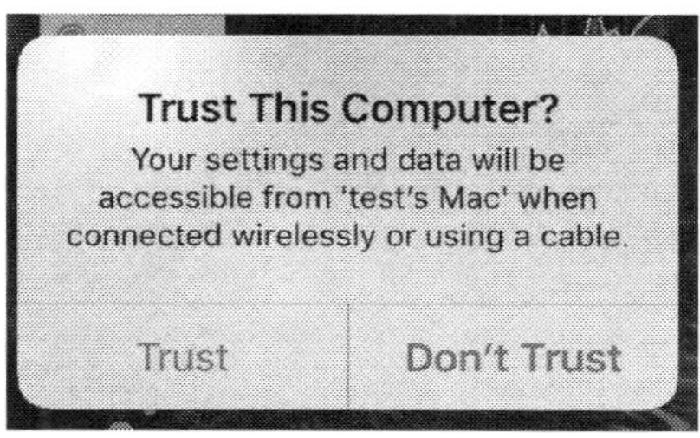

Click **Trust** and enter your device's password. Make sure your device's name is visible in the Xcode window on your computer.

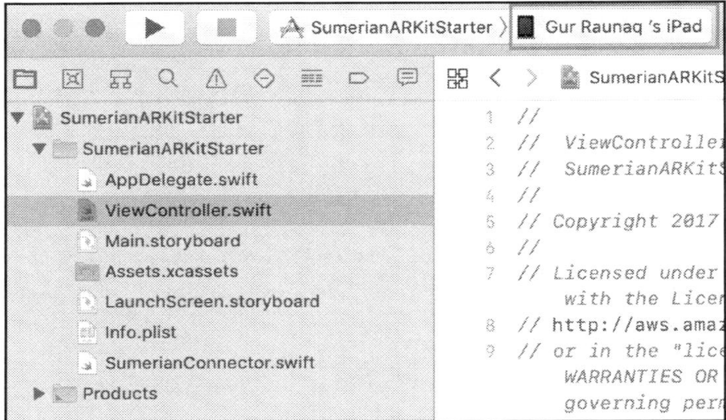

Before you can install and run the app on your iOS device, you need to sign in with your developer account. The signature tells the mobile device about the source of the app you want to install – which is you, in this case.

Signing your app with your developer account

From the menu bar, select **Xcode ▸ Preferences**, then select the **Accounts** tab.

Click the + button. From the drop-down menu, select the **Apple ID** account type and click **Continue**. Enter your Apple ID and password to sign in.

If successful, your account will now be visible in the list of Apple IDs in the Accounts window.

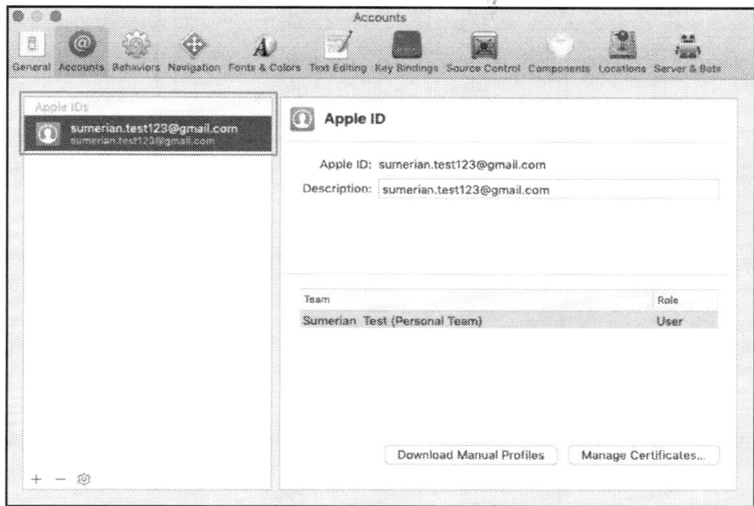

You've signed your app now, but it's still not quite ready to install. You have to specify some other properties first.

On the top-left side of the Project navigator window, click **SumerianARKitStarter** then select the **General** tab.

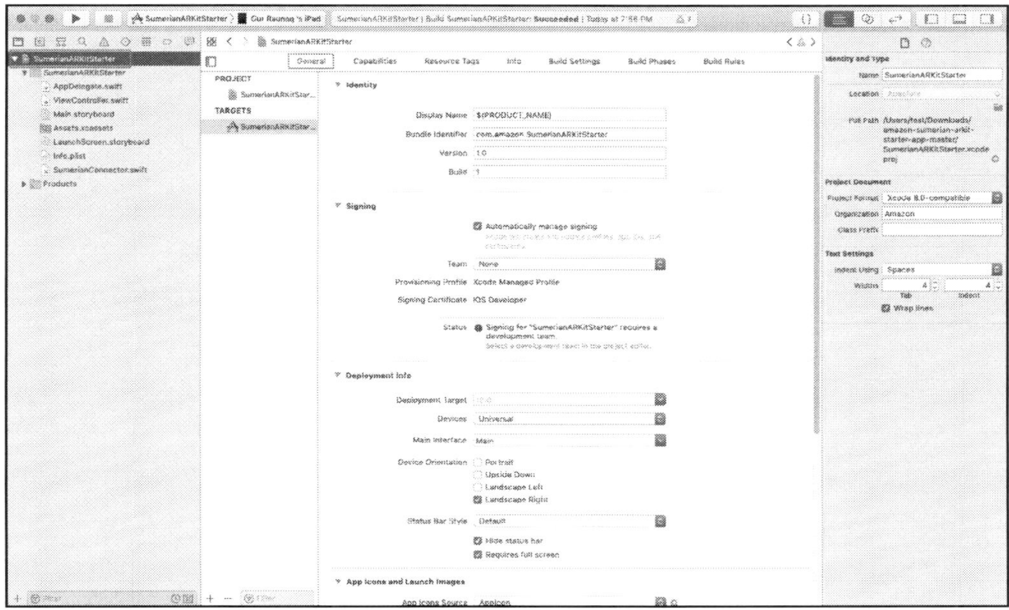

In the **Identity** section of **Project Settings**, change the **Display Name** to **MyARApp** and change the **Bundle Identifier** from **com.amazon.SumerianARKitStarter** to **com.<MY_DOMAIN_NAME>.<MY_SCENE_NAME>**.

Your bundle identifier *must* be unique. Replace **<MY_DOMAINB_NAME>** and **<MY_SCENE_NAME>** with something unique. For example: **com.raywenderlich.sumerianapp.shoes**.

Once you register the bundle identifier with your app, no one else can use it. If you try to use an existing bundle identifier, you'll get a build error.

Next, in the **Signing** section, click the drop-down next to **Team** and select **(Personal Team)**. The status should change to **Waiting to Repair**. After a couple of seconds, the error should resolve. The window should look something like this:

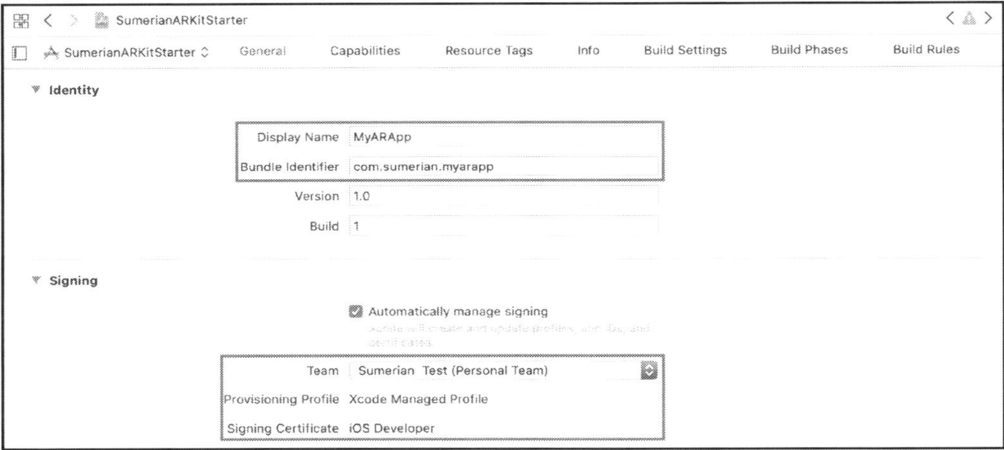

> **Note**: To learn more about signing, visit https://help.apple.com/xcode/mac/current/#/dev60b6fbbc7.

Building and running your app

Finally, from the menu bar, select **Product ‣ Run** to build and run.

If the build is successful, Xcode will try to run the app on your iOS device. At this point, you may encounter an error in your Xcode windows stating **Could not launch "SumerianARKitStarter"**.

To fix this, open **Settings ‣ General ‣ Profiles and Device Management** in your iOS device. In this window, you'll see an option under **DEVELOPER APP** with the Apple ID that you used to sign in.

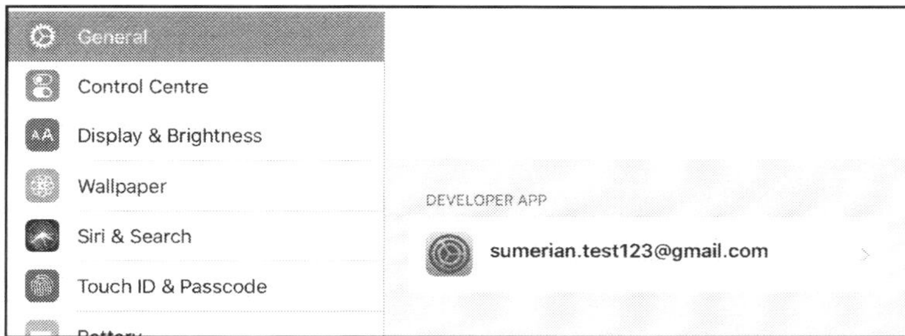

Tap on that ID and, in the next window, click on the blue text that reads **Trust <your-apple-id>.**

Still in the pop-up window, click the red **Trust** text.

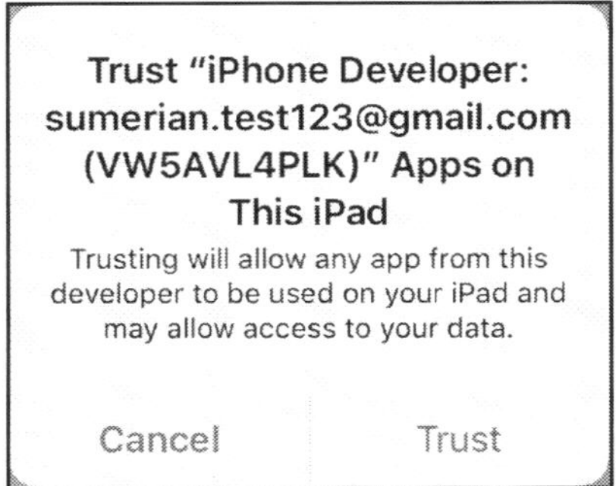

Back in Xcode, start the build and run process again using **Product ▸ Run**. This time, the install process will start without any errors and you'll be able to see the app in your device's app drawer. The app should load automatically.

Click **OK** to allow access to the camera when the app asks for it.

After you give the app permission to use the camera, the Sumerian scene should continue loading.

Once the scene finishes loading, check if you can see the camera viewfinder on your device. If so, it means you have successfully built and installed the app on your device.

You can only see the camera viewfinder at this moment since augmented reality uses your device's camera. Since you haven't added anything to the Sumerian scene, the camera does nothing at the moment.

Setting up your app on Android

To build the same app on Android, you'll need an ARCore-compatible device. ARCore contains all the code necessary for an Android device to create augmented reality experiences. To see the list of ARCore-supported devices, visit https://developers.google.com/ar/discover/supported-devices.

The process of running an augmented reality Sumerian scene on Android is the same as on iOS: You'll download the starter project, set up and install the IDE — Android Studio, in this case — and build!

Your first step is to set up Android Studio, which is the official IDE for Google's Android operating system. Unlike XCode, which is available only on macOS, you can download Android Studio for Windows, macOS, and Linux.

> **Note**: The following setup guide is just for Windows. If you are using Android Studio on a different platform, you may need to perform additional steps. See the documentation for your setup.

Downloading and setting up Android Studio

Open the official page to download the Android Studio setup file.

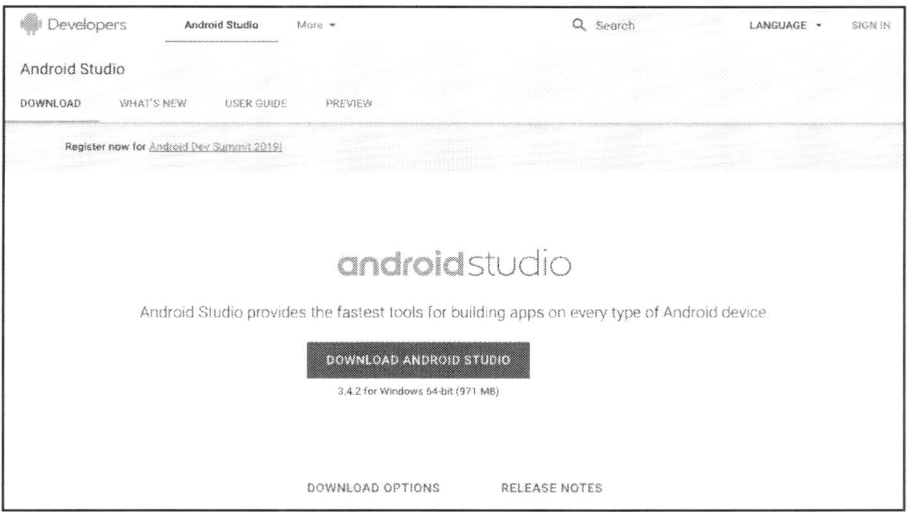

Click on **Download Android Studio** and a pop-up window will open. After reading the terms and conditions, check the **I have read...** option and then click on **Download Android Studio**.

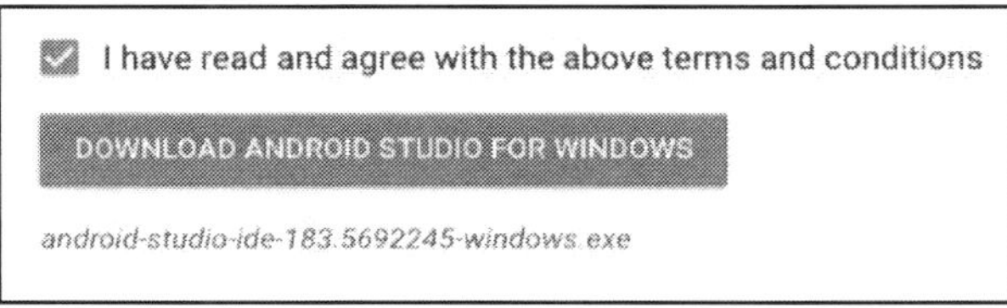

A file with a **.exe** extension will start downloading. Once the download completes, double-click the file to launch it. Follow the setup wizard in Android Studio and install any SDK packages that it recommends. Once the setup completes, click **Finish** to launch Android Studio.

The next window will ask if you want to import previous Android Studio settings. Select **Do not import settings** and click **OK**. While loading, the setup may download some SDK Tools that the IDE needs, so make sure your system has an active internet connection.

Finally, the **Android Studio Setup Wizard** window will open. Click **Next**.

In **Install Type**, select **Standard** and click **Next**. In the UI Theme, select **Darcula** then click **Next**. The setup will show the list of SDK components that you're about to download. Click **Finish** to download the required components.

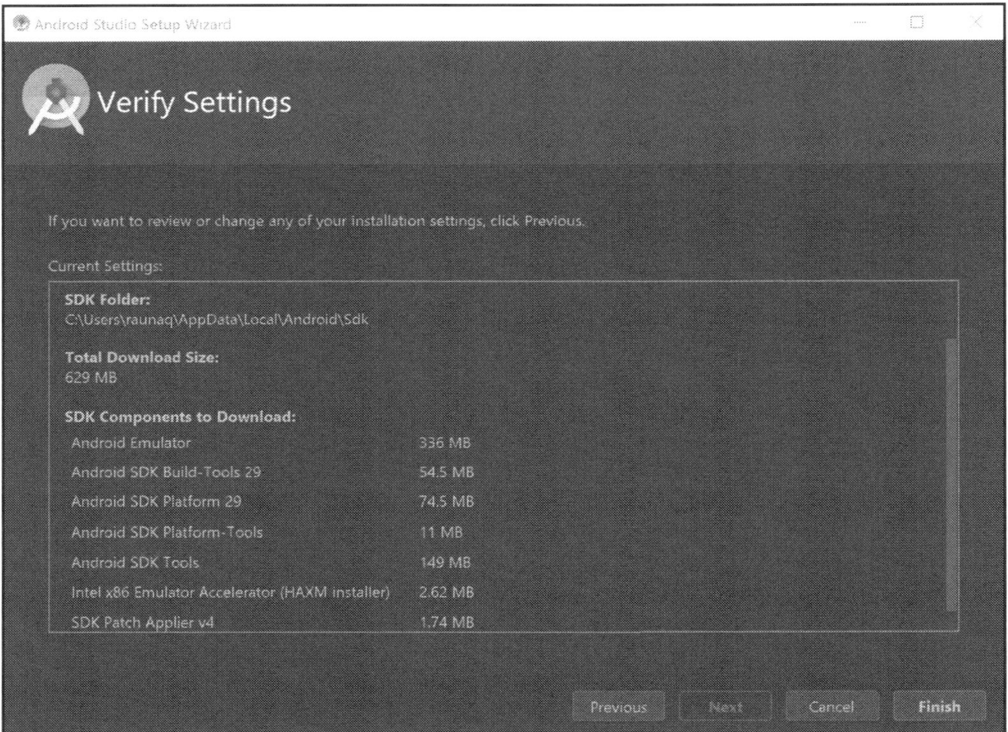

Finally, click **Finish** and the Android Studio welcome screen will open.

Setting up the starter project

Your next task is to download the Sumerian project files, which are different from your scene. The scene contains everything you build using Sumerian and the project files have all the code that you need for your scene to talk to ARCore.

Next, open the AWS Sumerian ARCore starter project page at https://github.com/aws-samples/amazon-sumerian-arcore-starter-app/tree/01131146b9345c24bad2c3f485df02b776b4dfef.

Download the project as a .zip file by clicking on the green **Clone or Download** button. When prompted, select **Download ZIP**.

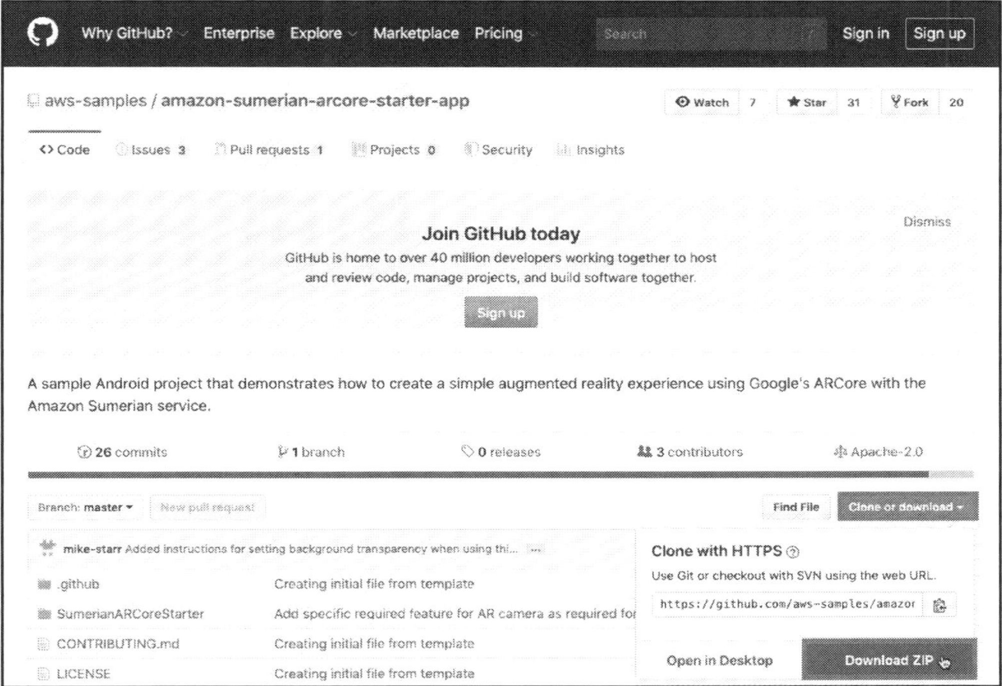

Next, select **Open an existing Android Studio Project**, browse to the directory where you downloaded the ARCore Starter project and open it in Android Studio.

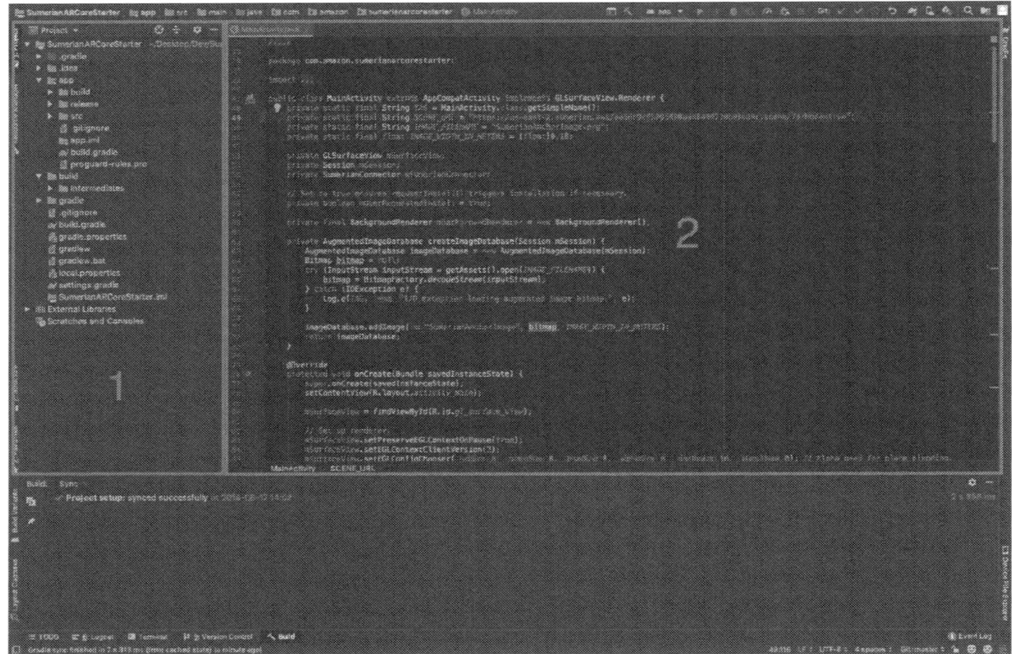

There are two key sections of the Android Studio IDE:

1. **Navigator**: Use this section to navigate to the different parts of a project.

2. **Editor**: When you click on a file to select it from the Navigator, its contents will open in this area so you can edit them.

There's much more to learn about the IDE, but for now, all you need to know is how to navigate around the project and where to make changes in those files.

The mobile app acts as an embedded web browser for the Sumerian augmented reality scene to load and run on your Android device. This starter project contains all the necessary files and packages to run a Sumerian AR Scene. All you have to do is change the default URL set in the project to the public link of your Sumerian scene.

In the Project Navigator panel, select the **Project** view.

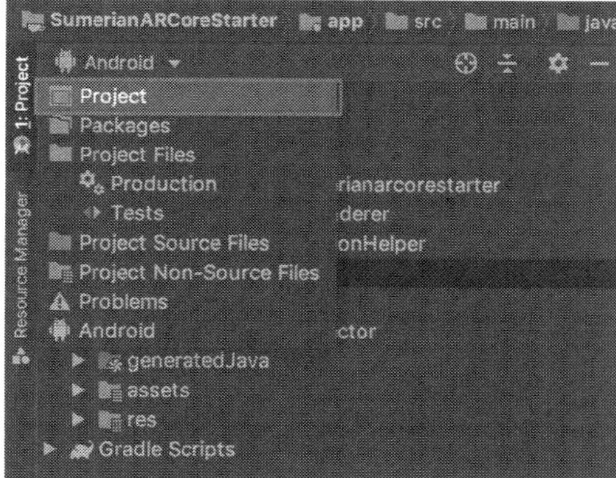

Then open **MainActivity.java** by navigating to **app** ▸ **src** ▸ **main** ▸ **java** ▸ **com** ▸ **amazon** ▸ **sumerianarcorestarter** ▸ **MainActivity**.

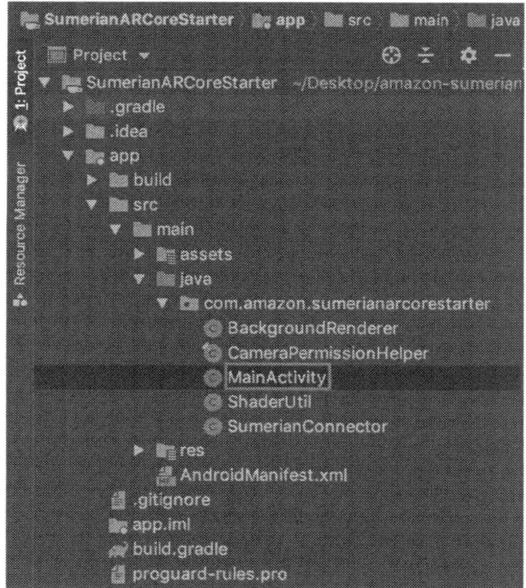

Change the value of `SCENE_URL` to point to the URL of your published Sumerian scene and append `/?arMode=true` to the URL.

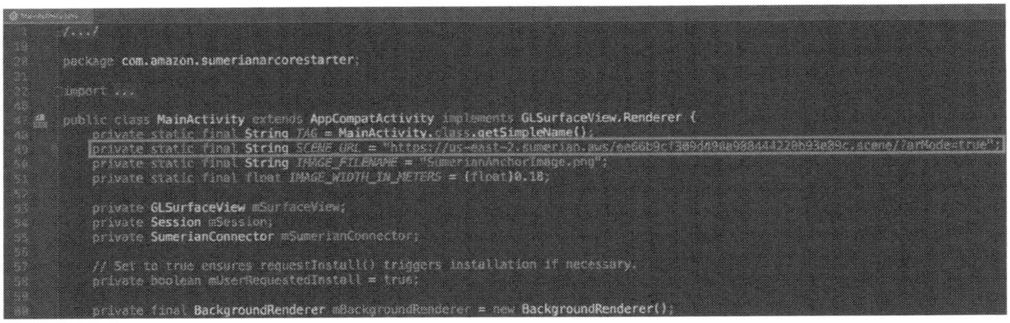

```
/.../

package com.amazon.sumerianarcorestarter;

import ...

public class MainActivity extends AppCompatActivity implements GLSurfaceView.Renderer {
    private static final String TAG = MainActivity.class.getSimpleName();
    private static final String SCENE_URL = "https://us-east-2.sumerian.aws/ee66b9cf309d49aa98844220b93e89c.scene/?arMode=true";
    private static final String IMAGE_FILENAME = "SumerianAnchorImage.png";
    private static final float IMAGE_WIDTH_IN_METERS = (float)0.18;

    private GLSurfaceView mSurfaceView;
    private Session mSession;
    private SumerianConnector mSumerianConnector;

    // Set to true ensures requestInstall() triggers installation if necessary.
    private boolean mUserRequestedInstall = true;

    private final BackgroundRenderer mBackgroundRenderer = new BackgroundRenderer();
```

Next, in the body of `protected void onResume()`, define a variable named `config`. Add `config.setFocusMode(Config.FocusMode.AUTO);` after the variable declaration.

```
// Create config and check if camera access that is not blocking is supported.
Config config = new Config(mSession);
config.setUpdateMode(Config.UpdateMode.LATEST_CAMERA_IMAGE);
config.setFocusMode(Config.FocusMode.AUTO);
if (!mSession.isSupported(config)) {
    throw new RuntimeException("This device does not support AR");
}
```

Save the project using **File ▸ Save All**.

These are all the changes you need to make in the starter project. However, you still need to do a few things to prepare your device.

Enable USB debugging

Before you can start the build process and run the app on your Android device, there are two things you must do: Enable USB debugging and download and set up the ADB tools for your OS.

USB debugging allows you to perform certain actions on your device through a USB-connected device which, in this case, would be your computer running Android Studio.

To enable this feature, you need to access a secret set of options: **Android Developer Options**. As the name suggests, these are principally for people who need additional functions to test software and apps they're writing for Android devices.

Since you're building a custom app for your Android device, you need to enable these options. Otherwise, you won't be able to install the app unless you publish it in the Google Play Store.

Open **Settings** on your device. For devices running Android 8.0 or higher, select **System**. Scroll to the bottom and select **About phone**. Next, scroll to the bottom and tap **Build number** seven times.

Click **Back** to return to the previous screen. Tap on **Developer options** near the bottom of the list.

At the top of the Developer options screen, click the toggle button to turn it on. If a pop-up window opens and asks you to confirm you want to **Allow development settings**, click **OK**.

Finally, scroll down and enable the **USB Debugging** toggle, then click **OK** on the confirmation pop-up window.

> **Note**: These steps should work for the most commonly-available Android devices on the market. If you can't enable Developer options with the above steps, visit the official documentation page to find the right solution for your device.

Next, you need to make sure that ADB (Android Device Bus) can discover your Android device through the USB connection.

ADB allows you to do things on an Android device that may not be suitable for everyday use, yet can improve your developer experience. Examples include installing apps outside of the Play Store, debugging apps and accessing hidden features.

In this case, you need to set up the ADB tools so that when you connect your Android device to your computer with a USB cable, Android Studio can discover your device and subsequently install the starter project on it.

After you've successfully enabled USB Debugging on your Android device, connect it to your computer with the USB cable.

Open the directory where you installed Android SDK during the Android Studio setup process, then open **platform-tools** to find the ADB executable. To open the directory, press **Windows Key + R**, then enter **cmd** and click **OK**. The windows command prompt will open.

Next, type **cd %HOMEPATH%\AppData\Local\Android\Sdk\platform-tools** and press **Enter**. The prompt will change the directory to the location of the **platform-tools** folder.

Type **dir** and press **Enter** to list the files and folders present in the current directory. You should see **adb.exe** in the output.

```
C:\WINDOWS\system32\cmd.exe
Microsoft Windows [Version 10.0.18362.175]
(c) 2019 Microsoft Corporation. All rights reserved.

C:\Users\raunaq>cd %HOMEPATH%\AppData\Local\Android\Sdk\platform-tools

C:\Users\raunaq\AppData\Local\Android\Sdk\platform-tools>dir
 Volume in drive C has no label.
 Volume Serial Number is FC59-0387

 Directory of C:\Users\raunaq\AppData\Local\Android\Sdk\platform-tools

07/04/2019  12:40 PM    <DIR>          .
07/04/2019  12:40 PM    <DIR>          ..
07/04/2019  12:40 PM         1,939,968 adb.exe
07/04/2019  12:40 PM            97,792 AdbWinApi.dll
07/04/2019  12:40 PM            62,976 AdbWinUsbApi.dll
07/04/2019  12:40 PM    <DIR>          api
07/04/2019  12:40 PM               140 deployagent
07/04/2019  12:40 PM         1,023,085 deployagent.jar
07/04/2019  12:40 PM         4,388,350 deploypatchgenerator.jar
07/04/2019  12:40 PM           190,976 dmtracedump.exe
07/04/2019  12:40 PM           362,496 etc1tool.exe
07/04/2019  12:40 PM         1,334,272 fastboot.exe
07/04/2019  12:40 PM            40,960 hprof-conv.exe
07/04/2019  12:40 PM    <DIR>          lib64
07/04/2019  12:40 PM           211,018 libwinpthread-1.dll
07/04/2019  12:40 PM           395,776 make_f2fs.exe
07/04/2019  12:40 PM             1,170 mke2fs.conf
07/04/2019  12:40 PM         1,007,616 mke2fs.exe
07/04/2019  12:40 PM           319,351 NOTICE.txt
07/04/2019  12:40 PM            17,783 package.xml
07/04/2019  12:40 PM                38 source.properties
07/04/2019  12:40 PM         1,239,040 sqlite3.exe
07/04/2019  12:40 PM    <DIR>          systrace
              18 File(s)     12,632,807 bytes
               5 Dir(s)  213,038,825,472 bytes free

C:\Users\raunaq\AppData\Local\Android\Sdk\platform-tools>
```

Type **adb devices** and press **Enter**. The output shows the list of attached devices, which should include your device's ID along with an authorization status.

If it says **unauthorized**, unlock your Android device. You should see a prompt to **Allow USB Debugging?**.

Click **OK**.

In the Windows command prompt window, type **adb devices** again. The **unauthorized** status should have changed to **device**.

```
C:\Users\raunaq\AppData\Local\Android\Sdk\platform-tools>adb devices
List of devices attached
b58e7944        unauthorized


C:\Users\raunaq\AppData\Local\Android\Sdk\platform-tools>adb devices
List of devices attached
b58e7944        device
```

Building and running your app

Now that you've set everything up, it's time to install the app on your device and run it.

Switch back to **Android Studio**.

From the menu bar, select **Build ▸ Make Project** to start the build process. This process creates an Android Package file that contains all the necessary files the app needs to run on a device. You can see the progress in the **Build Output** panel in the bottom-left of the window.

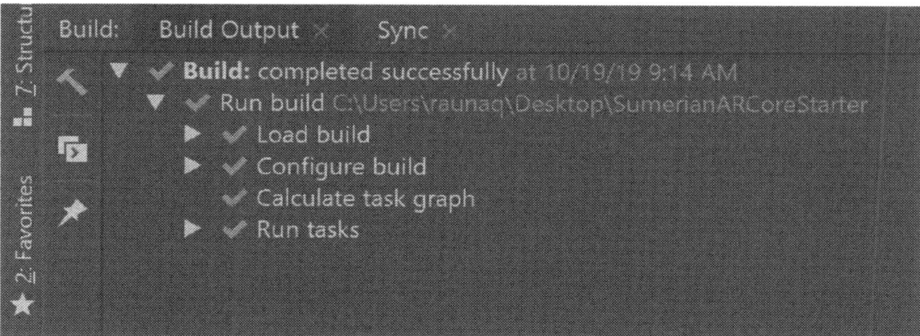

When the build output shows **Build: completed successfully**, select **Run ▸ Run 'app'**.

That opens the **Select Deployment Target** window, which will display a list of connected devices. Your Android device should be one of them.

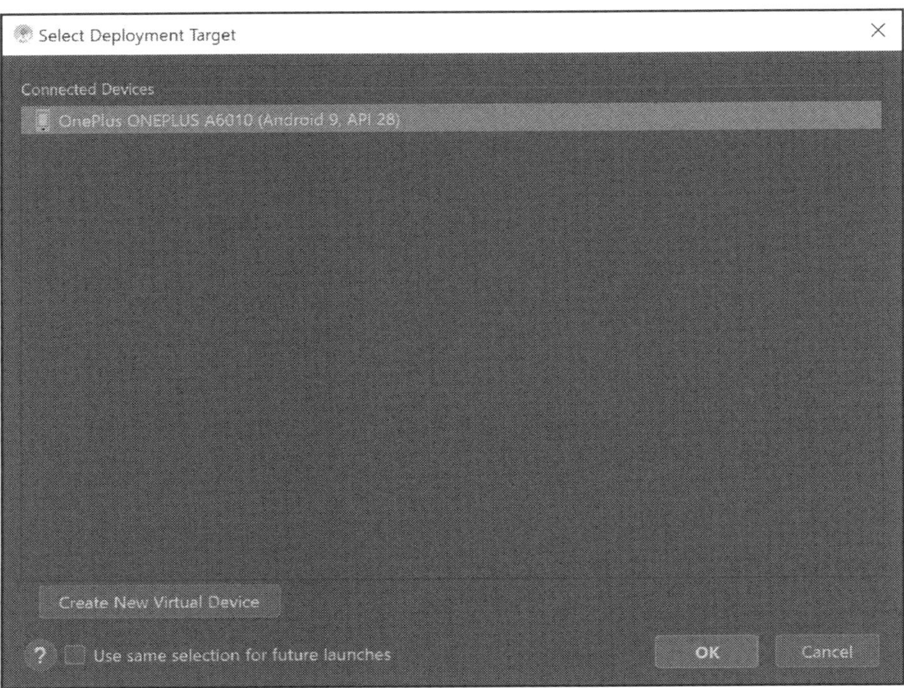

Select your Android device and click **OK**. This will generate the APK (Android Package) file, copy it to your Android device, then install and run it.

Once you've installed the app on your phone, it will start and will ask for camera permissions. Click **Allow**. Your Sumerian scene should load once the app starts. Make sure you've connected your Android device to the internet.

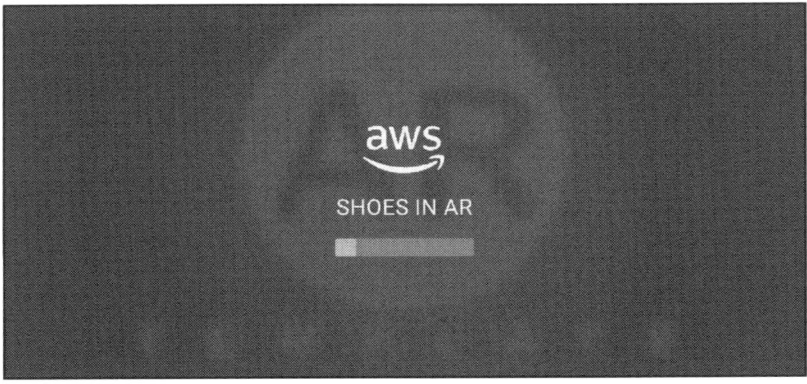

Once the scene finishes loading, check if you can see the camera viewfinder on your device. If so, it means you have successfully built and installed the app on your device.

You can only see the camera viewfinder at this moment since augmented reality uses your device's camera. Since you haven't added anything to the Sumerian scene, the camera does nothing at the moment.

> **Note**: If you have any issues due to unaccepted licenses, use the official user guide by Google to troubleshoot the device's connection issues.

Congratulations!

This was your first look at how to build a mobile app on Android or iOS. You learned the basics about how a mobile app goes from code on a computer to a functioning app on a mobile device. You also learned how to run a published Sumerian scene on a mobile device running iOS or Android.

Key points

- Creating an augmented reality scene requires that you **install the scene on a modern mobile device**.
- A Sumerian mobile app **embeds your published scene** into a web browser.
- You must **download the app project files** from Github then build them onto the device.
- iOS scenes require devices capable of running **ARKit**.
- Android scenes require devices capable of running **ARCore**.

Where to go from here?

Now that you have a working mobile app on your device, the next step is to start building your Sumerian scene, which you'll read all about in the next chapter.

Chapter 16: Augmented Reality in Sumerian

By Gur Raunaq Singh

Now that you have a development environment set up, and a running app on your mobile device, it's time to build your scene from the ground up.

For this experience, you'll build a scene that allows you to virtually try on a shoe. You place a reference image on the floor, point your device at it and a shoe will magically appear. You can put your foot in the 3D model to get a sense of how it will look.

Later, you'll incorporate several different types of shoes as well as allow the user to change the size of the shoe. Before you do any of that, you first need to display the shoe which is what you'll do in this chapter.

Components of the Augmented Reality template

Log into the Sumerian Dashboard, and open the **Shoe in AR** scene that you created in the previous chapter. You'll notice there are a couple of additional components present in the scene compared to an entirely new Sumerian scene.

There's an **AR Camera** entity present. This is similar to the Default Camera entity that is present in a basic Sumerian scene except that it has a script named **AR Camera Control** attached to it. The primary purpose of this script is to communicate with the **ArSystem**.

The **ArSystem** is a key component for building an AR compatible scene in Sumerian. It processes of all entities that are associated with an **ArAnchor** component attached to them. It also enables the use of device-specific augmented reality APIs — ARCore for Android and ARKit for iOS.

However, to build Augmented Reality apps with Sumerian, you don't need to know the nitty-gritty details of the internal workings on all these components. As you keep adding new features to this project, the details of what that component is and why it is important will be explained to you as you go. For now, it's time to start building the scene, starting with adding the 3D model, modifying its properties and building the scene to see how it looks in AR.

Importing 3D assets

Since you'll be adding custom 3D models of shoes that you want to be able to see in AR, you first need to import them into your scene.

> **Note**: If you are interested in learning more about models in Sumerian, please read Chapter 9, "Custom Models and Sound."

Click **Import Assets** to import **Shoe1.FBX** from the **resources** folder for this chapter. When uploading is successful, you'll see both of these in the Assets panel.

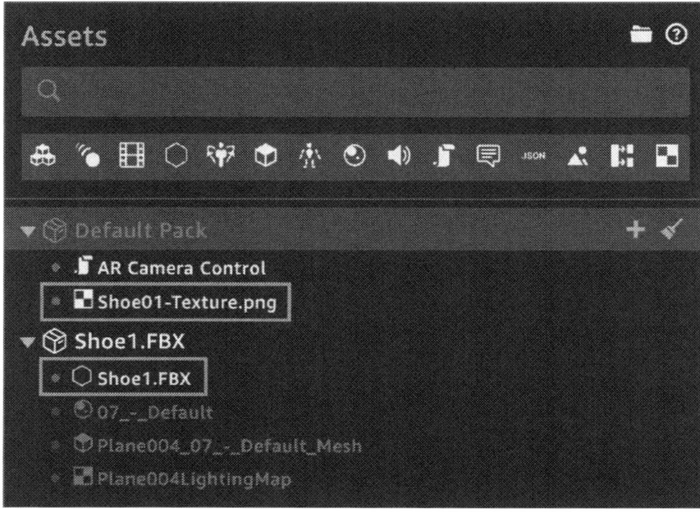

Next, drag the **Shoe1** entity onto the ARAnchor entity that already exists in the Entities panel. The 3D shoe entity should be visible in the editor.

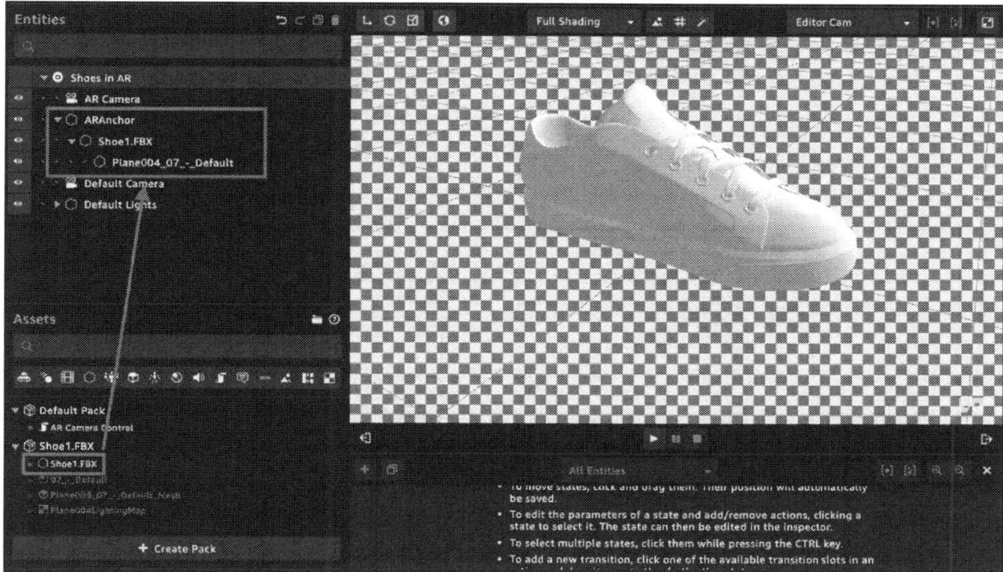

As you can see, the shoe is imported as an entity in your scene. You can pan around the scene to see it from different sides and different angles. But like all newly imported models, it's completely white, lacking any texture.

Within the Entities panel, click the arrow to expand **Shoe1.FBX** and select its child entity, **Plane004_07_-_Default**. With the entity selected, click **Material** within the inspector to expand that component.

Click **COLOR (DIFFUSE)** to expand the options, which you can see on the next page.

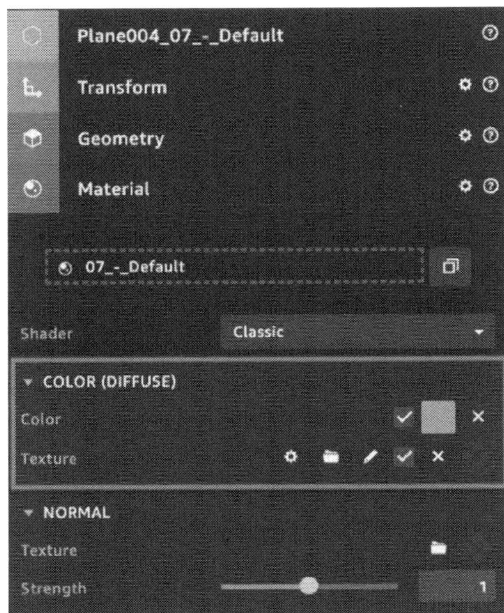

Next, click the **folder icon** next to Texture and select **Shoe1-Texture.png** to upload it.

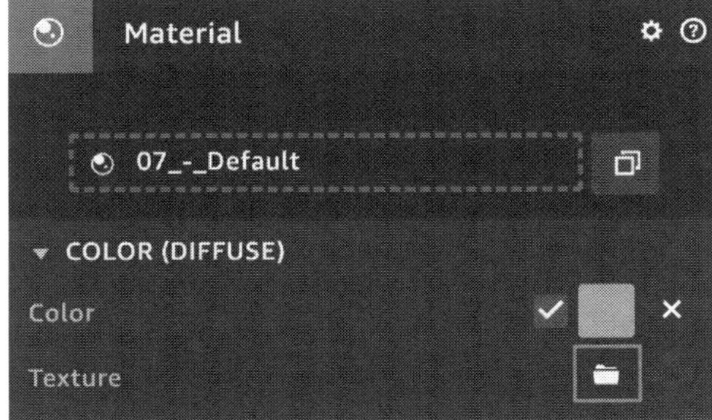

Once the file upload is successful, the texture is applied to the shoe. Your Sumerian editor window will look something like this:

Finally, select **Shoe1.FBX** from the Entities panel. Set the scale to **(0.1, 0.1, 0.1)**.

At this point, you can view the Sumerian object in an AR context. However, the object will sit stationary at the world's origin. That is to say, the shoe model would be stuck at the origin position of your device, and it will look like it's floating in the air. You don't want shoes just floating around in the air in your house, do you?

To see how this would look, republish your Sumerian scene by selecting **Publish ▸ Republish**.

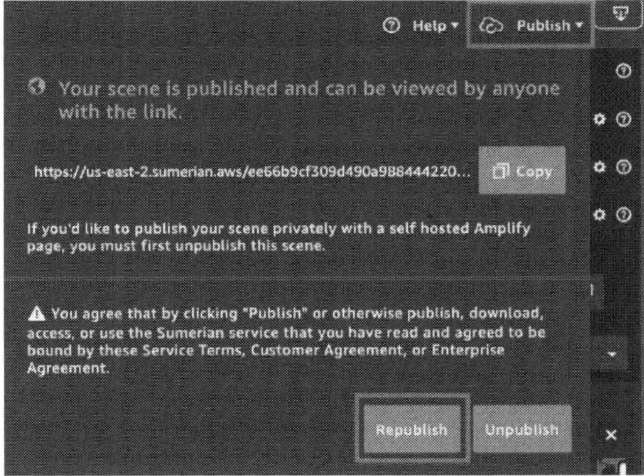

Notice that you don't have to build and install the app again on your mobile device. As you learned in the previous chapter, the mobile app serves as a browser for the Sumerian scene to load. When you make changes to your Sumerian scene, republish the scene, wait a couple of seconds and reload the app on your mobile device. Make sure that you force close the app before you open it again.

Once you have republished the scene, reload the app on your mobile device. If you move and rotate the device, you should see lines and boxes, something that might look like the inside of the shoe model.

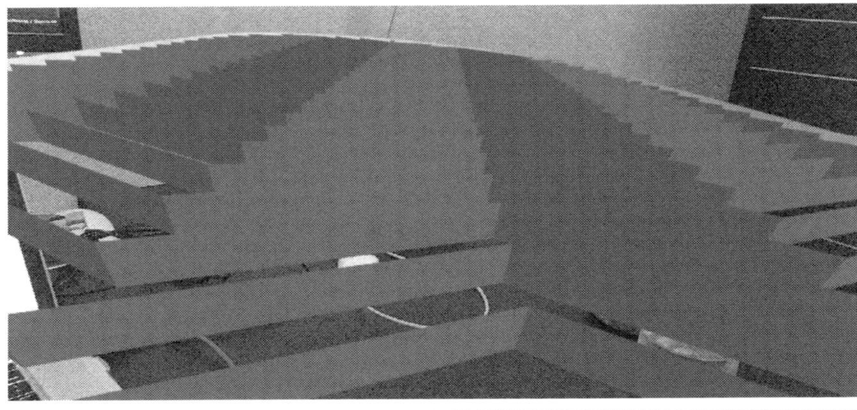

While this makes for some great abstract art, this is not the desired effect. You need to reposition the shoe.

Repositioning the Shoe model

To fix your position issue, you'll add a `Script` component to your scene that will handle the repositioning of this shoe in the AR World space.

Positioning the shoe is managed in two different ways. First, the user can point the device at a real-world surface and then tap on the screen. This repositions the object. Or the user can point the camera at a particular image that image will anchor the model.

First, you'll try to the surface detection method. This method is possible by adding a script to the `ARAnchor` entity. This anchor uses the Sumerian `ArSystem` to interact with the ARKit/ARCore SDK.

Currently, the shoe model is too big, so it's best to change its scale.

Select **Shoe1.FBX** from the Entities panel and set the scale to **(0.05, 0.05, 0.05)** and the rotation to **(0, 180, 0)**.

Next, you'll add a script to the `ArAnchor` entity that will reposition the 3D model based on-screen tap event.

Select **ARAnchor** from the Entities panel. In the inspector, click **Add Component** and select **Script**.

Click the + button. From the drop-down menu, select **Custom (Preview Format)** to add a custom script. Rename this script to **Object_Positioning**. The Inspector panel will look something like this.

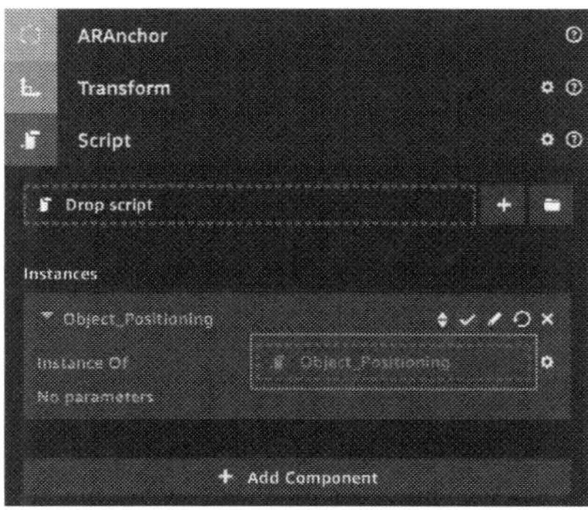

Open the **Object_Positioning** script for editing by clicking the **pencil icon** on top of it in the Inspector panel. Replace the contents of the file with the following piece of code.

Note: The following code uses "the old" API. This is the only way to access the AR components at the moment.

```
'use strict';

function setup(args, ctx) {
  // 1.
  ctx.entity.setComponent(new sumerian.ArAnchorComponent());

  // 2.
  const arSystem = ctx.world.getSystem('ArSystem');
  if (!arSystem) {
    return;
  }

 // 3.
  ctx.performHitTest = function(evt) {

    var pixelRatio =
      ctx.world.sumerianRunner.renderer.devicePixelRatio;

    var normalizedX =
        evt.changedTouches[0].pageX * pixelRatio /
        ctx.viewportWidth;

    var normalizedY =
        evt.changedTouches[0].pageY * pixelRatio /
        ctx.viewportHeight;

    arSystem.hitTest(normalizedX, normalizedY,
        ctx.hitTestCallback);
  };

 // 4.
  ctx.hitTestCallback = function(anchorTransform) {
    if (anchorTransform) {
      arSystem.registerAnchor(anchorTransform,
          ctx.registerAnchorCallback);
    }
  };

 // 5.
  ctx.registerAnchorCallback = function(anchorId) {
    if (anchorId) {
      ctx.entity.getComponent('ArAnchorComponent').anchorId
          = anchorId;
    }
  };

  // 6.
```

```
    ctx.domElement.addEventListener('touchend',
        ctx.performHitTest);
}
```

Here's how this code works:

1. Create and attach a Sumerian `ArAnchorComponent` to the current `ARAnchor` entity so that the `ArSystem` is aware of it.

2. Get the `ArSystem` component using `ctx.world.getSystem()` and save a reference to it in the newly created constant named `arSystem`.

3. Define a `performHitTest` function. This function gets called when the user taps the screen. The line after comment // 6. defines this function. It converts the event's coordinates into normalized screen coordinates (a value in the range 0.0 - 1.0). Then, it passes these values as parameters to the `ArSystem`'s `hitTest` function, defined below, which asks ARKit whether a surface exists at that location in the real world.

4. Next, the `hitTestCallback` function gets called and has the results of the hit test passed to it. If successful — meaning, a surface was detected at the tap location — an object of type `Transform` is returned representing the detected surface. Then, `registerAnchor()` of `arSystem` is called for it to register this transform as an anchor.

5. `registerAnchorCallback()` is called with the results of the anchor registration request, an anchor ID. If successful, the `anchorId` property of `ArAnchor` component is updated, which automatically updates the Transform values of the entity, essentially moving the shoe model to move to the location of the tap.

6. Finally, `ctx.domElement.addEventListener()` is called to register an event of type `touchend`, which is called when the screen is tapped.

Save the script file, republish the scene and, after waiting for a few seconds, open the mobile app again.

Once the scene is loaded, point the camera's viewfinder at a solid, well-lit surface, such as a tabletop, or floor, and tap the center of the screen. You'll see the 3D shoe model reposition to the location where you tapped the screen.

Positioning using image recognition

Another way to provide positioning is through the use of an image. This image is used as an anchor point in the world.

Companies have made great use of this approach. For example, one newspaper showed video footage of events when users viewed the paper with the newspaper's app. The app recognized the trigger images and projected video footage on top of them, creating an interactive experience.

In this section, you'll be changing the contents of the **Object_Positioning** script so that the shoe will reposition in AR when the camera viewfinder points to a specific image, which is referred to from this point as the **target-image**. This is known as augmented reality with image recognition.

From this point, the rest of the app will be built using this image recognition approach. This approach is better for building this particular app as you'll understand in the subsequent chapters.

Time to get started. Open the **Object_Positioning** script in the Text editor and replace the contents of the file with the following code:

```
'use strict';

function setup(args, ctx) {
    // 1.
    ctx.entity.setComponent(new sumerian.ArAnchorComponent());

    // 2.
    const arSystem = ctx.world.getSystem('ArSystem');
    if (!arSystem) {
        return;
    }
    // 3.
    ctx.imageAnchorCallback = function(anchorId) {
        if (anchorId) {
            ctx.entity.getComponent('ArAnchorComponent')
                .anchorId = anchorId;
            ctx.entity.show();
        }
    };

    // 4.
    const imageName = 'SumerianAnchorImage';

    // 5.
    arSystem.registerImage(imageName, ctx.imageAnchorCallback);
}
```

Here's the code breakdown:

1. A Sumerian `ArAnchor` component is attached to the current `ArAnchor` entity so that the `ArSystem` is aware of it.
2. Similarly, a reference to the the `ArSystem` component is set in constant variable `arSystem` in using the `ctx.world.getSystem()` method.
3. The `registerAnchorCallback` function is called with the results of the anchor registration request, an anchor ID. If successful, the `anchorId` property of the `ArAnchor` component is updated when the entity is detected. When the image is detected in the real world, `ctx.entity.show()` will be called and the `ARAnchor` entity will be visible again, and so will its child objects, the shoe.
4. A variable of type constant is defined, and a string value `SumerianAnchorImage` is set. This would be the exact name of the target image — the image on top of which the 3D Model will reposition — that you will define while setting up the mobile app later on in this tutorial.

5. Finally, `registerImage()` of `ArSystem` is called which registers a to-be-detected image in the environment in a Sumerian scene.

Switch back to the Scene editor and in the Entities panel, hide the `ARAnchor` entity by choosing the eye icon to the left `ARAnchor`. The shoe 3D model should not be visible now.

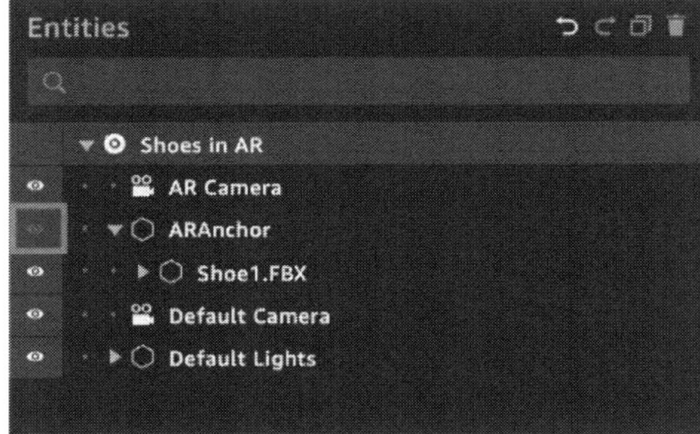

You're doing this because when your scene loads, the shoe will be hidden by default. Only when you point the camera viewfinder on the target image will the shoe be visible and positioned on top of the image.

Save the scene and republish it. Now that you have changed the **Object_Positioning** script, you need to set the target image on top of which the shoe model will reposition.

Proceed to either the Android or iOS sections depending on your platform of choice.

Adding an anchor image in Android

Open the **amazon-sumerian-arcore-starter-app** you downloaded and set up in the previous chapter in Android Studio.

In the Project navigator panel select the **Project** view.

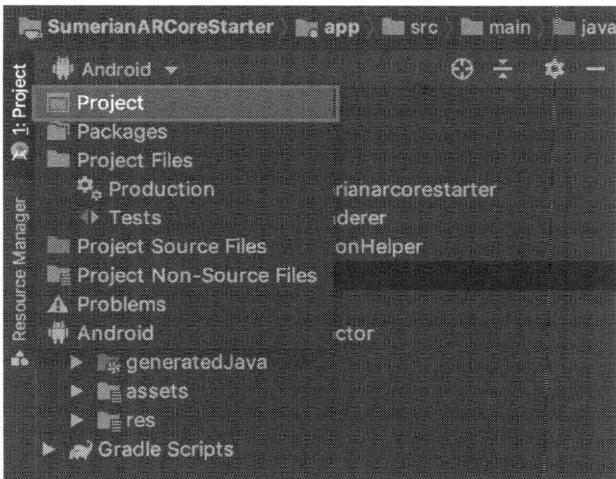

From the Project navigator window, select the **assets** folder by navigating to **app** ▸ **src** ▸ **main** ▸ **assets**.

Right-click on it and, from the drop-down menu, click on **Reveal in Finder** (macOS) or **Show in Explorer** (Windows) option to open the directory.

There should only be a **SumerianAnchorImage.png** image file in this folder.

Replace this image with **SumerianAnchorImage.png** from the **resources** folder from that are part of the assets for this chapter.

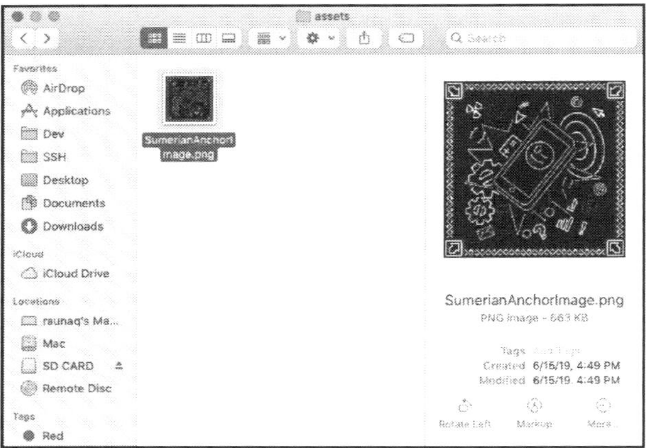

Next, open the **MainActivity.java** file by navigating to **app ▸ src ▸ main ▸ java ▸ com ▸ amazon ▸ sumerianarcorestarter ▸ MainActivity** and change the value of `IMAGE_WIDTH_IN_METERS` to the width, in meters, of your custom image in the real world.

Taking the example of an A4 size sheet of paper, set the value to `(float)0.20`.

```
public class MainActivity extends AppCompatActivity implements GLSurfaceView.Renderer {
    private static final String TAG = MainActivity.class.getSimpleName();
    private static final String SCENE_URL = "https://us-east-2.sumerian.aws/ee6b9cf309d
    private static final String IMAGE_FILENAME = "SumerianAnchorImage.png";
    private static final float IMAGE_WIDTH_IN_METERS = (float)0.20;
```

Finally, save the project by selecting **File ▸ Save All** and then build and rerun the project by connecting your Android device to your computer and selecting **Run ▸ Run** in Android Studio.

Notice you are building and installing this project again because, in addition to the changes in the Sumerian scene, you've also made changes in the contents of the mobile app itself. Such as replacing the **SumerianAnchorImage.png** file with your own.

Adding an anchor image in iOS

Open the **amazon-sumerian-arkit-starter-app** you downloaded and set up in the previous chapter in Xcode.

In Xcode's Project navigator, select **Assets.xcassets**. Next, click the **AR Resources** folder to expand its contents. You should be able to see that an image **SumerianAnchorImage** already exists.

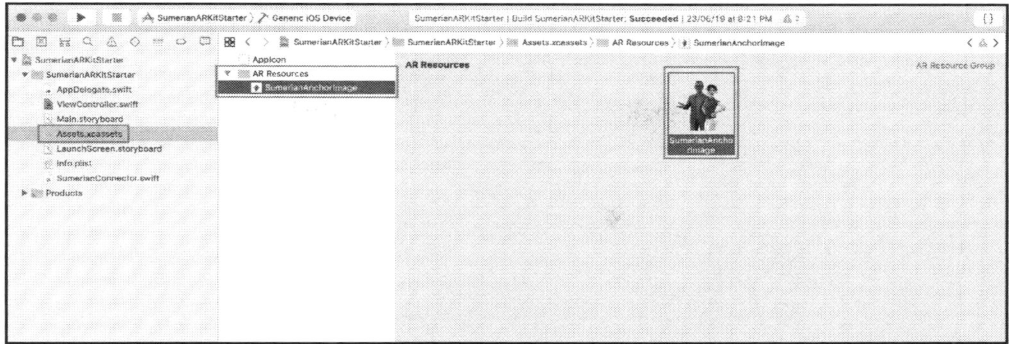

Right-click on **SumerianAnchorImage**, and click **Remove Selected Items** to delete it. The window should show **"No AR Items..."**.

From the **resources** folder containing the assets for this project, drag and drop **SumerianAnchorImage.png** into the Xcode window.

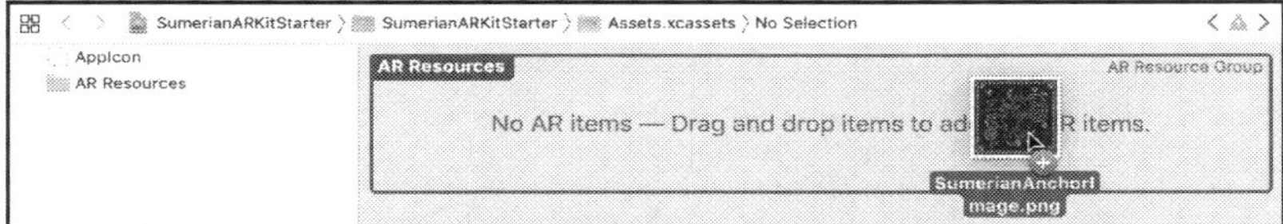

Next, you need to set the real-world dimension for the target image. Using an A4-sized sheet of paper as an example, set the dimension to 20x20 cm.

In the Xcode window, select the target image and click the **Attribute Inspector** button. Set Units to **Centimeters** and then set both height and width to **20**.

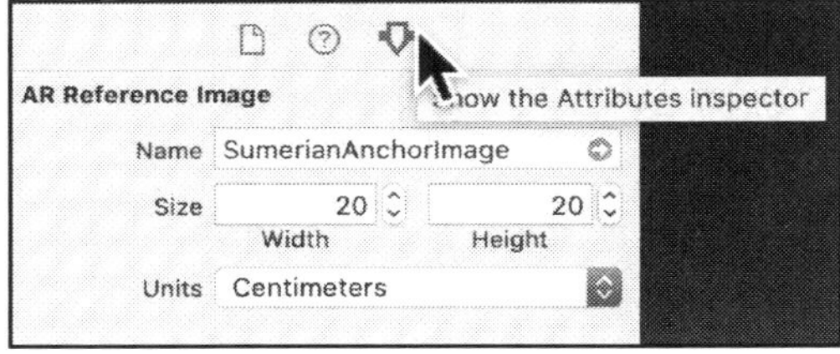

Running the app on a device

Now you're ready. You set the anchor image and you put the code in place to recognize it and display the shoe on it. Connect your iOS device to your computer and, run your app.

Once the Sumerian Scene has loaded on your mobile device, the camera viewfinder will open. You'll notice that no matter where you point your camera, you cannot see the shoe 3D model.

Point your camera viewfinder on a copy of the target image that you set in this chapter.

> **Note**: If the shoe 3D model does not appear on top of the image, or appears only temporarily, completely close the app on your iOS device and open it again. Also, make sure your device is connected to the internet.

It's best to take a colored print out of that image and point your camera at it. You should see the shoe on top of it.

You can try moving either the image or your mobile device from different angles, making sure it is still pointed at the image, to see the shoe from varying angles and distances.

Key points

- To create an AR scene in Sumerian, you must use the AR project template.
- The **ArSystem** manages all the components in an AR scene.
- The ArSystem processes all the entities with an **ArAnchor** component attached to them.
- Models can positioned in AR using **surface detection** or **image recognition**.
- Anchor images must be added to the app project.

Where to go from here?

Congratulations!

This was a first look at how to build a simple augmented reality scene with Sumerian. In this chapter, you learned about the basic components of the Sumerian Augmented Reality template, how to import 3D assets, and how to build and run the app on your mobile device.

You also learned how to use image recognition. If you'd like, you can try setting your custom image — it can be anything you want — and set it as the target image for the app. You can even experiment with how changing the value of the image width in the project properties affects the size of the shoe model in AR.

In the next chapter, you'll learn about the basics of databases and how to use the Amazon DynamoDB service within your Sumerian scene.

Chapter 17: Fetching Data from DynamoDB

By Gur Raunaq Singh

Your virtual shoe store is coming together. You've added a shoe and provided an anchor image for your shoe to appear. Unfortunately, there's no information about the shoe. You can add all that information inside of the scene, but this adds unnecessary work.

Think about it. Imagine you were having a sale and you wanted to discount your shoes by ten percent. This change requires you to load up the Sumerian scene and then search for all the prices. This means searching in your canvas as well as checking all your behaviors. For small scenes, this may not take much time but for larger scenes with dozens of behaviors containing hundreds of states, this is a process fraught with error.

A better approach is to maintain that information outside of the scene. That way, instead of modifying your Sumerian scene to apply a discount, you can just update the price from a web page. AWS contains a great tool for to use. It's called DynamoDB and in this chapter, you'll put it to work.

Introduction to databases

DynamoDB is a database provided by AWS. The term database is used to describe an organized collection of data. This is where you can store all your records about your shoes.

In the digital world, it is simply a location where data is stored in the form of one or more numbers of files in a structured way. A common way to store data is in the form of a table.

For example, a spreadsheet document is basically one large table, with rows and columns, where the column defines the characteristics of a data point, and a row defines a record of data. A database can have hundreds or even thousands of tables and are usually related to each other in some way.

The main benefit of storing data this way is that you can query (lookup) the data fast, or connect data from two or more different tables to each other. For example, if you have a database of sales information, you could do relatively simple things such as find out how much money you were taking in each day, or track your inventory of any given product, so you know when to buy more.

An example of a non-digital database can be a filing cabinet, which can be used to store massive amounts of information in an organized, methodical manner. Since several databases can connect, think of them as a series of filing cabinets right next to each other. When you go to look up some information, you can find it easily and quickly, as well as information pointing to other files that may be used in reference.

Once you have data stored in a database, you need a way to interact with the data — fetch data, add data, remove data, etc. — in an efficient way. This is known as a **Database Management System (DBMS)**.

For this app, you'll use Amazon DynamoDB, a fully-managed database management service that will allow you to interact with the information about the different models of shoes that you'll be adding in your augmented reality app.

Before you access DynamoDB from within Sumerian, you'll need to create a set of credentials within your AWS Account. Mainly, you have to:

- Set up an AWS Cognito Identity and get it's Identity Pool ID.
- Create corresponding IAM Roles.
- Attach access policies to the IAM Role.

You'll start by setting up AWS Cognito.

Getting started with Cognito

Amazon Cognito is an AWS product that controls user authentication and access for mobile applications on internet-connected devices. The service saves and synchronizes end-user data, which enables the developer to build the app instead of the back-end infrastructure.

Since you want users other than yourself to be able to get shoe details from DynamoDB with your Sumerian AR app, you need to set up AWS Cognito. Perform the following steps to create an AWS Cognito Identity pool.

Open the Amazon Cognito page located at https://console.aws.amazon.com/cognito/home and enter the credentials for your AWS account. Once signed in, you should be redirected to the Amazon Cognito service page. Click **Manage Identity Pools**.

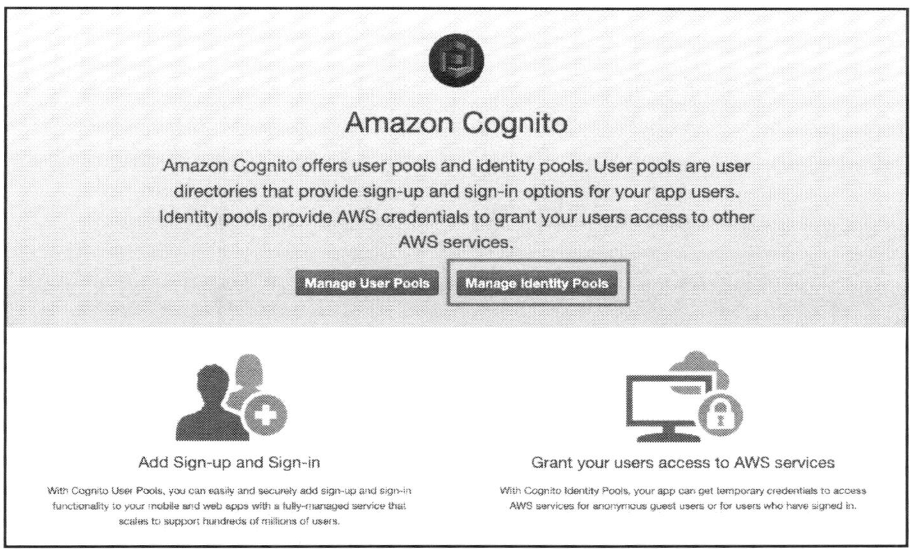

The **Getting started wizard** should open, allowing you to create a new identity pool. You can also open the wizard directly using the following link: https://us-east-2.console.aws.amazon.com/cognito/create.

For the Identity pool name, enter **Shoes_in_AR**. Place a checkmark in the box next to **Enable access to unauthenticated identities**. With this option enabled, all users will have access to the app without having to log into AWS.

Finally, click **Create Pool**.

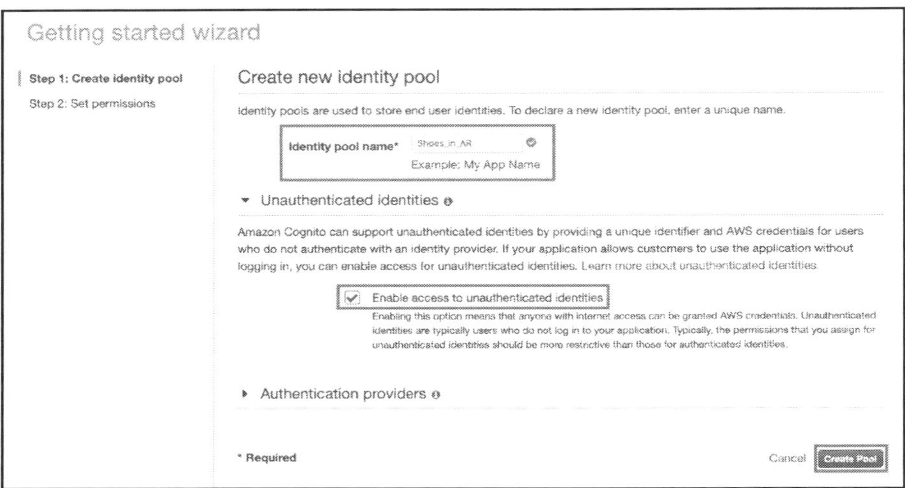

On the next page, you'll be asked to assign **Identity and Access Management (IAM)** roles. In review. An AWS IAM role is an IAM identity that you can create in your account that has specific permissions. To refresh yourself about IAM roles, check out Chapter 1, "Getting Started with Amazon Sumerian."

Click **View Details** to see the complete details about the created IAM roles. Click **Allow**.

Once the IAM roles complete, you should be redirected to a page displaying the AWS Credentials.

▾ Get AWS Credentials

```
// Initialize the Amazon Cognito credentials provider
CognitoCachingCredentialsProvider credentialsProvider = new CognitoCachingCredentialsProvider(
    getApplicationContext(),
    "us-east-2:669267cd-04d1-451a-88e6-1b18936540b1", // Identity pool ID
    Regions.US_EAST_2 // Region
);
```

Copy the **Identity pool ID**, in red text, and save it someplace safe as this is the unique ID you'll be using in your Sumerian scene later.

Attaching policies to IAM roles

IAM roles are a secure way to grant permissions to entities that you trust.

Once you have created IAM roles, you need to attach certain **policies** to them for them to access a particular AWS Service. Since you'll be storing and fetching data from a DynamoDB table, you'll need to attach specific policies so that your app can read data from DynamoDB.

To start, open the AWS IAM Roles page located at https://console.aws.amazon.com/iam/home. Based on your AWS usage, you may or may not see some items in the table on the page.

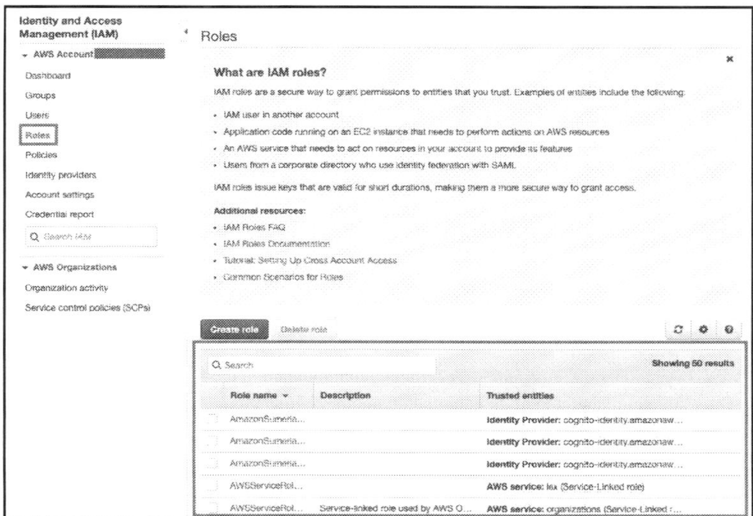

In the table, you might see a long list of roles, a description, and their respective trusted entities. In the search box just above the table, enter **Shoes_in_AR**, which is the AWS Cognito ID pool name that you created in the previous subsection.

You should be able to see two role names in the table.

Here, you only need to attach policies to the **Cognito Unauth Role** since you want to allow unauthenticated access to your app so that the DynamoDB table can be queried.

In the filtered list, click **Cognito_Shoes_in_ARUnauth_Role** to see a summary of the role.

On the **Summary** page, click **Attach policies**.

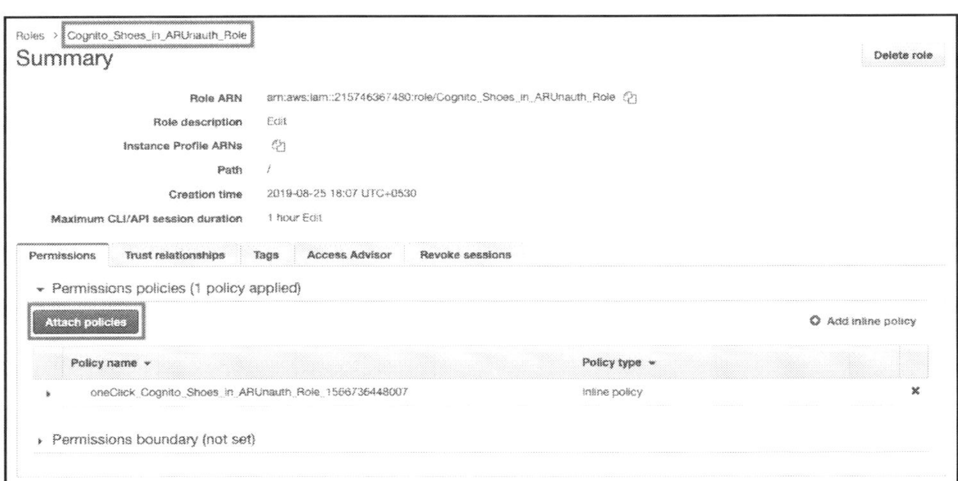

You should be redirected to a page in which you'll see a list of policies that you can attach to your IAM role. In the search box, enter **dynamodb**. You should see a list of policies related to the DynamoDB Service on AWS.

In the list of policies, place a checkmark in the box for **AmazonDynamoDBReadOnlyAccess** and click **Attach Policy**. Since you only want to be able to read data from DynamoDB table, you only need to attach this policy.

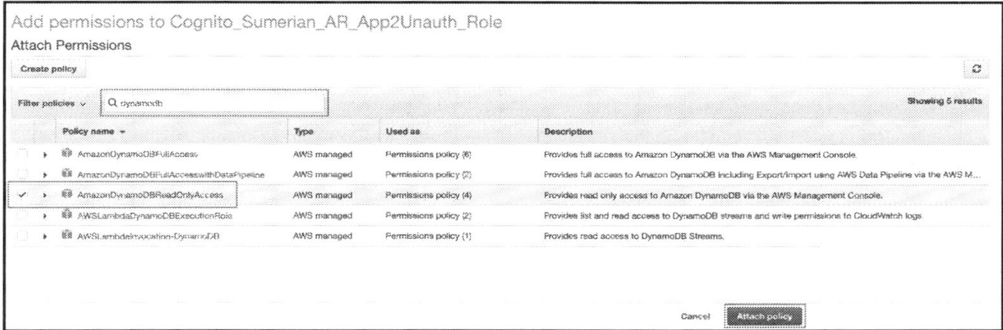

You should be redirected to the Summary page with a notification of successful policy addition. You should also be able to see the attached policy in the Permission policies list.

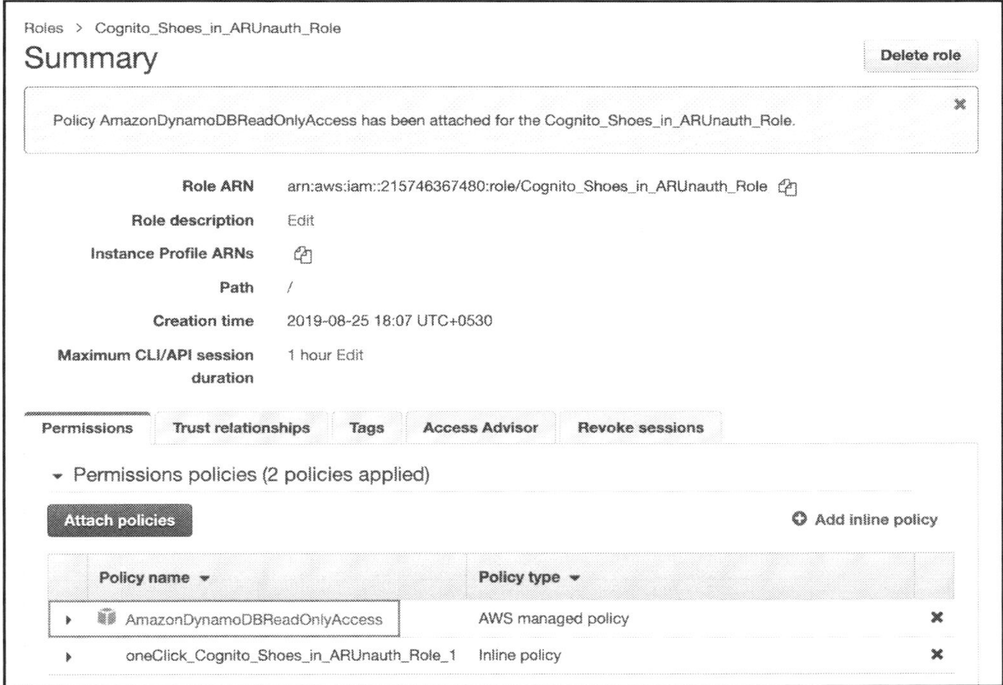

And that's it. Now you'll be able to fetch data from DyanamoDB Tables in your Sumerian AR Scene.

Setting up DynamoDB and adding data

With your IAM all configured to use DynamoDB, you are now ready to dive into it!

Open the AWS DynamoDB console located at https://console.aws.amazon.com/dynamodb/home and click **Create table**.

Enter **shoes** for the Table name, and for the Primary key, enter **shoe_id**. A primary key is a column used to identify a row of data and it is meant to be unique.

For example, you may contain a table that represents a person. The table may contain fields such as first name, last name, address and so forth. All these fields may duplicated. For instance, there are multiple people named John Smith.

You could use a social security number as a primary key but that's sensitive date. A better approach is to create an id field that increments with each person added to the database. This lets you know that the John Smith with an id of 10 is different from the John Smith with an id of 32.

Finally, select **number** from the drop-down.

In the **Table settings** section, ensure the **Use default settings** option is checked. Once you have everything set, click **Create**.

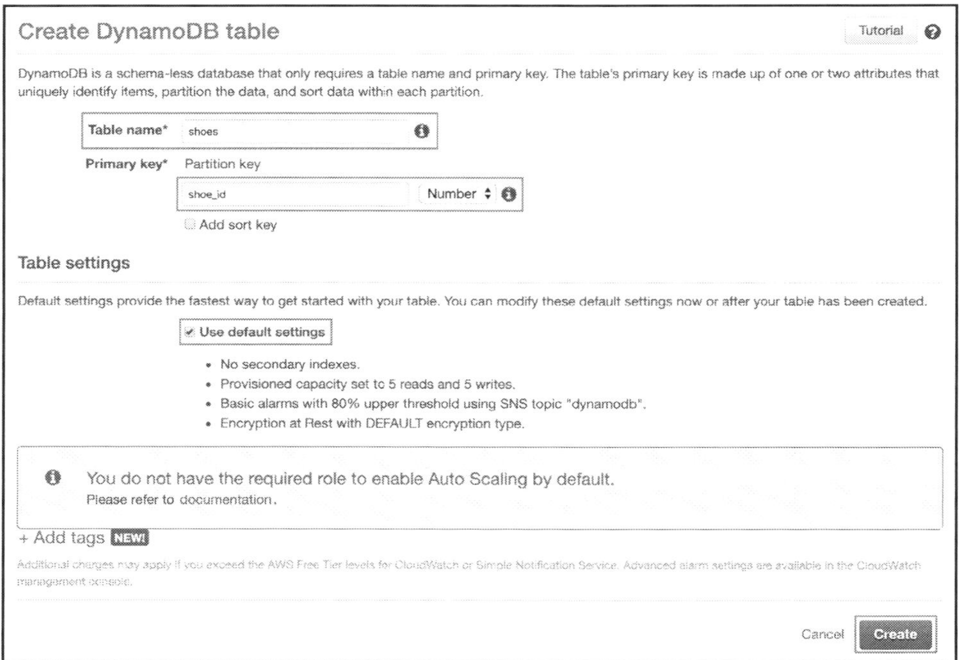

It should take a few seconds, after which your table will generate. Once done, click the **Items** tab. You should see an empty table.

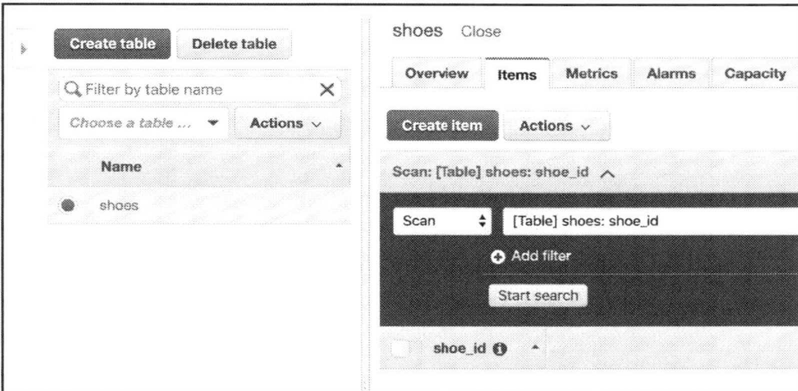

Click **Create Item**. The Create item window should open.

There are two ways to add data to the table. The first way involves using the interactive menu options by clicking on the + button.

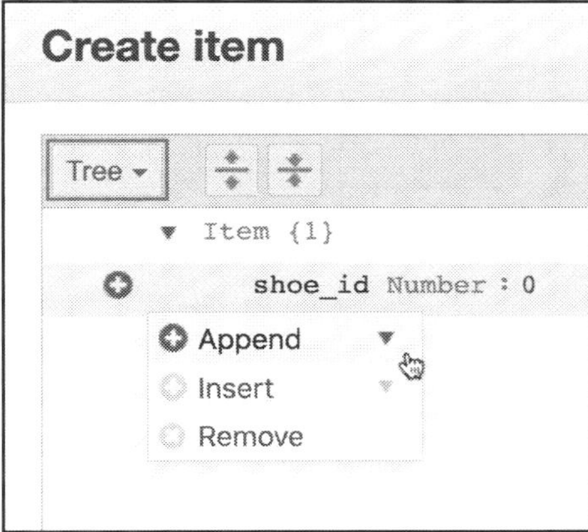

The second way is by organizing your data in a JavaScript Object Notation (JSON) format and pasting it in the window with the text option selected.

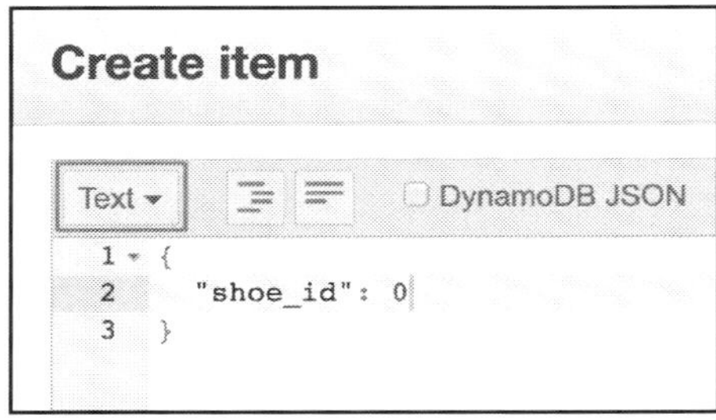

You'll be using JSON to add data to the table. All this means is that you'll be expressing your data with JavaScript objects. This is the same JavaScript that you've used throughout this book.

If you need a refresher, refer back to Chapter 11, "Introduction to JavaScript."

Switch the drop-down selection on the top-left of the Create item from Tree to **Text**. Now, replace the text inside of the box with the following:

```
{
  "shoe_id": 1,
  "shoe_type": "Sneaker",
  "shoe_color": "Black-Orange",
  "shoe_price" : 39.99
}
```

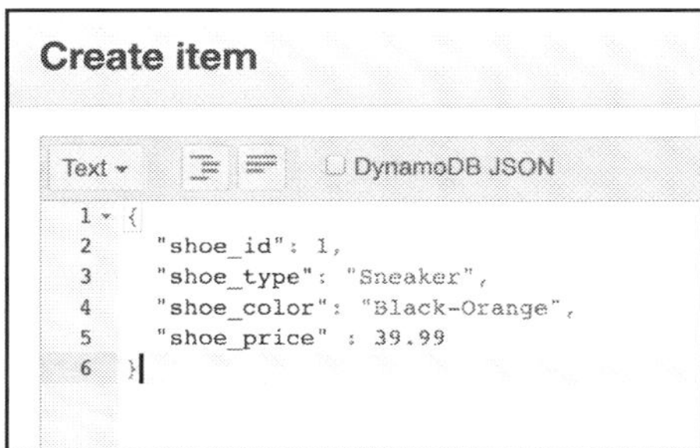

This JSON simply defines an object with some values. An object is created by using the curly-braces {}. Inside the object, you defined four properties. A property must have a name and a value. This name and value combination is separated by the colon. Properties are separated by commas.

Note: If you want to play around with JSON, head over to https://jsonlint.com/.

Click **Save** to add the item to the table. You should be able to see that there is now one item in the table.

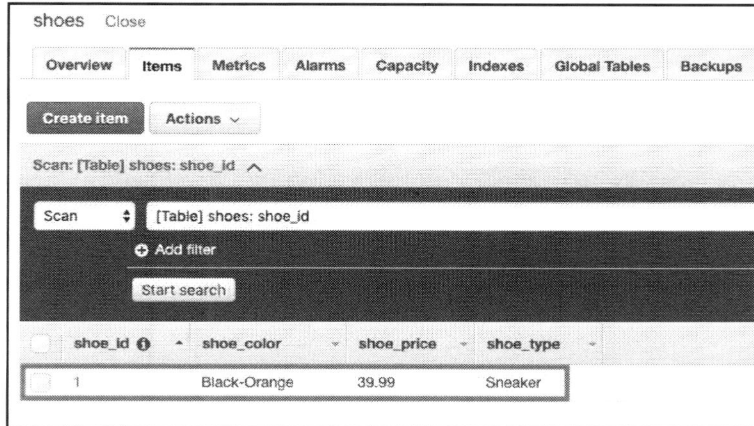

Similarly, add two more items by repeating the above steps.

```
{
  "shoe_id": 2,
  "shoe_type": "Formal",
  "shoe_color": "Brown",
  "shoe_price" : 49.99
}
```

```
{
  "shoe_id": 3,
  "shoe_type": "Sports",
  "shoe_color": "Grey",
  "shoe_price" : 79.99
}
```

The table should look like this:

shoe_id	shoe_color	shoe_price	shoe_type
1	Black-Orange	39.99	Sneaker
2	Brown	49.99	Formal
3	Grey	79.99	Sports

And that's it!

With the Cognito ID pool, IAM roles and shoes table set up, it's time to move on to the Sumerian scene and learn how to fetch the data so you can display it in your app.

Fetching data from DynamoDB and displaying it

Before writing the code to fetch data and display it on the screen, here's an overview of the different components you'll be adding the flow of data between them.

First, you'll create an html button. When the user clicks the button, Sumerian will ask DynamoDB for the shoe information. It will get this information based on the `shoe_id`.

When DynamoDB finds the information, it will send the information back to Sumerian. Once Sumerian receives the information, it will show the information to the end user. It will do this using an HTML entity.

Creating the button HTML entity

Perform the following steps to create a 2D HTML entity, in which the contents of data fetched from the DynamoDB table will display.

Open up your Sumerian scene. Click **Create Entity**, and add an **HTML Entity**. Rename the entity to **Scene_UI**.

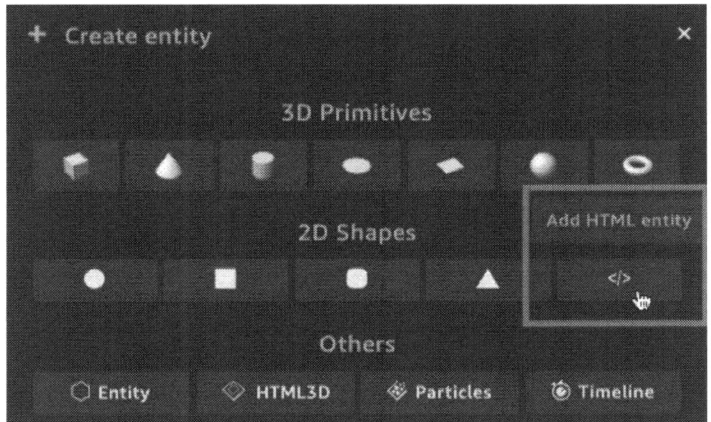

Next, drag the `Scene_UI` entity into the `ARAnchor` entity, making it a child of `ARAnchor`.

Your Entities panel should look like this:

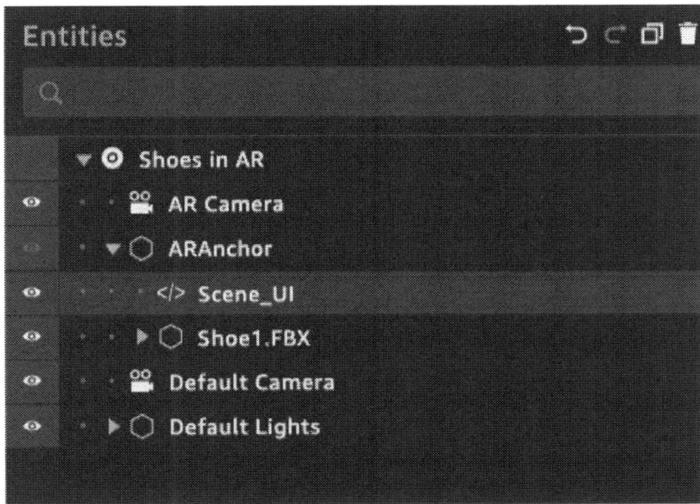

Click the **eye** icon next to ARAnchor to enable its visibility. The HTML entity and the 3D shoe model from the previous chapter should be visible now.

With the Scene_UI entity selected, look at the Inspector panel. Expand the **HTML** component and disable **Move with Transform** by removing the checkbox. When you check this checkbox, the element moves to the upper left corner of the canvas.

This removes the HTML element from the 3D space of the scene. Changing the position won't affect the element at all. Instead, you place the element using traditional CSS properties.

This allows you to create user interface elements that remain fixed in the same position regardless of where the camera is pointed.

Click **Open in Editor** to edit the contents of the HTML entity.

Replace the existing HTML code with the following:

```
<style>

    #myContainer {
    width: 100vw;
    height: 100vh;

    }

    .shoe-info-p {
        font-size: 18px;
        padding: 5px;
        border-radius: 3px;
        margin: 0;
        font-family: calibri;
        font-weight: bold;
    }

    .shoe-info-bg-div{
        background-color:white;
        margin-left: 15px;
        margin-top:  15px;
        border-style: solid;
        border-width: thin;
        border-radius: 5px;
        max-width: 200px;
    }

</style>

<div id="myContainer">

    <!-- Defining a main div of class "shoe-info-bg-div" -->
```

```
        <div class="shoe-info-bg-div">
            <h2 class="shoe-info-p">
                <b> Shoe Info</b></p>

                <!-- 3. Defining entities of type span. -->

                Type : <span id="shoe_type"></span></p>
                Price : <span id="shoe_price" ></span></p>
                Color :  <span id="shoe_color" ></span></p>

            </h2>
        </div>

    <div>
```

This HTML code creates a simple user interface. However, notice the three `<span>` elements with ids `shoe_type`, `shoe_price` and `shoe_color`. By adding ids to these spans, you'll be able to populate each one using the data from the DynamoDB table you created earlier.

Click **Save** to save the file. At this point, you should have an HTML entity in the scene.

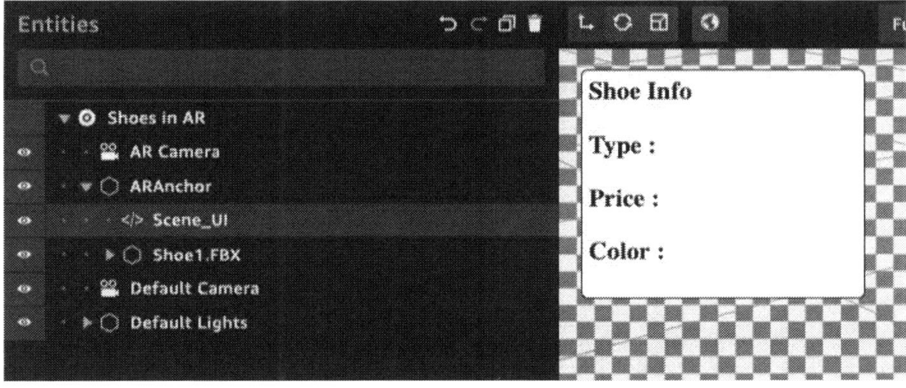

Next, you need to add a button that, when clicked by the user will trigger an event that will fetch data from the DynamoDB table and display in the 2D HTML entity defined in the previous section.

Open the `Scene_UI` entity in script editor and add the following code snippet in the body of the `<style> ... </style>` tag.

```
    .shoe-button-style{
        position: absolute;
        left: 5%;
        bottom: 10%;
```

```
    background: transparent;
    border:none;

}

.shoe-button-img{
    max-width:100px;
}
```

The body of `<style>` should look something like this:

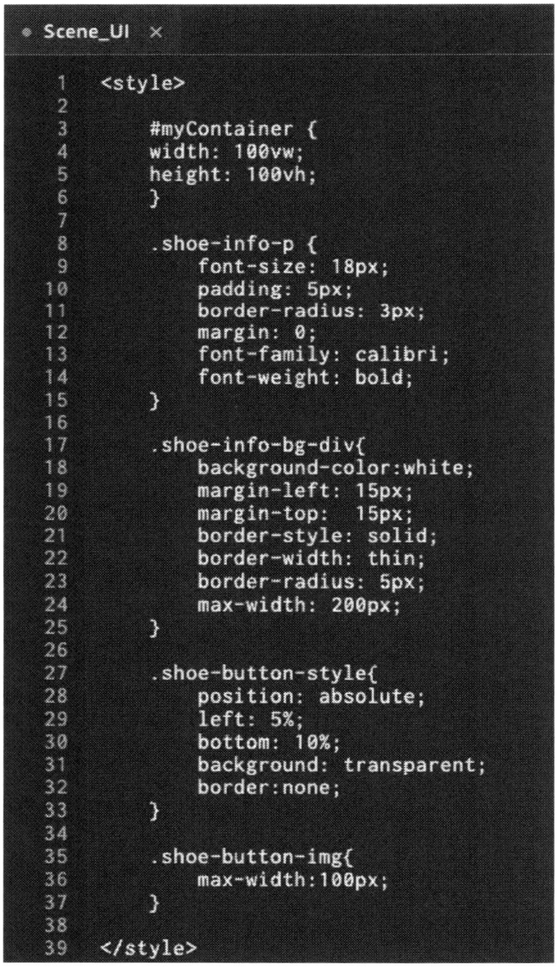

```
Scene_UI ×

1   <style>
2
3       #myContainer {
4       width: 100vw;
5       height: 100vh;
6       }
7
8       .shoe-info-p {
9           font-size: 18px;
10          padding: 5px;
11          border-radius: 3px;
12          margin: 0;
13          font-family: calibri;
14          font-weight: bold;
15      }
16
17      .shoe-info-bg-div{
18          background-color:white;
19          margin-left: 15px;
20          margin-top:  15px;
21          border-style: solid;
22          border-width: thin;
23          border-radius: 5px;
24          max-width: 200px;
25      }
26
27      .shoe-button-style{
28          position: absolute;
29          left: 5%;
30          bottom: 10%;
31          background: transparent;
32          border:none;
33      }
34
35      .shoe-button-img{
36          max-width:100px;
37      }
38
39  </style>
```

Next, add the following code snippet in the body of the `<div id="myContainer"> ... </div>` tag:

```
<!-- Adding button to get information for Shoe with id="1" from
DynamoDB -->
<div class="shoe1-button-div">
    <button class="shoe-button-style" id="shoe1button">
        <img class="shoe-button-img" data-id=""/>
    </button>
</div>
```

This is an HTML code snippet adding a `<button>` of class `shoe-button-style` and id `shoe1button`. The `id` tag can be used to uniquely identify an HTML entity, which you'll see in the upcoming sections.

Notice that in the `<img>` tag, the value of `data-id` is empty.

All assets in a Sumerian scene can be uniquely identified and references by a **data-id**. Here, you will set an image to act as the button in your Sumerian.

Save the script and go back to the scene editor. The button you just added is missing. That's because the `data-id` value is empty. So, how do you get id?

When using an image as part of your HTML code, you need to upload the image. Once successfully uploaded, a data-id generates for that image which you can use in your scene.

Once again, open the `Scene_UI` entity in the Text editor, and click **Browse**. Select the **shoe1.jpg** image from the **resources** folder for this project to add it to the project.

Once the image is uploaded, an HTML element of type `<img>` should be added at the bottom of the script. It would look something like this:

```
<img data-id="5eebf7b56cb8d453bcd17e55d05960e0965b2528.jpg"/>
```

Finally, copy the value of the `data-id` tag from the line that was added to the script when you uploaded **shoe1.jpg** and paste it next in the body of the `<img>` element from the above code snippet.

Then, delete the line that was added automatically when you uploaded `shoe1.jpg`. The body of `<div id="myContainer">` should now look something like this:

```
43  <div id="myContainer">
44
45      <!-- Defining a main div of class "shoe-info-bg-div" -->
46      <div class="shoe-info-bg-div">
47          <h2 class="shoe-info-p">
48              <b> Shoe Info</b></p>
49
50              <!-- 3. Defining entities of type span. -->
51
52              Type : <span id="shoe_type"></span></p>
53              Price : <span id="shoe_price" ></span></p>
54              Color :  <span id="shoe_color" ></span></p>
55
56          </h2>
57      </div>
58
59      <!-- Adding button to get information for Shoe with id="1" from DynamoDB -->
60      <div class="shoe1-button-div">
61        <button class="shoe-button-style" id="shoe1button">
62          <img class="shoe-button-img" data-id="5eebf7b56cb8d453bcd17e55d05960e0965b2528.jpg"/>
63        </button>
64      </div>
65
66  <div>
67
68
```

Finally, save the script and go back to the scene editor. You'll notice that a button is now present:

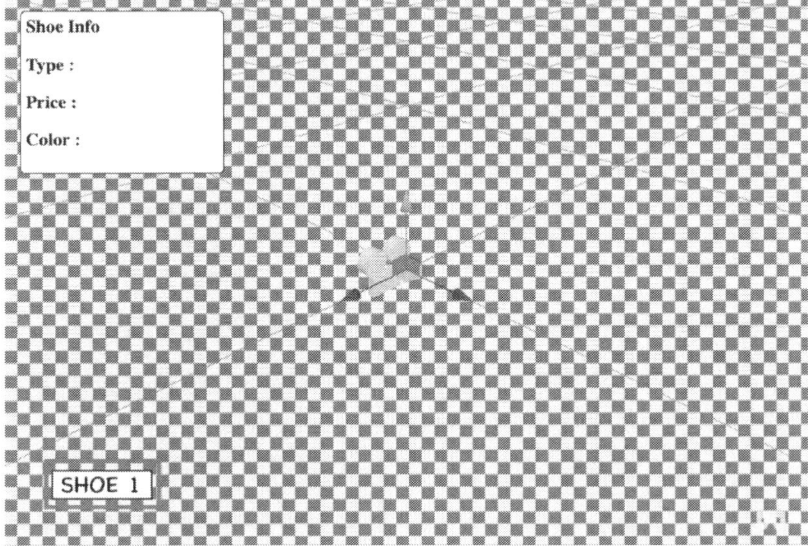

Now that you have added a trigger to fetch data from the DynamoDB table, the Button element and a way to display the contents in the Sumerian scene, it's time to write the script that will execute all of this.

Connecting Sumerian with DynamoDB

To connect to and make use of other AWS Services, you need to provide the Cognito pool ID to your Sumerian Project. In the Entities panel, select the top-level entity, **Shoes in AR**.

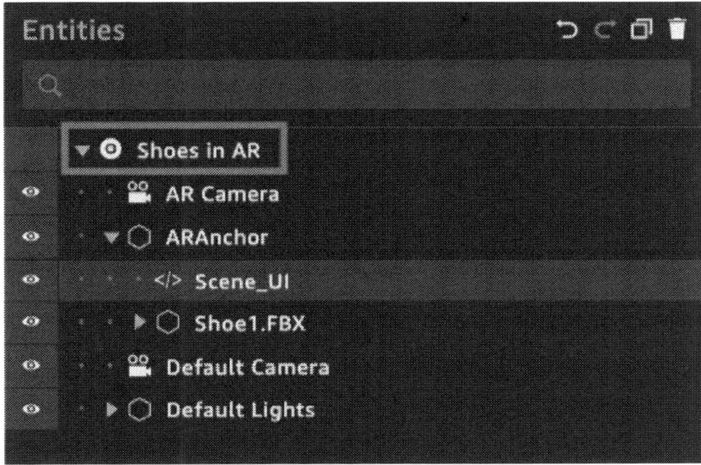

Now, in the inspector, expand the AWS Configuration component, and paste the **Cognito Pool ID** you saved earlier. It should look something like this:

Now that you can access AWS services from within your Sumerian app, the next step is to write the script to query the data from the DynamoDB table and display it within the Sumerian scene.

Creating a script to fetch data

Create an empty entity and name it **Scripts**. Then, add a new **Custom (Preview Format)** script and name it to **SceneManagerScript**. Drag the **Scripts** entity into the **ARAnchor** entity to make it a child.

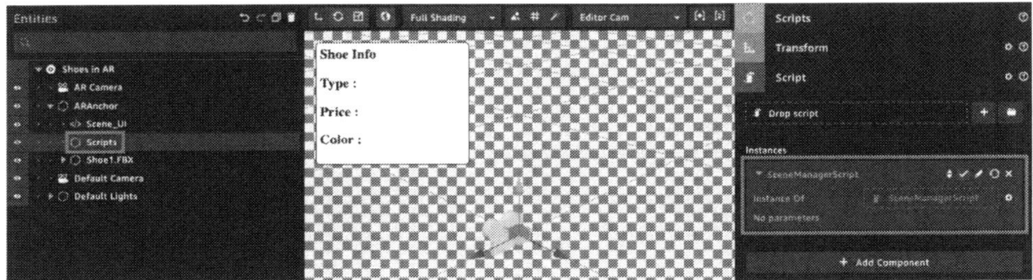

Open the **SceneManagerScript** script in the text editor, and replace the contents with the following piece of code:

```
import {DomEventAction} from 'module://sumerian-common/api/dom';
```

This is another way to import the Sumerian API. You can import the entire framework, or you can import just a part of it. In this case, you import just the parts that deal with the Document Object Model.

Now to add the initial action.

```
export default function SceneManagerHandlerAction(ctx) {
    ctx.start(
        [AddEventListenerToShoeButtons, {shoeID: 1} ]
    );
}
```

The `SceneManagerHandlerAction` functions calls the `AddEventListenerToShoeButtons` action. Doing so, it passes the 'shoe_id' into it. The `shoe_id` is passed in a plain old JavaScript object.

Now create the `AddEventListenerToShoeButtons` action.

```
function AddEventListenerToShoeButtons(ctx, {shoeID}) {
```

This creates function header. Notice the `{shoeID}`. This is a feature of the JavaScript language called a destructuring assignment. It assigns a value of the object to a `shoeID` variable.

Complete the method so it looks like the following:

```
function AddEventListenerToShoeButtons(ctx, {shoeID}) {
    ctx.start(
        [DomEventAction, {
            eventName: "mousedown",
            querySelector: '#shoe' + shoeID + 'button',
            onEvent: () => {
                getShoeData(shoeID);
            }
        }]
    );
}
```

This creates a new `DomEventAction` object. It listens for a mouse click event. The query selector determines when the mouse click event will fire. In this case, it fires when a shoe button is clicked. When it does fire, it calls `getShoeData()`, passing in the `shoeID`.

Now comes the time where you connect to DynamoDB. Add the following function:

```
function getShoeData(shoeID){
    var ddb = new AWS.DynamoDB();
}
```

This defines the function, taking in a `shoeID`. The first thing you do in the function is get an instance of the DynamoDB.

```
var params = {
    Key : {  shoe_id : { N : shoeID.toString() } },
    TableName : 'shoes'
};
```

You use `params` to tell DynamoDB what values you'd like to retrieve. First, the `Key` sets the key you are searching, passing in your `shoeID`. Being your `shoeID` is a number, you call `toString()` to convert it into text.

Next, you set the `TableName` for the search.

The only thing left to do is to query DynamoDB. Add the following:

```
ddb.getItem(params, function(err, data) {

});
```

`getItem` performs the actual query. It takes your `params` object and a function. This function is called when your query completes. Notice it provides two variables: `err` and `data`.

The `err` variable contains any errors that may have been returned. The `data` variable holds your returned data.

Now add the following inside `getItem()`:

```
if (err){
    console.log(err, err.stack);
} else {

}
```

This checks to see if an error is returned. If this is case, it prints the error to console.

Add the following to the `else` clause:

```
document.getElementById('shoe_type').innerHTML =
    data.Item.shoe_type.S;

document.getElementById('shoe_price').innerHTML =
    data.Item.shoe_color.S;

document.getElementById('shoe_color').innerHTML =
    data.Item.shoe_price.N;
```

If the query is successful, `data` is populated with keys and values. The keys is the column names and the values is the actual data.

To set the respective value, a reference to the HTML entities is get by calling the `document.getElementById()` method and the inner HTML contents are replaced by the respective corresponding value.

Setting the value is done by accessing the column name followed by the attribute type. The `N` indicates a number and the `S` indicates a string (text).

Here's the complete script:

```
import {DomEventAction} from 'module://sumerian-common/api/dom';

export default function SceneManagerHandlerAction(ctx) {
    ctx.start(
        [AddEventListenerToShoeButtons, {shoeID: 1}]
    );
}

function AddEventListenerToShoeButtons(ctx, {shoeID}){
    ctx.start(
        [DomEventAction, {
            eventName: "mousedown",
            querySelector: '#shoe' + shoeID + 'button',
```

```
                onEvent: () => {
                    getShoeData(shoeID);
                }
            }]
        );
    }

    function getShoeData(shoeID) {
        var ddb = new AWS.DynamoDB();
        var params = {
            Key : { shoe_id : { N : shoeID.toString() }},
            TableName: 'shoes'
        };
        ddb.getItem(params, function(err, data) {
            if (err){
                console.log(err, err.stack);
            } else {
                document.getElementById('shoe_type').innerHTML =
                    data.Item.shoe_type.S;
                document.getElementById('shoe_price').innerHTML =
                    data.Item.shoe_color.S;
                document.getElementById('shoe_color').innerHTML =
                    data.Item.shoe_price.N;
            }
        });
    }
```

Save the script and go back to the scene editor. Hide the `ARAnchor` entity using the hide/show toggle button. It looks like an eye.

Finally, re-publish the scene by clicking **Publish** > **Republish** and open the mobile app on your Android or iOS device.

Once the scene is loaded, point the camera viewfinder at the AR target image. Both the shoe 3D model and the UI elements should be visible. Finally, click the **Shoe 1** button, wait for a few seconds and voila!

The details of the shoe should be updated on the UI box in the top-left corner of your screen, which you can see on the next page.

Key points

- A database is an **organized collection of data**.
- DynamoDB is online accessible that allows you to **save data** in JSON format.
- A **primary key** is a unique column in your data.
- To access DynamoDB in your scene, you need to **create a Cognito identity pool** and attach the **necessary permissions to your IAM role**.
- **Reading and writing data** is handled by JavasScript in your scene.

Where to go from here?

DynamoDB is a powerful tool provided by AWS. In this example, you added data to the database and read it back in your scene. That said, DynamoDB is a two way street. This means you can write to it from Sumerian and read data back from it. Using just a little code, you can create a complete chat room, save user registration data and anything else that you need to persist data.

To learn more about DynamoDB, check out the official site for documentation and tutorials. You can find it over here: https://aws.amazon.com/dynamodb/

Chapter 18: Completing the Augmented Reality App

By Gur Raunaq Singh

Your shoe store is almost done. With all the shoe data contained in a database, you can easily update information about the shoes without having to touch the scenes. To finish your store, you need to add more shoes. Your store also needs a way for the user to change the shoe sizes. After all, not everyone has the same sized foot. Adding these improvements employs everything you've learned so far in this section.

Time to get started.

Adding more shoes to the project

In Chapter 16, "Augmented Reality in Sumerian," you added a 3D model of a single shoe to your project. Now, you'll add more shoes to your project. This will give it some variety and show how you use DynamoDB to store and fetch data from multiple items of the same type. You could add any number of shoes to a project like this, but for the sake of simplicity, you'll only add two more models now.

The process of importing shoes and adding textures is similar to what you learned in the previous chapters. Here's a quick recap of how to do it.

Open the Sumerian scene and click **Import Assets**. Then, click **Browse** and select **Shoe2.FBX** and **Shoe3.FBX** from the **resources** folder to import the shoe 3D Models into your Sumerian scene.

Once you've successfully uploaded the models, you'll see them as items in the Assets panel.

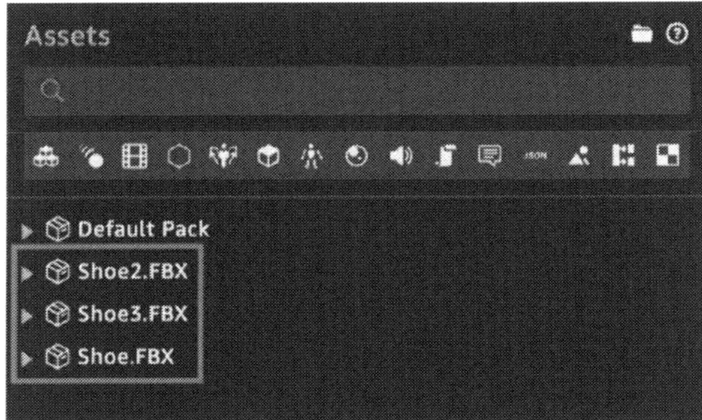

Next, **create three empty entity objects** and rename them to **Shoe1**, **Shoe2** and **Shoe3**, then drag them into the **ARAnchor** entity to make them its children. At this point, your Entities panel should look like this:

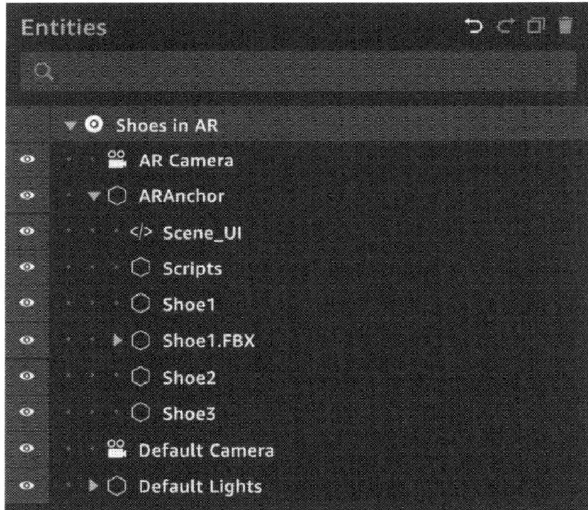

Drag the **Shoe2.FBX** and **Shoe3.FBX** 3D models from the Assets panel into the Entities panel. You can see the newly-added shoe models in the editor window.

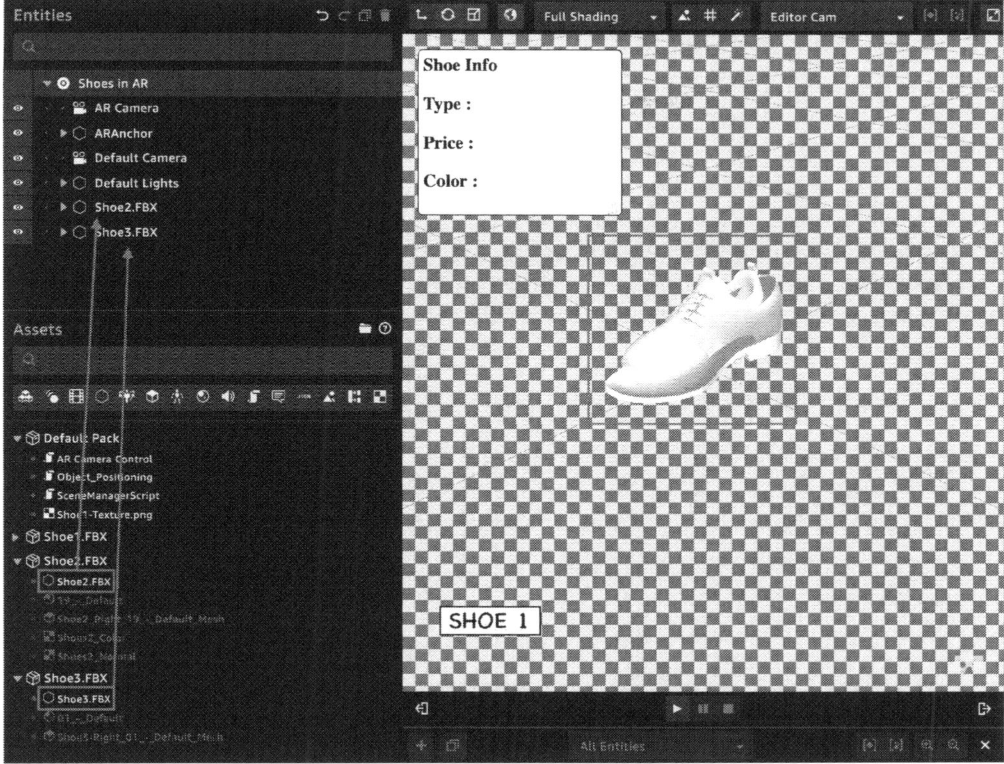

Next, drag these entities into the ARAnchor entity to make them its children.

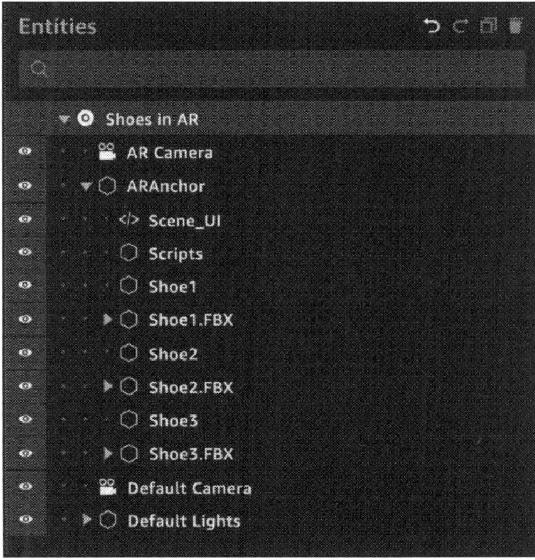

Finally, you need to apply the appropriate textures to each shoe entity. Select the child object of Shoe2.FBX named **Shoe2_Right_19_-_Default** and expand it by clicking the **Material** component in the inspector. Then, click the **COLOR (DIFFUSE)** property to expand it, click the folder icon next to Texture and select **Shoe2-Texture.png** to upload it. Once the upload finishes, Sumerian will apply the texture. You can see the results in the editor.

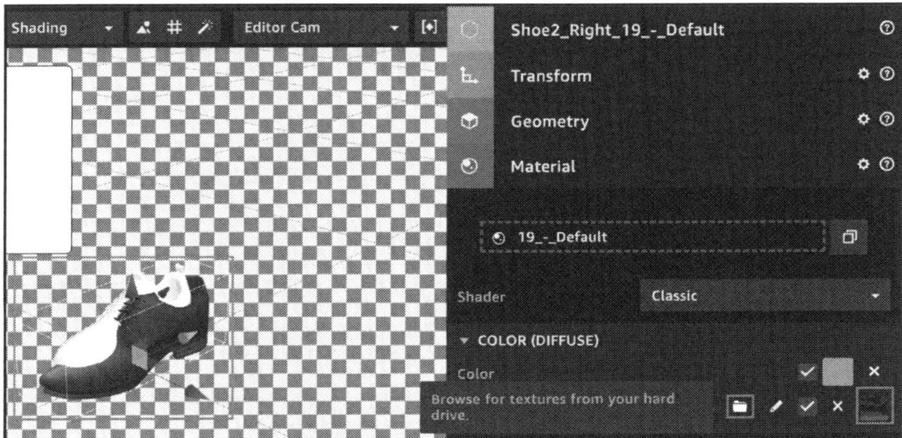

The shoes look weird right now because they overlap each other, but don't worry about that at the moment. You'll fix that later.

Repeat the same steps for Shoe3.FBX by selecting its child object, named **Shoe3-Right_01_-_Default**, and selecting **Shoe3-Texture.png** from the **resources** folder.

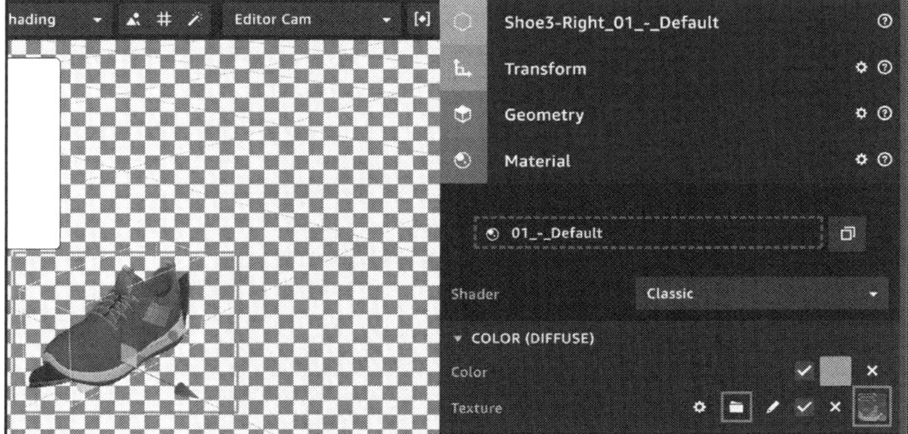

For your next step, you'll set the Transform properties of Shoe2.FBX and Shoe3.FBX to the same values as Shoe1.FBX:

- **Transform**: (0, 0, 0)
- **Rotation**: (0, 180, 0)
- **Scale**: (0.05, 0.05, 0.05)

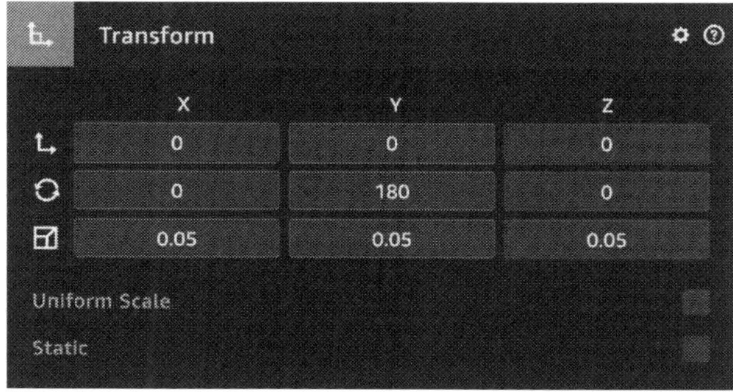

You want to set all of the entities' Transform values this way so they always appear in the center of the augmented reality target image when the user views them through the mobile app.

Next, drag the **Shoe2.FBX** and **Shoe3.FBX** entities into their respective empty entities: Shoe1.FBX to Shoe1, Shoe2.FBX to Shoe2 and Shoe3.FBX to Shoe3.

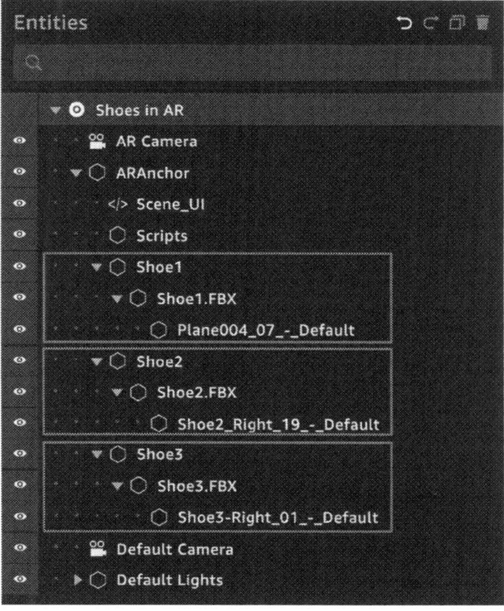

Now, create another empty entity, rename it **Shoe_Entities**, and drag the parent shoe entities you made in the previous step into this entity to make them its children. Completely expanded, your Entities panel should look like this:

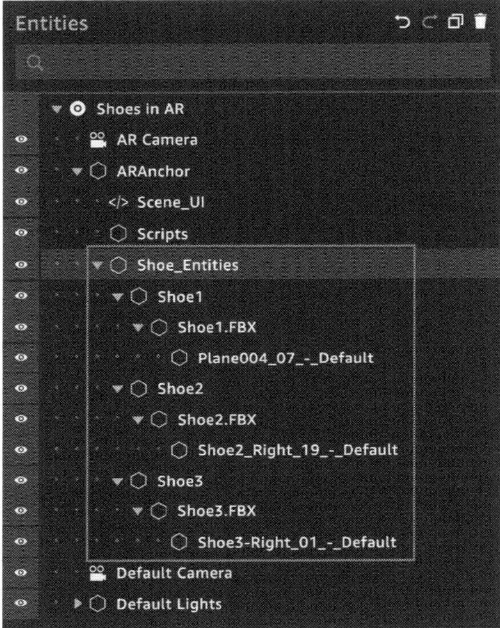

It's good practice to organize the entities this way, but it also makes it easy to interact with the entities. You'll use it when you write scripts to change Transform properties when you change shoe sizes and also to set only one entity to be visible when you add more shoe buttons.

Speaking of which, it's time to add those buttons now.

Adding 2D HTML buttons for new shoes

In the previous chapter, you added a button in the Sumerian scene which fetched the data for **Shoe ID: 1** from the DynamoDB table when the user clicked it. Now that you've imported two more 3D shoe models into your scene, you need to add the corresponding buttons for them.

Get started by opening the **Scene_UI** script in the Text editor.

Similar to the previous chapter, you need to add the HTML code for the buttons in the body of `<div id="myContainer">` and their corresponding CSS code in the body of `<style>`.

Add the following code in the body of `<style>` after `.shoe1-button-style{ ... }`:

```
.shoe2-button-style {
    position: absolute;
    left: 20%;
    bottom: 10%;
    background: transparent;
    border:none;
}

.shoe3-button-style{
    position: absolute;
    left: 35%;
    bottom: 10%;
    background: transparent;
    border:none;
}
```

Here's how the body of `<style>` should look:

```
18        .shoe-info-bg-div{
19            background-color:white;
20            margin-left: 15px;
21            margin-top:  15px;
22            border-style: solid;
23            border-width: thin;
24            border-radius: 5px;
25            max-width: 200px;
26        }
27
28        .shoe1-button-style{
29            position: absolute;
30            left: 5%;
31            bottom: 10%;
32            background: transparent;
33            border:none;
34        }
35
36        .shoe2-button-style{
37            position: absolute;
38            left: 20%;
39            bottom: 10%;
40            background: transparent;
41            border:none;
42        }
43
44        .shoe3-button-style{
45            position: absolute;
46            left: 35%;
47            bottom: 10%;
48            background: transparent;
49            border:none;
50        }
51
52        .shoe-button-img{
53            max-width:100px;
54        }
55
56    </style>
```

Next, add the following code snippet inside the body of `<div id="myContainer">`, after the ending div tag of `<div class="shoe1-button-div">`:

```
<div>
  <button class="shoe2-button-style" id="shoe2button">
    <img class="shoe-button-img" data-id=" "/>
  </button>
</div>

<div>
  <button class="shoe3-button-style" id="shoe3button">
    <img class="shoe-button-img" data-id=" "/>
  </button>
</div>
```

Here’s how it should look:

```
73
74        <!-- Adding button to get information for Shoe with id="1" from DynamoDB -->
75        <div>
76          <button class="shoe1-button-style" id="shoe1button">
77            <img class="shoe-button-img" data-id="5eebf7b56cb8d453bcd17e55d05960e0965b2528.jpg"/>
78          </button>
79        </div>
80
81        <div>
82          <button class="shoe2-button-style" id="shoe2button">
83            <img class="shoe-button-img" data-id=""/>
84          </button>
85        </div>
86
87        <div>
88          <button class="shoe3-button-style" id="shoe3button">
89            <img class="shoe-button-img" data-id=""/>
90          </button>
91        </div>
92
```

Notice the `data-id` elements are empty because you haven’t added the image files for the two new shoe buttons to the project. It’s time to do that now.

In the Text editor window, click **Browse** to upload **shoe2.jpg** and **shoe3.jpg** from the **resources** folder. This will add an `<img>` with the corresponding `data-id` to the end of the code file. You’ll see a preview in the Images panel.

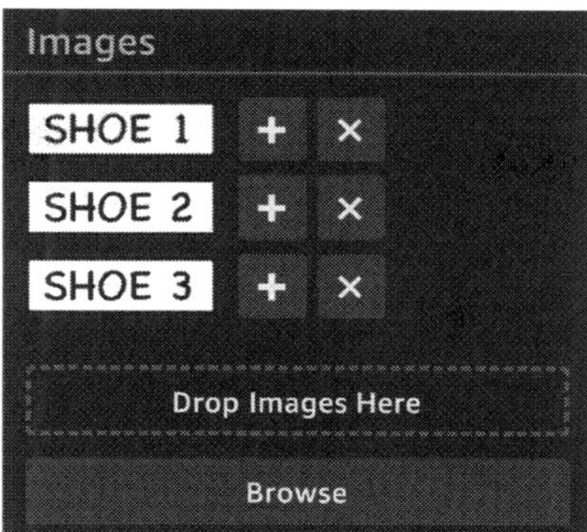

Copy the respective `data-id` from the <img> you added when you uploaded and paste it in the `data-id` tag in the <div> tags you added in the previous step.

```
73
74      <!-- Adding button to get information for Shoe with id="1" from DynamoDB -->
75      <div>
76        <button class="shoe1-button-style" id="shoe1button">
77          <img class="shoe-button-img" data-id="5eebf7b56cb8d453bcd17e55d05960e0965b2528.jpg"/>
78        </button>
79      </div>
80
81      <div>
82        <button class="shoe2-button-style" id="shoe2button">
83          <img class="shoe-button-img" data-id="9ba7465f8a3b714daac82ae84a06c86797e4d2aa.jpg"/>
84        </button>
85      </div>
86
87      <div>
88        <button class="shoe3-button-style" id="shoe3button">
89          <img class="shoe-button-img" data-id="6eb1ad4718e2473013f2bdbbf0b7c9692ba9768b.jpg"/>
90        </button>
91      </div>
92
93  <div>
94
95
96
97  <img data-id="9ba7465f8a3b714daac82ae84a06c86797e4d2aa.jpg"/>
98  <img data-id="6eb1ad4718e2473013f2bdbbf0b7c9692ba9768b.jpg"/>
```

Finally, delete the <img> tags at the bottom of the file and save the file.

You should be able to see three buttons in the Scene editor window, which you can see on the next page.

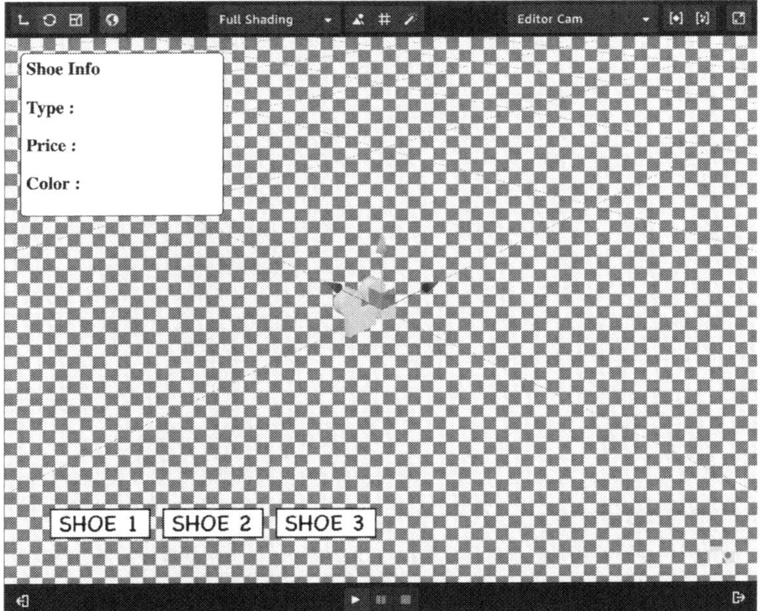

Now that you've added the code to display the buttons for Shoe2 and Shoe3, it's time to write the code that will make them work when the user clicks them.

Adding functionality to the shoe buttons

You've added the HTML buttons, but you still need to add the logic in your scripts to make them function as expected.

First, you need to duplicate the Shoe1 button, which fetches the data from the DynamoDB table and displays it when the user clicks it.

Start by opening the **SceneManagerScript** script in the Text editor.

In the previous chapter, you added an event listener by calling `AddEventListenerToShoeButtons()` in `ctx.start()` of `SceneManagerHandlerAction()`.

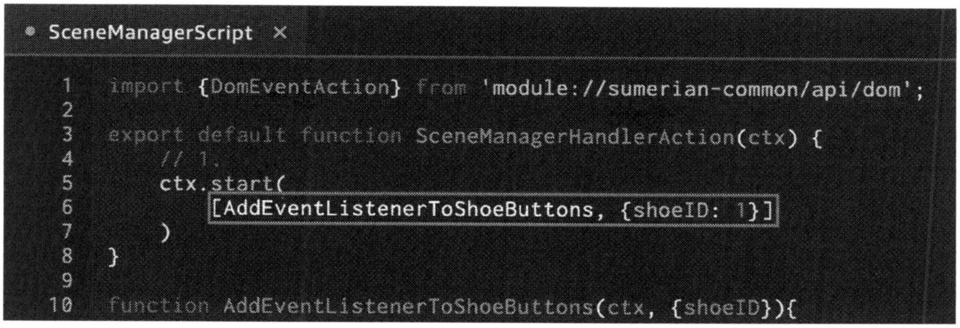

```
• SceneManagerScript ×
1   import {DomEventAction} from 'module://sumerian-common/api/dom';
2
3   export default function SceneManagerHandlerAction(ctx) {
4       // 1.
5       ctx.start(
6           [AddEventListenerToShoeButtons, {shoeID: 1}]
7       )
8   }
9
10  function AddEventListenerToShoeButtons(ctx, {shoeID}){
```

These buttons work in a similar way. They will get data from the DynamoDB table to return the `shoe-id`. To enable this, all you need to do is add two more actions, one for each new `shoe-id`.

Add the following lines of code in the body of `ctx.start()`, making sure that each function call is comma-separated:

```
[AddEventListenerToShoeButtons, {shoeID: 2}]
[AddEventListenerToShoeButtons, {shoeID: 3}]
```

It should look like this.

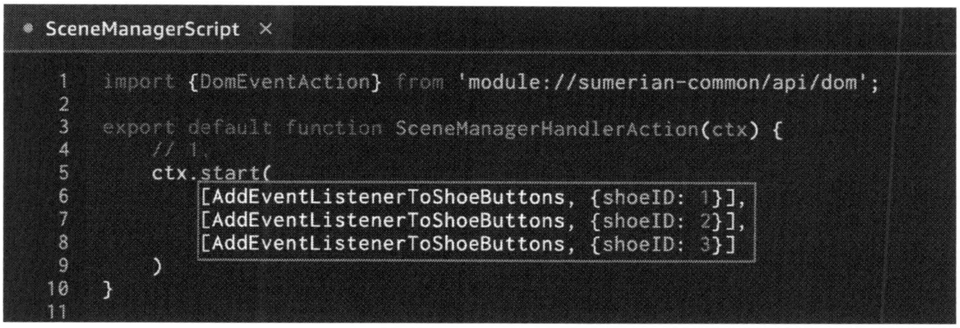

```
• SceneManagerScript ×
1   import {DomEventAction} from 'module://sumerian-common/api/dom';
2
3   export default function SceneManagerHandlerAction(ctx) {
4       // 1.
5       ctx.start(
6           [AddEventListenerToShoeButtons, {shoeID: 1}],
7           [AddEventListenerToShoeButtons, {shoeID: 2}],
8           [AddEventListenerToShoeButtons, {shoeID: 3}]
9       )
10  }
11
```

Save the script and return to Sumerian, then click the Play button to play the scene.

Click any of the three shoe buttons. You'll notice that it will fetch the data of the corresponding `shoe-id` from the DynamoDB table and display it on the shoe infobox.

For example, if you click the **Shoe3** button, Sumerian will fetch the data of **shoe-id: 3** and put it on the **Shoe-UI** box.

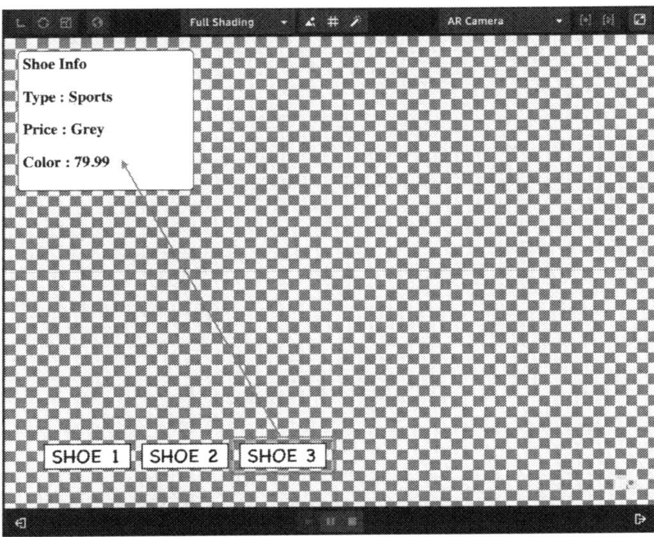

Now that you've added the buttons to fetch the correct `shoe-id`, all that's left to do is write the functionality to display only one shoe at a time.

To achieve this, you'll add code that will first disable the visibility of all three shoe entities, and then display only the button whose ID is passed to it as a parameter.

First, add the following code at the end of **SceneManagerScript**:

```
function makeShoeVisible(ctx, shoeID){

    // 1. Get a reference to each shoe entity
    const shoe1 = ctx.world.entitiesWithNames("Shoe1").single();
    const shoe2 = ctx.world.entitiesWithNames("Shoe2").single();
    const shoe3 = ctx.world.entitiesWithNames("Shoe3").single();

    // 2. Hide all three shoe entities
    shoe1.hide();
    shoe2.hide();
    shoe3.hide();

    // 3. Show the shoe entity of shoe-id only
    const shoe_to_show = ctx.world.entitiesWithNames("Shoe" +
        shoeID).single();
    shoe_to_show.show();
}
```

Here's a brief explanation of the above code:

1. To hide an entity from the Sumerian scene, you first need to get a reference to it. `ctx.world.entitiesWithNames("Shoe1").single()` searches for the entity with the name "Shoe1" in the Sumerian scene and returns a reference to it, which you store in the variable `shoe1`. Similarly, you store references to entities "Shoe2" and "Shoe3" in variables `shoe2` and `shoe3`.

2. To keep the logic simple and the code clean, you disable the visibility of all three shoe entities in the Sumerian scene. You do this using `hide()`.

3. Finally, you store a reference to `"Shoe" + shoeID` in `shoe_to_show`. You'll pas shoeID to the function as a parameter. Then you call `show()` to show the corresponding entity in the scene.

For example, if the value of `shoeID` is **2**, variable `shoe_to_show` stores a reference to the entity named Shoe2 and then calls `show()` on it, making it visible in the Sumerian scene.

SceneManagerScript should look like this:

```
57  function makeShoeVisible(ctx, shoeID){
58
59      // 1. Get a reference to each shoe entity
60      const shoe1 = ctx.world.entitiesWithNames("Shoe1").single();
61      const shoe2 = ctx.world.entitiesWithNames("Shoe2").single();
62      const shoe3 = ctx.world.entitiesWithNames("Shoe3").single();
63
64      // 2. Hide all three shoe entities
65      shoe1.hide();
66      shoe2.hide();
67      shoe3.hide();
68
69      // 3. Show the shoe entity of shoe-id only
70      const shoe_to_show = ctx.world.entitiesWithNames("Shoe" +shoeID).single();
71      shoe_to_show.show();
72  }
```

Now, you need a call to this function within the script. The ideal place for it would be in the body of `onEvent` of function `AddEventListenerToShoeButtons`. This way, when the user clicks any of the shoe buttons, Sumerian will not only fetch the data from DynamoDB, but also set the corresponding shoe entity to visible.

Add the following line of code in the body of `onEvent` in `AddEventListenerToShoeButtons`:

```
// Set visible the corresponding shoe
makeShoeVisible(ctx, shoeID);
```

The body of `AddEventListenerToShoeButtons` should look like this:

```
function AddEventListenerToShoeButton(ctx, {shoeID}) {
    // 2
    ctx.start(
        [DomEventAction, {
            eventName: "mouseDown",
            querySelector: '#shoe' + shoeID + 'button',
            onEvent: () => {

                    // Get Shoe Data from DynamoDB of shoe with id : "shoeID"
                    getShoeData(shoeID);

                    // Set visible the corresponding shoe
                    makeShoeVisible(ctx, shoeID);
            }
        }]
    );
}
```

Go ahead and test this. Back in the Scene editor, make sure the ARAnchor entity is not visible. Also, click the **eye** button to hide both **Shoe2** and **Shoe3**. By default, only the first shoe entity will be visible in the camera viewfinder. Make sure the Entities panel looks like this:

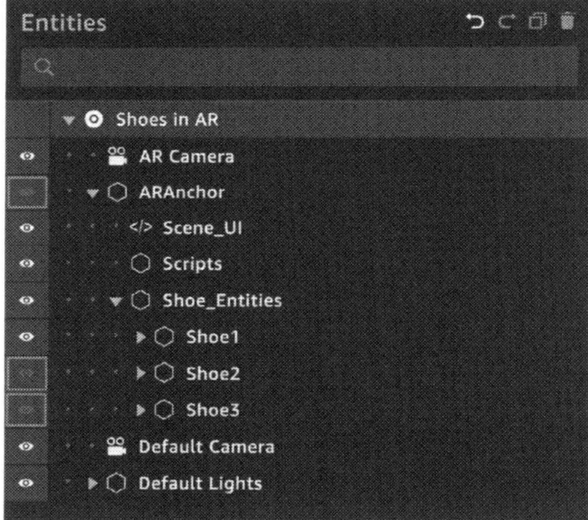

Time to test.

Re-publish the scene, then load the mobile app on your Android or iOS device. You now see three shoe buttons. Clicking them will display each shoe and its information.

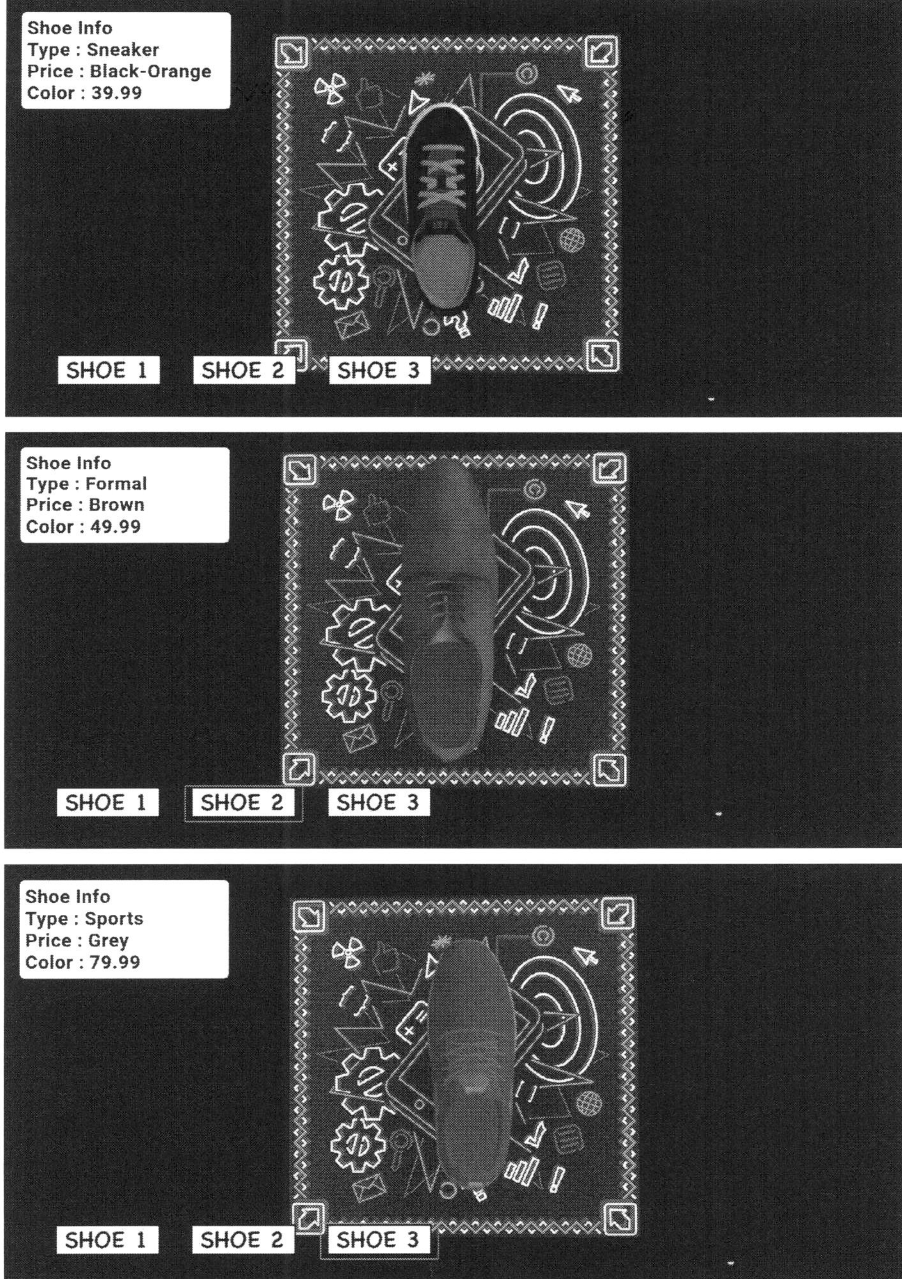
Shoe Info
Type : Sneaker
Price : Black-Orange
Color : 39.99
SHOE 1
SHOE 2
SHOE 3
Shoe Info
Type : Formal
Price : Brown
Color : 49.99
SHOE 1
SHOE 2
SHOE 3
Shoe Info
Type : Sports
Price : Grey
Color : 79.99
SHOE 1
SHOE 2
SHOE 3

Now, take a printout of the augmented reality target image, point the camera viewfinder at it and put your foot in the center of the sheet to see how the shoe looks on your feet.

However, shoes come in a range of sizes and no shoe fits two different people exactly the same way. Therefore, in the next and final section, you'll add buttons to set the size of the Shoe models in AR.

Changing shoe sizes

The idea behind modifying the shoe size is simple: Changing an entity's Scale makes it look bigger or smaller in AR.

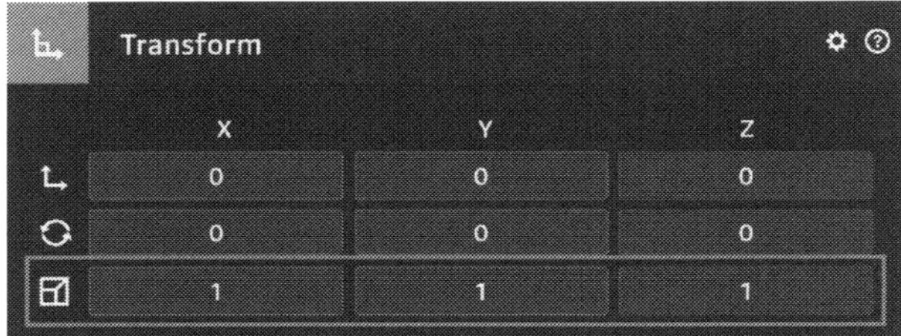

Building this functionality is similar to what you did when you added buttons that fetched data from DynamoDB. You need to:

- Write the HTML and CSS to display the buttons for the different sizes.
- Add event listeners, which execute a function when a user clicks a particular button.
- Write a function that changes the scale of an entity.
- Add a UI component to display the current shoe size.

You'll add four buttons to the scene, one each for setting the shoe size to **7, 8, 9** and **10**. Later on, you can experiment by adding or removing buttons from the scene, but for the sake of simplicity, four sizes are enough for now.

Open **Scene_UI** in the Text editor.

Add the following code in the body of `<style>`, which defines the style properties of the buttons:

```
.shoe-size-button-image{
    width:100%;
    max-width:50px;
    background-color: white
}

.shoe-size-button-div {
    background: none;
    border: none;
    position: absolute;
    right: 60px;
    padding: 15px;
}
```

It should look something like this:

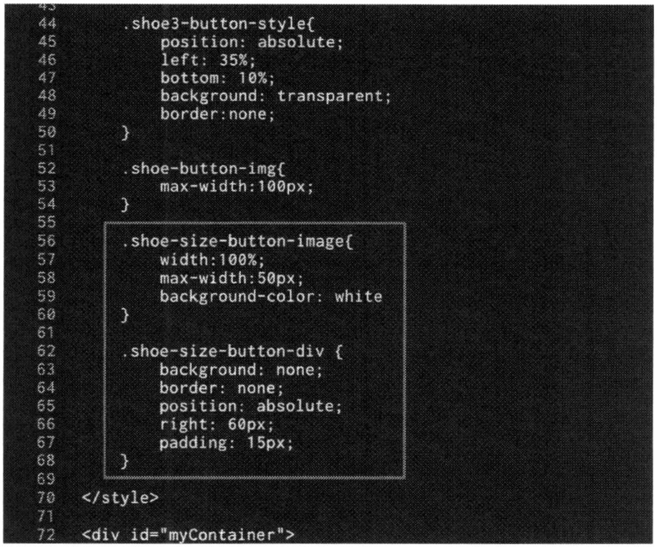

```
44      .shoe3-button-style{
45          position: absolute;
46          left: 35%;
47          bottom: 10%;
48          background: transparent;
49          border:none;
50      }
51
52      .shoe-button-img{
53          max-width:100px;
54      }
55
56      .shoe-size-button-image{
57          width:100%;
58          max-width:50px;
59          background-color: white
60      }
61
62      .shoe-size-button-div {
63          background: none;
64          border: none;
65          position: absolute;
66          right: 60px;
67          padding: 15px;
68      }
69
70  </style>
71
72  <div id="myContainer">
```

Then, add the following code in the body of `<div id="myContainer">`, which is the HTML code for the buttons themselves:

```
<button class="shoe-size-button-div" id="shoesize7button"
style="bottom: 80px;">
    <img class="shoe-size-button-image" data-id=" "/>
</button>

<button class="shoe-size-button-div" id="shoesize8button"
style="bottom: 130px;">
    <img class="shoe-size-button-image" data-id=" "/>
```

```
</button>

<button class="shoe-size-button-div" id="shoesize9button"
style="bottom: 180px;">
    <img class="shoe-size-button-image" data-id=" "/>
</button>

<button class="shoe-size-button-div" id="shoesize10button"
style="bottom: 230px;">
    <img class="shoe-size-button-image" data-id=" "/>
</button>
```

Now, it should look like this:

```
101        <div>
102          <button class="shoe3-button-style" id="shoe3button">
103            <img class="shoe-button-img" data-id="6eb1ad4718e2473013f2bdbbf0b7c9692ba9768b.jpg"/>
104          </button>
105        </div>
106
107        <button class="shoe-size-button-div" id="shoesize7button" style="bottom: 80px;">
108            <img class="shoe-size-button-image" data-id=" "/>
109        </button>
110
111        <button class="shoe-size-button-div" id="shoesize8button" style="bottom: 130px;">
112            <img class="shoe-size-button-image" data-id=" "/>
113        </button>
114
115        <button class="shoe-size-button-div" id="shoesize9button" style="bottom: 180px;">
116            <img class="shoe-size-button-image" data-id=" "/>
117        </button>
118
119        <button class="shoe-size-button-div" id="shoesize10button" style="bottom: 230px;">
120            <img class="shoe-size-button-image" data-id=" "/>
121        </button>
122
123    <div>
124
```

Notice that the value of data-id is empty because you haven't uploaded images for these buttons, which you need to do separately. Note that the key difference is style="bottom: <number> px;", which you define in the body of the <button> definition. This makes the buttons display in increasing height from the bottom.

Upload the shoe button images files: **ShoeSize7.jpg**, **ShoeSize8.jpg**, **ShoeSize9.jpg** and **ShoeSize10.jpg**. You'll find them in the **resources** folder.

Once uploaded, copy the value of data-id from the <img> added to the respective data-id in the definition of <img class="shoe-size-button-image">. Then, delete the <img> tag that you added after the upload.

```
106
107         <button class="shoe-size-button-div" id="shoesize7button" style="bottom: 80px;">
108             <img class="shoe-size-button-image" data-id="2a7ea28b853fdcbbda8af5fab565d24f3aa5782a.jpg"/>
109         </button>
110
111         <button class="shoe-size-button-div" id="shoesize8button" style="bottom: 130px;">
112             <img class="shoe-size-button-image" data-id="01576d042bbccfaf7cb8a339de0bc5ba60034142.jpg"/>
113         </button>
114
115         <button class="shoe-size-button-div" id="shoesize9button" style="bottom: 180px;">
116             <img class="shoe-size-button-image" data-id="186e6f7407a2ae182e3d204e5f74720e33bdae7f.jpg"/>
117         </button>
118
119         <button class="shoe-size-button-div" id="shoesize10button" style="bottom: 230px;">
120             <img class="shoe-size-button-image" data-id="de4112b57771959c481a1d5af76642329592fc2d.jpg"/>
121         </button>
122
123     <div>
124
125
126     <img data-id="2a7ea28b853fdcbbda8af5fab565d24f3aa5782a.jpg"/>
127     <img data-id="01576d042bbccfaf7cb8a339de0bc5ba60034142.jpg"/>   <------Delete these
128     <img data-id="186e6f7407a2ae182e3d204e5f74720e33bdae7f.jpg"/>
129     <img data-id="de4112b57771959c481a1d5af76642329592fc2d.jpg"/>
```

Finally, save the file and switch back the Scene editor. With the ARAnchor entity set to visible, the buttons should look like this in the editor:

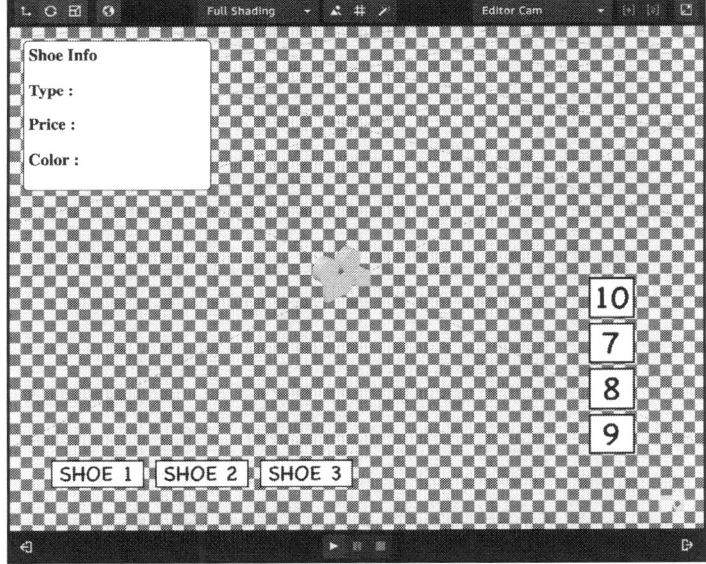

At this point, if you click these new buttons, nothing happens since you haven't added an event listener for them. Before doing that, you'll add another UI element that displays the current shoe size and changes as the user clicks the different shoe size buttons.

Adding a shoe size indicator

Open **Scene_UI** in the Text editor and add the following code in the body of `<style>`, which defines the style properties of the current shoe size box:

```
.shoe-size-current-div {
    font-size: 18px;
    padding: 10px;
    border-radius: 3px;
    margin: 0;
    font-family: calibri;
    font-weight: bold;
    bottom: 5%;
    right: 5%;
    position: fixed;
    background-color:white;
    border-style: solid;
    border-width: thin;
    border-radius: 5px;
}
```

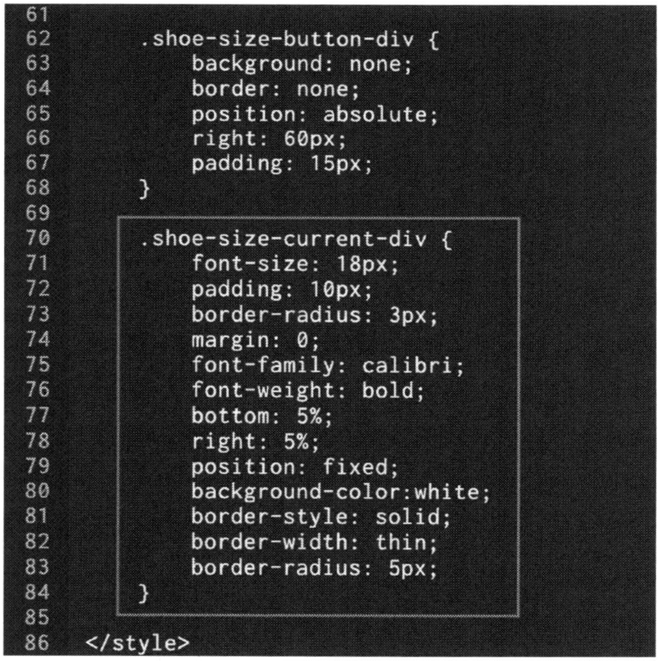

```
61
62      .shoe-size-button-div {
63          background: none;
64          border: none;
65          position: absolute;
66          right: 60px;
67          padding: 15px;
68      }
69
70      .shoe-size-current-div {
71          font-size: 18px;
72          padding: 10px;
73          border-radius: 3px;
74          margin: 0;
75          font-family: calibri;
76          font-weight: bold;
77          bottom: 5%;
78          right: 5%;
79          position: fixed;
80          background-color:white;
81          border-style: solid;
82          border-width: thin;
83          border-radius: 5px;
84      }
85
86  </style>
```

Then, add the following code in the body of `<div id="myContainer">`, which is the HTML code for the shoe size div:

```
<div>
    <h2 class="shoe-size-current-div">
          Shoe Size : <span id="current_shoe_size"> 7 </span>
    </h2>
</div>
```

The body of **Scene_UI** file should look like this:

```
134        <button class="shoe-size-button-div" id="shoesize10button" style="bottom: 230px;">
135            <img class="shoe-size-button-image" data-id="de4112b57771959c481a1d5af76642329592fc2d.jpg"/>
136        </button>
137
138        <div>
139        <h2 class="shoe-size-current-div">
140              Shoe Size : <span id="current_shoe_size"> 7 </span>
141        </h2>
142
143    </div>
```

This code is pretty straightforward. All it contains is the text displaying `Shoe Size :` and then a `<span>` element. A function in **SceneHandlerScrip** updates the current shoe size value and changes the text inside `<span>` to match.

Save the file. Your Scene editor should look like this:

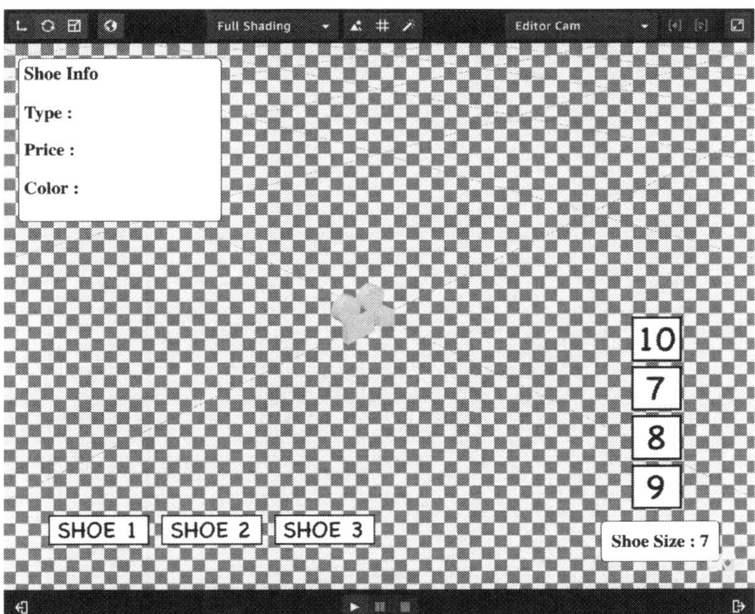

Finally, all that's left to do is to add Event Listeners for the buttons, then execute the required function.

Adding functionality for shoe size buttons

Open **SceneHandlerScript** and add the following function after the definition of `AddEventListenerToShoeButtons()`:

```
// Adding Event Listeners for Shoe Size buttons
function AddEventListenerToShoeSizeButtons(ctx,
    {shoe_size, scale_value} ) {

    ctx.start(
        [DomEventAction, {
            eventName: "mousedown",
            querySelector: '#shoesize' + shoe_size + 'button',
            onEvent: () => {

                // Get a reference to Shoe_Entities
                const shoe_entities = ctx.world
                    .entitiesWithNames("Shoe_Entities").single()
;

                // Set the Scale
                shoe_entities.scale
                    .setDirect(scale_value, scale_value,
                    scale_value);

                // Change the value on the Shoe Size UI
                document.getElementById('current_shoe_size')
                    .innerHTML = shoe_size;
            }
        }]
    )
}
```

The body of **SceneHandlerScript** should look like this:

```
29  // Adding Event Listeners for Shoe Size buttons
30  function AddEventListenerToShoeSizeButtons(ctx,
31      {shoe_size, scale_value} ) {
32
33      ctx.start(
34          [DomEventAction, {
35              eventName: "mousedown",
36              querySelector: '#shoesize' + shoe_size + 'button',
37              onEvent: () => {
38
39                  // Get a reference to Shoe_Entities
40                  const shoe_entities = ctx.world.entitiesWithNames("Shoe_Entities").single();
41
42                  // Set the Scale
43                  shoe_entities.scale.setDirect(scale_value, scale_value, scale_value);
44
45                  // Change the value on the Shoe Size UI
46                  document.getElementById('current_shoe_size').innerHTML = shoe_size;
47              }
48          }]
49      )
50  }
```

Take a look at what this function does:

- ctx.start() calls DomEventAction(), which adds an event listener to a given query selector. This is similar to AddEventListenerToShoeButtons() that you added previously, which handled the button click event for shoe buttons.
- The function requires two inputs: shoe_size and scale_value. You use the shoe_size parameter to define the complete querySelector argument, for example, if shoe_size is 7, then the value of querySelector will be shoesize7button. This is the value of the button with id : shoesize7button and the data-id of image **7.jpg** in the **Scene_UI** file.
- Secondly, scale_value contains the value to which you'll set the Scale of the Shoe_Entities. Since Shoe_Entities is the parent of all the entities containing the shoe 3D models, you only need to change its Scale. Changing the Scale of a parent entity will make a proportional change in all its child entities. In this case, that's all three entities containing the shoe 3D models.
- Then, in the body of onEvent(), you store a reference to Shoe_Entities in the shoe_entities variable. Then the Scale value is set using scale.setDirect(), which takes three values, one for each axis: X, Y and Z.
- Finally, you set the value of <span id="current_shoe_size"> to indicate the current value of shoe_size.

Now that you've added the key function, all that's left to do is add an EventListener for all four buttons.

Add the following lines of code in the body of ctx.start() in the body of SceneManagerHandlerAction(), making sure that each function call is comma-separated:

```
[ AddEventListenerToShoeSizeButtons, {
    shoe_size: 7, scale_value: 1.0} ]
[ AddEventListenerToShoeSizeButtons, {
    shoe_size: 8, scale_value: 1.2}]
[ AddEventListenerToShoeSizeButtons, {
    shoe_size: 9, scale_value: 1.4}]
[ AddEventListenerToShoeSizeButtons, {
    shoe_size: 10, scale_value: 1.6}]
```

It should look like this:

```
• SceneManagerScript ×   • Scene_UI ×

1  import {DomEventAction} from 'module://sumerian-common/api/dom';
2  import {World} from 'module://sumerian-common/internal';
3
4  export default function SceneManagerHandlerAction(ctx) {
5      // 1.
6      ctx.start(
7          [AddEventListenerToShoeButtons, {shoeID: 1}],
8          [AddEventListenerToShoeButtons, {shoeID: 2}],
9          [AddEventListenerToShoeButtons, {shoeID: 3}],
10
11         [ AddEventListenerToShoeSizeButtons, { shoe_size: 7, scale_value: 1.0}],
12         [ AddEventListenerToShoeSizeButtons, { shoe_size: 8, scale_value: 1.2}],
13         [ AddEventListenerToShoeSizeButtons, { shoe_size: 9, scale_value: 1.4}],
14         [ AddEventListenerToShoeSizeButtons, { shoe_size: 10, scale_value: 1.6}]
15     )
16 }
17
18 function AddEventListenerToShoeButtons(ctx, {shoeID}){
```

Notice that you should put a comma after an item in `ctx.start()` only if there's another item next to it.

Also, the values of `scale_value` that correspond to each `shoe_size` are just a sample of calibrated values for this particular app. Feel free to experiment and try different models of shoes and to adjust the values of `scale_value` on your own.

Save the script and return to the Scene editor. Then, make sure you've disabled ARAnchor's visibility by clicking the **eye** icon next to the ARAnchor entity in the Entities panel. Republish the scene.

Finally, load the mobile app on your Android or iOS device and point the camera viewfinder at the AR Target Image. Voila!

Try switching between any of the three types of shoes and see how their information updates in the top-left UI box. Then tap on any of the shoe size buttons to change the size, and see the change reflected in the UI Box at the bottom-right of your screen.

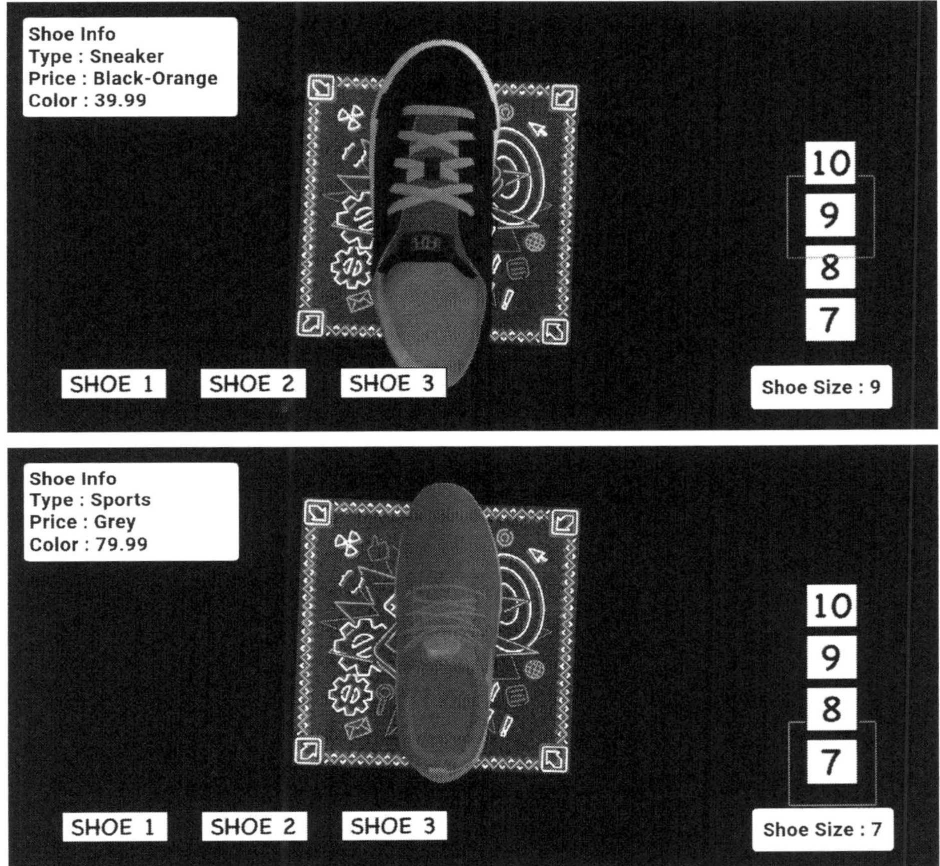

Key points

- The basics of augmented reality and the components used to build an AR Scene in Sumerian.
- How to set up your computer and build a simple mobile app on Android or iOS.
- The basics of a database including how to set one up and how to use Amazon DynamoDB.
- How to add 2D HTML elements to display information and buttons to interact with different components of a Sumerian scene.

Where to go from here?

Congratulations! You just created a complete mobile augmented reality app using Amazon Sumerian. You've created a way to try on shoes without leaving your house. In the process, you learned the following:

With the knowledge you've gained, play around with the different components of this project. Keep experimenting and learning more things! But now's not the time stop reading. In the next section, you'll continue to leverage AWS by creating a virtual travel agent that can talk with the end user.

Section IV: Creating a Virtual Travel Agent

There are many 3D engines on the market that allow you to create experiences similar to Sumerian's. However, these engines are usually aimed at professional developers; they can take years to truly master.

Sumerian allows you to get up speed rapidly. You can even do everything in your web browser – and that's not all. Sumerian offers a feature out of the box that would take months of development time with another engine: The ability to create a host.

A host is a virtual person that provides a "human" touch to your scene. Hosts speak, perform gestures and, with a little AWS magic, even chat with the end-user.

You can use hosts for a variety of purposes such as walking a user through a registration form or acting as a virtual tour guide for a real art gallery like the Getty Museum.

In this next project, you'll create a virtual travel agent. This travel agent will ask you questions that you can verbally answer. In doing so, you'll see how AWS can turbocharge an experience.

These chapters cover the basics of creating a virtual travel agent:

Chapter 19: Basics of a Sumerian Host: This chapter introduces you to the host and shows how easy it is to add one to your scene.

Chapter 20: Speech in Amazon Sumerian: You'll learn how to leverage Amazon Lex to provide the "brains" behind your host.

Chapter 21: Audio Input & Lex: Once you get your host talking, you'll naturally want users to respond. This chapter covers the basics of recording voice input. Your host will use this input to respond to the user.

Chapter 22: Integrating Amazon Lambda with Lex: In this final chapter, you'll leverage AWS Lambda to query a database and return a list of "must visit" places for a particular city.

Chapter 19: Basics of a Sumerian Host

We hope you are enjoying the early access version of Amazon Sumerian by Tutorials! This chapter will be available in the final release, but here's an overview of what it will cover.

This chapter introduces you to the host and shows how easy it is to add one to your scene.

Chapter 20: Speech in Amazon Sumerian

We hope you are enjoying the early access version of Amazon Sumerian by Tutorials! This chapter will be available in the final release, but here's an overview of what it will cover.

You'll learn how to leverage Amazon Lex to provide the "brains" behind your host.

Chapter 21: Audio Input & Lex

We hope you are enjoying the early access version of Amazon Sumerian by Tutorials! This chapter will be available in the final release, but here's an overview of what it will cover.

Once you get your host talking, you'll naturally want users to respond. This chapter covers the basics of recording voice input. Your host will use this input to respond to the user.

Chapter 22: Integrating Amazon Lambda with Lex

We hope you are enjoying the early access version of Amazon Sumerian by Tutorials! This chapter will be available in the final release, but here's an overview of what it will cover.

In this final chapter, you'll leverage AWS Lambda to query a database and return a list of "must visit" places for a particular city.

Conclusion

We hope this book has helped you get up to speed with Sumerian! This is a flexible engine that allows you to create unique experiences for a variety of applications.

Part of the fun of creating experiences is sharing them. If you created an experience, head on over to the Amazon Slack channel (http://amazonsumerian.slack.com). Paste a link to your experience in the Showcase Channel and show off your work.

If you have any questions or comments as you continue to use Git, please stop by our forums at forums.raywenderlich.com/c/books/amazon-sumerian-by-tutorials.

Thank you for reading our book. We hope you make some amazing experiences.

– The *Amazon Sumerian by Tutorials* Team

Made in the USA
Middletown, DE
23 November 2019